The Audacity to Win

The
Audacity
to Win

The Inside Story and Lessons of
Barack Obama's Historic Victory

David Plouffe

Viking

VIKING

Published by the Penguin Group

Penguin Group (USA) Inc., 375 Hudson Street, New York, New York 10014, U.S.A. • Penguin Group (Canada), 90 Eglinton Avenue East, Suite 700, Toronto, Ontario, Canada M4P 2Y3 (a division of Pearson Penguin Canada Inc.) • Penguin Books Ltd, 80 Strand, London WC2R 0RL, England • Penguin Ireland, 25 St. Stephen's Green, Dublin 2, Ireland (a division of Penguin Books Ltd) • Penguin Books Australia Ltd, 250 Camberwell Road, Camberwell, Victoria 3124, Australia (a division of Pearson Australia Group Pty Ltd) • Penguin Books India Pvt Ltd, 11 Community Centre, Panchsheel Park, New Delhi – 110 017, India • Penguin Group (NZ), 67 Apollo Drive, Rosedale, North Shore 0632, New Zealand (a division of Pearson New Zealand Ltd) • Penguin Books (South Africa) (Pty) Ltd, 24 Sturdee Avenue, Rosebank, Johannesburg 2196, South Africa

Penguin Books Ltd, Registered Offices: 80 Strand, London WC2R 0RL, England

First published in 2009 by Viking Penguin, a member of Penguin Group (USA) Inc.

10 9 8 7 6 5 4 3 2 1

LIBRARY OF CONGRESS CATALOGING IN PUBLICATION DATA

Plouffe, David.
    The audacity to win : the inside story and lessons of Barack Obama's historic victory / David Plouffe.
        p. cm.
    ISBN 978-0-670-02133-8
    1. Presidents—United States—Election—2008. 2. Political campaigns—United States. 3. Obama, Barack. 4. Plouffe, David. I. Title.
    JK5262008 .P55 2009
    324.973'0931—dc22   2009030176

Printed in the United States of America
Set in Berkeley • *Designed by Carla Bolte*

For Olivia, Everett, and Vivian

Contents

Prologue

David Axelrod and I left the Obama campaign headquarters election bunker in Chicago at 10:30 p.m. central time to humbling cheers from the knot of staffers who had been prepared for a long night of data crunching and narrow margins. Instead, they were downing beers and celebrating, having just watched all the networks announce the election of their boss as the forty-fourth president of the United States of America.

It was the end of long road. Axelrod and I had begun the journey walking together through an airport in November 2006, en route to our first meeting about the far-fetched prospect of Barack Obama's running for president. At the time we figured it was probably the only meeting that such an unlikely endeavor would yield.

Yet here we were, walking down the hallway of the high-rise that had housed our campaign for almost two years, on our way to greet the president-elect. As we departed the elevator and stepped into the lobby, the security guards broke into raucous cheers and tearful thank-yous. Their joy hit me with a jolt of reality that blaring televisions and hours of encouraging results from battleground states had somehow failed to convey.

"I'm having a hard time actually believing this," I said to Axelrod as we made our way into the street.

"I know," nodded Ax. "It's too big to comprehend right now."

We had just elected the president of the United States—an African American man, born to a Kenyan father and a Kansan mother, just four years out of the Illinois state senate. He had defeated the gold standard in both parties, Hillary Clinton and John McCain, to win in one of the biggest upsets in American political history.

The elation of these security guards, all African Americans, struck me powerfully. Later I learned that this same celebratory scene was playing out all across the country, in groups large and small; black, white, and brown; suburban, urban, and rural. Americans were expressing not merely satisfaction at the victory of a political party or candidate, or relief that the lesser of two evils had prevailed, but something deeper and more profound. Their reactions were closer to a kind of primal joy at seeing wrongs righted, at having risen up to achieve something cynics said couldn't be done. For most of us under a certain age, any prior familiarity with this feeling came secondhand, from history books. Now we owned it.

Ax and I crossed the street to the Hyatt Regency where the next president, his family, and Joe and Jill Biden were watching election results. The advance team directed us up some back stairs, to a blocked-off elevator and eventually down a hall to the Obama suite. Members of the road show—the staff that had spent two years with Obama on the road, living every minute of this amazing and improbable journey—lined the hall. Reggie Love and Marvin Nicholson, both giants, swallowed me in their emotional embrace.

As Ax and I slipped into the suite, Obama was on the phone with President Bush, receiving his congratulations. I shivered, as another jolt of reality shot up my spine. Right before we walked in, Obama had received the historic concession call from Senator John McCain, our vanquished opponent. The next minutes were a blur of hugs and happiness: embracing the Bidens; Michelle's brother, Craig Robinson; and then a wonderful high-five with Michelle. Michelle's mother was radiant, holding hands with her son-in-law, the next president of the United of the States. Then Obama was done talking to Bush and crossed the room toward me. He and I embraced for a long time. He pulled Ax and Robert Gibbs in for a beaming photograph, a treasured memento.

I suddenly noticed how quiet the room seemed. There were no shrieks or champagne corks popping or screams of delight. Perhaps because of exhaustion, relief, or a sense of elation that was more quiet and private than boisterous, we were a remarkably subdued bunch for a party of victors. An outside observer might not have immediately known if we had won or lost the election.

I could not relax. Though victory was sealed, there were still states to be called, and these states were like my babies—I couldn't rest until they were all put to bed, hopefully tucked under a blanket of Obama blue. I stared intently at the suite's TVs and checked results religiously on my BlackBerry.

The press coverage and reports from our advance staff told us the crowd at nearby Grant Park was enormous and crackling with energy. We piled into a waiting motorcade and screamed down Lakeshore Drive; before it seemed possible, we began to see the crowd. The throngs on the outer edge of the park saw the motorcade approaching, and a roar of cheering supporters followed us all the way down the drive until we reached the security entrance. Axelrod, Gibbs, and I did not want to watch Obama speak from backstage, so we asked the advance staff to get us out with the crowd. We wanted to be swept up in the human wave of energy.

As I watched Barack Obama emerge onto the stage with his beautiful family, I found it difficult to contain my emotions. Was this really possible? Was this our next first family? Obama delivered a phenomenal speech; at one point he thanked me and Ax personally, which was as surreal as it was embarrassing.

Then it was over. The Obamas and the Bidens embraced and joined hands, waved to the crowd, and strode off the stage.

Two years earlier, this historic moment would have seemed little more than a fantasy. It strained credibility—required a certain audaciousness, you might say—to believe that Barack Obama could wrest the Democratic nomination from the Clinton franchise, much less go on to win the presidency with 365 electoral votes, 7 million more popular votes than anyone who had ever run for president, and a higher vote percentage than any Democratic candidate besides FDR in 1936 and LBJ in 1964.

The remarkable Obama for President campaign, led by a once-in-a-generation candidate, had the audacity to win—and not just to win, but to do so with guts, defying conventional wisdom time and again. We talked to voters like adults and organized a grassroots movement of average citizens the likes of which American politics had never seen.

It was not easy. At the beginning it was a stretch just to find office space and fill it with computers and phone lines. Taking the first halting steps of the Obama for President journey, most of us, me included, were more resolute than starry-eyed. We could hardly have realized, in signing up to work for this political long shot from Chicago, that we had gained a unique perch from which to watch American history unfold.

1

Yes or No

The week before the 2006 congressional elections, my business partner, David Axelrod, and I were sitting in an editing suite in Chicago, putting the final touches on a series of television ads for various Democratic clients. We were seven or eight hours into a sixteen-hour session at the studio.

"I can't wait for this goddamned election to be over," I grumbled. "I want it to be over more than I want to win."

It was a biannual complaint. By October of each election year, everyone in the business has pulled too many all-nighters, been on too many conference calls, and read too many polls. If the whole profession could put the campaign in suspended animation and sleep for a week, it would.

Ax fiddled with some music selections for the spot we were working on. "Well, then you won't like this," he said. "Barack wants to meet in Chicago the day after the election to talk about the presidential race. And he wants you there. So don't get too excited for Election Day."

"Really?" I said. "Shit."

———

Obama's book tour that fall for *The Audacity of Hope* had unexpectedly turned into a presidential draft. Independent groups calling for him to run had sprung up across the country, generating tens of thousands of rabid potential supporters. There was clearly enthusiasm on the margins. It seemed to me to stem from a hunger for something new and a desire to turn the page not just on the Bush era, but on our own party's recent history.

The crowds and chatter around the book tour in turn bred a great deal of speculation in the political community and the media about a possible Obama candidacy. Obama would be appearing on *Meet the Press* one Sunday in October, and it was expected that host Tim Russert would press him on whether he was going to run. The question was complicated by the fact that Obama had been on the show in January 2006 and made a Shermanesque statement about not running in 2008.

The Saturday before his October *Meet the Press* appearance, Axelrod and I got on the phone with Obama and his press secretary, Robert Gibbs. Obama and Gibbs were driving down the New Jersey Turnpike toward Pennsylvania, in between rallies he was attending for Democratic U.S. Senate candidates. In 2006 Obama was the most in-demand speaker for Democratic candidates in every part of the country, thanks to the fame resulting from his stirring 2004 Democratic National Convention speech in Boston and the success of his two books.

Ax, Gibbs, and I were trying to find the right turn of phrase to reconcile what Obama had said in January with where he stood in October: while a presidential candidacy was, as he said to us privately, "unlikely," the response to the book tour, the state of the country, and his profound sense that we needed a big change in leadership had caused him to give the race some consideration.

We started by throwing out some of the standard nonanswers: "Tim, my focus now is helping Democrats win back the Congress in 2006," or "We haven't even had the 2006 election, so let's settle down a bit; there will be plenty of time to discuss 2008 down the line."

Obama listened and then offered a novel approach. "Why don't I just tell the truth?" he suggested. "Say I had no intention of even thinking about running when I was on the show in January but things have changed, and I will give it some thought after the 2006 elections."

That kind of straightforward answer may sound unremarkable, but politicians always twist themselves into knots denying the obvious on these shows. His instinct to drop the charade and just say what he was thinking was enormously refreshing.

When the strategy session ended I called Ax and said, "That was impressive. It sounds silly but I think if he answers the question that way people will be even more intrigued. Because it will sound so nonpolitical."

"That's what makes him unique," Ax replied. "He doesn't have that political gene so many of them do. He's still a human being."

Ax had known Obama since 1992, when Barack was running a voter registration drive in Chicago and Ax was emerging as the city's preeminent Democratic political consultant. They stayed in touch over the years, and even though Ax never worked for him in a political capacity, they built a strong friendship. He often said Obama was one of the smartest people he had ever known—maybe the smartest.

Ax and I were partners in a political consulting firm. We met in 1994 when I was managing a U.S. Senate race in Delaware and he was hired to serve as our media consultant. His firm produced our television and radio ads and served as campaign advisers on strategy and message.

I thought David was unique among political consultants. He was not slick—in fact, whatever the opposite of slick is, Ax was its poster child. He and his partners did not take on too many races, choosing instead to pour themselves into a handful of worthy efforts. Ax took great pride in his work, opting for quality over quantity, and he had a healthy disregard for Washington, which I found appealing. He also had a great sense of humor, was a legendarily poor dresser, and was profoundly disorganized. And he was one of the smartest people I had ever met.

We lost the Delaware race—as did just about every Democrat facing the Republican tsunami of 1994—but I thought Ax did an excellent job for us, and we stayed in touch. In 2001 he asked me if I'd be interested in joining his firm as a partner. The idea appealed to me; I was interested in learning a new discipline—advertisement production—and respected the firm's focused approach. I agreed to join but would work out of Washington instead of the Chicago headquarters.

The firm—which became AKP Media in 2007—had a meeting in late 2002 to discuss business options for 2003 and 2004. The main topic of conversation was the 2004 Illinois senate race, which would be an open seat.

The two main Democratic contenders were Blair Hull, a very wealthy businessman who had vowed to spend millions on his campaign, and Dan Hynes, the state controller, who would have the endorsement of the state party and many labor unions and was considered a strong favorite. Both candidates had approached us about working for them, and David had sat down with each man to size him up.

But at our meeting he announced that he did not want to work for either. Instead, he thought we should work for a little-known state senator named Barack Hussein Obama, who was given zero chance to win by the political establishment. Just fourteen months after September 11, most believed his name alone would sink his candidacy.

"One of the others will probably win," Ax told us. "But Barack Obama is the kind of guy who should be in the U.S. Senate. He's bright, principled, skilled legislatively, and committed to a politics that lifts people up. I think that's who we should work for."

"Let me get this straight," summed up one of our colleagues. "We should work for the candidate with no chance, no money, and the funny name?"

"As I keep telling you guys," Ax wryly replied, "I am a terrible businessman."

So that was that. Ax had been the lead political reporter for the *Chicago Tribune* before transitioning into politics and had since elected mayors, senators, and congressmen throughout the state. He was considered the godfather of Illinois Democratic politics, from the operative side of the fence, and had great latitude on any decision the firm made involving Illinois.

I was not heavily involved in the day-to-day of Obama's 2004 Senate race, having other projects that I was primarily responsible for, but I attended some meetings and wrote his initial campaign plans for the primary election and then, when he won the primary in a stunning landslide, for the general.

My first meeting with him came at Ax's request in the spring of 2003. I flew into Chicago from D.C., and the three of us had breakfast at my hotel on Michigan Avenue. My mission at the breakfast was simple: convince Barack that he could not run for U.S. Senate and simultaneously serve as both his own driver and scheduler. The fledgling campaign was struggling with this as well as a host of other remedial issues: he was not spending enough time making fundraising calls. He was not closing the deal effectively enough with potential political supporters. And he was generally having a hard time allowing his campaign staff to take more responsibility for both the campaign and his life.

"You just have to let go and trust," I told him. "Your staff will inevitably screw up. But the most precious resource in any campaign is time. The candidate's time. Your time. You have to be the candidate. Not the campaign manager, scheduler, or driver."

"I understand that intellectually," he said, "but this is my life and career. And I think I could probably do every job on the campaign better than the people I'll hire to do it. It's hard to give up control when that's all I've known in my political life. But I hear you and will try to do better."

It was my first exposure to Obama's significant self-confidence. We chatted about the race for the rest of breakfast. I was struck by his intelligence and ease, and noticed that he lit up more when talking about policy than politics. I also noted his thoughts on campaign strategy—he was determined to win not with thirty-second ads and clever sound bites, but by building a grassroots campaign throughout Illinois. With rare exceptions, that was not the way politics was done anymore. Maybe Ax is on to something here, I thought. This is the kind of person we need in politics—and that we desperately need in Washington.

Still, had I been asked to gauge the likelihood that three and a half years later we'd be discussing whether Barack Obama should run for president, I wouldn't have taken the question seriously. At that time, with the country still shaken from 9/11, and the Republicans entrenched in power, it would have seemed insane.

But by 2006 the suggestion had gained a hint of plausibility. The political playing field had shifted dramatically, and one of the reasons was the mood and state of the country. President George Bush was deeply unpopular. Iraq, the economy, divisiveness in Washington, and the erosion of our moral leadership around the world had sent both Bush's and the Republican Party's stock plummeting.

As a result, Democrats scored a resounding victory in the 2006 congressional election, winning the House for the first time in twelve years and winning enough Senate races, coupled with the defection of a moderate Republican senator, to control that chamber for only the second time in twelve years. It was an electoral bloodbath for the GOP.

Historically, the sixth year of a two-term presidency can result in big losses for the incumbent's party. In 2006 something deeper was at work, and it was related to the feeling that the core leadership had turned rotten. Voters believed the Democrats' argument that Republican majorities were engaged in a culture of corruption, with lobbyists like the felonious Jack Abramoff calling the shots, showering their political patrons with money, and getting the desired results for themselves and their clients. Meanwhile, the people were getting hosed. Voters wanted a clean break.

The 2006 election swept many Republicans from office, but it did not quench that appetite for fundamental change. Voters wanted more and the presidential race was their chance to complete the job. Without this hunger for change, driven by a belief that Washington was fundamentally broken, the idea of a Barack Obama candidacy could not have taken flight.

Against this backdrop the nascent Obama organization had its first meeting to discuss the presidential race. Ax and I had spent election night of 2006 at the Democratic Congressional Campaign Committee (DCCC), the committee in charge of U.S. House races for the Democrats. We had poured our hearts into the effort for the past two years, partly because it felt personal. Rahm Emanuel, one of Ax's oldest friends, was the DCCC's chairman, and I had run the DCCC in 2000, coming a few thousand votes short in a razor-close national battle for the House. Six years later the job was finally done. We were ecstatic.

It was the kind of night that deserved a few days to soak in. Instead, after a few hours of sleep, we boarded a flight for Chicago to discuss the slimmest possibility, an Obama for President campaign.

My sense was that we would go through the process over the next couple of months and he would decide not to run. Almost every major presidential candidate in recent memory had been doing rigorous planning and laying groundwork for years before jumping in. Even long-shot candidates who eventually don't run still do the legwork. Most of the major Democratic contenders in 2008 spent the previous two years—and sometimes longer—on the hustings in Iowa and New Hampshire, building relationships, acquiring quiet offers of support, and familiarizing themselves with these sometimes-quirky states. Biden, Warner, Dodd, Edwards, and Bayh—all had been relentlessly planning and precampaigning. Hillary Clinton was in rarefied air all her own; armed with assets built up over twenty years, she was content to allow lesser candidates to bounce around Iowa. She would take things by storm at the moment of her choosing, when her army would gather and take the field.

I approached this meeting skeptical that a campaign would materialize, doubtful one should, and a little cranky that less than twelve hours after one election had ended the next one was beginning. Unless Obama decided that afternoon not to run, the time that I had planned to spend with my family would instead be spent writing memos and doing analysis that would likely lead nowhere.

Our initial meeting was small and consisted of Barack and Michelle Obama; their close Chicago friends Valerie Jarrett and Marty Nesbitt; Obama's Senate chief of staff Pete Rouse; his spokesman, Robert Gibbs; his scheduler and political hand, Alyssa Mastromonaco; Steve Hildebrand, a Democratic operative; and Axelrod and me.

We were a motley crew. Gibbs had left John Kerry's presidential campaign in 2003 during a purge and had entered a form of political purgatory. When Obama won the primary for the Senate race in 2004, we set out to enhance his campaign with more seasoned hands and brought Gibbs on board. He was from Alabama, a die-hard Auburn fan who had served as the top communications staffer in a number of campaigns and Democratic organizations. He was known as a tough enforcer who skipped the velvet on his hammer. Signing up with Obama helped rehabilitate his promising career. Despite their different demeanors and upbringings, over the course of the Senate campaign and then two years in the Senate, Gibbs and Obama grew quite close. Obama leaned on him for his political and media judgment, and would clearly want him to play a major role if he decided to run.

From his first days in the Senate, Obama drew top talent. Rouse had been the chief of staff for Tom Daschle when he was the Democratic leader, and Rouse had gained such respect and clout that he became known as the 101st Senator. When Daschle lost his reelection race in 2004, Obama courted Rouse hard to be his own chief of staff. Pete originally demurred but eventually gave in, providing the invaluable assistance of a skilled guide as Obama made his way in the Senate. Alyssa had been the scheduler for John Kerry's presidential campaign; doing a similar job, albeit with additional political responsibilities, for a freshman senator would normally be seen as a backward career move but she was drawn to Obama's potential.

Steve Hildebrand had been running Democratic campaigns for years and was one of the most respected managers and organizers in the party. He knew Iowa well, having run Al Gore's caucus campaign there in 2000. He originally got involved when he accompanied Obama to the Harkin Steak Fry in Iowa in October at Rouse's invitation, where the excited reaction to Obama added to the intensity of the speculation about his plans; after a few outings with Barack, Hildebrand had become a true believer, and relentlessly pressed him to make a presidential bid.

Valerie and Marty were both close personal friends of the Obamas and had been around Illinois politics for some time. Valerie had served as the finance chair for the 2004 Obama Senate race. I got the sense that after the meeting was over, Valerie, Marty, Barack, and Michelle would have a separate discussion to evaluate how it went. They would be important sounding boards throughout the campaign.

We met in a small room at AKP Media. Crowded around a conference table, we all waited to hear for the first time exactly what Obama was thinking. Within minutes it was clear he had given this a lot more thought than most of us had realized. He laid out why he was considering a run: the country needed deep, fundamental change; Washington wasn't thinking long term; and we had big challenges like energy and health care that had languished for decades; the special interests and lobbyists had too much power, and the American people needed to once again trust and engage in their democracy; the country was too divided; and the middle class and those trying to get into the middle class,

especially their children, ran the risk of having less opportunity than generations before. His question for us—before we got to any of the politics—was
whether he offered something distinct enough from the other candidates in
terms of addressing these challenges that it merited a campaign. I thought his
answers a pretty strong rationale for a candidacy and a strong campaign message. We had done some baseline research on where the race stood, but no
message testing, and we hadn't taken any polls to derive that message, which
was exhilarating in itself. I was also struck that his initial assessment of the
race was all about substance, not about politics. I have been in very few meetings with candidates or potential candidates where this was this case.

Barack did ask questions about the politics, and to a person we all said that
Hillary Clinton was an enormously strong front-runner. In fact, at this point,
it was tough to see how she could lose. We spent some time on the other candidates, but only briefly, discussing John Edwards's strength in the first contest,
Iowa, and how that was a complicating factor; because we could not assume
the role of alternative to Clinton there, we'd have to earn it. She was the eight-
hundred-pound gorilla, with organizations in every state, 100 percent name
recognition, and a fund-raising machine ready to be switched on at a moment's
notice. We had none of this. Nothing, nada, zilch. Any political conversation
about the 2008 primaries started and ended with Hillary Clinton.

Michelle Obama had questions about what this would mean to their family.
How often would Barack be campaigning out of town? Could they still have
many weekends together? Would the family be able to campaign together?
How much would she need to do and how would that work with her job and
looking after their daughters?

This was the first time I had met Michelle and I was impressed by her di-
rectness and the no-nonsense focus of her questioning. She clearly wanted all
the facts, and I could tell that running was not going to be solely Barack's
decision—they would decide together.

Other than Hildebrand, who was the cheerleader in the room and offered
a dubious fairy tale about not campaigning on Sundays and a lot of time at
home, no one had good news for Michelle. There could be no shortcuts. It
would be grueling and then more grueling. The candidate would only be home
for snatches of time and when he was, there would be calls to make and
speeches to review. And it would last at least a year if we lost. Two if we won.

I felt satisfied that there was no window dressing. They needed to make
their decision with open eyes and all the facts. But hearing is different than

living; we couldn't control how they received the message. I knew they could rationalize that the obstacle course was manageable, only to find themselves stuck midcourse.

The consensus concerning Michelle's involvement was that the campaign, if it existed, would want to use her as much as possible, but that she would tell us when she could travel, and we would utilize that time, with no pressure on her to do more. The Obamas made clear they would not outsource the care of their two young girls, so we would work around the family schedule, not the other way around.

At the end of the meeting we agreed we would reconvene in a couple of weeks and each of us would produce something to move the discussion forward—a sample schedule so the Obamas could see what their lives might look like day to day and month to month; an initial overview of the calendar and our provisional electoral strategy recommendations; fund-raising estimates; and an overview of what the first three months' imperatives and benchmarks would be.

Obama said he would spend time with Michelle discussing whether they could make this work as a family. He made it clear that the campaign's message—the rationale he had laid out at the meeting's outset—was not negotiable. So the Obamas would report on their ruminations about the family and lifestyle issues, and the rest of us would spend the bulk of our time discussing, in his words, "whether we can build not a winning campaign, but a credible one." That was our bar. It may seem low. But given our starting point, it was alpine.

I still believed the undertaking was largely a theoretical exercise, but Obama was more serious about running than I had anticipated. I called Ax on my way to O'Hare to get his take. "I think he wants to run, but he's drawn more to the idea of running than actually running," he said. "We'll see how he processes the reality of what this will mean, how hard it is, and how long the odds are. Michelle is the wild card. If she is opposed, there is no way this is going to happen. And I can't read yet where she'll come down."

I sighed. "Well, all I know is I was supposed to be at Disneyland with my son next week but we'll have to postpone that to pull together everything he asked for. But I was impressed by him. He clearly has a good sense of why he might want to run, and it's not about power or politics or some long-held ambition. I still think he doesn't do it—how many people have just sort of, last minute, with no planning, rolled the dice and jumped into a presidential race against maybe the strongest front-runner in history? With young kids to boot?"

"It's likely all our work will be for naught," Ax agreed. "But we owe this a real solid effort so at least he has everything he needs to make the decision."

In the interim before our next meeting, Obama organized a gathering with some of his key Senate staff, friends, and outside advisers in Washington. It was like a Harvard Law School reunion. Axelrod and I attended, and we listened as Obama explained his current thinking and asked everyone in the room to offer their thoughts, opinions, and concerns.

I was impressed by the thoughtfulness of the responses. Most centered on concern about what this would mean to his family; some flatly said they thought it was too early; others said he should run before he spent too much time in Washington and got senatoritis. Others thought it would be difficult to put together a campaign in such a short amount of time. I found it noteworthy that Obama surrounded himself with a fairly selfless crew, all the more remarkable given the type A ambitions often associated with a roomful of Harvard Law grads. I didn't get the sense that any of them were offering their opinions based on what was in it for them—the chance to be close to a new and exciting presidential candidate.

Toward the end of the meeting, Obama turned to me and asked me to outline what would be required to get a presidential campaign up and running and how it might operate. I spent about fifteen minutes ticking through the immediate imperatives were he to commit: launch a cutting-edge website, recruit talented senior staff, develop a plan and budget. I also talked about how strong Clinton was, and our need to focus on the early primary states in order to reset the race—when front-runners stumble early, they have generally been visited with great peril, though they almost always win anyway. We had not discussed electoral strategy in depth, but I thought it was important for his friends to understand from the get-go this would not be a sexy pursuit filled with grand white papers and big crowds in major metropolitan areas; we'd likely have to grind it out one voter at a time in Iowa to have any chance of winning. I made the point that to beat Hillary we'd have to run a perfect campaign. And even if we came close to doing that, the odds were still heavily in her favor.

The room was quiet during my spiel and I got the sense the theoretical had become more real—for Obama, too. It also dawned on me that if he ran, he might ask me to manage his campaign. Instantly, I thought I should have kept my mouth shut.

For the past five years I had been a consultant, with Axelrod as my partner. I got paid to give advice, not to be responsible for every facet of a sprawling organization. Before getting into consulting, I had managed two U.S. Senate races, a congressional race, and a national party committee. I knew exactly what managing was—a pain in the ass.

There is a heady side to it, sure, but the job encompasses a lot more than just developing electoral theories, obsessing about metrics, and spending lots of money creatively. It also requires dealing with myriad personnel issues, mediating internal disputes, and worrying about things like office air-conditioning costs and how much to reimburse staff for mileage—stuff I had not had to worry about for a long time but remembered as a grind. The manager has to be on top of every aspect of the campaign—when the candidate calls, he or she can't say, "I haven't been paying much attention to (fill in the blank). Let me talk to the staffer who has." As I had told Obama, there are no shortcuts. The manager's ass is on the line every minute of every day. The campaign has to be all-consuming.

I had not managed since 2000 and aside from knowing I would be rusty, I was not sure my family or I could handle it. I grew very uneasy at the prospect the more I thought about it. My wife and I had a two-year-old son, we had just moved into a new house, and we had family plans for 2007. My wife had a successful career and was applying to graduate school for the fall. We were also hoping to add another baby to the mix. A campaign would upset the whole apple cart.

Standing on the street outside the gathering, I said to Ax, "I see where this is headed. I am the logical choice of the folks around him to manage this. Well, I don't want to and I'm not even sure I'm a good choice. We better come up with some other options. Fast."

"You go right ahead," Ax said, smiling sweetly. "But I am going to tell him you are the only and best choice. We'll be in this boat together, even if it goes down."

———

In retrospect, our embryonic team entered this possible race having witnessed in 2004 and 2006, from different perspectives, some of the new techniques and political currents that would emerge so forcefully in 2008. Axelrod and I had worked on the tremendously long-shot gubernatorial campaign of Deval Patrick of Massachusetts in 2006, where we worked with a campaign that was doing some fascinating and new stuff using the Internet to organize and communicate message—from scratch, like we would have to do.

Obama's own 2004 race showed us the enormous power of his television presence directly communicating with voters. We realized without even having to discuss it that our most powerful weapon would be the candidate, unfiltered.

The fact that all of the initial inner circle—Gibbs, Ax, and me—had done presidential politics in 2004 (for three different candidates) was incredibly important for how we viewed the conventional wisdom about 2008—and was another huge advantage over the Clinton campaign. Few of her inner circle had been involved in the 2004 Democratic primaries. Ax and I had seen improbable outsiders win congressional primaries and races in 2006 while we were working closely with Rahm Emanuel and the DCCC on the effort to win back the House while in 2005 Gibbs was traveling with Obama, seeing a startling passionate reaction to him in very unlikely places all across the country. Of course, most important, Obama was absorbing these lessons as well. All four of us were in the right spots to see a new potential out there to match the changing mood of the electorate and new technological advances that could help us build a campaign to tap into the winds of change. Many of these lessons ran counter to conventional wisdom about how to run for president, so it was a good first test to see if we could ignore the evidence before our eyes, trust our gut, and start with a clean sheet of paper, not try to rerun the campaigns of the past.

When we gathered in Chicago for our next meeting with the smaller initial group, Michelle Obama opened things in very surprising fashion. She declared they had worked through all the family issues and had decided they would run if they thought they could mount a credible effort. They still wanted time to make a final decision on the family side of the ledger, but our conversation that day would focus more on politics than personal life.

We spent a lot of time at this meeting, and during this period, discussing the political calendar. We viewed the race not as national campaign, but as a sequence of states—beginning in Iowa in January and running through Montana and South Dakota on June 3—with the belief that what happened in any one contest had the distinct ability to affect the next. Essentially, this was a momentum theory, and valid or not, we really had no choice but to embrace it. We were thirty points behind Clinton; a head-on race fighting on multiple fronts across the country would be quick and painful. Prior campaigns lent some credibility to our approach. Momentum had historically been crucial in these early contests: winners generally kept winning, at least for a time. A loss was hard to turn around, though front-runners could sometimes stumble and recover due to their strength in other states and financial and organizational superiority.

The year 2008 marked the first time the Democratic Party would add two states to the early primary calendar: Nevada and South Carolina. These would follow Iowa and New Hampshire, in that order. February 5, the first date in the so-called window (those states not granted an early primary date), was also beginning to take form, but we did not know then it would become the twenty-two-state monster that was Super Tuesday.

Before we even knew the contours of the final calendar, we pounded Obama with the mantra that the first contests held undue influence. If you stumbled as an insurgent candidate, you were done. "If you run," we told him, "you are going to spend all your time doing two things: raising money and campaigning in one of these four states, most often Iowa." Though this strategy would be tested vigorously at times, in hindsight having it pinned down and clear at the outset could not have been more important.

Our strong strategic sense was that Hillary Clinton had to be disrupted early in the primary season for us to have any chance of derailing her. Ax and I gravitated to the same place on this pretty quickly, and the rest of the team concurred. There were no long drawn-out discussions. It just made sense.

It would take discipline to stick to the path, but the necessity of doing so was not really rocket science. We were running against such a formidable front-runner that if she won the first few contests, the race would be over. We would never be able to erase her big leads in the latter primary states, and at that point, her organizational and financial advantages would really kick in, as she looked to be the all-but-certain nominee and we campaigned in states where we had spent little time or resources.

As Ax told me over a breakfast in Chicago one day during this period, "I really don't think we have a choice. It's Iowa or bust."

I suspected that if you ran a computer simulation of the primary, ninety-five out of one hundred times, Hillary Clinton would win. Edwards would win a couple of the remaining five. That's how narrow I believed our path to be. And while there was no guarantee that our strategy would lead to victory, back-tracking or zigzagging would unquestionably lead to a precipitous fall off the electoral cliff.

Our first cut on these states—before any in-depth survey research was conducted or the final field of candidates was known—was the following (as always, Clinton was the main focus of our analysis):

We thought Iowa could be potential quicksand for Hillary. Bill Clinton never campaigned there in the primaries—in 1992 Senator Tom Harkin ran a favorite-son candidacy (on which I worked), and in 1996 Clinton was unopposed. Unlike in most other states, the Clinton operation, though likely to generate a formidable surge of early endorsements from elected officials and major Democratic activists, was not impregnable. None of her core senior team had any Iowa experience whatsoever. They did not have residual volunteers in every corner of the state from Bill's 1992 primary campaign as they did elsewhere. And many Iowans were strongly antiwar—including many Republican voters—so we thought her vote and stubborn position on the Iraq War could give her problems. Iowa was also historically friendly to outsider and long-shot candidates if they spent a lot of time in-state, had a resonant message, and organized well.

Of course, we had no assets in Iowa—Obama had close to zero relationships there. But many of us around the table—me, Hildebrand, Axelrod, Alyssa—had extensive experience in Iowa or had dealt with Iowa through the prism of a national campaign. We understood the quirks of caucuses, the nuances of the electorate, and that its voters historically paid little attention to the national media (they would make their own judgments, and take their time doing so). We knew we could count on a fair hearing in Iowa. I did not fully appreciate at the time the advantage such broad Iowa caucus experience gave the Obama headquarters, but looking back I can imagine that at Clinton headquarters, it must have seemed somewhat like foreign territory.

New Hampshire was the next state, and the first primary, and home of Bill Clinton's "Comeback Kid" resurrection in 1992. The state had a special relationship with the Clintons. Despite that, we thought New Hampshire could be fertile ground. Independent voters can make up a huge percentage of the primary electorate, and our sense was that Clinton would be very challenged to earn a healthy share of their support. The Granite State also had a history of tripping up front-runners—Walter Mondale and George W. Bush most famously—so if we could come out of Iowa as the main alternative to Hillary, we thought New Hampshire could be competitive. For Hillary Clinton, losing New Hampshire could be a damaging, if not fatal, blow.

Nevada was one of the new kids on the block; the Silver State would be holding a caucus for the first time. Our first cut at Nevada was the haziest, but our sense was that this would be a hard state for us, as the Democratic establishment would likely have outsized influence in a first-time caucus. Even in the spring training portion of the campaign, it was also clear that Hillary Clinton would have real strength among Latino voters, whom we expected to compose 10 to 12 percent of the Nevada electorate. We thought Nevada would be the least important of the first four contests in terms of the trampoline effect. I figured we would need serious momentum coming out of New Hampshire to have any chance of winning it.

Conversely, we were thrilled that South Carolina would be the gateway to the rest of the calendar. African Americans made up about 50 percent of the primary electorate, and though Hillary Clinton had a huge lead in the African American community at the moment, we believed that if we could show competitiveness through 2007, and if voters became familiar with Obama (most African American primary voters had no idea who he was or knew only his name, whereas the Clinton name was the gold standard in many of these households), our support levels would increase. If we could topple Clinton in Iowa or New Hampshire, our support in this community would skyrocket. And if we didn't do what we needed to in Iowa and New Hampshire, it was moot anyway; we'd probably be out of the race by South Carolina. We also believed that only one, Obama or Edwards, would be alive by the time South Carolina rolled around; if it was Obama, we would have a terrific opportunity to attract the support of progressive white voters in the Charleston area and rural white men whose support Clinton might have a tough time securing.

But it started and ended with Iowa. If we did not win there, our chances were probably zero. When you got under the hood in Iowa, it was a daunting challenge. Our first poll there had us firmly in third place. Edwards was polling 38, Clinton 25, and Obama 18. Edwards remained very popular in Iowa after his strong second-place finish in 2004 and had a strong core of organizational support. A look beneath the top numbers showed that our task was even harder than we initially realized. To win Iowa, we thought we'd probably need 35 percent of caucus attendees. If Edwards really faded, which looked unlikely but possible, the win number could jump up higher as his vote percentage dropped.

From the get-go it was clear we could not win if the caucus universe was the same as it was in 2004. And it had been that way pretty much every year since Jimmy Carter won in 1976, propelling him to the presidency. To win, we would have to attain the holy grail of politics—a fundamentally altered electorate.

Say you are a business trying to expand your percent of market share against an established brand-name product. Your competitor's customers have been buying their product for decades and are unlikely to sample something new. How do you outsell that competitor without converting their customers? You have to recruit new buyers.

We had to grow the share of the electorate we believed would be most supportive of Obama. The 2008 caucuses would have to be younger, attended by more minorities (though they constituted a small percentage of the population in Iowa, every voter mattered), and have a higher percentage of independents and Republicans participating than had historically done so.

It sounded great in theory. The reality was terrifying. In every recent caucus, twice as many people over sixty-five had turned out as people under thirty. We'd have to narrow that considerably, doing something most political observers thought was impossible—get young people interested and get them to show up. Republicans and independents could attend the caucuses but had to reregister as Democrats to do so—a huge barrier to participation. We'd have to find a way to create a permission structure to make this easier.

At our second meeting and in subsequent conversations, some other key assumptions were developed and decisions made that would help guide us out of the box if Obama gave the go-ahead:

We would be headquartered in Chicago. There was some dissent about this—he was a senator and would frequently be in Washington; some thought that we would have trouble attracting staff to Chicago for an underdog effort. I felt strongly that our base should be in Chicago. D.C. is a swamp of conventional wisdom and insiders that can suck a campaign down, and we needed to think differently, to care more about volunteers than political endorsements, to focus more on Iowa field numbers than the national Gallup poll, to be strategic more than tactical, and to not traffic in gossip and internal campaign politics. As far as attracting talent, I thought people who moved to Chicago would be committing themselves to the campaign, not fitting the campaign around their lives. And most simply, it was hard to sell an outsider candidate who was based in Washington. Obama raised splitting the headquarters—basing some functions in D.C. and some in Chicago—to accommodate those who couldn't move. I quickly shot this down as a potential disaster in the making. Even in the age of technology, it is invaluable to have everyone under one roof. Nothing is a substitute for human, in-person contact for hatching plans and hashing things out.

We would strive to be a grassroots campaign. That meant volunteers. This was a prime motivation for Obama to run, the belief that the American people needed to reengage in their civic life. He laid out a clear dictate that we needed to build a campaign that had this at its core. As a former community organizer, Obama felt in his gut that if properly motivated, a committed grassroots army could be a powerful force. Over time the volunteers became the pillars that held the whole enterprise aloft, but at the outset, we thought the grassroots could play three pivotal roles for our campaign. One, we hoped our volunteers could help fund our campaign with small contributions to a greater degree than any previous presidential candidate had succeeded in doing; two, we wanted them to organize their local communities for the campaign—the best way to get new people to caucuses and polls was to have a family member, friend, or neighbor ask them to go; and three, we needed them to help deliver our message, person to person, which was critical—trust in and attention paid to traditional media sources seemed to be dwindling rapidly.

Obama's desire to mount a grassroots effort answered neatly the looming question of how to run against the strongest establishment front-runner in our party's history; we would build a ragtag militia to compete against her regular army.

Technology, like the grassroots focus, would be at the core of our campaign from the start. In order to build a grassroots movement, it was clear that the only way to get to scale quickly enough was to use the power of the Internet to sign people up and ask them to get involved. I also made the point that many of our early supporters were likely to be fairly technologically savvy, as was more and more of the general population as well.

"So many people are living their lives through technology—how can we expect their interaction with politics to be the one exception?" I asked.

Because of the lead time required, we decided to green-light the building of a website, heavy on video and tools for our supporters to organize and raise money and have discussions and find each other—our own social-networking site. If he didn't run, this work would largely go down the drain, but we knew that the moment he indicated he was running, we would need a website that could absorb the interest and help propel our campaign.

We would follow the Bush model in one area. Obama was running largely to be a national antidote to George Bush, but he had read enough and studied enough about recent presidential elections to know that the Bush people did one thing very well: they had a tight circle involved in key decisions and none of those people talked out of school. Obama wanted the same along with a clear chain of command.

"I don't want to be involved in a campaign where everyone is leaking on each other and we have to worry that the contents of conference calls and meetings will show up on the Drudge Report or in the *New York Times*," he said. "I want to be inclusive on many matters in the campaign, so people feel listened to, but on big decisions, I want the circle small. So we can trust each other.

"And," he added pointedly, "we'll have fewer suspects to interrogate if there is a leak."

Ken Mehlman, who was Bush's manager and Obama's law school classmate, told him the Bush people had a rule that their campaign inner circle would never expand. If they wanted to add someone new, someone else had to be kicked out. Our tight circle initially consisted of me, Axelrod, and Gibbs, talking through key strategic matters with him. Some staff told me having three white guys as the most inner core in the beginning was the source of some internal tension, and I understood why. The circle would need to get more diverse and grow a bit down the line. But for now, that was the unit.

Fifty million dollars was our initial fund-raising target. That was the number we thought we could raise in 2007 based on initial estimates of fund-raising events, online contributions, and direct-mail contributions. It was a conservative estimate; if we built momentum and looked viable down the line—a big if at that point—we could expect it to grow, but it served for our initial budget. The budget allowed for strong campaigns in the first four states and that was it. We would need to use strong showings in Iowa and New Hampshire to quickly raise the money needed to compete in the February primaries. This underscored how perilous our path to the nomination was—we assumed Clinton would raise at least $100 million in 2007 on top of the $10 million she was transferring from her Senate account (we were transferring next to nothing, because his Senate account had next to nothing), that she would outspend us in the early states and also be better prepared in the later states.

The last point may not seem strategic, but it ended up being important. And we would try to have fun. It became clear in these discussions that Obama did not have a pathological desire to be president. He was a grounded, sane, and relatively happy person who would be just fine if he never became president or even a presidential candidate. If he ran in 2008, it would be because at this moment, he thought he had something to offer in terms of leadership and priorities that matched what the country needed. We did not spend much time talking about 2008 versus 2012 or 2016. Obama was not searching for the best time to run. Because of this, we did not have the stifling pressure that came with expectations or unhealthy ambitions. As Obama said at one of our initial meetings in Chicago, "I'm putting all my chips in the middle of the table and letting it ride. If I win, great. If I don't, I won't be personally crushed."

Given all that, when he insisted that we also should have some fun, it did not ring hollow. We'd strap on the armor, battle our way across the country-side, and see what we could accomplish without getting weighed down by overseriousness. This also led to the "no asshole" rule, so popularized in our campaign by Axelrod. We stated from the outset we would try to build a col-legial team, where everyone was in it for something bigger than him- or herself. We would not staff positions with merely the best talent available. Of course our people had to know what they were doing—but how they went about doing it was equally important. Presidential campaigns are brutal affairs in the best of circumstances; when the internal dynamic is corrosive and not filled with trust, it can be unbearable. We were determined to avoid that from the beginning.

Campaigns are no different than any other organization—they are collec-tions of human beings. The clarity of the mission and the culture of the group may not outweigh strategy and resources in determining eventual success, but they're awfully close. We would strive to build a campaign where people did not scream at each other, where performance was measured objectively, where crises were dealt with calmly, and where the team was there to serve the cause, not personal ambition.

A healthy culture was hard to quantify in terms of its eventual impact on the election. But we thought it would be a big factor. The Clinton inner circle was notorious for infighting, backstabbing, and jockeying for position. Our approach could offer an important competitive advantage.

The formations of a campaign strategy were taking shape, as were some core principles that would define how we would operate and what would be impor-tant for us to focus on in creating a start-up organization at warp speed.

I was in Chicago a few days before Obama left for Hawaii on his long-planned family vacation in December. AKP Media was soon to have a meeting to plan out the next two years; most of the conversation would revolve around how we would adjust if Obama ran. The night before the meeting, Obama called and asked me to come to his house. I had a sinking feeling that he was going to ask me to manage his campaign if he jumped in.

I arrived at the Obamas fairly late in the evening, and after saying good-night to Michelle, he and I settled down in the den with a couple of beers to review the current landscape. I was more or less the operational hub in this strange period, so I updated him on various areas: potential staff, machinations of the other candidates, timelines we would need to meet if he were to run. After we chewed on all that, he got around to the subject I'd been dreading.

"So, David," he said. "I won't make a final decision until the Hawaii trip. But I think it is all but a certainty that I'll run. And if do, the most important role I need to fill is campaign manager." Here it comes, I thought. "I've been impressed by your judgment, temperament, organization, and strategic sense over the last few weeks. There are lots of bigger names out there, and maybe I should have canvassed for other possibilities. But I think you and I would work well together, and it's clear you can work well with Axelrod, Gibbs, and the other likely staff. So I want you to manage the campaign."

I took a big chug of my beer before replying. "There are not many people in our line of work who would not jump at this opportunity, win or lose. But I have two huge stumbling blocks. First, I have a young son. I'd rarely see him. And my wife and I want to have another child, ideally pretty soon. So that will be put off at least another year, and I'm already pushing forty."

"I had my youngest when I was forty," Obama piped in helpfully.

"I understand," I said. "But what if we do the improbable and win the primary? It'll be two years. And it's not just that. My wife's career will be affected too. She'll be marooned here in Chicago with no support network and a husband who is a ghost. It's a personal loser all the way around.

"I'm also not sure I will do a good job. I haven't managed in eight years, since the DCCC. My last stint as campaign manager for a candidate race was the 1996 U.S. Senate race in New Jersey. I will be terribly rusty from a manager's standpoint, and I've gotten used to pontificating and giving advice and counsel, not being responsible for everything from the budget to electoral strategy to personnel headaches. I'm not sure I want to go back to that world and, even if I did, that I would be any good at it."

He nodded. "Well, I understand the hesitation on both fronts. They are valid and you need to wrestle with them. On your last point, I know there will be some rust, but I have faith you'll shake it off quickly. You've never managed a presidential campaign either. But I can see you understand the rhythm and contours of a race like this. I've never been a presidential candidate. Hell, I've never had a negative ad run against me. So I think we'll be a good team, in some ways much more so than people who have been around the track a bunch of times in their current roles. We can look at everything through a fresh set of eyes and be more agile."

"Just making it up as we go along," I added.

Obama laughed. "I prefer the way I put it. It sounds more appealing."

We agreed that I would talk it over with my wife and I would call him in Hawaii to tell him my decision. If it was no, I would have some other candidates lined up for us to consider, and if I didn't manage, I'd work on the race from my firm and spend as much time on it as I could.

On the ride back to my hotel I reported to my wife that the offer was indeed made. She sounded as angst-ridden as I felt. I don't think I had ever before agonized over a job in my life, whether it was cleaning chimneys, selling knives door-to-door in college, or my many political jobs. Things made sense immediately or they didn't. I accepted or turned down jobs very quickly. This one would take longer to work through.

The day before Obama left for Hawaii he met with Ax, Gibbs, and me in the same AKP conference room where our initial meeting about running had been held the month before. "I am ninety percent certain I am running," he reported. "Maybe even higher. You guys should proceed quietly as if I am, and keep making progress on planning and sizing up potential personnel. I had hoped to have a final decision by now, as you know, but I want to mull it over a bit more while I'm away. When I get back in early January, I'll give you the final green light."

I thought this bout with normalcy might cause him to pull back. Spending two weeks in Hawaii, frolicking with his kids, feeling the weight of the looming possibility that his life would be changed for the next year if not forever—it would be a sobering experience.

Meanwhile, I had my own decision to make. My wife and I debated the pros and cons, weighed the move to Chicago and the impact on the family. It was difficult to find any kind of clarity until my wife finally opened the door for me.

"I have watched you struggle through campaign cycles for years now," she said. "Your heart hasn't been in it since Gephardt took a pass in 2000. You tell me Barack Obama is authentic, one of the smartest people you have ever met, and in it for the right reasons. You say that you'll try to run a different campaign, getting people involved, especially young people and minorities. This seems like the kind of campaign you idealize. Sure, he probably won't win. But won't it be hypocritical if, after all the bemoaning of politics today, you don't answer the call here and try to do something about it?"

It took me aback. She had plenty of valid reasons to oppose this step for us, but now, to my surprise, she was challenging me to live up to my rhetoric. And what's more, she was dead-on. This was a gut check. And if she thought we could potentially make it work, with all the sacrifice it would entail for her and our son, it would be fraudulent of me not to address my own cynicism by doing all I could to change it.

She added, "We'll have to figure out housing, preschool, and my work. I guess it would mean putting off grad school again. We just signed on to a new mortgage and we'll have to swing Chicago rent on top of it. It makes no sense for us right now. And frankly, I'm not sure a guy who was in the state senate three years ago has any business running for leader of the free world.

"But we've been making a living in and around politics and government for a long time, complaining all the while about how nasty it is. You believe in this guy. I believe in you. We can muster the courage to make this leap. I can figure out the finances, the logistics, and the family stuff. You just make sure we are part of a campaign that's worth it."

I called Obama in Hawaii to tell him. "Against my better judgment," I said, "I've decided to accept and manage this nutty enterprise. All-in. I'm yours until we win or lose. "

"I am very grateful," he responded. I'll do my best to make sure you don't regret it."

Then he became wistful discussing his vacation so far. "For the first time, it's hard for me to move about the island—I'm getting stopped everywhere I go, people asking for pictures, asking me if I'm going to run. I guess this is what it will be like everywhere if I run." He asked if I thought he could get to Hawaii next year; I said it would be difficult. That prospect clearly made him unhappy. If he knew that pictures of him shirtless would appear on newsstands days later, he probably would have decided right then not to run. I thought I was hearing a guy experiencing huge second thoughts. Maybe I'll get to have my cake and eat it too, I thought to myself—agree to manage the campaign, get out of my comfort zone and belly up for the greater good, and never have to see it through.

But I tried to give him some clarity. "I figured being over there would cause some doubts to creep in," I told him. "That's what you are giving up. Normalcy and time with your family. You have to own that. You should not feel like you have to do this, that you are on some inexorable path here. We will be ready to charge out of the gate if you tell us it's a go. But you can still pull up. Because the worst thing would be for you to get in this when you still have lingering doubts. You'll be twisting in the wind for a year and hating every moment of it and we'll almost assuredly lose."

I think he appreciated the candor. He said he was still much more likely to run than not but would need to spend more time thinking about it during the remaining days of his vacation.

Yet when he landed in Chicago in early January, he still had not made a final decision. He called Axelrod to get together and the two of them spent a couple of hours reviewing the bidding. Ax called me afterward and said he had done a lot of listening. He now thought it was no better than 50-50; Obama was having a hard time taking the final leap. We had all the rockets on the launch pad, ready to hire the first wave of staff and to plot out and execute the first moves of the campaign. But now everything ground to a halt, and we idled by for a few days as he wrestled with this momentous decision.

On January 6, Obama called me late at night (that's when Obama usually called, after his kids went to bed) and said he had crossed the Rubicon.

"It's a go," he said. "You can start hiring some core people quietly, but swear them to secrecy. We should all get together in the next couple of days to hash out how we announce I'm running and what the first few weeks will look like."

"Okay," I replied. "I have a memo that Ax and I worked on that lays out a lot of thoughts on this. I'll send it to you and we'll get together to discuss it. I feel confident that you went through a rigorous process about deciding. As did I. So why don't we make the best of this and win this thing."

"I think we can," he said resolutely. "Let's get to work."

Just like that we were off to the races. It had been only sixty days of contemplation, planning, and decisions, but it felt like six months. Barack Hussein Obama, forty-five years old, a United States senator for two years, born to a Kenyan and a Kansan, was running for president of the United States. With little more than hope in his sails.

We had a presidential campaign to get off the ground. And quickly. And a mountain named Hillary Clinton in our path that we had to find some way to scale, get around, or blow a hole through.

2

Taking Off While Affixing the Wings

Barack Obama was running for president. Now his team—such as it was—had to figure out how to get his campaign aloft without crashing and burning.

Our short-term goals through the spring of 2007 were clear and daunting: achieve a clean lift-off with a strong announcement of his candidacy and take no blows to the engine—external shots or self-inflicted wounds—that might stall our momentum; raise at least $12 million in the first quarter, a number we thought would give us a solid foundation and put us on pace to make $50 million for the year; flesh out our core message and provide some substance—like health care and energy plans—to go along with the hype; begin to build a grassroots movement, most aggressively in the early states, and figure out the best way people could be helpful beyond giving money; assemble a top-shelf campaign organization marked by camaraderie, collegiality, and discretion; and somehow survive the fusillade we would be facing from the press and our opponents.

The last of these goals was complicated by the fact that we had done zero research on our own candidate beyond a small and incomplete package from the 2004 Senate race. With this lapse, we were violating a central rule of politics—know more about yourself than your opponents and the media do. Since we had not scrubbed every quote, vote, speech, and donor of Obama's, we knew we'd be getting questions we couldn't foresee, and unless he remembered each incident and vote precisely, we'd be scrambling to mount a defense.

Our goals were all derived through the prism of our electoral strategy: their attainment was necessary for us to successfully execute that strategy—focus like a laser on Iowa and the other early states. The plan was clear and logical. It just seemed nearly impossible to carry out in the infancy of the Obama campaign.

First, we had to decide how to let the world know that Obama was running for president. Our initial recommendation was that he tape an online video announcing that we were forming an exploratory committee but that left no question he was running. Then he could follow up a few weeks later with a video saying he was officially in. We thought he should postpone a formal announcement speech and tour until after the first quarter, in April, when we would have our sea legs under us.

Obama readily agreed to the exploratory committee taping—our lawyers said we needed to get that set up as quickly as possible so we could legally begin taking care of the thousand things necessary to get the campaign up and running (raising money, opening accounts, spending money and tracking that spending, and having a process in place to hire people, quickly). But he insisted that he needed to give a speech laying out the rationale for his candidacy as soon as possible, certainly before April.

"We just can't wait to begin laying out why I'm running—not fleshed-out plans but principles," he insisted. "I'm going to be hyped to the *n*th degree, and I need to make sure the voters and the press corps understood why I'm running before somebody else fills in that canvas for us."

It made sense, and, moreover, he had 99 percent of the voting shares in this particular decision. That this would be extraordinarily difficult to accomplish in a month was beside the point. The whole endeavor was so improbable that we could afford to be cavalier and shoot for the stars. Axelrod and I compounded the degree of difficulty by insisting that we couldn't just do one speech at one location. We'd have to cover at least Iowa, New Hampshire, and South Carolina in addition to whatever kickoff we did in Illinois. If our strategy was about the early states, we'd have to be there from Day One or it could get some noses out of joint—and we needed to begin building our organizations in these states. From scratch.

Unfortunately, you can't just say you're running and have everything fall into place. There are a million little things to do and a few important ones. In addition to getting the campaign particulars functioning—the website, a system to receive and respond to e-mails and phone calls, office space, equipment for all the employees, a way to process contributions and generate thank-you letters, and ensuring everything is done legally—we also had to get the organization functioning. Who was going to do what and who would report to whom? We also had to make sure everybody we hired understood our strategy and message so they could internalize it and default to those touch points when making decisions.

We wanted to keep the campaign structure simple so it would work smoothly once assembled. Our operations department dealt with human resource issues, maintaining the budget, preparing Federal Election Commission reports, and a gazillion other items. In essence they administered the campaign. We had a finance department. A new media department. A scheduling and advance team. Press and communications. Opposition and self-research. A team managing our polling and paid media efforts. A political department to deal with elected officials and constituency leaders around the country, excluding the four early states. A field department to interact with our volunteers in the non–early states, complementing new media's online organizing. The information technology department. And then, finally, our state operations.

The heads of each of these departments reported directly to me, though some I dealt with much more frequently than others; Hildebrand spent a lot of time with the political and field departments in the beginning so I could focus on press, message, fund-raising, and Iowa.

I would have drowned if not for one of the best hires I made early on. Katie Johnson was technically my assistant but really the glue of the entire campaign. She kept us all organized and facilitated internal communication, setting up many of our meetings and conference calls, often on her own initiative. Katie had served as Rahm Emanuel's assistant at the DCCC in the 2006 cycle, while he was chair. Rahm makes a hurricane look like a spring breeze. I figured if Katie could thrive under that force of nature, she could handle a presidential campaign no sweat. I was right.

One of the most important things Katie did was keep me from getting into a logjam; she developed a great sense of what I needed to deal with personally and what could or should be handled by others. It was critical to the successful management of a seemingly unmanageable torrent of tasks. With Katie's help, my first cut at every call, e-mail, or request was to determine who else could handle it. Managers have to keep most things off their desks, so they can focus on execution in the moment and still have time to look around the bend and keep ahead of unfolding events.

Delegation kept my plate relatively clean, but I also wanted the senior staff to be empowered in their interactions with the outside world. Whether it was a donor, reporter, or politico, I wanted the people who worked with us to understand who their internal contact was, and that there would be no end runs. The buck stopped with whichever department head their business fell under. If our finance director, Julianna Smoot, wanted me to talk to a donor, or Gibbs to a reporter, they made that decision and delivered me on their own terms. This policy and our discipline in enforcing it helped our organization run smoothly and gave our senior staff necessary muscle.

It held for internal matters too. If a junior staffer came to me with an idea or complaint, I told them, "Talk to your boss," or just forwarded the e-mail to the appropriate senior staffer. We needed a clear chain of command and awareness throughout the campaign that there was no daylight between members of the senior team—no court of appeals.

As we prepared for the announcement, the campaign still existed mostly on paper. We had no campaign office. No internal e-mail. No staff in the early states. No polling or policy work. We didn't yet have the ability to get campaign credit cards, so our staff out in the states and advance staff working on the announcement were forced to charge everything to their personal cards and file for reimbursement. And Obama wanted to write much of the announcement speech himself. The odds of crashing were getting higher by the moment.

The campaign infrastructure consisted of a few of us in a temporary office in D.C., some others in D.C. working from home, and a few living in Chicago, including Ax. Every problem proved a good reminder that even with technology, there was no substitute for being able to run down the hall and discuss issues with your colleagues. We were a disorganized mess, communicating by e-mail chains and conference calls. Our goal was to find space and get settled in our Chicago headquarters by early February, but until March about sixty of us were packed in three to a desk in temporary space that would have made OSHA's head spin. A few people were crammed in the tiny Hopefund space in D.C., which housed Obama's hole-in-the-wall political committee and from where he now made his fund-raising calls. Basically those days were a total shitshow—the term, introduced by Alyssa, that we used to describe the times when things seemed completely off the rails.

Our senior staff met in D.C. in mid-January to discuss the announcement and decide where the kickoff speech would be. Obama suggested Springfield,

Illinois, as a location, specifically the Old State Capitol, where Lincoln had given his famous "House Divided" speech. Obama had served in the state legislature in Springfield for eight years and had been unusually successful at bringing Democrats and Republicans together, which made it a good choice in terms of alluding to his record. It also bolstered the midwestern-values-versus-Washington-values contrast we would highlight in the announcement speech and throughout the campaign.

Ax wrote the first-draft script for the short video that we would release online to announce Obama's intention to run. I made a few small changes, but it hardly needed them. From Day One, David had in his gut and at his fingertips the core elements of our message—change versus a broken status quo; people versus the special interests; a politics that would lift people and the country up; and a president who would not forget the middle class.

The video was shot in Chicago at a supporter's home. Obama, as he always did when filming an ad, changed the language and improved the final product even while they were shooting.

Ax e-mailed the clip to me a few hours later. When I did not respond immediately, he called me three times in ten minutes, leaving increasingly urgent messages. Ax got this way when putting together an important creative piece; desperate to know what others thought, he'd seek immediate feedback.

I called him and innocently said, "What's up?"

"You know what the hell is up," he replied. "Have you seen the video?"

"Video? Oh, the announcement video. I'll get to it soon," I replied.

"Look at it now!" he all but screamed into the phone.

I laughed, dropping the ruse. "I have. It's terrific. We have a provisional core message that should carry us through for some time. And the fact that it feels more casual, not like an Oval Office address, is dead-on. It looks less contrived."

We released the exploratory video on January 18 and it instantly became a YouTube phenomenon, driving hundreds of thousands of people, to our embryonic website. This was an important moment: it heightened our belief that the Internet could become both a message tool that would let us speak directly to voters as well as an organizational net—and hopefully more. In the video Obama laid out the CliffsNotes version of his candidacy. (I think it says something about the depth of his beliefs that almost three years later he still uses much of the same language and makes the same arguments.) He also stated flatly that on February 10 he would share his plans with the nation in Springfield, Illinois—there was no ambiguity. We wanted to make clear we were in, for good.

Obama spent much of those early days calling potential contributors and fund-raisers, and we were surprised by the positive response from a mixture of fund-raising graybeards and new talent. We were on our way to having strong people in place in all the major finance cities. Many of them had been with the Clintons for years but were ready for something new. It didn't hurt that these donors were intensely motivated, having infuriated the Clintons by jumping ship. If Obama failed to win, they faced eight years in political Siberia.

Alyssa ran daily countdown calls on the announcement to make sure everything was coming together. How was building the crowd going? What press access needed to be granted around the announcement and when? Who would speak at these events? What political meetings or calls should Obama do at each stop? What would the staging and pictures look like?

We had no phone numbers in any state, so we set up temporary phone numbers that flowed to a call center; if someone from Iowa called and expressed interest, we could capture their information and get back to them once we had staff on the ground. By the time we assigned people to begin working through the list, we had a backlog of more than ten thousand e-mail questions and offers of support. It took us two months to get caught up.

One of my most important hours during this time was spent over a couple of beers at D.C.'s Union Station with Paul Tewes, the leading candidate to become our Iowa state director. Tewes was eccentric, a strong leader, and passionate about Obama. He also had excellent credentials; he was business partners with Steve Hildebrand, our deputy manager, and had run Iowa for Gore in 2000 and served as a key strategist at the committee charged with running U.S. Senate races. A Minnesota native, he was partial to the late senator Paul Wellstone's style of grassroots politics.

Tewes and I got into an intense discussion about what our strategy and approach should be in the Hawkeye state. We sketched out the blueprints for an organization that would go after every voter, place a huge staff on the ground (Tewes's first budget draft could have funded the Iraq war), and put a premium on local volunteers. As we talked about this, Tewes said something that sold me on his ability to do Iowa right: "A staff is not an organization. A staff is there to support a local organization." That would be our strategy: Iowans talking to Iowans. We'd have to build that kind of network to have any chance of winning this state—or any others after it.

Our staff was as motivated as our donors. We attracted people who wanted to be there for the right reasons. No one was joining Obama for President because they thought it was the best avenue to a White House job. In the dark recesses of our minds we all knew that Hillary Clinton would likely be the nominee. Nevertheless, a wonderfully talented and committed staff materialized, many of them uprooting their lives to do so. Some were drawn to the chance to be part of making history; some liked Obama's call for a new politics; others were excited by the clear stirring in the country about his candidacy; yet others, myself included, while grateful for the good the Clintons did in the 1990s, felt it was time for a change of the guard. Twenty-eight years of Bushes and Clintons would be too much. Our country needed a fresh start.

Tewes came on board and began to fill out his Iowa staff. Mitch Stewart, an up-and-coming talent with a strong organizing background, was brought on as our caucus director, overseeing the organization. He worked with Anne Filipic, our Iowa field director, who managed many of the field organizers, the young kids working with our volunteers. Emily Parcell, our Iowa political director, had helped the Iowa senate turn Democratic for the first time in over a decade, and had great credibility throughout the state. We needed a balance of novices and grizzled hands, and Emily identified our best political targets and whom Obama should spend time courting. Tewes brought in Marygrace Galston to serve as his deputy and occasional therapist. Tewes had ten ideas a day, nine of them nutty, and Marygrace sorted for the daily stroke of brilliance while generally keeping the operation on track.

One of Tewes's ideas was to make sure we were working every community, no matter how small. African American, Latino, high school kids, Republicans—we had staff assigned to all of the demographics, months ahead of our competition. It gave us a real leg up.

Singling out all that our heroic and skilled campaign staff did right would fill an encyclopedia. But I will mention some structural decisions we made that in hindsight were very important to our success.

First, we imposed a salary cap. No one in our campaign, with the exception of our finance director, made more than $12,000 a month. Now, that is a lot of money. But in many statewide campaigns, never mind presidentials, staff can make twice that. In addition to conserving money, the cap also took all the drama out of salary negotiation. We eventually had salary bands for more-junior staff, so new hires were offered what their peers made—take it or leave it. We also instituted a no-raise policy, unless someone was taking a new job with more responsibility. This was not ideal; people were working hard and we were succeeding. From a management perspective, though, deciding who would get a raise and how much they'd get could cause serious internal discord and suck up valuable time. Because we were a campaign with a set end time—and not a business with a longer horizon—we were able to put this policy into place without too loud an outcry.

Obama heartily agreed with the salary cap, which signaled to him from the get-go that I would watch our funds carefully. I tended sometimes to go beyond careful to downright miserly. People weren't always happy with my decisions, but once they were made, the issue was settled. This was critical, in fiscal instances and in others. We did not have a lot of time to build up trust with one another. We had to make dozens of decisions a day, and not all of them would be optimal. But we were a start-up in the truest sense of the word, running against a behemoth, and we did not have the luxury of wallowing in hard decisions or overanalyzing things. We had to move, move, move. Through that process, Obama and I developed a good sense of what decisions he needed to be involved in, and he trusted that we were doing the blocking and tackling well enough that he could focus less on the "Did we do this?" "Did you think of that?" "When is that getting done?" and spend the majority of his time on the major responsibilities of a presidential candidate—improving delivery and fine-tuning message, executing political and fund-raising asks at a high level, and getting to know the states and the rhythms of what was a shockingly new experience for him.

Axelrod brought in Larry Grisolano, a talented, longtime Democratic manager and strategist, to oversee our paid media and polling teams, which became an increasingly important part of the campaign as we got closer to elections. Larry had Iowa experience, working for Tom Harkin twice (we were roommates in Des Moines as kids on Harkin's Senate race in 1989), but he had also managed major races in California and other states. Ax is brilliant and has many strengths; knocking off a to-do list every day is not one of them. To his credit, he identified this as a challenge early in the campaign and insisted we bring in Larry; it made a huge difference. We would have languished without a strong person in that role.

The new media group (online communications, Web-page development and maintenance, texting) in most campaigns reports to the communications department, and its department head is not considered an equal of other senior staff. But I saw how important the burgeoning online world was to our overall success; new media would touch just about every aspect of our campaign. So I had that department report directly to me. To find us new talent we enlisted one of Barack's law school classmates, Julius Genachowski, who was steeped in the technology world. He identified our director of new media, Joe Rospars, a veteran of Howard Dean's revolutionary new media effort in 2004. Joe seemed to relish the challenge of marrying digital technology and strategy with a strong grassroots campaign.

Julius also found the former chief technology officer of Orbitz, Kevin Malover, to be our CTO. Kevin saw things from a large corporate perspective in terms of our infrastructure needs. From the start we had a wealth of technology geniuses supporting us, and our new media and technology staff held weekly conference calls with them to generate ideas as we refined our plans and tried new things. Though the rest of the world was zooming forward at a rapid digital clip, for some reason political campaigns were in many respects stuck in the Dark Ages technologically. With the help of supporters like Eric Schmidt of Google, we dramatically improved our digital strategy and execution, and I'd say we were competitive digitally with any business-world start-up.

Julianna Smoot had been the chief fund-raiser for the Senate Democrats in 2006 and knew many of the major Democratic donors in the country firsthand. Julianna had our entire national finance operation up in a matter of days and hired a slew of fund-raising staff who were deeply loyal to her. Her North Carolina roots showed in her accent, but Julianna's soft drawl camouflaged a hard-charging, take-no-prisoners mentality. She rode her staff hard to meet their goals and did not take guff from our fund-raisers around the country.

Steve Hildebrand did a terrific job of finding our lead staff for the first early states. We preferred hungry people for whom a proposed role on the Obama campaign might be a bit of a stretch, as opposed to people who might coast because they had been a state director in a presidential race before. We were fortunate that most of the Clinton campaign apparatus was set in stone; because they had been planning to run for a long time, they knew who was playing what roles, and this froze out many talented players. A mixture of availability and faith in Obama led a huge number of very qualified and motivated staff to come knocking at the Chicago HQ, despite the long odds.

I set the tone early, at our first staff meeting, by decreeing that all of us in Chicago should view our job first and foremost as supporting the states. Most presidential campaigns operate with the mentality that headquarters knows best and that that's where the major action is. My view was there were no voters in headquarters. I wanted the staff to wake up every day and see their job through the prism of "What can I do today to help us win the Iowa caucus?" I sought to instill that discipline throughout the organization. We would not waste time or bounce from strategy to strategy. We would all align in the same direction and work as hard as we could.

Even as our staff was coalescing at breakneck speed, there were reminders every day that we weren't shooting free throws; we had defenders in the lane. On a Saturday morning in late January, Hillary Clinton released her own video, and then a press release, proclaiming, "I'm in it to win it."

I understood the strategy behind those words: she presented herself as the inevitable nominee. Hillary is going to win, her campaign insisted, so why would any donors, activists, or elected officials support one of the other campaigns? We thought it was a terrible misreading of the electorate—inevitability doesn't speak to a hunger for change—and they certainly misread the electoral terrain of the primary. The early states *really* do not like to be told the election is over before it has started. They like to soak up every ray during their quadrennial moment in the sun, and that requires a competitive race.

That said, we all had enormous respect for the Clinton political machine and assumed they were three steps ahead of us. The Clinton campaign may have underestimated us, but we never made that mistake regarding them. We knew what we were up against—or thought we did.

We knew Clinton's campaign would be run by loyal, longtime lieutenants. Patti Solis Doyle was my counterpart. She had been with Hillary in various roles going back to 1992, as a scheduler and then as director of her political action committee and her 2006 Senate race. Originally from Chicago, Patti was known as a tough and organized operative, though she had no experience managing competitive elections.

Mark Penn, a pollster with a long history with both Clintons, played the role of lead message strategist, the rough equivalent to Ax in their campaign. Penn was known to develop strategies geared toward the center of the electorate, and he was a believer in microtargeting, an approach spelled out in his book *Microtrends*. We thought this was an election with one big macrotrend—change—and thought Penn's penchant for slicing and dicing the electorate could come back to bite them. Or so we hoped.

Howard Wolfson, whom Ax and I both knew well from previous campaigns, was Hillary's über-communications director, their answer to Robert Gibbs. He was skilled in the black arts of politics—leaking information, setting traps for opponents—and was deeply respected by the press corps, which seemed to think, not without reason, that Howard was always two steps ahead of everyone else.

Their fund-raising was led by Terry McAuliffe, considered the best fund-raiser in Democratic Party history, and Jonathan Mantz, who had worked for me at the DCCC and knew every donor in America, having served as chief fund-raiser for both the House and Senate Democrats.

Some pundits called it the dream team of presidential staffs.

Barack and I had a long conversation the morning of Clinton's announcement. We were both underwhelmed by her message, which put a little bounce in our step. "In it to win it?" he said. "Seems awfully political. Maybe the base will like it though. They're hungry to win."

"Maybe," I said. "But it's an awfully cold message. I think you need to warm folks up a bit with your vision and where you want to lead before essentially calling the race over." I had already talked to Axelrod at least three times that morning, and he concurred. Barack and I quickly moved our discussion to the myriad things we had to get buttoned up before the formal announcement and in the weeks following. Despite the jaw-dropping challenge all this entailed, we were both grasping onto a bit of fleeting normalcy. It was my last weekend in Washington before moving permanently to Chicago and leaving my family behind for six weeks. Barack had a down day in Chicago and was planning to spend time with his kids and work out. Even with our chief rival officially throwing down the gauntlet, we were pretty relaxed. The respite was brief.

In Chicago, two days before the announcement, the high temperature was five degrees. It was not much warmer in Springfield. Our inclement weather site in Springfield was an old, dank building. Any event held there would be cramped and depressing, hardly a great first impression.

Michelle Obama questioned whether we should scrap our outside plans altogether. While the Saturday forecast called for highs in the mid- to high teens by the afternoon, we'd probably be hovering around ten degrees at speech time. She was rightly concerned about her own girls being outside in the cold and was especially concerned about all the kids that would come with their parents and might be standing outside for hours.

We started rolling out emergency relief—hand warmers, hot chocolate stations—but it was a tough call. Barack was torn, like the rest of us.

"I get the appeal of being outside, speaking before thousands of hearty souls," Obama said, "but there's a thin line between hardy and foolish. This could be the biggest case of mass frostbite in history. Not to mention, it may not matter how good a speech we create if I'm chattering the whole time." He paused. "But I'm still inclined to roll the dice here and hope the forecast is right and it warms up a bit. Pray it gets all the way up to a balmy eighteen."

We conferred and decided the upside of being outside was so great—the specter of thousands of Americans braving the cold to witness his announcement would not be lost on people, as well as the echo of Lincoln—that we should stay outside.

I reported this back to Obama. "Okay, we'll give it a go," he replied. "I just better not see any of you guys huddled around the heaters inside that day."

Thus began a trend. Throughout the campaign, whenever we embraced risk, we were rewarded, a lesson that eventually became a touchstone when making hard decisions. I think seeing him refuse to play it safe reminded voters he was different, as was our campaign. It was also good internal motivation to attempt really difficult, unconventional things. We would have to come together as a campaign family, link arms, and try to succeed, knowing the downside would far outweigh any upside.

Michelle and Barack were satisfied we had worked through all the angles, but Obama said he'd have to wear an overcoat and gloves. That's all? I thought. No problem. All too often in politics operatives are concerned about things like this. They have an image of John Kennedy standing outside during his inaugural address in just a suit jacket, in bitter cold, and insist their candidate do the same. I thought that kind of attitude was crazy. Anything that kept our fledgling contender from chattering through his speech was fine with us.

Besides, we had bigger problems with the speech itself. As of Thursday, we still did not have one. Barack and our speechwriter, Jon Favreau, were going back and forth on drafts. Favreau had served as a deputy speechwriter for John Kerry in 2004 before being recruited by Gibbs to join Obama's Senate staff. Favreau was a brilliant writer, and he and Obama had a great collaborative rhythm. Jon understood Barack's voice and, unlike many speechwriters, was open to feedback and constructive criticism on his speech drafts. He did not treat them like sacred texts, but as living organisms that would change many times from start to finish. Now the draft sat with Obama, who wanted to add a few lines and spend some time refining the entire speech. It was unusual that the best writer in the campaign was the candidate, but that was definitely our situation. It was a huge asset, not only because it produced effective and powerful speeches but also because by participating so thoroughly in the writing of major speeches, he internalized and owned the material, resulting in better delivery.

We finally received what he considered his final draft—it was a beautiful speech with a crystal clear message. And it arrived in my inbox on Friday at two or three in the morning.

―――――

Later that Friday morning, a bunch of us caravanned from Chicago to Springfield. The Obamas were scheduled to arrive from Chicago relatively late that night. We had just crossed the city line into Springfield when everyone's BlackBerry began going nuts. Whatever this is, I thought, it can't be good.

It wasn't. The Reverend Jeremiah Wright, the Obamas' longtime pastor, had said some inflammatory things in a *Rolling Stone* interview that was released that morning. The article quoted Wright's profoundly critical statements about the United States: "We are deeply involved in the importing of drugs, the exporting of guns and the training of professional KILLERS. . . . We believe in white supremacy and black inferiority and believe it more than we believe in God. . . . We conducted radiation experiments on our own people. . . . We care nothing about human life if the ends justify the means!"

This would be problematic in a normal campaign situation, however that's defined. On this day in particular it was horrific. Wright was slotted to perform the invocation at the announcement. We could not afford to have Obama's message about coming together swallowed up by the controversy over his fiery and divisive pastor's comments.

We were looking at our first crisis.

Ax looked stricken. "This is a fucking disaster," he said. "If Wright goes up on that stage, that's the story. Our announcement will be an asterisk. The Clinton campaign will ensure it."

Gibbs, Ax, and I got on the phone with Obama, and Ax laid it out for him.

This would obviously be a painful call to make, but he immediately agreed it was no longer tenable for Wright to give the invocation. "I'll call him and tell him it will overshadow everything," said Obama. "I still want him to come, maybe he can do a private prayer with my family before I go out to speak."

We breathed a sigh of relief. The crisis had been averted. For the moment.

The incident should have prompted an immediate scouring of the Reverend Wright and all he had said over the years. There will be plenty of time for the reverend later, but it's worth noting that our systemic failure to deal with this issue properly started the day before Obama's announcement. I still kick myself for how terribly we mishandled our internal Wright work.

Obama was scheduled for a few run-throughs of the speech Friday night in the basement of the Old State Capitol. He was also interviewing with *60 Minutes* from some of the ornate and historical rooms upstairs. The interview ran long and he was tired. The speech rehearsal did not go well. We all felt like he was just going through the motions, "Don't worry," he said, "I'll nail it tomorrow. I just need to get some sleep."

When he left, Ax immediately shot me a concerned look. I shrugged my shoulders.

"Well," I said, "I guess we'll see what the hell we get tomorrow."

Obama was not much of a practice player. But when the red light went on, and he had strong material (which usually meant he had written or had a hand in it), he would hit the clutch shot. He was secure in almost every way but, like most people, he did not enjoy the harsh lights of scrutiny. "It's easy for you guys just to sit there and criticize every little thing I do," he would sometimes say. "But you're not out there giving the speeches and doing the interviews. So I need to take what you say with a grain of salt."

After that practice we walked into the cold Illinois night and gazed at the setting for the morning's speech. It was beautiful. Our lighting gave the Old State Capitol an ethereal glow, shedding warm light on the mammoth American flags hanging down the facades of buildings around the square. The scene was set. The estimated crowd count was now well over ten thousand. All we needed was a knockout performance from our candidate.

We put our heads down and walked the few blocks to the hotel through the frigid air, knowing that things would never be the same after tomorrow.

By 9:00 a.m. there were well over fifteen thousand people packed into the grounds around the Old State Capitol. I went with Emmett Beliveau, our advance director, as he briefed the Obamas and their extended family about the movements for the day and the program. Obama seemed to be in a great place, very relaxed and jovial. This was a good sign.

But last night's ho-hum speech practice was still playing in my head on repeat. As Obama took the stage in the chilly Springfield morning, I looked at Ax nervously. "What do you think?" I asked. "Is he going to deliver?"

Ax shrugged. "I have no idea. But I choose to be an optimist, just this once."

Obama launched into his opening lines and instantly our fears dissipated. The tired, uninterested speaker we had seen the previous night had vanished, replaced by a man who filled the stage and seized the moment. It looked great on TV, but most important, the message was a clear and distinctive frame for his candidacy. Obama had been spot-on about the need to go public early.

The rest of the announcement tour hit Iowa, New Hampshire, South Carolina, and a stop in Chicago, all sandwiched into the space of two days. Ten thousand people attended our two Iowa stops, which was fewer than in Springfield, but keep in mind that only 120,000 people attended the Iowa caucuses in 2004. To have almost 10 percent of that entire total show up at the beginning of the campaign was remarkable. Some attendance was spurred by curiosity, certainly. Many longtime caucus attendees go to dozens of events for all the candidates before deciding whom to support. But because people had signed up online for tickets and we did sign-in at the events, we could match these people to the Iowa voter file we had purchased and see who they were. What it told us was music to our ears: lots of young voters. A surprising number of independents and Republicans. Many Democrats who were regular voters but not caucus attendees. And a healthy number of people not registered to vote.

It was the start of the group portrait we would build our campaign around. There in Iowa, on Day One of the campaign, it was already on full display.

———

The week after the announcement, Virginia governor Tim Kaine endorsed us. Obama and Kaine did not know each other well but had bonded during one of their few conversations over their shared belief in pragmatism, their common Kansas origins, and Kaine's missionary work and Obama's community organizing. His endorsement was a nice piece of news; Kaine could be a helpful surrogate voicing the change message, and while political endorsements were not key to our strategy—we assumed Hillary would land the bulk of them—it showed that some people would be willing to go out on a limb for us. It said not everyone expected this to be a coronation.

In hindsight, what's most striking about Kaine's endorsement is that when he gave it, most people, our team included, thought the race would likely be over by February 5. This meant that the Virginia primary a week later on February 12 would be meaningless. At that point Virginia was not even in the discussion about general-election battlegrounds. The future would tell a different story on both counts.

We had our first serious exchange with the Clinton folks around this time and learned a lot about both of our campaigns in the back-and-forth. The media mogul David Geffen, who had been exceedingly close to the Clintons during the 1990s, had decided to support Obama and help us raise money. Obama had met him in 2006 but they were not close. Geffen told our California finance staff that he wanted to host an event, which we considered a coup.

Geffen invited *New York Times* columnist Maureen Dowd to his fund-raiser and granted her an interview, in which he said some particularly unflattering things about our chief rival, most memorably, "Everybody in politics lies, but [the Clintons] do it with such ease, it's troubling." The Clinton war room gurgled to life for the first time and Howard Wolfson called on Obama, as the purveyor of a politics of hope and congeniality, to condemn his donor's remarks and apologize.

Obama was in the air heading back from California when we received word of Wolfson's challenge. For us, the Clinton missive quickly ratcheted things up to DEFCON 1. The press was in a frenzy, salivating at the inklings of the primary's first fight. We decided we could not wait until Obama landed to offer our response. Ax, Gibbs, and I huddled to plot our strategy.

"This is a test," I said. "We should ignore them most of the time. But if we let them pound us for something we had nothing to do with, it will send a signal that we are too weak for the fight."

Gibbs, who was Wolfson's equal in terms of tenacity, flashed a grin. "I've been waiting for this moment," he said. "Game on. But seriously, we have to say something back or people will just believe the Clintons can walk all over us."

I wrote the meat of our broadside, which didn't follow our usual division of labor, but I was raring to go. I threw it right back at the Clintons and said Geffen was their lifelong friend; he had spent nights in the Lincoln Bedroom during the messy 1990s, and they should take up whatever beef they had with him.

My thinking was that while this was not the approach or tone we should take normally, we needed to assert that we would not be cowed; they had to know that "Obambi," as Dowd called him, would fire back. The exchange was also an opportunity to inject into the news some of the less flattering aspects of the Clinton tenure, which we knew bothered voters.

We hit Send and the political world went nuts. In the next hours, we received a lot of feedback saying that it was the right thing to do.

But when Obama landed he was furious.

"Can I not get on an airplane anymore without you guys launching cruise missiles?" he asked the three of us with exasperation over speakerphone. "I understand your instinct. But going the Lincoln Bedroom route just gets us playing in the muck, where they are more comfortable than we are. Run this stuff by me from now on, at least until we get in stride in terms of tone."

He was right. The crack was gratuitous and had moved the game to their playing field. I still think there was value in our punching back, done properly. But it was a good object lesson: anytime we joined candidates on the low road, we took a blow, because it flew in the face of the kind of politics Obama felt passionate about trying to present.

The exchange did show us that the Clinton folks had a hair trigger. Our reaction may have lacked grace, but theirs had been overheated. Despite regularly dismissing our prospects to the press and insisting we would flame out, they had mounted a full attack at the first perceived provocation, even when doing so drew attention to their own weak spot. Whether they were more worried about Obama's candidacy than they admitted or were dangerously thin-skinned, it was an illuminating moment. We tucked that nugget away for future war gaming.

Another moment during this period revealed surprising weakness in the Clinton camp. The campaign had barely begun and all the candidates were bombarded with invitations to debate and make joint appearances. Every interest group and news organization was hatching ideas for the candidates to appear together. We all had dozens of requests. I convened a discussion with Patti Solis Doyle, my counterpart in Clintonland, and Jonathan Prince, an Edwards representative, to hash out whether there was a coordinated approach we could take to minimize the headache of sorting out the avalanche of requests, and we fervently agreed that if we did not gain some control, we would all end up bogged down with planning for and attending joint appearances. We each would lose both flexibility and control of the most important asset in any campaign, our candidate's time.

The three of us decided we would decline all upcoming requests and send out a joint message saying that we wanted to work with the DNC, the Democratic National Committee, to set up an orderly debate calendar. The schedule would include a healthy number of sanctioned debates, and these would be the only ones any of us attended.

The first joint appearance invitation that every candidate received was to a forum in Nevada hosted by AFSCME—the American Federation of State, County and Municipal Employees, a government-employee union. In February 2007, AFSCME had partnered with George Stephanopoulos, who would moderate the discussion. News organizations and interest groups commonly co-sponsored debates or forums to make it harder for candidates to say no. Here was the first test of our arrangement. Patti, Jonathan, and I agreed we would decline the AFSCME event and do so by explaining our joint effort to bring order to the debate process. Obama was on board, and my counterparts said their candidates were, too.

We all told AFSCME we were not attending. The next day I receive a sheepish call from Patti, who had infuriating news: they needed to reverse course and attend after all.

"I'm sorry," she said. "I tried to stick to the plan but I got overruled. Not at the staff level." I assumed she was talking about Bill, who was exceedingly close to AFSCME's president after receiving a big endorsement from him during the 1992 primary.

"So, we are going to the forum," she concluded.

I was deeply frustrated. "Our first test, and you guys blinked? Now we're going to have to do them all, a damn debate a week, maybe more."

Patti sounded resigned. "I know. We tried. That's all I can say."

I was boiling over. I called Prince and he said he would talk to his candidate, but that he was hoping to hold tough. We assumed the Edwards campaign would be pretty disciplined, having been around the track once before. With a clear electoral strategy of winning Iowa and hoping lightning would strike, they knew time was precious.

A few minutes later, he called back with bad news. They were really pissed about it, but if Hillary went, they felt like they needed to as well, or they were essentially ceding AFSCME's endorsement to her.

Just like that, our debate deal was out the window and the whims of outside groups were threatening to drive a large part of the campaign. Now we had a decision to make.

We stuck to our guns. While the other candidates shared a stage in Nevada, we elected to spend the day in Iowa instead, with Obama's support. "Plouffe," he said to me when he got word of our decision, "I assume it was not in your plan to cede the AFSCME endorsement, which I suspect we will have done by not showing up, but I'll stick to our plan here."

"Our plan to win doesn't really take endorsements into account," I responded. "We should assume that we'll get few if any institutional endorsements. And anyway, AFSCME is a lost cause as far as I'm concerned. Their president is thick as thieves with the Clintons."

Watching it play out, I knew we'd made the right move. It was not even a close contest in terms of who did more that day to further their chances of winning the nomination. We signed up Iowa caucus-goers. The other candidates—a total of eight went to the forum—were yakking on a stage for only ten minutes each. And they blew most of a day traveling to and from Nevada.

We stood alone in our decision. Most first-time presidential candidates would have folded in a minute. It speaks to Obama's discipline that he went along, as well as to his belief that we should try to run our campaign on our own terms.

This AFSCME affair was a very illuminating exercise, and it boosted my confidence. The Clinton folks were not showing the discipline and resolve that we had expected. Political pressure could clearly get them to change course, even if doing so went against their strategic interest. It was a strong indication of weakness; given their strength in the race, any sign of faltering was welcome. If we could count on our discipline being matched with reactivity on their part, it gave us a leg up.

We did agree to attend the next candidate forum, on health care (also in Nevada), sponsored by SEIU, the Service Employees International Union. We structured our event schedule so we would be out west anyway and wouldn't have to waste travel time, but I think we showed weakness here on two fronts. First, by going at all. We should have stuck to our guns when it came to denying requests. That one acceptance revived the hopes of countless other groups and made future events that much harder to decline. Over time we declined many more appearances than the other candidates, and eventually some order was established, but we did buckle from time to time. Second, Obama's performance, by his own admission, was very weak. He rambled, got very defensive when pressed on certain issue-related questions, and was generally off his game—particularly in comparison to Clinton, who was sharp and had her bullet points down. He even took the bait on why his website still lacked a detailed health care plan (because we didn't have one!); instead of simply laying out his health care reform principles and promising a fleshed-out plan in due time, Obama said his campaign was new and if "we didn't have a plan on there in a couple of months, we'd be in trouble."

It was not a good day for the home team.

His performance showed we had a lot of work to do. Obama's chief takeaway was that he needed to get all his policy plans completely developed right away. This became a constant struggle in the months ahead. Axelrod and I knew that of course we needed to develop white papers, but we viewed these early multicandidate forums largely as message exercises. What are your priorities? Who are the special interests standing in the way of progress? What is your criticism of Bush in that area? How are you going to get it done? And when it came to these questions, Obama already had a solid framework for just about any answer. To spend time developing complex policy positions now would drain resources we needed to maintain our momentum. The lesson was valuable, but it was still a blow to Obama's confidence.

He called me after the forum, very dejected. "I just whiffed up there, and Hillary was exceptional. I am not there yet."

It was the first time I sensed that he might be realizing what taking on Hillary was going to mean.

But there were many other reasons for him to feel confident. Our grassroots base was growing very quickly. Online sign-ups were progressing nicely and reached 450,000 by the end of March. We had taken the unusual step of holding rallies in cities around the country, and this was very educational. I had initially pursued rallies to maintain the perception of the campaign as grassroots-driven. We spent most of the first few months fund-raising, while much of our organizing took shape online and in living rooms. Free rallies provided a nice balance to the Geffen-style high-roller events, and the database was growing every day.

We held rallies during this period in Los Angeles, Cleveland, and Austin. All were well attended, but the Austin event drew over twenty thousand people, an enormous crowd for a primary event. We didn't ask for money at the rally, but we followed up with e-mail and mail solicitations. The response was terrific. At the end of March, the county with the largest number of Obama contributors was Cook County, Illinois, not surprisingly. Number two, though, was not Manhattan or Miami Dade or Marin County, California. It was small-by-comparison Travis County, Texas, home of Austin.

One of the beauties of technology and data is that you can track the contribution history and volunteer performance of people all the way through the campaign. On November 4, 2008, we knew how each person at the Austin rally had performed through the entire campaign. How many times did they contribute? Did they volunteer? Did they vote in the Texas primary and attend the Texas caucus? Are they part of an online group? This type of data made establishing metrics much easier and allowed us to track what people responded to and what they didn't.

The rallies were a big part of our growth during the spring. Many people got involved through our website on their own initiative, and we had great success in encouraging people to ask others to sign up. When people asked how they could help, we told them that nothing was more important than getting additional people signed up on the site so we could communicate with them and try to convert them to donors and volunteers. All this was happening before we had done any large-scale online advertising to drive people to our site. It was remarkable organic growth that revealed a core of passionate early devotees.

The Texas swing also marked the end of our days flying commercial. We spent the first weeks on passenger jets, two or three legs a day. It was brutal, but we were concerned about money. Obama himself cited cost reasons to reject the notion we should be flying private more often. As each day passed, however, it became harder and harder just to get through the airport. He was being mobbed by people who wanted to take a picture with him. Many were also running into nearby airport bookstores to buy one of his two books, generally on prominent display, so he could sign them. We had private security traveling with us, but they could do little to help speed things along. Obama called me the morning after Austin from the airport.

"There's a sea of people here. I've barely moved in a half hour," he quietly said into his phone as he signed books. "I'm just going to have to make a run for it toward security if I'm going to make the flight."

I could hear the hum of the crowd through the phone.

"The people are all very nice, but we are going to have to get to airports two hours early at this rate. The upside is, I'm selling a lot of books. My publisher will be happy."

He seemed more bemused than irritated by the situation, but we decided we needed to make a travel change. And with that, Southwest's brief tenure as the unofficial airline of the Obama campaign had come to an end.

Another unique decision we made during this time period was to try some low-dollar fund-raising events. This idea came from a supporter in Kentucky, Matthew Barzun, who was one of our larger fund-raisers. We were holding a fund-raiser for high-dollar contributors in Louisville, and Matt's team wanted to add an event with ticket prices of around $25 so that more people could see Obama. Most high-dollar fund-raisers would never have considered this, but it spoke to the commitment our core early fund-raisers felt to the cause and the excitement they were picking up on the ground.

Our initial inclination was to decline; a low-dollar event added time and was labor intensive, and we would be lucky to break even. Kentucky was not an early primary state, so the organizational value was very limited.

But they persisted and said they could do all the work themselves; we would just need to send a few e-mails to people in the area and set up an event page online where people could sign up. Matt and his group would shoulder the load so our staff could keep its focus on the big-ticket event generating the bulk of the revenue. Trusting our ground team, we agreed to give it a shot.

The event was a smashing success. Three thousand people came, all paying, to hear Obama. True to their word, the local folks took care of pretty much everything. And, as in Texas, many attendees gave again when we solicited them online.

We carried this model across the country. Through dozens of events like it we grew our list and donor base, and many of these low-dollar contributors became our best volunteers down the line. It also provided a nice local press hit wherever we happened to be. Holding only a high-dollar dinner would generate a local-news story that Barack Obama was in town raising money, but when we added the low-dollar event, the report would also include footage of Obama delivering his message speech and excited supporters at what looked like a rally. It gave viewers strong images to associate with our campaign. And Obama really enjoyed them; he drew energy and motivation from the crowds, and appreciated the organizational strategy behind them.

This was also the beginning of what might be called "citizen fund-raisers." In most campaigns there are people who give a small amount in response to an e-mail appeal or direct-mail letter, and then there are people at the higher end who host big events or collect large checks from wealthier contributors, a process called bundling.

In our campaign, grassroots supporters started to raise money. Generally, they brought in relatively small amounts—$100, $500, $1,000—using a tool on our social-networking site to keep track of the money they raised and to ask others to contribute.

Over time this grew into a powerful force. We treated these citizen fund-raisers as no less important than our larger raisers. They were asked to join conference calls with Barack, me, and other senior staff so we could thank them for what they were doing and give them updates on the campaign. They believed their effort was valued—and it was—so they dug deeper and kept raising. This was not a tactical relationship. It was authentic. And that authenticity became a very powerful driver in the connection between Barack Obama and his supporters.

I suspected from the beginning we would have a core of rabid supporters who wanted Obama paraphernalia. Being in the T-shirt business along with the election business is kind of a pain in the ass, and most political campaigns outsource this task to a vendor. The campaign doesn't make any money if they do, but a service is being provided to supporters who want a T-shirt or a bumper sticker. I asked our lawyers if we could keep the merchandising in-house. There were two complications. First, we had to buy all the merchandise up front. It would be considered an illegal corporate contribution for us to pay the vendor for only the stuff that sold. So if we planned poorly we would be stuck with expensive inventory, tying up our money in mugs and hats gathering dust in a closet at HQ. Second, it added a layer of complexity to our campaign finance reporting; since these purchases would be contributions, it meant someone who had already given us the maximum allowable amount of $2,300 could not buy merchandise. Taking this on would require detailed tracking.

I decided to plow ahead anyway, and we ended up netting millions from sales of Obama merchandise during the campaign—and I am convinced we actually expanded our base at the same time. Some in the press scoffed at this, suggesting that including merch sales in contributions inflated our donor numbers. I thought the opposite was true. If someone felt strongly enough about Obama to buy merchandise, they would probably also be receptive to nonmerchandise solicitations, and more likely to volunteer. And, of course, they were wearing Obama stuff around town, which had value as well.

"Can I get a cut of all the money we're making off my name and face?" Barack joked.

"No," I told him. "Just consider this a down payment on the private plane."

I often kidded Barack that at any moment I might step down as manager and open up the Obama Store kiosk at O'Hare. There were plenty of days when the notion was appealing.

We also experimented with live streaming video during this early period. Our first and most significant effort was to live stream a small-town Obama event in western Iowa to all of our supporters around the country. It would ground them in our campaign's strategy—all about Iowa. We needed to condition our supporters to understand our electoral strategy and path so they would not feel dejected by national polls showing us losing big in later primary states where Hillary had a huge lead.

Despite a few technical issues, the live stream grabbed a significant number of people, and it became a sharp tool in our arsenal. Rospars and his new media team increasingly looked for events that lent themselves to the live-streaming option, another way we could try to make barackobama.com a "home," where supporters could find valuable content and comprehensive information about the campaign with one click of the mouse.

But it was not all forward progress. Our opponents and the media were going through every phase of Obama's life, trying to unearth any inconsistent facts. Our own preparatory research on Obama was still way behind schedule; it should have been completed before he announced, and we were scrambling to catch up. In the meantime, not a day went by without a reporter or opponent confronting us with a new question about something we were unaware of, like so many cats delivering dead mice to our door. This was probably the hardest part of getting the campaign off the ground. We were routinely blindsided and had to decide quickly what information we had and didn't have, what we needed to get, and how to respond. It was brutal, and the time spent putting out these fires added to every day.

_____

The biggest moment and metric of the entire first quarter of the campaign was release of the candidates' fund-raising reports, which covered the period through March 31. The press had circled this date on their calendar from Day One, and we had worked hard to make sure we had positive news to report. This early in the campaign, fund-raising is viewed as a test of viability and potential. Too much is probably read into these numbers by the press, but a poor report certainly can endanger a candidate's prospects.

It became clear as we moved into March that we would exceed our $12 million goal. Then it became clear we would obliterate that number. The take from our events was blowing by the goals we had set, sometimes doubling or tripling them. Almost all of March was a succession of fund-raisers, sometimes four or five events a day. Our online money was still modest, so almost all of this came from our finance staff and our core, early fund-raisers across the country. They put us on their shoulders.

It was unlike anything any of us had ever seen. Our finance staff was both amazed and struggling to keep up. We had to keep finding bigger venues to hold all the people willing to pay to hear Obama. This was the quarter when we were most reliant on old-fashioned fund-raising. Penny Pritzker, our finance chair, was a prominent businesswoman, new to this level of politics; the head of Hyatt, she earned people's respect immediately with her poise and leadership qualities. Penny and Julianna and her staff did a great job of lining up talented raisers, many of whom had never met Obama or did not know him well.

Our pitch was not based on access, titles, or future jobs or influence. That resonated with a lot of people. We simply put forth that Obama was the right candidate for the time, and that we had a strategy to win that was more plausible than people might realize. We also made it clear that we were a democratic organization, without a lot of hierarchy. This contrasted with the Clinton campaign, where only the top dog in a region was afforded special fund-raiser treatment.

Most finance committees are a pain in the ass, offering ideas on everything, trying to monopolize time with the candidate, and generally thinking they should be running the show. Ours was anything but, a great mix of young and old, experienced fund-raisers and novices, and an important ingredient to our success. There was a great esprit d'corps, and like the rest of the staff, none of the finance people joined Obama because they had picked out the ambassadorship they wanted; they were there because they believed in him and the promise his candidacy held.

We raised $4 million online, a significant amount but far less than our fund-raisers wanted. Our new media team and I were very careful about how often we asked people for money by e-mail. We wanted our online contributors to have a balanced experience with us, thinking that if they felt part of and connected to the whole campaign, they might be more generous over time. The fund-raisers, who felt the pressure I was putting on them to post a big number, wanted to ask for as much as possible, as often as possible, starting right away. These were some of the tensest disputes I had to navigate throughout the whole campaign, and they left a lingering sore spot that did not heal for over a year. The finance team really believed that the new media team was underperforming financially, and the new media team thought the finance team viewed them and our supporters as an ATM.

On April 1, Hillary reported raising a total of $26 million, only $19.1 million of which could be spent in the primary (the other $6.9 million could be spent only if she became the nominee). This perplexed us. They clearly were raising a lot of general-election money just to boost their overall number, to cement the perception of their fund-raising strength. It was also easier to get someone to write a $4,600 check, a max out for the primary and general, than to get them to write $2,300 and find someone else to write another $2,300 check. But general-election money is funny money during a primary; it can't be spent until the game is over.

We strongly discouraged our donors from raising general-election money and went so far as to say any general-election money raised during the primary would not count toward their membership in the National Finance Committee, which required raising at least $100,000.

There was a practical reason for this: primary money was the only money we could use during the nomination fight. But the theory behind it had real implications. It was clear from our discussions with the press that they understood the importance of the distinction, so the Clinton campaign would receive far less mileage from their large overall figure. We spent a good deal of effort making sure the press accepted the metric of primary money.

We intentionally held off releasing our finance numbers until April 3 to build suspense. It worked. We reported raising almost $26 million, all but a few thousand of it primary money. Obama had outraised Clinton in primary money by $7 million. This news sent shockwaves through the political community, especially in early states like Iowa. People who had been on the fence, waiting to see if we could really put together a viable campaign, were now convinced we could and jumped on board.

Without that big first quarter, I'm not sure we could have won the nomination. It showed once and for all we could compete with Hillary on what was considered her home court. And it demonstrated that something powerful was stirring across the countryside.

Clinton had constructed a campaign of inevitability, built on a foundation of financial dominance. Those early contribution levels were important markers, and they showed that we had the power to weaken that foundation.

We ended the first quarter in stronger financial shape than we had dreamed possible. We exceeded our own expectations in other areas as well. The size of our e-mail list was well ahead of schedule. Our presence on the ground in Iowa was much stronger and deeper than Clinton's; she was organizing at a remarkably slow pace there. In the other early states we were either matching her activity (New Hampshire and Nevada) or exceeding it (South Carolina). We had a strong top-line change message, which was very distinct from the inevitability and experience message Clinton was employing. And we had survived—so far—the scrutiny of our candidate.

We were off to a strong start. The plane lifted off the runway and did not explode in flames. We weren't soaring but we were on an upward trajectory.

3

Building Blocks

As we rolled into spring of the 2007 primary season, we could no longer consider ourselves a start-up. We were still years behind Hillary Clinton in terms of policy planning, political relationships, and national donor base, but we were now a fully formed campaign. We had staff and organizations in place in the first four primary states. We had a donor network around the country. Our website and its social-networking component were heavily trafficked and becoming a real resource for our supporters. Internally, we had clear lines of authority and were establishing a calm, respectful operating rhythm.

It was time to take it to the next level.

We needed to put some policy meat on the bones, starting with health care. We needed to continue our aggressive compiling of supporter e-mail addresses, volunteers, and contributors. Our early-state organizing and political activities had to accelerate. We had to start building large volunteer networks in these states and begin to lock down support, voter by voter. And we had to continue to gel as an organization and cement a campaign culture that could carry us through what promised to be an increasingly brutal race. The turbulence of takeoff was nothing compared to the white-knuckle moments that lay ahead.

During the first several months of the campaign, none of us had time for much reflection. We had been shot from a cannon—Obama especially—and our efforts had been focused entirely on getting our bearings and surviving the launch. As we caught our collective breath, the implications of what we were doing started to sink in.

In mid-April, Axelrod slumped into a chair in my office and asked, "Is it ever going to slow down? It feels like it's the week before the election, not ten months out from the primaries. I don't know if I can sustain this pace."

55

"I know," I wearily replied. "I misread this. I thought we'd be moving helter-skelter to get up and running but then things would calm down and we'd have somewhat of a lull—or at least a more modest pace until the fall." I sighed. "The press is going to cover every sneeze and hiccup 24/7. Plus it's going to be an arms race out there, each of us trying to escalate financially and organizationally. I don't think it will slow down a bit."

"A marathon at sprint pace," Ax observed. And he was right. None of us was prepared, most significantly our candidate, whose attitude about the whole enterprise took a sharp turn for the worse as we headed toward summer.

The spring months were tough for Obama. By most external—and internal—measures the campaign was ahead of schedule. But with the rush of his first weeks as a presidential candidate now in the rearview mirror, he had enough perspective to realize that this was going to get only more difficult over the next nine to twelve months. He already missed his family. He spent much of his time fund-raising. He found most coverage of the race banal. And there wasn't nearly enough time for his favorite part of the campaign—noodling over policy, or as he called it, think time.

Gibbs was on the road with Obama more and more, a duty that eventually claimed him full time. The two men shared a close bond, and Gibbs was brutally honest with Obama when he found his performance or outlook flawed. In the end, Gibbs's transition to the road greatly benefited the campaign. It helped to have a senior person with Obama at all times to ensure that coordination between the road show and HQ was smooth and that someone on the ground could make things happen when we needed to call an audible.

Gibbs had excellent instincts when it came to reacting in the moment, offering sage advice as we navigated any number of unforeseen situations. The desk work of communications, including planning and management, was less his strength. We brought Dan Pfeiffer, who was Gibbs's deputy at the time, in off the road to take over management responsibilities at the HQ.

Pfeiffer was from Delaware, like me. Coupled with all our South Dakotans—Hildebrand, Pete Rouse, and a bunch of junior staffers—it had to be the greatest representation of tiny three-elector states in presidential campaign history.

I never asked Pfeiffer directly, but I still wonder if he was at all relieved to escape for a while from our increasingly sullen candidate. During a flight leg in April, Gibbs tried to have a heart-to-heart with Obama. "Are you having any fun at all?" he asked him.

"None," Obama flatly replied.

"Do you see any way we can make it more fun?" Gibbs replied.

"No."

Reggie Love, who was listening in on the conversation, piped up, "Well, if it's any consolation I'm having the time of my life!" Reggie, a former basketball player at Duke, was renowned for working hard and playing hard, as befit a single twenty-four-year-old who seemed to require zero sleep. As Obama's "body guy," or close, full-time personal aide, Reggie would experience the campaign from a unique perch and always with a great outlook and sense of wonderment for the ride he was on.

Obama still didn't flash a smile. He hadn't embraced campaign life, and it was beginning to cause concern. The early-state staff in particular thought he was not locked in on the trail, either in his remarks or in his solicitations of political support. We weren't sure if Obama would turn out to be Secretariat, but we suspected he had some thoroughbred political talent; it just wasn't on daily display. During his 2004 Senate race and in flashes on the presidential campaign trail, Ax, Gibbs, and I had seen his ability to move a room, to hold a crowd in thrall. His was never a fire-and-brimstone style; he quieted a room, until everyone was listening so intently that all else fell away. This command was on full display during his 2004 Democratic National Convention speech, and it had catapulted him onto the national stage. He was also strong when working one-on-one or in small groups, where he could be more focused and convey a sense of urgency. But the reports from Iowa were that he was mostly going through the motions. After one event, Tewes called me and laid it on the line. "Unless he gets better, we might as well just not have him meet with people," he said. "They tell us afterward, 'He really never put the squeeze on me. It was a nice enough conversation but he doesn't seem like he really wants it.'"

We needed to address this, and fast. In April, Axelrod, Rouse, and I arranged a dinner with Obama at a restaurant in downtown D.C., ostensibly to talk about next steps in the campaign. While we did some of that, our main purpose was to let him know he had to find his inner motivation—or at least better disguise his weariness. As we unfolded our critique, he seemed bemused at first. Then he grew irritated. Eventually, though, he accepted we had a point.

"You're right," he said. "I am struggling a bit out there. And only I can fix that and I will try. But you guys also need to make sure the things I ask for—

like more time to kick ideas around with policy experts—get taken seriously and get scheduled." We agreed to try to do our part better.

This in no way solved our candidate issues—he'd have to find that spark himself—but thereafter he did a better job of keeping his doubts and perhaps even second thoughts about running to just a few of us. "Maybe you shouldn't have run," I told him later. "But you did, and the one thing that won't happen is that you'll quit. So let's at least give it a go, try to enjoy ourselves. Worst case, in eight or nine months we'll be out and have nothing but time on our hands. This is hard enough firing on all cylinders—it's unbearable if your heart is not one hundred percent in it."

He thought about it for a moment. "I guess it's like being in the middle of the ocean. It's the same distance to swim back as to keep heading across. Just tell me this is going to get more fun."

"When you finally own Iowa," I said, "really own it, think about it 24/7, get competitive, and see how everything you're doing comes together—then I think you will. Plus, summer in Iowa and New Hampshire is a lot of fun. Outdoor campaigning, lots of good food. But that's all I have to offer you."

He laughed. "Well, I'll work on having fun if you work on your pep talk skills."

Barack is a logical guy. Later that spring he wrote a memo about his own state of mind and performance to close an internal memo about his overall view of our progress and challenges overall in the campaign. In it, he was as unsparing and clear-eyed about his own struggles to date as he was in expressing concerns about other aspects of the campaign.

"Many of the difficulties that we have had over the past five months are my responsibility," he said, with disarming candor. He acknowledged that he had been slow to adjust to the pace and demands of the campaign, and that his ambivalence had had a negative "impact on staff morale."

He panned his first debate performance, which he said, after reviewing it on tape, "was worse than I realized at the time." And despite the constrictive nature of debate formats, which he felt could often lead to mindless and pat answers, he vowed to, if not master the discipline, improve.

But most of all, Barack said he needed to find his authentic voice and reconnect with the fundamental concerns that drew him into the race in the first place. He had run to challenge the bankrupt and conventional politics of Washington, not master it. He would never win a race by trying to beat the insiders at their own game. But, he said, "if I can muster the discipline, the energy, and the confidence to consistently speak the truth as I best understand it, and the campaign can help me do that, then I don't think we can be stopped."

It was hard not to run through a wall for this guy. Few people are this self-aware, fewer still politicians at the highest levels. It was a trait I thought would be invaluable in the campaign and, if we won, as president.

As we moved through spring, he dug out of his funk and began to locate the motivation that would see him through the day-to-day grind and let him kick into a higher gear when the moment required.

Though Obama's understated personality and demeanor sometimes made it difficult for him to transition to high-energy moments, it also played a pivotal role in grounding our campaign. In most of the campaigns I've worked on—and in most principal-driven endeavors of any sort—the principal's moods, reactions, and operating style become the focal points of the enterprise. Everyone becomes accustomed to saying things like, "He's going to be pissed about this"; "She blew her top last time this happened, we'd all better duck"; "He's going to lose his shit." We've all been there.

That was never the case with Barack. Sure, sometimes he'd think his schedule was too long or didn't make sense, or that an event could have been better organized, but he would make his point and move on. His normalcy wasn't a dominant reason for our success, but it proved a major factor. We were free to focus on doing our jobs, knowing that any criticisms he offered would be on the merits and made without histrionics. Ours was a healthy campaign environment; we never woke up dreading his reactions. In politics that is the exception, not the rule.

———

We finally nailed down a debate calendar sanctioned by the DNC in the spring. Or so we thought. Before the cement could set, one more early debate was quickly added, to be held in April at South Carolina State University, a historically black college, and broadcast nationally by CNN. None of the major candidates was eager for the first formal debate to be this early, but Congressman Jim Clyburn, the most powerful Democrat in this newly pivotal early state, put enormous pressure on the candidates. We all buckled.

Debates were considered hugely important by the press and dominated campaign coverage for three days: speculation and expectation setting the day before, debate day itself, and scoring and postgame analysis the day after. Most primary voters were oblivious to these early showdowns, but a lot of core

Democratic activists, elected officials, and donors tuned in. For this reason, the opinions of the general electorate were of less concern in our preparation than the echo chamber of insiders.

A good performance would be helpful with the political community and foster a sense of momentum and strength. But a bad performance would have a much stronger adverse impact. Accordingly, our first imperative was to do no harm.

Historically, Obama was not a strong debater, so we tried to work him harder in the run-up. We prepped him over and over, reviewing likely questions and practicing answers and exchanges he might have with the other candidates. These sessions did not inspire a great deal of confidence. Obama thought the whole exercise of boiling down complex answers into thirty- or sixty-second sound bites was silly and rewarded glibness, not depth and complexity. It was definitely going to be a challenging night. A big part of managing debate coverage was setting and then meeting expectations. We tried to set our bar as low as possible so it would be easier to surpass.

At debates, each campaign is afforded a walk-through in which the candidate and his staff are allotted time to take the stage and get comfortable with the lectern, lighting, and stage positions of the other candidates and moderators. This generally happens a few hours before the debate, so the producers can lock down the set and prepare for the broadcast, while the candidates go off for a few hours of rest and last-minute prep.

Obama was loose as we took our tour. As we surveyed the professional staging and the avalanche of media, he joked to Gibbs, Ax, and me that the scene was just a bit different from his last debate, with the gadfly Republican Alan Keyes during the 2004 Senate race. "I guess I should consider it a step up that I'm now debating Hillary Clinton," he noted wryly.

We wanted to check into our lodgings to let him rest, review his debate materials, and do some light "pepper" before the debate. There were no hotels in Orangeburg, South Carolina, just a series of motels, a grim line of rundown doors looking out on dreary parking lots. This was one of our first trips with Secret Service, but our driver got lost and couldn't find the motel where we had reserved rooms. We went the wrong way for several miles, turned around, and then finally pulled into a motel parking lot—the wrong one.

I was riding with Obama, who remained surprisingly relaxed. "Maybe we were better off back when we had volunteer drivers using MapQuest," he cracked.

As we looped through the rear parking lot on our way back to the main road, we came across one of our primary opponents going through his own version of prep. In what appeared to be an approximation of exercise, Governor Bill Richardson of New Mexico was shuffling—and that may be too kind a word—along the motel sidewalk in a velour sweat suit, trailed by what must have been a couple of very large New Mexico state troopers, his regular entourage. He looked, as I said at the time, a bit like Tony Soprano. We were howling with laughter as we pulled away, because it was such a bizarre sight, and we would have missed it had we not wandered into the wrong motel parking lot.

We later found out Richardson was severely under the weather, and we felt bad about our reaction, but we definitely appreciated the laugh we got in the tense predebate hours.

Back at the site, the atmosphere was crackling. Supporters for all the candidates lined the streets, waving signs, chanting corny slogans, and singing songs. Our South Carolina staff had recruited a drum line from a local high school to be part of our visibility contingent. Pulling back onto campus, Obama saw our throng of supporters and the band and asked the driver to stop. The motorcade screeched to a halt and he jumped out and shouted his thanks to everyone. The band roared to life and Obama danced with them for a moment.

In the days leading up to the debate, he had confessed to being nervous about it. Generally, he had enormous self-confidence, but he was also deeply self-aware. He knew that the ways debates were judged—glowing press coverage went to whoever got off the best zinger—did not play to his strengths. It seemed an awfully good sign that he had been loose and having fun throughout the day. But as the debate approached, I could sense he was getting a bit tighter; he seemed more and more detached, which I took as a sign of nerves.

Ax and I were in Obama's holding room moments before the candidates would take the stage, the three of us forming a tight circle as Ax and I took turns giving him last-minute advice.

"Don't forget to smile," Ax told him.

"Iraq is an economic issue, too," I added.

"And remember the experience riff."

He tolerated this for a few minutes then held up his hands. "Guys, enough," he said. "You're junking up my head. All I will be thinking about is what you just told me I had to do and I'll be tight."

Every candidate is different. Some thrive on that last-minute banter. Some want to talk before, but about anything but politics. And some just want solitude. Obama seemed to prefer a relaxed, off-topic conversation, and we never again made the mistake of larding him up with too much information at the last minute. We backed off.

The debate, on the whole, was uneventful. Obama's performance was solid; not a ten strike by any means, but he more than passed muster.

"Well, that could have been a lot worse," said Ax as the debate ended. "It was a lot better than I'd thought we'd do." Ax tended to see calamity lurking around every corner. When Obama had left the hold room an hour earlier to take the debate stage, Ax had turned to Gibbs and me with a look of deadly seriousness and said, "This could be an unmitigated disaster."

More significant was the postgame reaction. Most of the pundits thought Clinton had won, and she did have a fine night from a traditional debate perspective. They did not view our performance nearly as favorably, but our sense was that Obama's performance would be welcomed by viewers because he was not parroting prewritten talking points. He certainly had a message he was trying to communicate consistently, but he was also providing thoughtful, honest answers on issues like Iraq, Afghanistan, and health care.

Much of the research we saw on viewer reactions backed up our belief. This became a pattern throughout the primary debates: the voters generally gave us much higher marks than the pundits, and gave Clinton lower marks than the pundits. This proved quite meaningful as the primary wore on and provided further evidence that voters were looking for something new, a candidate who did not seem to be following a worn script. It gave us renewed confidence that we could connect directly with voters and have that guide our strategy, as opposed to obsessing over the media filter.

From a standing start we had made striking headway in the early states. As planned, Obama spent most of his time in Iowa, and we tracked metrics of progress there closely. We made an aggressive gamble and staffed up to huge numbers very quickly. Presidential campaigns usually hire in waves for the caucuses, with most staff brought on toward the end of the campaign when people are beginning to pay closer attention. We took the opposite approach— not an insignificant budget risk at the time—and placed more staff in more communities earlier than any campaign in caucus history.

This upending of Iowa tradition was the brainchild of Paul Tewes and Mitch

Stewart. As I've mentioned, we had no preexisting organization or relationships in Iowa, so we had to build a network from scratch, and fast. Since Obama was not well known on the ground, Paul and Mitch thought it imperative that our organizers become embedded in the local community as soon as possible, to build up relationships and trust. Many Iowa caucus attendees actually met some of the candidates personally in 2007. But for most, their determinant and consistent contact with our campaign would be with our young organizers.

Tewes established a motto for our field staff philosophy: "Respect. Empower. Include." We wanted to be the nicest, most attentive, and most creative staff in the field.

Though Obama was new to the state, it was clear from the outset that he had an enthusiastic if small base of Iowans. Our early hires never had time to twiddle their thumbs; they had volunteers to manage and empower immediately.

In the spring and summer of 2007, our organizers were focused on developing relationships and beginning to recruit the volunteer leaders in their areas of responsibility—initially about two dozen precincts per organizer. This was a lot to handle, but the number would decrease as we got closer to the caucus and hired more staff. We called these volunteer leaders precinct captains. They served as the head volunteers in their precincts, essentially the face of the Obama campaign to their neighbors and friends. Their tasks included recruiting volunteers, persuading voters to support Obama, and building crowds for events attended by Barack, Michelle, or other surrogates.

We treated our precinct captains like gold. Obama spent time with them on the phone and in person before and after events, to keep them motivated. For him, it was more than a business transaction; he really loved these volunteers. "The thing I get the biggest boost from in the whole campaign is meeting and spending time with our Iowa precinct captains," he told me once. "They don't care about how far behind we are in national polls, or what line I did or didn't use in a debate. They just focus on what they can control. And I'll put our captains up against anybody's."

They included people like John Powers from Cedar Rapids, a strong Republican, who gave in to his wife's hounding and reluctantly attended an Obama event. He was intrigued but not sold after his first encounter. He attended another event, stopped by our local office to ask a few more questions of our local organizer, and, satisfied by his research, eventually agreed to become a precinct leader. This was John's first time getting involved in politics to such a degree, and he no doubt convinced many of the large number of Republicans from that area who caucused for us to join him.

Or Jerre Grefe, a grandmother from small, rural Hampton, Iowa, who also had never been involved with politics but spent just about every weekend going door-to-door. In addition to her precinct duties, she also organized women throughout her county for the Obama campaign.

The unprecedented early investment in people that allowed us to find and recruit John and Jerre and thousands more like them flowed directly from our strategy in Iowa and some of the realities on the ground.

We believed from the outset that we had to expand the electorate or we were cooked. We had to look for caucus attendees under every rock. Most caucus campaigns talk to a narrow group of Democrats, those who have attended prior caucuses. In our case, that was just the opening bid. We needed to find young voters, sporadic voters, people who were not registered independents, Republicans. We had to grab them anywhere and any way we could.

In some counties, folks might see Obama in person once or twice at the most. Their interaction with our campaign—and with all the other campaigns—would be primarily through staff. There was huge value in our organizers showing up at charity events, eating at the local coffee shop, drinking at the Main Street bar. Countless key supporters signed up for the campaign because of their positive interactions with our organizers—these Iowans were drawn to and impressed by Obama, but the staff pulled them over the line.

We knew we were attracting top-shelf staff talent at the organizer level. This speaks to both Obama's appeal to younger people (almost all of our organizers were under twenty-five) as well as the appeal of organizing for a campaign and candidate who actually believed in, well, organizing. Our people knew they would not be field scum, as I was called when I started out as an organizer in 1988. In many ways, they would be the embodiment of our campaign.

We married these unprecedented investments in staff with others in good old bricks and mortar. Usually, campaigns establish regional offices in Iowa that the staff can use as bases. Staff members work out of the regional office and regularly drive out to the counties they are responsible for. Then, at the very end of the race, they finally descend full time on their areas.

We envisioned a much more comprehensive network of Obama offices throughout Iowa. Tewes and Marygrace made the case for this real estate empire by stressing two points: First, it was another way to ground Obama in these communities, which had not yet had much exposure to him. Second, from an efficiency standpoint, it was a big plus to have locally based staff spend their time working instead of driving. Nine or ten months from caucus day, I was skeptical that we needed all these offices. But it turned out to be one of our smarter moves and a lesson we carried forward.

At the end of May, I flew from Chicago into Moline, Iowa, to join up with Obama on the road for a few days, which I liked to do from time to time just to assess our events, staff, and the feel on the ground. It was my fortieth birthday, and my parents had flown out to Chicago to see me before I left. Bidding them good-bye as I took off for Iowa, I didn't realize it would be more than a year until I saw them again.

During my time in Iowa, we hosted an invite-only Memorial Day evening event in the Quad Cities for veterans and their families. Several hundred people turned out, an impressive crowd. As with most of our audiences, a hefty percentage had never caucused. Obama gave an understated, nonpolitical, and off-the-cuff speech about America, its veterans, and how, as president, he would view his relationship with both our active-duty military and veterans. As at many of Obama's events, there was little applause. The room was quiet and still except for the occasional head nod, as the crowd took in and weighed his words. Afterward, many attendees signed up on the spot. It was this type of organization building that was our only hope to win Iowa.

Also at this event, Bill Gluba, soon to be mayor of Davenport, came up to me and produced over twenty supporter cards—signed pledges by people to attend the Iowa caucuses for Obama—that he had collected as he bounced around the day's picnics and barbeques. As picayune as it sounds, this was exactly what we were trying to do; it was a small but symbolically important sign to me that things were moving in the right direction. We needed to have thousands of Iowans eventually living and breathing the campaign every day. Our supporters' involvement couldn't end at making calls or knocking on doors from preapproved lists; they had to approach everyone they could, no matter their electoral history, and make a personal case for why their targets should support Obama. It was the surest way to expand the electorate in our favor.

———

The other early states were also progressing nicely. In New Hampshire, we were playing a huge game of catch-up with Clinton, whose organization was just-add-water. In South Carolina, we were much more aggressive than Edwards or Clinton—at this point, we were doing the only organizing in the state. All the other candidates were engaged in top-level politics exclusively—signing up political insiders, elected officials, and ministers, and hoping they would convert supporters and get voters to the polls. That's historically how it was done in South Carolina—you put local big dogs on the payroll, gave them money around election time, and kept your fingers crossed that they would turn out the vote for you. We resisted this approach; we were happy to have political support and received a lot of it, but our consistent core strategy was to build a locally grown organization.

Most politicos in South Carolina thought we were nuts. But we stuck to our guns and refused to engage in many of the bidding wars for support of political figures. This became a source of tension for some of our more traditional supporters, who wondered why we were so focused on volunteers instead of the warlords who had been getting taken care of for decades and had proved they could turn out the vote with some degree of success.

Our South Carolina staff was pilloried for not playing the game. Stacey Brayboy, our state director, came to us from Virginia governor Tim Kaine's most recent campaign and had worked in South Carolina previously. She and Anton Gunn, our political director, a former offensive lineman at the University of South Carolina and now a community organizer (which is why we hired him—I liked that his orientation was organizing, not old-school politics), asked me to come down to South Carolina to take some arrows and help convince our political supporters that our approach was sound. They were holding the line, but it was getting harder.

The meeting with our statewide leadership turned into a very spirited discussion.

"We have been running and winning races down here for years," they told me. "We put ourselves on the line for Obama and now you are telling us you'll do it a different way—you people who have no idea how to win our elections."

My response was polite but firm. "Look," I told them, "we need to drive up turnout, find new and young voters, appeal to independents. We need a huge volunteer organization to accomplish this. In combination with the leadership of the people in this room who know the ropes, it will be a very powerful force."

A prominent local elected official responded with agitation and a little heat:

"If you don't do it our way, you will lose," he said. "There are no volunteers in South Carolina politics. You need to pay for your help—and your turnout."

I stood my ground. I said I appreciated their position but we had an established approach, focused on the grassroots, and we had great faith in its potential success. Most of our leadership was relieved we stood our ground; they were hungry for a new way of doing things; it was the reason they were committed to Obama in the first place. But a few of our key supporters dropped away at that moment and never reengaged, or did so only very late in the game. They just didn't believe in what we were doing. The word in South Carolina political circles, spread by our opponents, was that we were trying to run an Iowa campaign in South Carolina and that it wouldn't work.

But we had our game plan and stuck to it. This was a hallmark of our campaign: because our strategy and approach were settled, decision making was fairly uneventful, which I think is important in any organization. When an issue or question arose, we asked ourselves whether it supported our strategy and whether it was consistent with our tactics. If the answer was no—and most times it was—there was no debate or drama. We simply demurred, as in the South Carolina situation. This allowed us to spend more time on execution and less on hand-wringing over decisions.

In Nevada, all the campaigns were off to a slow start compared with the other early states. No one was sure yet how important the state would be in the end. But by spring we were up and running statewide, and in April more than three hundred people came out to the opening of our office—a tremendous turnout, especially as the only headliner was me. It told me that our ground game could be potent, even in a state with no history of holding caucuses and where Obama could not spend much time.

The night's more relevant lesson came from a great idea on the part of our Nevada staff. As I wandered around the office, I noticed that all the walls were lined with street maps. I asked a staffer what they were for.

"It's so people can find the street they live on and their precinct name or number," he told me.

"Most people don't know?" I asked.

"Well, in most states, people do," he replied. "But here in Nevada, we've had an influx of new residents in the last few years. Plus, it's our first time as a caucus state. So a lot of people have no idea."

I thought this sort of close-to-the-ground strategy could pay big dividends for us. It was fascinating to watch person after person write down their precinct as if it were a strange phone number. In Iowa, voters knew it as well as their kids' names.

———

All political campaigns consume lives—presidential campaigns especially so. The normal things in life—movies, sports, books, uninterrupted time with family and friends—fall away almost entirely. People who sign up for a presidential campaign should know that they are putting their personal lives on hold. If they don't know, they will learn so painfully, and quickly enough. Our staff and their families regularly made sacrifices large and small to accommodate the campaign; the same was surely true in our opponents' camps. For the most part, as the campaign wore on, we were too absorbed by what lay before us each day to think about what we were missing of the lives that continued around and without us. What was abnormal became normal. But on that trip to Nevada I was reminded of the personal toll of my prolonged absence from my loved ones.

My wife and I had a dog, a beloved pet that was simply a member of the family. On our first date we discovered we had both always wanted a dog named Marley; by the time our son was born, the Rhodesian ridgeback puppy we had picked out together years earlier was jokingly referred to as our "firstborn." Marley had made the trek to Chicago with my wife and son in March, and we had all settled into a condo not far from the campaign office.

The morning after our Nevada office opening, my phone rang at 4:00 a.m. Vegas time. This was not unusual and I answered my phone. My assumption was that there was some crappy press story to deal with. Instead, it was my wife, her voice tight with concern.

"Marley woke me up and then collapsed by the bed," she said. "He's still sprawled on the floor. If I leave the room he tries to struggle to his feet but can't make it. He's whimpering and his breath is labored." We'd had prior health incidents with Marley, so we knew to be calm and roll with the punches, but I sensed this time was different. I could tell my wife did, too. "I am going to put the phone up to Marley's ear so you can talk to him," she said.

"Good boy, Marley, everything will be okay, buddy," I promised him; she said he perked up a bit. I heard my son in the background, very distressed, his two-year-old voice insisting, "Marley, get up right now!" Somehow by this time my remarkable wife had already arranged for a babysitter to watch our son while she found a pet ambulance to help her carry Marley outside and drive them to the veterinary hospital.

I hung up and got ready for a breakfast meeting at my hotel with the most important labor official in Nevada and some members of his union. I had to force myself to focus. Usually I am adept at compartmentalization, but I desperately wanted to get on a plane and be with my family.

While the union leaders and I were deep in a discussion of the race and Nevada's role in it, my phone rang. It was my wife. I excused myself and stepped out onto the terrace, which was strikingly warm in the desert sun.

Through sobs from the animal hospital, she asked me to say good-bye to Marley. That was all she could get out. I did so, barely holding it together on the outside, torn up on the inside. "We just lost him," she whispered. "He is gone."

I gathered my composure, did the best I could during the rest of the meeting, and headed off to the airport in a daze. Stricken with my own grief, I was also beset by knowing that for my wife and son, losing our beloved dog would not make it any easier for them to adjust to Chicago while I worked around the clock.

We eventually got the endorsement of the labor official and his union—and when we did, all I could think about was that horrible morning, my wife dealing with the death of our pooch all alone, my son terrified, and me thousands of miles away and of zero help.

That's what life is like on presidential campaigns. There is little time to get diverted from the mission. Dedicated staff become more machine than human, not by choice but because the reality of the challenge and the pace demand it.

———

When we entered the race, we talked a lot about trying to run a different kind of campaign. The odds of our electing a president were against us; our only hope of success depended on breaking free of the standard political paradigm and becoming a movement. Ax and I discussed this often, frequently with Steve Hildebrand. One of Steve's roles was to manage our relations with elected officials, constituency groups, and organized activists, forces that constantly pressured us to take conventional routes. They wanted us to seek endorsements, attend events that did not fit our strategic needs, and meet the demands of narrow but seemingly powerful interest groups.

Our determination to run a campaign that eschewed these machinations became shorthand for us; "If we do this, how is that running a different kind of campaign?"

What precisely did we mean? Above all, it meant a change in tone. We wanted to avoid engaging in the snarky tit-for-tat that had consumed our politics for years, and to put the grassroots—the people—before interest groups and endorsement politics. We wanted to reach voters individually rather than expect some group or person to deliver them.

Our dogged refusal to be led around by the nose by insiders and interest groups was driven by a few factors: We had no margin for error; We knew we wouldn't run the perfect campaign, and we didn't, but we could not be cavalier in making decisions on resource allocation—whether time, money, or message. We had none of them to waste. Because we were trying to expand the electorate and attract new and younger voters along with independents and Republicans, we could not afford to spend time at events where there would solely be a very limited audience of traditional Democratic activists.

This caused great stress to our early state and political staff, which time and again had to convey Obama's polite refusal to incredulous party and constituency leaders unused to being rebuffed by major presidential candidates.

For our break-the-rules strategy to work, we all had to remain faithful to its principles all the time. If we were turning down a traditionally important event in one state, we couldn't cave on another. We had to be consistent and clear, or our schedule would soon be out of our hands. Allocation of the candidate's time is the most important decision any campaign has to make. How the candidate is spending time, day in and day out, ought to be the clearest reflection of a campaign's strategy and priorities.

Our strongest preference when it came to Obama's time was avoiding the pack. Orchestrated Democratic events involving all the candidates produced no unique or meaningful press coverage; the story was always "Dems Gather in Cedar Rapids, Woo the Faithful." We believed that at best 25 percent of our eventual caucus supporters would pay fifty or a hundred dollars to attend a Democratic party dinner; attending these types of events robbed us of days we could run the show our way.

In Iowa our staff had to deliver the bad news that we were not going to one of the Iowa Democratic Party's major fund-raisers or the second-biggest county's annual Democratic Party dinner. All the other candidates were attending both, and the grief was raining down on us not just from party leaders and the press but also from some of our own more traditional supporters in the state, who couldn't fathom what we were doing.

On the phone with Hildebrand and me, Tewes pleaded for some relief. "Guys, you know I agree with the premise. But we're getting killed out here.

People are starting to say we are arrogant and don't care about the party." From his voice, we could tell just how much grief he was taking. "Please," he continued, "just find a way to give us a few more days in Iowa?"

I had great sympathy for him. But the allocation of Obama's time was a complex dance between fund-raising, all the horrid debates (the reason we tried to limit them from the beginning), time in other early states, and his need to be in Washington for key Senate votes. There were simply no extra days floating around.

I told Tewes to let HQ be the bad guy, as I had in South Carolina, so that down at the state level they could claim, honestly, that they were trying to persuade us to attend some of these events. He did, and it gave me the chance to say, "Our state staff thinks we're nuts here in Chicago. They're beating the hell out of us to go, but sorry, we just can't be there."

As time went by, though, our in-state staff increasingly came to see the value of this iron-willed discipline. They also saw that the fallout from Obama's absence at certain functions was never as bad as had been predicted. The lead-up to missing an event was treated like a ten-alarm fire; afterward, there would hardly be a puff of smoke. Eventually, state staff led the charge to maintain our flexibility to do the types of events that best served us.

Obama deserves enormous credit for backing us up on these decisions. He got incredible grief about his absences from local pols in the states, usually couched in biblical terms; at the very least, they assured us that skipping their events would absolutely destroy any shot we had at the presidency. It must have been tough for him, but almost without fail he would diplomatically hold the line.

Our independence also enabled us to create our own large, untraditional crowds. The more events we did in the early states, the more we drew crowds that were substantial, diverse, and filled with the type of people who traditionally did not attend political events. We used our database to model those who attended our events, looking at past voting history and demographic information. It turned out to be a real representative sample of the population, not just a solid block of Democratic Party activists. So while some candidates were thrilled to have a big audience to speak to at an existing event, we were more interested in building events that would feed into our specific voter targets and that included trying to attract a lot of people who do not like to pay to go to a political event.

Of course, there were times we relented. One example was the International

Association of Fire Fighter's Legislative Conference in the spring. It was held in D.C.; Obama was already scheduled to be in town for a Senate vote the day of the convention, so he had to go. We decided, however, that rather than do what the rest of the candidates would do—rattle off a list of the firefighters' priorities and pledge undying devotion to them—we would refuse to pander. Instead, we would give a broader speech about Iraq, the toll it was taking on local communities and preparedness (firefighters, too, of course), and make a general call for bringing about fundamental change.

The other candidates received loud and sustained applause as they each recited the same talking points, hitting the obvious buttons. Obama's comments about Iraq and its implications were received politely but quietly. The political punditocracy, which attended all of these cattle calls and assigned them overblown importance, judged it an abject failure for us; some went so far as to say we bombed. Yet the coverage around the country in AP stories and local papers was actually quite positive; we had differentiated ourselves and gotten a compelling message out beyond the hall. Still, we had to concede part of the pundits' point: there must have been a better way to differentiate ourselves without creating stony silence in a cavernous hall.

The candidate thought so, too. After the event, Obama called me and said, "Listen, I signed off on this strategy and believe in it but there has to be a happy medium. I have to be able to give these groups some red meat so I can get their attention and then make our broader message points." He was clearly unhappy at having to sweat out the silence. "I just kept talking louder and louder but it was painful. They were just staring back at me."

We agreed that, going forward, we would play these events a bit more traditionally but not go as far as Clinton and Edwards, who were just playing up to the crowd—albeit to undeniable effect.

So all things being equal, other than the David Geffen episode in February, we had done a pretty good job of staying out of the deep muck. Until Punjabgate.

———

Our research team had put together a document that highlighted the voluminous examples of Hillary Clintons' expressing tacit support for outsourcing. We knew this could cause huge problems in Iowa with blue-collar voters, so we decided to send this background document around to select reporters in hopes of getting some stories written.

This is standard operating procedure—campaigns move research and story ideas around to introduce them into the campaign dialogue without having to launch the attack themselves. Sharing such information is meant to spur a reporter into doing her own research and reporting; get it right and you can draft behind a press story and not catch the arrows for doing the dirty work. We did much less of this than many campaigns did, but there were times when we indulged—it was our researchers who found John Edwards's infamous $400 haircut expenditures.

The document on outsourcing was titled "Hillary Clinton, D-Punjab," after an incident when Hillary Clinton was in India and she jokingly told a local official that should be her title because of her ongoing political interest in many things Indian. It was stupid and snarky; these research documents historically do not see the light of day, so communications staff doesn't treat them as though their language will be repeated. They are considered off-the-record and rarely get sourced. As a result, we were sloppy. But we got burned, and the *New York Times* broke the story that we were moving the D-Punjab document around the press world.

As soon as we got the first call from the *Times* we knew we were in deep shit. Our press secretary, Bill Burton, called me with the news as I was landing in Chicago, and my stomach sank. My first reaction was, "How on earth could they write a story off a paper that was clearly research, a background document?"

But that was blame shifting and rationalization. We had screwed up, and in a way that could be uniquely damaging. For other campaigns this would be a blip on the radar. But we had promised a different standard, and this was about as far as possible from the type of campaign we had pledged to run.

Obama was predictably furious when I talked to him after getting off the phone with Burton. Worse than that, he was disappointed. "This is the first time I am embarrassed by my campaign," he said. "How could this happen? Is staff going renegade?"

"No, this was distributed to the senior message staff before it went to reporters," I told him. "None of us objected because it was a research document and we didn't expect that material to surface or be printed by the press."

"I never want this to happen again," he said, making sure I had it clear. "I want controls in place and I want you to take personal responsibility for it. I don't care what the other campaigns are doing. We can't use that as a standard. Get control of it or I won't allow us to send anything but our schedule out to the press."

He was as short and upset as I had ever seen him. His campaign now looked jingoistic, simplistic, and engaged in the kind of politics he was running against.

Poor Gibbs was traveling with Obama and said that Punjabgate put Barack in the foulest mood he'd seen him in in three years. And much of it was directed at Gibbs, who was part of the command chain that was responsible for things like this and also happened to be in front of him all day long. Obama kept coming back to it. Gibbs took a lot of heat, but this one was my screwup; I should have killed the memo. I did a call with prominent Indian American activists around the country, who appropriately let me have it.

We changed course after this incident and sent out very few research documents; when we did, they were straightforward and fact-based. We set up internal controls so nothing got sent out without the right groups of us paying close attention and giving it a go-ahead. We had to control our message and make sure it was consistent, but we needed to pay even more attention to the tone of everything we were doing. This meant avoiding snark while still pointing out differences without abandoning decency.

———

In May, we had unveiled our first major policy proposal, the Obama recipe for health care reform. After the candidates' first joint appearance, when Obama felt disadvantaged because he did not have a formal plan, this issue shot to the front of the line. Along with energy independence, it was also the issue Obama consistently used as an example of what was wrong with Washington: every president since FDR has talked about health care reform that results in coverage for all. But far too little has been done in those six decades to bring it about.

Health care was also the top domestic issue for likely Democratic primary voters in the spring of 2007. We spent weeks getting ready for our health care offensive. Our policy staff, led by Heather Higginbottom, our Jill-of-all-trades who eventually became our policy director, was working around the clock and enlisting health care experts to help shape the choices for Obama. It was an arduous process but necessary, as our ultimate plan had many moving parts and aggressively attacked health care costs. One decision point in particular illuminates how Obama thought about it.

A few days before our formal unveiling of the health care plan, we had one decision left to make: would there be an individual mandate for all Americans over twenty-one forcing them to obtain coverage, even resulting in hefty financial penalties if they didn't?

Obama asked for the pros and cons on both sides. It was clear that the press—and our opponents—would default to a simple evaluation of our plan: whether it would provide "universal coverage" in the truest sense of the word. Gibbs was confident that factor would dominate the news. "We can argue till we're blue in the face," he said, "but if the referees say Edwards offers universal coverage, and we fall short, that will be the measuring stick. I am not advocating here, just laying out the facts."

He was right, which frustrated Obama. "So on a complex issue like health care reform, where there are cost, coverage, access, quality, and technology aspects, they'll just dumb it down to one evaluation?" he asked with exasperation. Even this far into the campaign, Obama still expressed surprise at the lack of depth in political reporting.

"I hear you," said Gibbs. "But I'm just the messenger here."

Barack fundamentally believed that before mandating coverage, costs had to be tackled. "I reject the notion that there are millions of Americans walking around out there who don't want health coverage," he said on this call. "They want it but can't afford it. Let's attack costs from every angle, provide incentives for small businesses and families to allow them to provide and buy coverage. I am not opposed to a mandate philosophically. But I don't think we should start there. It could be a recourse if coverage goals aren't being met after a period."

Heather's health care experts believed our plan could achieve near-universal coverage and universal access. Axelrod summed up, "We are just going to have to do our best to explain that this plan will cover just about everybody and does the best job by far of cutting costs."

Obama's pragmatic side was kicking in. Much has been written about Obama's "liberal" voting record, but a two-year U.S. Senate voting record is a poor measure of someone's ideology. Leaving aside the problem of the small sample size from such a short tenure, most votes in the Senate are highly partisan, constructed so that Democrats vote with Democrats and Republicans with Republicans. A more accurate representation would be his record during his tenure in Springfield, when he found common ground with Republicans on issues like health care, tax cuts, and death penalty reform. Obama has a deeply practical, results-oriented streak—grounded in progressive values—that was on display during our health care discussion.

Our health care plan was fodder for many attacks from the Edwards and Clinton camps during the rest of the campaign, but our research showed they never gained much traction. Few, if any, voters believed Barack Obama was secretly running for president to deny the American people health care coverage. Independents and Republicans, and some Democrats, preferred our more pragmatic approach, and progressive Democrats—on the whole, with some notable exceptions—had no question about Obama's sincere commitment to providing health care for every American. As is often the case in politics, when you make substantive decisions the right way, not based on polls and political wind gauging, you often end up on the high side of politics.

After we filed our stunning first-quarter finance report in April, we began to see huge growth in our online list. People now thought that this could be a real, sustained race, and many people who had been intrigued but hesitant to get involved finally jumped in with both feet. The unsolicited sign-ups were still exploding, and we began to do some Internet advertising around the Web to drive people to our site. In the beginning we had an optimistic goal of getting 3 million names on our list by the end of 2007. That number was based on what we thought was realistic, as well as what we thought we needed to support our original budget and provide us enough volunteers to execute the campaign.

We figured we wouldn't get to a million names until the fall and would then have to grow quickly in those last months before Iowa. Instead, we got to a million names in June, and remarkably, more than 250,000 of them had become contributors. This was an insane conversion rate, but it told us our base was larger than we realized and that these were not, on the whole, people dropping in casually to check out our website—they were trying to discover how to get involved, and, once they did, many became frequent volunteers and contributors.

We also learned a lot about the regular e-mail messages we were sending out. People wanted information, and a lot of it. We could send more e-mail than we originally thought advisable, which spoke to the heightened interest in the race and the commitment of our supporters. To keep things fresh, we varied the length and tone of the messages—some were long and informative, others quite short and informal. Perhaps most important, we learned that people responded very well to e-mails from Michelle Obama and that we needed to use Barack somewhat sparingly—when he signed an e-mail it always produced by far the biggest response, but we did not want this to become a stale event. So many of the e-mails came from me, though when we needed a big response to an ask—for money, volunteer time, or to watch an event—we made sure the e-mails came from the Obamas.

We ended the second quarter on June 20 having raised $32.5 million, $31 million of it for the primary. Hillary raised only $21 million for the primary—which would have been seen as astronomical but for our report—and the news created an uproar in the campaign world. No one, us included, would have predicted that we could match her in money this early, much less outraise her by $10 million in one quarter.

The Clinton money machine, over twenty years in the making, was the best our party had ever seen, and we had demolished it in our fifth month. We still raised most of our money the old-fashioned way, through traditional fund-raising events, direct mail, and people writing large checks for us. But the online money had spiked to more than $10 million. This was by far a record for online primary money in a quarter and spoke to the fact that our income from this channel could really explode down the line, as we had hoped. By comparison, Howard Dean's monster quarter in 2003 that propelled him to front-runner status raised only $7.4 million online.

Many of the online contributions were in small amounts, twenty-five and fifty dollars. And almost all of our contributors indicated to us that they also wanted to volunteer. We believed that making a financial contribution would lead people to feel more invested in the campaign and could result in higher degrees of activism. From the beginning, the two categories of people who made up the largest percentage of our donor pool were retirees and students, showing a very healthy generational span. We were even more encouraged that many young people seemed to be moving beyond showing interest to actually contributing and volunteering. This new turn would be absolutely essential to us down the road.

But our grassroots donors were of every age, race, and income group. Many had never participated in politics before, like Monique from Colorado Springs, whose husband had been sent to Iraq twice already and would likely return. She was motivated by Obama's commitment to end the war in Iraq as well as his refusal to accept money from lobbyists. Or Gene, a retired teacher from Dakota Dunes, South Dakota, who felt that Obama's time as a community organizer gave him the empathy and ability to help struggling families. The touch points and rationales for involvement ran the gamut, but what was being spun was a potentially powerful web of people who had not been involved much, or at all, in politics. These supporters were beginning to take ownership of the campaign, small piece by small piece.

More important, our overall donor base swelled to more than 255,000, with over 95 percent of them not yet giving the maximum amount of $2,300, meaning they could give again and again if they were so inclined. The Clinton campaign had a much higher percentage of their donors giving the maximum, but we had built a larger donor base. We had more total donors and more donors who could still give us money without reaching the cap.

It was a surprising position to find ourselves in.

I quickly added money to all the state budgets, and we upped the timing and intensity of our media plans in the early states; we would begin advertising earlier and more frequently, which would be very important to us because voters in these states knew very little about Obama at this point. Most of what they knew was surface information—he was a senator, gave a good speech in Boston in 2004, served in the Illinois legislature. We needed to fill in his life story, his values, accomplishments, and agenda. Now we had the resources to do a more thorough job.

Perhaps most important—and shocking, to us—we could afford to start planning for the states beyond the first four. I put $5 million aside to cover foundational expenses for the twenty-two states on Super Tuesday, and within weeks we began placing staff on the ground in all these states.

We had assumed we would be playing catch-up with the Clinton campaign after the first four contests. If we won Iowa, we thought, we'd immediately be scrambling to place staff, build organization, and mount competitive campaigns.

Now, it was not implausible that we could actually be better funded and organized than the Clinton campaign as we moved deeper into the race. In my mind, that made our Iowa strategy even more sound—and important. If we could pull off a win in Iowa now, we would not be doing so as the plucky, underfunded underdog who poured everything into one or two states but did not have the staying power to go toe-to-toe with the muscular front-runner. We were growing into a powerful force, capable of leveraging a win in Iowa in all the states where we were more active and organized, and better funded than the Clinton campaign. This was a strategic tipping point. And it made winning Iowa all the more important—our path was coming into clearer focus.

I somewhat excitedly laid out this revelation for Obama, who was pleased by our competitive advantages but remained cautious. "I still don't quite see how we erase thirty-point leads in all these states," he told me, "but I have faith in what you and Ax preach, that the race will reset after we win Iowa. I understand we find ourselves in a better position than we could have hoped.

You've asked me for some time to own Iowa. Trust me, that's going to happen. Every week I feel like I'm getting more in the groove out there."

The Iowa staff agreed; they reported that he was much better on the stump and in locking down supporters in June than he had been in April and May. But we still had a long way to go.

Even though we were raising a healthy majority of our money from the grassroots—and not taking any from federal lobbyists or PACs, a huge and important distinction from Hillary—we were wary of being defined by money and worked to spotlight other strengths of the campaign. Our opponents all held conference calls at the end of fund-raising quarters to tout and spin their performance. We shared the news first with our supporters through a post on our website, and the only spin we put on our performance was to emphasize the growth of our grassroots donor base, not the overall dollars raised.

This is very unusual. Almost every modern campaign proclaims their financial success from the rooftops, but we took the opposite tack. We decided to let pundits and insiders chew on it all they wanted; we would not strut or pontificate.

To try to get the press to see beyond our fund-raising ("Yes, he can raise money, but what else is there?"), the day our numbers became public I released this memo, laying out how we saw the race at that moment. Looking back now, you have to remember that this was the actual window through which we saw the race at this point. True, it was our interpretation, but I thought we put very little spin on the ball.

We targeted this memo to the press, the political elite, and our larger donors, and sent it to them directly, but I thought it would also be useful reading for our staff and grassroots supporters, so it was also posted on the website.

TO: Interested Parties
FR: David Plouffe, campaign manager, Obama for America
DA: July 1, 2007
RE: The State of the Race

Less than six months ago, we began this campaign with a mission.

Barack and all of us were determined to defeat the politics of cynicism and division that is so pervasive in Washington today and replace it with a politics of unity, hope, and common purpose.

The pundits and political insiders questioned whether a new leader and fledgling campaign could compete with the big money and massive organization of other candidates who have been preparing to run for years, and even decades.

Well, for the second consecutive quarter, you've helped send a resounding answer.

I'm thrilled to report that in the last three months, the Obama campaign has set a new record for fund-raising. Thanks to you, we raised at least $32.5 million including at least $31 million that we can spend on the battle for the Democratic nomination.

But as astonishing as that feat is, much more important is how we raised it.

To date, more than 258,000 Americans have contributed to this effort, much of it coming in small donations. This, too, shatters all records and sends an unmistakable message to the political establishment that the same old politics just won't do in 2008.

The American people are demanding real change, a politics of principle and not just expediency. They want to turn the page, and they're turning out and supporting this effort in unprecedented numbers. It has become more than a campaign. It is a movement.

Our financial success will provide the campaign important momentum. But there is practical application as well, which gives us a decided advantage in the nomination fight.

First, we are on a financial course that will allow us to both fully fund efforts in the early primary and caucus states, and also participate vigorously in all the February 5 contests, including large states like California, New Jersey, New York, Georgia, and Missouri.

Frankly, when we entered this race, we did not think that was possible. We estimated at this point of the campaign we'd be at least $20–25 million behind one of our fellow candidates. But due to the amazing outpouring of support from people all across the country, remarkably, we should be on at least even financial footing for the duration of the campaign.

Second, because so many states are holding early contests that may have significant impact on deciding the ultimate Democratic nominee, a winning campaign will need deep organizations in dozens of states to prevail. Our more than 258,000 donors provide us the foundation of an unprecedented volunteer army in all 50 states. We also have thousands more who are not able to contribute but are already volunteering or who plan to. For example, early in June, more than 10,000 Americans took part in our "Walk for Change"—canvassing neighborhoods in all 50 states, visiting more than 350,000 households.

We will have the largest and most committed grassroots organization in the race, allowing us to build our support, chase absentee ballots, conduct early vote programs, and turn out Obama supporters in any state we need to.

This is a tremendous asset and is one more manifestation of the "enthusiasm gap" we have over our rivals.

Six months into the race, we simply could not be in a better position. We have built a powerful, well-funded grassroots movement and strong organizations in each of the critical early states. Barack's call to change our politics and put government back on the side of the American people and our best ideals is resonating more strongly every day.

If you don't believe it, take a look at how so many of our opponents have in recent months embraced Barack's critique, positions—and even his language.

Some of our opponents have tried to deflect attention from the obvious power and momentum of the movement we're building by pointing to national polls that are all but meaningless. Indeed, at this juncture four years ago, Joe Lieberman had a solid lead in national polls. In the fall of 2003, the leaders were Howard Dean and Wesley Clark. You'll recall, none of these men were the nominee.

We're pleased to be running as strongly as we are in the national polls, but they are beside the point in a process that will be shaped by a series of early contests that will begin in Iowa.

One of our opponents is also the quasi-incumbent in the race, who in our belief will and should lead just about every national poll from now until the Iowa caucuses. Expect nothing different and attach no significance to it. It is clear you did not in this past quarter and we would encourage everyone to keep our sights focused on doing well in the early primaries and caucuses, and then using our organizational advantage nationally to clinch the nomination in February.

Just as a refresher, below are some Democratic primary national polls going back to 1980. You'll see how effective they have been as crystal balls.

* 2003: In August 2003, Joe Lieberman led the national polls, in September, Howard Dean led, in October, Wesley Clark led, and in December—one month before the Iowa Caucuses—a Wall Street Journal/NBC poll showed John Kerry, the eventual nominee, in fifth place trailing among others Joe Lieberman and Dick Gephardt. Yet after winning Iowa and New Hampshire, Kerry vaulted to 49% in national polls before the end of January. This has been true in nearly every previous Democratic nomination contest:

* 1992: According to a November 1991 Los Angeles Times poll, Bill Clinton was

in 3rd place with less than half the support of the then–frontrunner, Jerry Brown.

* 1988: A January 1988 New York Times/CBS Poll showed Michael Dukakis in fourth place with 6 percent.
* 1980: An August 1979 poll showed President Carter trailing Senator Ted Kennedy by 36 points

Time is a friend to our campaign.

While voters have a distinctly positive feeling about Barack, they don't have a great depth of knowledge about his life and history of leadership in Illinois and Washington. That history, which we have begun sharing in the early states, distinguishes Barack as someone who not only speaks about change, but who has spent a lifetime working to bring it about.

As we educate voters about Barack, we have strong reason to believe that our already impressive support in the early states will solidify and slowly build later in the year.

It is clear we have the most room to grow in the race, given that the majority of voters do not know much about Barack beyond what they have gleaned from news reports over the last few months.

We also remain the candidate most clearly synched up with the electorate, an electorate clamoring for change and ready for our relationships around the world to be repaired. The election is after all about the voters, and we are very confident that Barack Obama is the type of leader Democrats are looking for in the standard bearer.

If we prevail in the nomination fight, there is mounting evidence that Barack Obama would be the strongest general-election candidate. Barack is consistently the strongest Democrat with independents in general-election polling, who are the voters that are the pathway to the presidency. Barack also has a 2–1 fav/unfav with general-election voters, which is also the best score in the Democratic field. That strength with independents, plus what would likely be very strong Democratic turnout across the country as a result of an Obama candidacy, also likely puts more states in play. We cannot afford another election where we have to run the table to win the Electoral College. So, the point is this. We are off to a great start because of your help. We are going to keep our head down and focus on continuing to build a powerful grassroots movement, focus on the early states but plan for the states to come in early February and continue to both introduce Barack Obama and the kind of President he would be to the American people.

In a little over six months, the contest begins in earnest. We are ahead of schedule in every phase of the campaign. Let's keep it going and elect a leader who will transform our country.

Thank you again for all you have done in the last five months.

Later in the campaign we sent these state-of-the-race memos—often in video form—directly to our supporters via e-mail. At this point, though, we did not circulate them. My sense was that for many of our grassroots supporters, inside baseball like this would be of little interest, and might even turn them off.

I was dead wrong. It could not have been more important for our supporters to understand how we saw the race and to know why their money and time were so important, especially as the press narrative was still quite negative about our prospects. It would have been very useful for our supporters to have our version of reality show up in their in-boxes, so they would not grow distracted, dejected, or confused when they repeatedly heard elsewhere that our prospects were poor.

When we started sending these types of updates out to our supporters months later, we received a hugely positive response. There is a big difference between simply posting an important message on your site and pushing it out directly to your audience. We learned that lesson the hard way.

Despite the rosy news and our undeniable progress, we knew that we had not seen the full Clinton arsenal. Our impressive start had allowed us to gain sight of a slim possibility for victory. We knew the road would get rockier, and the Clinton campaign would retrench. We often joked that the race was like the Empire versus the Jedi resistance: we were winning some early battles, but wondered at what point they would fire up the Death Star and unleash holy hell on us. That was the Clinton way. We assumed we would see it soon.

Just a few short weeks later, we were essentially given up for dead.

4

The Empire Strikes Back

The first six months had gone well, but we knew we were sailing into stiffer winds as the first actual contests approached. We were about to run our first TV ads and move aggressively into building our hard count—the list of confirmed supporters in each state. And we now had to launch offensives in states outside the first four. Our opponents and the press were ready to fasten on any misstep.

A July debate—our fifth—provided one of those tests, creating real sparks and revealing a meaningful distinction that would impact both the primary and the general-election campaign. Obama was asked at the debate, hosted by CNN and YouTube, whether he would be willing to engage in diplomacy without preconditions with bad apples like Ahmadenijad, Castro, and Chavez.

"I would," he answered.

It was, simply, what he believed should be our approach on diplomacy. We knew that our opponents, especially Clinton, would pounce on it as an example of how he was not ready for this office and claim that the GOP would have a field day with statements like this in the general election. The news media, always looking for conflict and potential gaffes, would further hype the story line.

We decided to be pugnacious rather than defensive. Obama was with Gibbs while we were on the postgame conference call, and at one point he grabbed the phone from Gibbs's hand. "We will not back down one bit from this," he asserted. "If Hillary and the others want to defend the Bush-Cheney foreign policy approach, let 'em, but this is one of the big differences in the race. So let's make our case."

Predictably, our opponents and the political community worked themselves into a lather. They all thought we had committed a major gaffe that finally exposed our naïveté, political weakness, and inexperience.

Our sense was that Democratic primary voters would react quite differently. We had clearly telegraphed how we stood apart from the pack with a stance that was timely and forward looking. It was easy for voters to visualize distinctions in certain areas—Obama's freshness versus Washington's stagnation, generational change, the clear differences between us and Clinton on Iraq—but when it came to foreign policy writ large the differences were harder to grasp.

The diplomacy issue provided an illustrated guide. Hillary was defending a Washington salon foreign policy—as were the rest of our opponents—while Obama articulated a different view. People were clearly hungry for a foreign policy that invested in diplomacy and rejected the notion that giving our adversaries the silent treatment was somehow a show of strength. Not only did Obama embrace and give voice to that position, he also confidently stuck to his guns when he was attacked for it.

A clear contrast on foreign policy had now been established between the Democratic front-runner and her closest rival. It was a real difference and one that we thought was working for us. Our field staff in Iowa reported that the exchange had opened eyes and ears on the ground. One staffer told Ax and me about an encouraging postdebate discussion with a Democratic voter. "I wasn't sure there were any differences between them other than Iraq," the voter had said. "Now I see it runs much deeper than that."

Interestingly, the Clinton campaign clearly thought they had some ground to gain here and deliberately stoked the flames. Hillary called a newspaper reporter in Iowa, Ed Tibbetts, of the *Quad-City Times*, and launched a broadside, calling our position "irresponsible" and "naive."

This set the political world on fire. Conflicts always do. We welcomed the engagement and had Obama call the same reporter and say that what was naive was thinking we could keep doing the same thing as Bush and Cheney on foreign policy and expect a different result. In fact, it was just as naive as following George Bush into the Iraq War without first asking the tough questions.

When we polled this issue in Iowa, we discovered our side of the diplomacy fight was earning much wider support. More important, in focus groups we were discovering that it was a signal to voters that Obama represented change in these areas and Hillary did not.

Focus groups yielded the valuable insights of listening to voters discuss key issues, and we used them frequently. After the election I was told that, remarkably, the Clinton campaign conducted very few focus groups. If true, this is campaign malpractice of the highest order. It was one of several decisions by their chief strategist and pollster, Mark Penn, that gave us a huge advantage. I can only assume he preferred interpreting his own polls to determine voter sentiment over allowing Senator Clinton to hear directly from the voters who would decide her future.

Focus groups conducted by a professional moderator (not a pollster) and feedback from the field were two of our most important assets; we wanted to listen to voters every way we could to see how they processed arguments throughout the campaign. We did not use them to make policy decisions. We used them to gauge how the arguments in the campaign were being received and digested. It was about communication, not content. We were lucky to have Penn on the other side, because a more rigorous research regimen would have showed the danger in pushing this diplomacy fight. More generally, it would also have turned up some of the lingering doubts voters in Iowa and other states had about Hillary Clinton, all her strengths notwithstanding.

———

The August debate was the first to actually take place in Iowa. We knew it would receive strong viewership numbers among potential caucus-goers, our most crucial audience. It was the real deal—this debate could affect the outcome on the playing field we cared about most.

There were two large hurdles. First, we couldn't afford to take a lot of time out of the Iowa schedule for prep. August time in Iowa is invaluable; you can do outdoor (and therefore larger) events and still have time to shake hands at baseball games and county fairs, but that warm-weather window was closing fast. And college kids were back home where we ultimately wanted them to caucus, not on their campuses where their support would be diluted.

Our goal was to reach as many people as possible during this time. We scheduled a multiday bus trip heading into the debate and set aside snatches of time for more formalized prep, though most of it had to be done on the bus in hour-long chunks led by Axelrod. This was less than ideal given the importance of the debate. We knew the diplomacy fight would be front and center and we needed to win that exchange. But running for president does not allow you to compartmentalize priorities very often. Multitasking up on the high wire is the natural order.

The second concern was that this would be a morning debate, broadcast nationally on ABC in George Stephanopoulos's Sunday-morning time slot. The debate would start at 8:00 a.m. central time. The problem? Barack Obama was not a morning person. Quite the opposite, in fact. And the bus was not getting into Des Moines until after 10:00 p.m. the night before the debate. So our candidate would likely get a few hours of sleep at most and have to perform at a high level at his worst time of day.

I flew in from Chicago and trudged across the street from the Des Moines airport to the Hampton Inn, which had become our hotel when Obama overnighted in the center part of the state. He and the road show often wound up crashing at Super 8s or single-floor motels in small towns throughout Iowa when the schedule took him far afield and it was inconvenient to head back to HQ.

Interestingly, we later discovered that when Hillary Clinton was in Iowa she preferred to stay at the Hotel Fort Des Moines, a historic Democratic-owned hotel, and would often insist on returning there as opposed to staying out around the state. This gave us a small but important advantage—we had less travel time than she did, meaning over the course of the Iowa campaign we were probably able to squeeze in at least a dozen more events because we did not have to fly or drive back to Des Moines. This may seem tiny, but because we believed everything had to break our way to win, it was an unexpected advantage we valued.

As I reached the hotel, the traveling party pulled in. I went with Obama to his room to go over some nondebate issues and then back to the lobby where our advance staff had some beer in coolers. I sat down with Axelrod, Gibbs, and Jim Margolis, our media consultant who was also helping on debate prep. We were all tense. Our candidate was not prepped as well as he should have been, and we were petrified of the morning debate time. "This debate should be in Waterloo," someone said.

Oddly, Ax, who is never one to look for silver linings, wasn't entirely convinced we were heading for disaster; he thought we'd done a good job of scoping it out and had even armed Obama with a killer joke. This was disconcerting, because we were now so used to his disaster mongering that we just thought it was background noise. But his confidence notwithstanding, even after a couple of beers, none of us would sleep well that night.

The next morning, Ax and I got ready to ride over to the debate site with Obama. When he stepped into the SUV, I expected to hear how tired he was. Instead he was smiling.

"Are all the debates in Iowa going to be this early in the morning—being one with the farmers or something like that?"

We were relieved. He seemed loose and his head was in a good place.

We knew that he would be on the griddle, and Obama assured us he was more than ready. "This diplomacy debate is one I can and should win."

Our Iowa staff did an amazing job raising our visibility around the debate site. All the campaigns put up a lot of signs and have a horde of volunteers show up to try to suggest they have outsized momentum and support. In most cases, this is a completely overhyped waste of time. But in Iowa and the other early states, it did have some value in testing the organization. Would your volunteers and precinct captains show up to help? If not, that raised questions about their commitment and follow-through capabilities. Throughout the campaign, we carefully measured how well our organization performed at various junctures. This measurement was a hallmark of our organization: metrics, metrics, metrics.

Our Iowa staff had gathered at the HQ at 4:00 a.m. Joined by hundreds of our volunteers, they moved out and dominated the debate area. Many who came said they had not slept at all that night, either afraid to oversleep or simply too excited. It pumped up Obama to see a mass of his supporters as he rode in.

As predicted, the first ten minutes of the debate was all about our diplomacy position. Stephanopoulos went to all the candidates before calling on Obama, giving each a chance to swipe at us. Joe Biden even went so far as to repeat that he did not think Obama was ready to be president. When it was Obama's turn to speak, he was ready with a line to deflate the tension that he, Gibbs, and Axelrod had cooked up the night before: "To prepare for this debate, I rode in the bumper cars at the state fair." He had in fact done that with his girls recently, and the pictures played all over the state so it was a relevant reference point for local voters.

Unruffled, Obama concisely laid out his position and made the point that the Bush-Cheney approach of not talking to our enemies, in contrast to what strong presidents like Kennedy and Reagan had done, was a failure the country would do better to abandon.

We learned over time that Obama was an excellent counterpuncher in debates, much better than when launching his own broadsides unprompted. He found that sort of attack-first style inauthentic and it showed.

The debate was a home run for us. He was strong throughout, and this time both the voters and the pundits thought we had won. Afterward, Obama headed to the airport to fly home to Chicago for a few hours with his family before hitting the trail again. As Axelrod, Gibbs, and I walked with him to the motorcade, he wore a cat-that-ate-the-canary smile. "I really felt comfortable on the stage for the first time in any of these debates," he told us, "I think because we had real differences emerge, not forced or phony disagreements. I could have stayed up there for hours, having that diplomacy discussion."

"Guess we should fight to have all these debates at sunrise," Gibbs cracked.

Obama grinned. "Not on your life. Let's go home."

———

At Paul Tewes's request I headed to our Iowa HQ to thank the staff and do a rah-rah. The HQ was always alive, volunteers and staff all over the place, tripping over each other, pizza boxes and fast-food wrappers everywhere. Local Iowa volunteers had painted murals throughout the entrance to the office depicting lots of hope and change and even an Obama endorsement from the farmers of Grant Wood's *American Gothic*. Prominently displayed was Tewes's motto, in huge letters no one could miss as they came in: "Respect. Empower. Include."

I always enjoyed talking to our organizers in Iowa; these kids were laying it on the line and doing a great job.

"Our candidate just kicked ass in the debate," I said, to hoots and hollers. "He showed definitively today why he should be our nominee and the next president. But you showed how we're going to win. Once again, you outthought, outhustled and just plain wanted it more than the competition. And that's how we are going to win. We are going to keep it close and you are going to pull us over the finish line."

Ax and I called the Iowa team our field goal unit—we thought the organization they put together would be worth at least three points. They were our secret weapon.

The debate had been held at Drake University, home of the Bulldogs. As I was walking out of HQ, I saw a blue oversized bulldog mascot head. I couldn't believe it. These guys had thought of everything; our cheers had been lead by someone in a Drake Bulldogs mascot costume, rented for the occasion. I asked to meet our staffer who played the bulldog. The poor guy must have lost five pounds, sweating for hours in the outfit.

"Above and beyond the call of duty," I said to him.

"I'd wear it every day if I had to," he replied.

From there I headed out for a two-day trip in northern and eastern Iowa. I was going to smaller communities to meet with key activists and residents who were still undecided to try to persuade them to support us. Looking back, this is exactly the kind of approach that helped us succeed. We did not see the other campaigns' national manager or senior staff fan out across Iowa to small meetings, as we did with frequency. Rather than have campaign personnel like me camp out in packed urban areas like Des Moines or Iowa City, the Iowa staff sent us to smaller counties where senior staff did not traditionally spend much time, places where just showing up was greatly valued by the locals.

We believed nothing was more important to our success than local Iowans talking to local Iowans, persuading their neighbors, friends, and colleagues to caucus for Barack Obama. That Sunday night I was driving with a staffer to Iowa Falls, a small town a few hours north of Des Moines, in rural Hardin County, when a severe midwestern summer storm enveloped us. A tornado watch was in effect and there was spectacular lightning and pounding rain all around us. Off to the west, we thought we saw a funnel cloud in the distance, so my driver hit the gas just in case. We pulled into Iowa Falls and went to a small coffee shop that had closed hours ago but reopened to let us have the meeting. About six key political and community activists gathered, and we spent an hour talking about the campaign; the conversation ran the gamut, from issues to electoral viability in the general election.

Several of these folks signed up either that night or in the following days. These few people might seem inconsequential. But day in and day out, that's how you build in Iowa: a few people at a time.

On caucus day, Barack Obama won Hardin County.

Two days later, after another meeting, I spent the night in Decorah, in the northeastern part of the state. It is a small and beautiful town, hilly for Iowa. After grabbing some snacks for the night and settling into my hotel room, I pulled out my laptop and spent a couple of hours playing with numbers, looking at different scenarios in Iowa.

What would happen if turnout of voters under thirty was 17 percent of the electorate? What if it was 22 percent? What would happen if one-third of the turnout was new? How about 40 percent? How well did we need to do in the smaller counties out west to complement our strength in the east, where the border with Illinois gave us some familiarity and an initial boost?

I ran through these exercises frequently—sometimes at 4:00 a.m., according to my wife, while flailing in my sleep. Often it gave me comfort. Sometimes agita. But it was the one thing that was real to me about this process at this moment.

It was clear we could pull off a win in Iowa, but only with a big turnout and by holding our own in the smaller, rural counties. We could leave no stone unturned, anywhere in the state.

Our staff, precinct captains, and volunteers had begun voter contact in earnest over the summer. By September we had done enough that a picture of our supporters—at least those signaling their commitment this early—was coming into view.

It was exciting but terrifying. Even if our numbers picked up, we were going to be heavily dependent on people who had never before participated in a Democratic caucus. We adjusted accordingly, adding more media and Internet advertising geared exclusively to younger voters; we prepared to do a lot more instructional and informative work with our supporters so they knew how to caucus, while trying not to spook them; and we redoubled our efforts to attract support from conventional caucus Democrats so our newbies in certain precincts were matched with some grizzled veterans.

It was clear that we would win Iowa only on the backs of independents, Republicans, young voters, and new registrants—a scary proposition, to say the least.

———

As we were building in Iowa, however, the national narrative was becoming more toxic for us. The prevailing sense among pundits remained that Hillary Clinton was in impossibly strong shape. They granted that Iowa would be competitive but pointed out that she was leading by a wide margin in national polls and actually gaining ground after our temporary summer bounce. She led in all of the state polling at this point, too, with Iowa and South Carolina having the closest margins. She had big leads in New Hampshire and Nevada, the other two early states, and massive leads across the country, with Obama's home state of Illinois being the only real exception.

The talking heads began calling for Obama's second act. If Iowa is the linchpin of your strategy, why have you not pulled ahead? Even if you win Iowa, how on earth can you erase her big leads in the rest of the states?

It became overwhelming in September and October. Throughout the campaign we had tried to educate our supporters about our Iowa-forward strategy. Now, though, bombarded by naysayers in the press, our supporters began to get nervous. All they were seeing every day on cable, in newspapers, and on blogs was that Clinton was strengthening her position and we had blown our window to make a move.

These jitters were fueled by the intense scrutiny our supporters around the country—and much of the voting public at large—were giving the race. They visited sites like pollster.com and realclearpolitics.com and saw for themselves that, day after day, Clinton's national lead never wavered; if anything, it was growing. The only place where this did not seem to affect people was in Iowa. Because Iowans were seeing the candidates regularly in their towns and on the local news (and not through the eyes and words of the pundits), they were witnessing a much more competitive race. They also had a history of not allowing national dynamics to greatly affect their choice of candidate; this independence was one of the reasons we thought we had a pathway to victory there.

None of this surprised us. We stayed focused on measuring our progress in Iowa and the early states, and growing our fledgling February 5 operation. The $5 million we had set aside for those contests thanks to our strong fundraising was paying for staff and offices in all twenty-two states. In many of them, our grassroots supporters had already been organizing on their own through our social-networking site, my.barackobama.com, or MyBO. It made easier our decision to send a modest amount of staff into these states—they would not have to start from scratch with only a few assets to call in. Our volunteers had already made great strides, and with some more pointed goals and the tools to measure their performance they would only become more effective.

We actively encouraged our volunteers in the non–early states, even without staff on the ground to offer direction. Chris Hughes, a founder of Facebook who gave up working there to help us organize online, offered our supporters a clear message: "Get busy on your own. Take the campaign into your own hands."

In state after state, our supporters answered the call, organizing their communities for Obama. In places like St. Paul, Minnesota, Obama supporters in the area would find one another on MyBO and then hold an offline organizing meeting at a local library or bar. They would discuss how to build their group and get more people interested, usually settling on e-mail, though some also took clipboards to local community events; eventually they wanted to start calling and door knocking potential Democratic primary voters and distributing literature on Obama's message and plans.

Often they contacted Hughes or someone in our new media department to ask for voter lists, or for guidance on how to download and print literature. More often than not, they were cautiously seeking a green light, worried that the campaign might object to their organic activity.

We gave them the brightest green light imaginable. No one in our camp knew for sure, but we sincerely doubted that the same scenario was unfolding in the Clinton campaign.

Our "go for it" response to eager volunteer organizers was unusual. For most campaigns, command and control is normally the order of the day. But it was clear we had uniquely motivated and talented volunteers who could give us a huge leg up, so we tried to send the message that they should consider the campaign a movement—their movement.

To our great surprise, as we began to move into the fall, the Clinton campaign had not yet opened up offices or sent staff into most of the February 5 states. They completely ignored the caucus states until very late in the year. Almost daily I asked Jon Carson, our field director who was managing the February 5 operation, "Have the Clinton people shown up?" His answer always filled me a sense of wonder and gratitude: "Not yet."

The best explanation we could come up with for such obvious neglect was that they steadfastly believed the race would be over by then—that Clinton would sweep the early states and we would drop out. Or perhaps they thought that organizing on the ground in these states would not have a deep impact, that momentum and late campaigning and spending would be all that mattered. Whatever the reason, they continued to let us have the field to ourselves, much to our advantage.

Our situation in February 5 states like Colorado, Missouri, and Minnesota was no different than in Iowa: we needed to expand the electorate to win. We could not wait until four weeks out from the vote to start working these states. To have any chance of winning, we needed our local supporters out early and often, actively seeking nontraditional primary and caucus participants.

Our preliminary targeting decisions in February 5 states were based on a sense of how we thought we would fare in each one. Was the contest a primary or caucus? We thought our most fervent grassroots support could give us an advantage in the caucus states, even with Clinton at full strength. As it became apparent that her campaign would be late to the party, our expectations grew in terms of what we could accomplish. Could independents participate? We figured we'd carry independents; our polls in state after state showed they were much more skeptical of Clinton than Democratic primary voters. How expensive was it to run strong? Could we make a dent with a modest investment? We calculated the overall statewide cost of running a baseline effort and developed a cost-per-delegate formula that estimated the media, staff, and other organizational costs to assess how expensive acquiring a delegate might be in one state versus another (small, less expensive states, not surprisingly, jumped off the page as much more cost-effective). On a broader level, how did we see the delegate allocation unfolding, and was there anything we could do to affect it? Our delegate director, Jeff Berman, worked with Carson and me to come up with an initial assessment of how we might strengthen our delegate hand. This ended up playing a pivotal role in the ultimate outcome of the primary.

We did not expect—and did not get—much poll movement until right before the contests. What was moving the race to our advantage was an imperceptible force that was passing from voter to voter, and manifesting itself in the amount of ground we were able to cover in spreading our message.

We knew that doubts would be raised about Obama by the press and our opponents: he was too inexperienced; the GOP would chew him up; he should wait his turn. We believed local people talking to their neighbors, friends, and family, to address these doubts, could create a permission structure whereby voters rationalized, "Well, you're supporting him enthusiastically. We think alike, live the same types of lives. You see something in him, and that's important to me."

Thousands of these conversations were happening every day, out of the glare of the media spotlight and we thought it could be a difference maker. We believed we had genuinely widened the enthusiasm gap over Clinton. Our supporters were more passionate, meaning they would give more time and more money, and a higher percentage of them would do both. In states where organization mattered, we believed having a more committed and diverse volunteer network could make all the difference.

We talked often about the enthusiasm gap with the press, but since it was not easily digestible catnip like national tracking polls, nobody bothered to figure out what it might mean if it was true.

We were hitting or exceeding our internal metrics in the fall of 2007. Fund-raising was ahead of pace. Organization building in the four early states was on schedule, and we were making the number of phone calls and door-knocks we needed to meet our overall voter-contact goals. Our e-mail list growth was much more robust than our original projections. The website and MyBO were growing into a powerful force. Most surprising, we were much more advanced in the February 5 states than Clinton was. And we still thought our message best suited the times.

But the chorus of criticism and concern only got louder. Externally, and even internally, people continued to question our electoral strategy and mes-sage. We shouted from the rooftops that national polls didn't matter and that the race would reset after Iowa. We believed that to our core. But even some of our most steadfast supporters were getting shaky.

I attended a meeting of our top New York donors in September in the spar-kling and leather-laden conference room of one of our top fund-raisers. Our finance staff had done a very smart thing from the outset: they made sure that our communication with our donors wasn't just about the money but was a regular dialogue, so that they were in on the campaign's thinking and trajec-tory. We had many sessions in person and on the phone where I, Ax, or some-times Barack himself would remind people what the strategy was and that they needed to take the long view, not sit at their computers hitting Refresh until that day's national Gallup tracking poll came out.

Despite all that education about how we viewed the race, I felt like I was starting from scratch that day in New York. The fifty or so attendees were very nervous. All of them had gone out on a limb in supporting Obama and op-posing their home-state senator, whom many of them had known and helped for years. I got question after anxious question about national polls: Did we know it was settling in that she would win, which made fund-raising harder? Why weren't we doing more to answer the lack of experience charge? Even if we won Iowa, the polls in New Hampshire and Nevada were terrible; how would we make that up?

After taking several questions I calmly and flatly laid it out:

"Listen," I told them, "I know it's hard to be surrounded by political chatter every day about how Hillary is going to win and we are stuck. It's frustrating. The media seems to be covering a completely different campaign than the one we believe will unfold. As if events down the road do not have the ability to fundamentally alter the race. We believe this is an incredibly dynamic process. If we do not win Iowa, we probably can't win. But if we do, we believe the door will have opened, and we have a shot. Not a sure thing, but a shot." I paused to let this sink in. "We may not lead any poll in Iowa until the end, though. And if we do, don't pay too much attention to it. All that matters is if we enter caucus night with enough confirmed supporters to win at the turnout level we project. And those numbers and that view will never—ever—be visible in the media. You just have to trust us that this approach and this discipline is our only path."

I ran through the specifics of the four-state forward plan, then went wide. "Our fund-raising and grassroots support is deeper and larger than we could have imagined," I said, "allowing us to compete with her, if not exceed her, during a lengthy primary fight. Now, perhaps we can win three or four of the four first states; that's certainly our goal, and we may have essentially secured the nomination by that point." This brought smiles to a few faces. "But if not, we can be in this for the long haul. Despite Clinton's big leads nationally and in most states, she is only in the forties in most states. That means over fifty percent of the electorate is open to an alternative. And we will be that alternative."

My explanation helped mollify them to some degree, but many were still skeptical. "That all sounds good," someone piped up after I was done speaking, "but it seems to be a scenario only you guys believe will happen."

"That may be," I answered. "But this is our chosen electoral path. Yes, it is unquestionably narrow. But we believe it is the only one available to us. We have committed to it, and we need you to preach the gospel out there that it is doable, even if you harbor your own doubts. Please trust me—at some point the coverage of the race will move from the national abstract to the early states. The coverage will shift then because the media will finally encounter voters in those states who see how close the race really is, voters who have never accepted the national media spin that someone is unbeatable. So just hang on for a couple more months and the tenor of the coverage will change."

Phew. I was relieved to head back to Chicago that day, but it would not be the last time I faced a nervous and skeptical room of our donors. Julianna had me go out to many of the major fund-raising cities like Los Angeles and Washington to calm everyone down and get them refocused and confident. But my talks were no better than a Band-Aid; only a drastic shift in political perception would create a better fund-raising environment for our major donors. They had already tapped all the people in their close circle of contacts. To get new recruits to contribute and raise money, we needed to foster a sense that we could actually pull this off. At this stage, potential recruits would not get that from perusing the political coverage. It was then easy for someone to say no to a financial solicitation—"I like him and will vote for him," went the rationale, "but it's not easy for me to get involved financially and I just don't see how he wins." Our fund-raisers were hearing versions of this every day.

Obama dealt with all this in a very healthy way. At one point in September he called a meeting with some of the senior team in order to make sure there was not another electoral path available to us. I thought he was doing this in order to be able to assure his friends and political supporters—who were obviously chewing on him about it—that he had rigorously explored other avenues but come to see that an Iowa-and-early-states strategy was our best shot.

"The Iowa strategy makes sense to me," he said in the meeting. "If Hillary wins Iowa, she will be next to impossible to stop. But should we be doing more in the other states, and nationally, to decrease her lead and help change the narrative even if it's only for optics? I don't know about you guys, but it's no fun to be told dozens of times a day you don't know what you are doing and have no shot."

We had a healthy discussion about what types of things would be required to move numbers nationally and in states. And all of them—national advertising, advertising in big states like California, more candidate time on the ground in those states, more national media appearances—led to the same problematic result: it would take time and money away from Iowa and to a degree the other early states, in direct opposition to our strategy. We would have to make cold-blooded choices about how to allocate resources, financial and human. Axelrod summed it up: "This is a zero-sum game. The clock is ticking, and every minute we spend somewhere other than Iowa gets compounded as we draw closer to the caucus."

"We're not sitting on surplus cash," I added. "To spend more nationally we would have to take from the early states and our initial February 5 spending. We can do that, but we need to be clear about the tradeoffs that would entail."

"Okay," said Obama. "We are going to stick to the game plan. I just wanted us to make sure we weren't getting too comfortable or lazy, not willing to adjust." I relaxed for a moment, thinking it was settled. But Obama wasn't finished. "I'm going to ask for one concession that should not harm our Iowa efforts," he said. "We are doing good African American politics in the early states. And that's as it should be, that's our focus. But I am going to insist that we start spending more time on African American leaders in states down the line. One, we will need their help eventually. Two, it's just psychologically draining for me to get e-mails and calls from people about how upset they are that we lost another prominent African American to the Clintons and that it appears like we really don't care. Win or lose, I just can't have that. We have to do more."

This was a conversation that had been going on for some time. I knew he felt I was being too stubborn by insisting that we did not have time for what I viewed as extracurricular campaigning when we did not have a dime or a minute to spare. And though it went unsaid, it was clear to me that he was viewing his base politics more through the prism of losing than winning. He did not want to lose and be charged with ignoring the African American community. Ever pragmatic, he knew how steep the next few months' climb would be.

He called me on his way home from the meeting. "Look, Plouffe," he said, "your focus and discipline are an important part of the campaign. Without it, we'd be tilting at windmills too often. But you can also be too stubborn in trying to enforce that discipline. Yes, Iowa is the pathway. I am in one hundred percent agreement with that and we'll just have to ride out the naysaying." He paused for a moment. "But if you want me to perform in Iowa, I need to have this burden lifted."

I told him I would try to do better with the African American community and would make sure we picked up our game in this regard. And we did. Valerie Jarrett began holding a daily call with our staff and key supporters involved in outreach, which helped to instill more discipline and allowed us to track progress more closely. Each day, Valerie had people on the call report on their conversations with various African American political targets and what their next steps would be.

The results didn't change much immediately in terms of endorsements, but all the contact helped freeze some leaders who might have gone over to Clinton and would now wait to see how the first states unfolded.

On our postmeeting phone call, he raised one other idea. He was fairly sheepish about bringing it up, so I knew it wasn't his idea but something a friend had brought to him. "What if we bought national ads on BET for a few weeks?" he asked. "We might be able to spike our numbers enough that it could erode her national poll lead to some degree."

I quickly did the math. "Even if we could easily move a bunch of African American voters," I said, "and I don't think we can, because the Clinton name and brand is strong and these voters probably won't break for you in big numbers until after you win Iowa and/or New Hampshire, proving your viability—if we went from thirty percent support to sixty percent support, it would move the national horse race a total of one point, because African American voters represent only fifteen percent or so of the national Democratic primary electorate."

And that was that. But it became clear to all of us that day how much pressure and criticism Obama was getting from all sides. It speaks volumes about his discipline and sense of the race that he refused to jettison elements of our electoral strategy. Most candidates would not have weathered this storm as well. They would have insisted we make some changes to satisfy the hungry hordes. That he did not, especially as a first-time candidate around the national track, increased my sense that Obama had unique leadership abilities.

———

Sometimes the quiet events that happen largely out of sight can have as much or more impact on the outcome of a campaign—or any endeavor—than the headline-grabbing moments. Our belief that a lot would have to go right for us to win and that therefore we had to treat any barrier to our success with intense focus was on display in two critical moments during the late summer and fall.

The first was the Florida-Michigan primary situation. The DNC rules stated that Iowa, New Hampshire, Nevada, and South Carolina would be allowed to hold early primaries or caucuses. All other states had to hold their contests on February 5 or later or risk being sanctioned, meaning their delegates would not be seated at the Democratic convention. The GOP had similar rules.

Despite the threat of sanctions, the states of Michigan and Florida decided to move up their primaries. Michigan chose January 15, and Florida, January 29. Upset by this, the four early states announced that they would also move up their contests, with both Iowa and New Hampshire threatening to go in December, before Christmas, which was uncharted waters for the primary (and really nuts in my view).

Chaos ensued, and it was deeply frustrating to all the campaigns not to have this schedule nailed down tight.

The DNC's Rules and Bylaws Committee, an otherwise obscure group of thirty party insiders, would decide the fate of Michigan and Florida, and the final primary calendar. Our campaign had been surgically designed to maximize our success in the original schedule, and we vastly preferred having South Carolina rather than Florida play the role of the final gateway to Super Tuesday.

For one, we had built an organization in South Carolina, and it was sizable enough that we thought our infrastructure could make a difference. There would also likely be close to 50 percent African American turnout, which we thought would benefit us if we came in having performed well in Iowa. If Edwards did not win Iowa, by South Carolina he would be out of the race or severely weakened, and we thought this would give us a good shot at capturing a healthy number of progressive whites and white males.

South Carolina was also small enough that Barack, Michelle, and our surrogates could cover the state pretty well, and it was becoming increasingly clear to us that time on the ground mattered a great deal. Where we campaigned, we built support. In South Carolina, we could campaign just about everywhere.

Conversely, we could spend thirty straight days in large, complicated Florida and barely make a dent. And under a scenario in which Florida held a January 29 primary, we might get to spend only five or six days there, tops. Advertising would cost at least $6 million. And Hillary would start with at least a thirty-point lead, making it next to impossible for us to overtake her.

Given this, it was clear to us that Florida's becoming the last state before February 5 would be a severe setback. And since from the start our operating philosophy was that we were always one step away from falling off our narrow path, we set out to see what we could do to influence the outcome of the DNC's calendar.

In short order we realized that the answer was not much. The Rules and Bylaws Committee was made up of at least a dozen firm Clinton supporters. Many had been appointed to their posts during Bill's tenure in the 1990s, and two members currently served as senior advisers to the Clinton campaign. The deck was firmly stacked in her favor, but, remarkably, they ultimately voted unanimously to sanction Florida and Michigan at 100 percent—there would be no delegates awarded, and these contests would not affect the race for the nomination. This was the outcome we desired, but it was bittersweet because these were two important battleground states whose voters were now being punished. I figured the state parties would now back off and run their primaries later—I was terribly wrong about that.

Rules are rules. And I must give the members of the rules committee who were Clinton supporters enormous credit for putting their service on the committee ahead of their candidate's interest. But in my view it further underscored how unconcerned they were by our candidacy.

The Clintons have proven through the years to be politically savvy and relentlessly tough. If they fretted about these calendar issues as much as we did, there is no way they would have allowed their supporters on the rules committee to go along with having the Florida primary eliminated from the equation. Had the rules committee decided to not sanction these states 100 percent, we thought we could come close in Michigan or even win narrowly. But Florida was a bridge too far, and losing it would have sapped whatever momentum we had built up in the early states. We assumed the Clinton campaign would share that view and would do whatever it took to have Florida, not South Carolina, serve as the gateway to the February 5 contests.

But at this point in the campaign we did not look like a serious threat, at least not on the surface. Underneath the surface, though, they had great reason for concern, but apparently they never felt it. Clinton led narrowly in Iowa and had huge leads in the other three early states. But these races are never static. They should not have allowed us the opportunity to build up a head of steam going into February 5. Letting Florida move up its primary likely would have prevented that. Now that opportunity was lost for them.

Emboldened by the drift of the rules committee, we took it to the next level. I asked Steve Hildebrand to go on a secret diplomatic mission to speak with the four early-state party chairs, encouraging them to ask all the candidates to sign a pledge stating they would not campaign in any states (Florida and Michigan) that had violated the rules and were threatening the approved early states' primacy. Yes, this was in our self-interest. But it was also in theirs. If these two big states were penalized as severely as possible, and we all committed not to campaign in them, then the role of the early states was protected with no ambiguity.

From our perspective, this would be the final nail in the coffin. The pledge would make the first four states sacrosanct, and by signing it the Clinton people would box themselves in; they could not claim at a later date that Michigan and Florida were somehow valid contests.

The early states took the ball and ran, though we weren't sure what would come of it. Soon after the rules committee sanctioned Florida, the four early states asked all the candidates to agree that we would endorse the rules committee's decision by not campaigning in the renegade states.

This was a Friday, and Bill Richardson, Christopher Dodd, and Joe Biden all quickly signed. I called my counterpart in the Edwards campaign and asked what they were going to do. He said of course they were going to sign, and right away. Now, we were by no means in league with the Edwards campaign. But on this issue, we had common ground. Edwards would have even more trouble competing than we would if additional large and expensive states were suddenly relevant early. I suggested to the Edwards rep that it would box in the Clinton campaign more effectively if we waited a day to announce our intentions. If we all said we would sign the early-state pledge on the same day, she could say no, and though she would undoubtedly get grief in these states, it would be easier for her to wriggle off the hook.

My plan was this: if we let the other candidates go first, and the three "first tier" candidates left the pledge hanging for a day, it would increase press interest and draw the story out. Then if both Obama and Edwards signaled the next morning that they would sign, it would put enormous pressure on Clinton to do the same. Edwards was fading in Iowa and, despite having won South Carolina four years ago, was now mired in third place there, but he was still a threat. While the press generally viewed Obama as the default alternative to Clinton, Edwards still was given small odds of possibly emerging—if we failed—as the candidate in a one-on-one showdown with Clinton after the early states. So our campaigns signing on together would create a huge amount of interest and coverage, and raise the stakes for Clinton.

They agreed, and on Friday we each told inquiring press that we needed time to mull it over. We held our fire until Saturday morning and then sent out statements that we would sign the pledge. The ball was in Clinton's court. Within hours she had no choice but to say she would sign as well.

The deed was done. We had our preferred calendar and also a window into the thinking of the Clinton campaign—they still didn't seem that concerned about us. It was useful to know.

As this was going down, I was on Cape Cod for a week with my family before all hell broke loose in the fall. The week turned into a full working vacation but was a much-needed break nevertheless. Obama was also on vacation that week (the timing of my vacation was not coincidental), across the sound on Martha's Vineyard.

I tried not to bother him too much, but after Clinton signed the pledge I put my son in the stroller and went for a walk through the quiet New England village streets. While we walked, I called Obama to tell him about the Florida-Michigan news. He was thrilled but also curious. "Why would the Clinton folks allow that to happen?" he asked, as I often did. "Are they up to something we haven't figured out yet?"

"I don't think so," I told him. "The outcome here is a clear win for us. They must think we'll be out of the race by late January. None of it matters if we don't win Iowa, but I think we will look back and remember this as a pivotal day, if we can somehow pull this off."

"We are catching some breaks here," he agreed. "But speaking of Iowa, I'm not sold on this slogan you guys have cooked up. 'Change We Can Believe In.' Do you really think it says enough? Nothing about issues at all."

Axelrod and his message team had come up with dozens of slogan options and sent Obama a memo recommending we go with "Change We Can Believe In." We had not had a slogan up to this point but felt that we should have something for the stretch drive. A slogan rarely outlasts the campaign it was created for, but a good one can effectively reinforce your core message.

I was not sold on "Change We Can Believe In" at first—it seemed a bit awkward and perhaps ephemeral. But it also had potential because it was a bit unusual and could reinforce our message. Few politicians were actually saying they would fight for you, the voter, and change Washington, or at least do so convincingly, and we hoped it would make people stop and think. Cynicism was one of our chief obstacles in convincing voters that Obama could bring about change. Our research showed that most voters believed Obama was authentic about his desire for change; they even thought someone not bound by the ways of Washington was more likely to bring it about than experienced Beltway hands.

But sadly, many voters weren't sure anyone could really change the foul atmosphere in Washington. We hoped this slogan would forcefully suggest that Obama could be trusted to try—and that he might just succeed. The slogan also had the value of serving as an implicit contrast with Clinton. Fair or not, a healthy amount of voters still suggested they had a hard time fully trusting her. So there was a character component to the phrase, at least un-consciously, and I had become quite enamored of it.

"Well, let's give it a try," he said. "I'm still not sure, but we can't spend an-other week or two on it."

The slogan ended up being one of the signature pieces of the campaign. We unveiled it for the first time in September, at one of our grassroots fund-raising events in Arizona. The finished signs and banners had arrived just before that event, and we thought there might be some value in testing it off-Broadway before we brought it to the big stage—Iowa. Perhaps most important, the slogan signage looked great on TV and online, as we could see on Alyssa's and Emmett Beliveau's monitors in the scheduling and advance department.

We had always anticipated that third-quarter fund-raising would be dif-ficult. July and August are notoriously difficult months to raise money, as people head off for vacation and spend less time attuned to politics. Because of that we held fewer fund-raisers in this period, and the ones we did hold were largely packed into September. For this reason, we had to be more reliant on our grassroots donors during this quarter than the previous two.

We had hoped to raise $20 million on the high end and just barely hit that target, with $19 million of it primary money. Internally we were pleased, hav-ing now raised $24 million more in 2007 to date than our original projections had estimated. The surplus was having a profound impact on our ability to prepare for a campaign that could go on for some time. And we believed our fund-raising through the first three months of the fiscal year (October through December) as the early contests drew closer would be at least $25 million. This would put us on track to raise $100 million for the year, allowing us to run Ferrari-like campaigns in the early states and invest heavily in Super Tuesday.

October 2 was the five-year anniversary of the now-legendary speech Barack Obama had given in Chicago in 2002 at a rally opposing the Iraq War. This speech had cemented his opposition to the invasion that all of our main pri-mary opponents had supported; it had been a huge engine for our candidacy since Day One, and we often distributed copies of the speech at events. It wasn't simply that Obama spoke out against the war, but that he had delivered a well-constructed and remarkably prescient overview of what he feared would happen down the line if we invaded Iraq—a lengthy occupation, great human and financial costs, and a burden that America would have to bear for a very long time. He also famously said in this speech, "I am not opposed to all wars; I'm opposed to dumb wars."

That forthrightness resonated with voters, as did the fact that Obama had seen clearly what would happen in Iraq while Clinton and others gave Bush the authority to proceed down a perilous path. Many voters pointed to this as an answer to Obama's lack of Washington experience. "Well, he got Iraq right when just about everybody else got it wrong," they would say. "Seems like he had the best judgment and that was more important than Washington experience."

This was music to our ears. In this electoral climate, change and judgment versus inevitability and experience were matchups that worked very much in our favor.

So we planned to mark the anniversary of the speech by having him speak in Chicago and then Des Moines on Iraq and the way forward. We figured the speech would get outsized coverage but would also educate voters or serve to remind them how his judgment five years ago had proved more well founded than Clinton's and Edwards's. At this point, well over a third of early-state primary voters still did not know Obama had opposed the Iraq war. We thought we'd have a huge footprint that day.

But the Clinton campaign had something up its sleeve. They'd had a very strong fund-raising quarter and decided to release news of it just hours before our Iraq speech in hopes of crowding out our coverage. It was a very clever tactical move, the sort of thing at which Wolfson and company excelled.

And it worked. They reported raising a whopping $27 million, and for the first time only a fraction of that ($5 million) was general-election money. This was the first quarter during which they outraised us in primary money, and it was the most primary money they'd raised in a quarter to date. Doing that during the summer doldrums was quite an accomplishment.

The impression it gave fit perfectly with the overall narrative of the race at that moment: we were stalled and Clinton was pulling away. That's how it was couched in reporting. What I really cared about was that we were hitting our own internal projections, but no one relished the thought of another piece of bad news we'd have to fight through.

The coverage that day and in the days following was all about how tactically brilliant they were to wash out the coverage of our Iraq speech; this move showed once again that she was in the driver's seat. I was traveling with Obama the day of the Iraq speech, and he handled it with his usual healthy perspective.

"Well, we're getting real good at lowering expectations," he joked.

Yet where it mattered most, the story was a bit different. His Iraq speech got terrific coverage in the Des Moines market, which at that moment was for us by far the most important market in the country, and much more key to our prospects than national coverage. Explaining this to the press was like whispering into a gale force wind. The national narrative had taken hold— Clinton was up, Obama was down—and our obsessive focus on Iowa would not be part of that story. That's pretty much how we entered the last three months before Iowa: defiant, if a bit defensive; convinced that our electoral path was real if not properly understood; and fighting through a toxic political environment that left very few people in the political community giving us much chance at all.

Clinton was now exactly where she wanted to be—the clear and close-to-inevitable front-runner. If they got through Iowa unscathed, they would be next to impossible to stop.

5

Win or Go Home

Hillary Clinton could do no wrong through much of the fall. Then two events, minor in their moments but instantly magnified, began to change the national narrative. More important, they caused real damage with voters in Iowa.

It seemed like we were debating every other day. After our attempt at a joint deal fell apart, we were dragged in every direction, just as I had predicted. The cable networks were drawing high ratings when they hosted Democratic primary debates, so they were constantly trying to lure the candidates on stage by partnering with Democratic constituency groups and local media outlets to generate more of them. It was a moneymaker for them and a schedule killer for us.

We finally put our foot down and unilaterally declared that from September forward we would participate only in the two remaining DNC-sanctioned debates and a few in Iowa and New Hampshire that we had already agreed to, like the historically important Des Moines Register debate and one in New Hampshire sponsored by WMUR. This decision upset many groups that were planning to hold their own cattle calls, but it wasn't our problem. We would have preferred to make the decision in conjunction with our opponents, but we had tried that once and seen they could not be trusted to follow through. Forging ahead on our own allowed Clinton to free up her schedule without bearing the political cost of rejecting debates, but it couldn't be helped. Our strategy required six public events a day in Iowa, not spending whole days prepping and debating. The clock was running out.

The next DNC-sanctioned debate was in Philadelphia on October 30. The proceedings were largely unremarkable until the last few minutes, the "garbage time" of debates when very little of consequence usually happens and many reporters have already tuned out to write and file their stories.

Tim Russert and Brian Williams were moderating, and Russert asked Clinton a question about a proposal by New York governor Eliot Spitzer to provide illegal immigrants with driver's licenses for the purpose of dealing with issues like traffic accidents; under current law an undocumented worker was not held responsible. Many local law-enforcement officials were also asking for some kind of identification program that would allow them to track undocumented immigrants.

Clinton said that the federal government had failed on immigration reform, forcing states to address the problem on their own. This answer seemed to express support for Spitzer's plan. But Russert followed up, trying to nail her down as firmly supporting or opposing it; once again her answer left the impression that she was supportive, but she danced around the question a bit more and refused to answer with a straight yes or no.

Russert then asked for a show of hands of all the candidates who supported allowing undocumented immigrants to have driver's licenses. Obama raised his hand; he had voted in the Illinois state legislature for a proposal similar to Spitzer's. The issue was not a priority for him, but he supported allowing states to pursue it if they desired, as Bill Richardson had done in New Mexico.

Chris Dodd, who had not raised his hand, uncharacteristically piped up to state his opposition to the driver's license idea and then, to everyone's complete surprise, chastised Hillary for not answering Russert's questions directly. This spurred Clinton to once again speak very positively about Spitzer's proposal but avoid saying clearly whether she did or did not support it. The tension in the air grew thicker.

And like that, the story of the debate was rewritten. It was Hillary's first major unforced error in any debate and the press pounced on it. Fed with oxygen from the media, the spark quickly turned into a firestorm for the Clinton camp. There was no need for us to fan the flames; we stood back and watched the carnage.

The next day her debate gaffe dominated the television coverage. The campaign tried to put out the fire by releasing a statement saying she was opposed to Spitzer's plan, which had the added effect of putting them in contrast with us on this issue.

But this response only made things worse, because it seemed highly inauthentic. Voters who had watched her three stabs at answering the question the previous night might not have been totally clear on her position, but they certainly wouldn't have come away with the impression that she was *against* the Spitzer proposal. Now her debate performance looked highly parsed.

———

This driver's license contretemps may seem a small thing in the scope of the entire campaign, but often things that start small end up having a profoundly outsized impact. The problem for Hillary was that she had turned a simple question about driver's licenses into a deeper question about her motives. It became a character issue, and the data and anecdotal information we got back from the early states showed that it dramatically slowed her momentum. This was also reflected in the national narrative: it was now Hillary Clinton's turn to be sent to the press penalty box. After months of coverage that cast her as inevitable, finally there was a crack.

The license debacle was soon followed by "Plantgate" in Iowa. A college student reported that at a forum at Grinnell College the Clinton staff had approached her about asking Hillary a question. She had something in mind but was told by the staff that the questions were already written out. She was then handed a piece of paper with a question on global warming. Naturally Clinton called on the student from a crowd of over four hundred people. When the student read her question, she winked theatrically at the end. It made for great TV.

Her story became a media sensation across the country and was covered extensively in Iowa. The Clinton camp tried to clean it up by calling it an isolated incident, but no one bought this feeble spin. Their ruse ruffled the feathers of Iowans, who prided themselves on asking tough questions and demanding spontaneous answers of the candidates. Trying to make an end run around this was a big no-no.

In the early stages of the campaign, voters continually pressed Clinton to explain why she would not apologize for her Iraq War vote; in response to this hounding she had eventually all but ceased taking questions, a move that had earned her sharp criticism. Plantgate bolstered the notion that she would take questions only if her campaign could control what was asked. Our early-state staff reported back that it exacerbated some basic, gnawing doubts among voters. They were concerned Hillary was too calculating and her decisions politically expedient.

———

We had expected to approach the November 10 Jefferson-Jackson (J-J) Day dinner with the wind in our faces. The J-J dinner is a yearly Democratic Party event in Iowa that historically has played an important role in the presidential primary. There would be close to ten thousand Democrats in attendance, and the ripples from the impressions made there would carry across the state: a prime opportunity for us to reshape the race.

The two recent kerfuffles hardly cleared a path to victory for us. "As things stand," Barack said to Ax and me in the lead up to J-J, "I feel like we'll end up doing better than people expected, put a scare or two into Hillary, but come up short. We have got to shake things up a bit or in a couple of months we'll be heading back to Chicago with a nice handshake and thanks for playing."

The J-J dinner has two main components. The first is the candidates' speeches. The media and the Iowa Democratic political community scrutinize each speech intently. What was the crowd's reaction? Was there new material? Would the speech provide new momentum to the campaign? At the 2003 dinner, John Kerry unveiled a tough new speech that established an implicit contrast with the front-runner at the time, Howard Dean; many saw this as the start of his unlikely climb from a stagnant third to eventually clinching the nomination.

Second, the event is viewed as a test of organization. Who got the most people there? Who had the biggest presence outside the hall? If undertaken properly—not just by building a crowd of bodies but by forcing your statewide organization to produce attendees—it could also be a very useful internal measuring stick for the health of the campaign.

Jon Favreau started working on the speech with Axelrod a few weeks out. We decided we had to offer the clearest distillation yet of our message and of the leadership contrast we were offering with Hillary Clinton. During a conference call, Ax laid out the strategic needs of the speech. "We have to shake people and remind them that the kind of change we're offering can't be replicated by Clinton," he said. "Barack Obama can unite disparate elements of our country; Clinton will be more polarizing. Obama can really challenge the ways of Washington; Clinton is comfortable in the muck. And Obama will challenge the country to deal with long-term issues, not play small-ball politics.

"This is not about issue differences, other than Iraq," he summarized. "It's about leadership qualities and vision. That's what we have to punch through at the J-J."

We went through several drafts, with Obama's input, and about two weeks before the dinner, Favreau, Ax, Obama, and I met in the Chicago HQ to start nailing things down. We went over the speech line by line as Obama munched on a tuna melt and made more changes. He began to practice reading through it; teleprompters were banned at this speech, so he would need to know his speech cold. Axelrod and I had been stressing the import of the J-J dinner to the point of probable annoyance, but by the end of the session it was clear that he understood the stakes.

"This is a very good speech," he said. "I need to give my best speech of the entire campaign at this dinner, so for the first time I'm going to memorize the whole thing, word for word, so it's crisp and delivered powerfully, and so I don't leave anything out." Memorize. Word for word.

This was music to our ears. His stump performance to date, when he was not reading a speech, had mostly been workmanlike. But this was a long speech. And at this point the J-J was just ten days away and our schedule was packed.

"We're all for that," I enthused. "But when are you going to be able to internalize this? Ax will be traveling with you so you guys can practice, but there's no down time set aside for memorization. Do we need to scrap some of the schedule?"

"No," he replied. "I'll spend time with this on drives between events and late at night at the hotel. And I'll practice some by myself and some with Ax and Favs. I get how much we have riding on this speech and dinner. I need to step it up."

Our Iowa staff had a monster plan for accomplishing the second imperative of the J-J dinner, demonstrating organizational strength. Their initial budget for the event was $250,000, which I quickly rejected. But we agreed that spending close to $100,000, though still a sizable risk, was a gamble worth taking for the shot in the arm it could give us. The budget included transportation to Des Moines for our supporters across the state, new signs and banners, and a pre-event concert with John Legend to get everyone psyched.

One organizational complication was that the J-J is a fund-raiser. Many supporters had to buy a ticket to come, and the cheapest one was $100, no small amount for most people. Some of our National Finance Committee members bought larger blocks of tickets to be distributed to our volunteers who could not afford it. All the campaigns did this, but we were extremely diligent about providing tickets only to people who were confirmed Obama supporters and volunteers. This was not just a tactical exercise for us—filling seats with people who would casually wave Obama signs did us little good. So we tasked our precinct captains from around the state with finding committed supporters in their area to attend the dinner.

It was clear the Clinton people were going all out as well, though perhaps with a bit less success. An e-mail surfaced from their camp asking out-of-state volunteers to come to Des Moines—something that struck us as very significant. They were a big campaign with a lot of support in Iowa, but if they could not fill their seats with local Iowans, it implied a lack of enthusiasm among her supporters.

J-J Day has the atmosphere of a college football game. All the campaigns host big "pre-events"—like tailgating. We held the John Legend concert, which drew thousands. At the concert's end, our supporters, lively and pumped up, marched through the city of Des Moines to the auditorium several blocks away. Barack and Michelle led the crowd, dancing part of the way. It was an impressive display. Our new media team cut a short video of the massive crowd that we shared on the Web and via e-mail with our supporters around the country, so they could get a taste of the enthusiasm and organization in Iowa.

In the hall itself, we clearly had the most supporters, each one of them committed to caucusing for Obama. Clinton's crowd was a somewhat distant second, and Edwards's way back in third. Our folks were ready to let loose and holler for their candidate.

The problem was they would have to wait four hours. There had been a drawing for speaking order and we drew the last slot. This was a concern; we needed an inhumanly strong reaction to his speech and were worried that by the end of the night, we would be lucky if most of the crowd had not nodded off.

The program dragged on and on and on. Every elected official in Iowa spoke—at length—in addition to the candidates, each of whom had been assigned a strict ten minutes and proceeded to ignore that limit completely. When at last Hillary took the stage, she used her moment to unveil a new shtick, a call and response. The main thrust of her speech was that she was tough enough to take on the Republicans. She asked the crowd, "And when the Republicans engage in fearmongering, and saber rattling, and talk about World War III, what do we do with them?" And her supporters, as instructed by her staff, shouted out, "Turn up the heat!" as they waved yellow signs emblazoned with the same phrase and repeated like a chorus throughout the speech.

I had stayed in Chicago for the J-J because we had a lot of planning to get done that Saturday at HQ. Back at our apartment, my wife and I watched the late-night events unfold on TV, which was how most Iowa voters would take in the speeches. "That just seems awful," I said to her as Hillary riled up the crowd. "Even for a Democratic Party dinner it's awfully political and partisan."

I e-mailed Ax my thoughts and asked how it came across in the auditorium. His reply: "Other than her supporters people are stone silent." It seemed like they let a desired tactic—an audience call and response—drive her speech instead of focusing on a clear, contrasting message. She delivered some solid lines—change isn't easy, without experience and hard work it's just words—but the clear takeaway for those in the hall and in the media was the "turn up the heat" nonsense. It was by no means a disaster for her, just a missed opportunity, and an important one.

Well after 11:00 p.m., Obama was finally welcomed to the stage. His entrance music was something Ax and I had cooked up late one Friday night in the office. We got the beloved Chicago Bulls announcer Ray Clay to tape Obama's introduction using the famous Bulls music from the Michael Jordan era. Instead of "From North Carolina, a six-foot-six guard, Michael Jordan," the music was accompanied by Clay intoning, "From our neighboring state of Illinois, a six-foot–two-inch force for change, Senator Barack Obama!" Obama was a rabid Bulls fan, and we knew that music would pump him up. Just as important, it pumped up our supporters, who had been sitting there for hours.

He delivered the speech of his life. The whole crowd was riveted. Gibbs and Ax sent me a stream of e-mails noting that even the "jackals," as we called the press, were impressed. I sat quietly with my wife and knew we were witnessing a very meaningful moment. He delivered the speech better than it was written, and it was one hell of a speech. He just nailed it. "We are in a defining moment in our history," he told the crowd. "Our nation is at war. The planet is in peril. The dream that so many generations fought for feels as if it's slowly slipping away. We are working harder for less. We've never paid more for health care or for college. It's harder to save and it's harder to retire. And most of all, we've lost faith that our leaders can or will do anything about it.'"

His speech raised the stakes of the election. Turning to the same old leaders in Washington was like rearranging the deck chairs as the ship headed toward an iceberg. "And that is why the same old Washington textbook campaigns just won't do in this election," he continued. "That's why not answering questions 'cause we are afraid our answers won't be popular just won't do. That's why telling the American people what we think they want to hear instead of telling the American people what they need to hear just won't do." Implicit in the text, and lost on no one that night, was that our main opponent would be more likely to play it safe and political.

In response to the speech, Mandy Grunwald, Hillary's campaign media strategist, told the press that Mark Penn had said disparagingly of our supporters that they "look[ed] like Facebook," while Hillary's looked more like traditional caucus-goers. And Penn himself made a comment to the media that should go down in political infamy: "Only a few of their people look like they could vote in any state." Even less than two months out from the Iowa caucuses, they were oblivious to the growing danger of our grassroots organization.

Our initial takeaway was that we had gotten out of the J-J exactly what we needed, both organizationally and from the impact of the speech. We were thrilled. Ax's e-mail to me after the speech was succinct: "Fucking home run."

I talked to Obama very late that night, after 1:00 a.m. He was really keyed up, which was unusual. "Sorry for calling so late," he said. "I just can't sleep. I'm talking quietly because Michelle is asleep. So you liked it, huh?"

I had sent him an e-mail as the speech ended saying our odds of winning Iowa just jumped because of his performance. "It was okay," I joked. "Hard to stay awake through it, but I guess it'll do."

We both laughed. This was a big moment in the campaign and not only had we survived it, we had thrived. He and I spent at least half an hour on the phone, reliving the night, critiquing Hillary's and the others' speeches, and talking about the road ahead.

"The only problem for you is now we all know you can memorize," I told him. "So next time you say we have to stop handing you a couple of late-breaking new lines for your speech, you'll get no sympathy."

He laughed. "True, but it's the big red-light moments I rise to."

Before we hung up I told him I was very proud of what he had done that night. Clearing the event's high bar and giving a great performance were both impressive, but so was the text of the speech itself, which he had molded into a compelling articulation of why he was running and offered our clearest explanation yet of the choice in the primary election. The whole campaign now had its rallying cry for the stretch drive.

"I wished you had been here tonight," he said. "We've come a long way."

"I'll be there with you the night we win."

J-J Day marked the beginning of the stretch drive in Iowa. Had the caucuses been held that day, I think we would have finished a close second to Clinton with Edwards posting a surprisingly poor third-place showing. But we had two months left to close the gap, and all of our pacing, spending, advertising, and strategy were predicated on trying to be at our strongest point on January 3. Our candidate was really hitting his stride and had just delivered a closing argument to voters as he began to crisscross Iowa at a breakneck pace. I would say we were anxious but optimistic.

In early December on a Saturday night (the night of yet another debate, the Black & Brown Presidential Forum in Iowa, which is a mainstay and a must-attend), all thoughts turned to the *Des Moines Register* poll, which was scheduled for release in the next day's paper.

The *Register* may have the biggest impact of any paper in the primary process, and its poll has tremendous influence beyond Iowa's borders. It is regarded as one of the most accurate polls in caucus history, and its results not only shape the press narrative about who has momentum and who is stalled or fading, but they also have a real impact on the ground in Iowa. Local officials endorse based on it, potential caucus-goers weigh it in pledging their support, and it can provide a motivational boost to an organization—or sink its hopes.

Generally, polls are a dime a dozen in a presidential race, and the sheer number of them makes each one seem less important. But the release of the *Register* poll is considered an event. Time stops and waits for the results.

My first experience with the poll was in 1990 when I was working on Tom Harkin's Senate race. This was before the Internet, so if you wanted the scoop on the poll you had to go down to the *Register*'s loading docks around midnight and persuade one of the truck drivers to give you a copy before he left on his route. Harkin's campaign manager called me into his office on a Saturday afternoon and told me to stay out of the bars that night and instead to go down to the *Register* building at midnight, get a copy of the paper, and then call him at home (cell phones were just large, toaster-sized oddities in those days) to give him the results and read him the story—then he would call the senator.

Sounds pretty pro forma and uneventful, but to a wet-eared twenty-three-year-old kid it was a high honor; it made me believe I must be doing a good job to be trusted with such an important task. Since then I have never seen a *Register* poll without thinking of that night and of how seemingly insignificant moments like that can have an outsized impact on your professional trajectory. Now I got to play the old hand: I told our mostly under-thirty staff about how we used to get the *Register* poll down at the docks because there was no Internet, and they would roll their eyes and look at me like I had escaped from the set of *Cocoon*.

The *Register* poll updates about every couple of months during the campaign season, and the previous results had been released in October, showing us at 22 percent, with Clinton at 29 and Edwards at 23. In the "when it rains it pours" category, we happened to be holding our National Finance Committee meeting (all of our top fund-raisers from around the country) in Iowa on the very Sunday that the poll came out.

I had half joked to our finance staff that we should buy up and burn every copy of the *Register* at the airport and all the convenience stores along the route to our meeting. The *Register* polls are always blared across the paper's front page, and the October poll edition had pictures of Clinton, Edwards, and Obama with their polling number and arrows for whether they were up or down from the last *Register* poll in the summer.

In that poll we were down a few points, Edwards was steady, and Clinton was up. So all of our donors were greeted with a big down arrow next to the picture of their candidate in the biggest paper of the one state we told them mattered most. Unsurprisingly, the meeting that followed was one of our roughest moments with donors pre-Iowa.

But we were in a very different place now, thanks to our continued organizational efforts, Clinton's gaffes, and our knockout showing at the J-J dinner. So as we awaited the results of the December poll, we had a lot to be optimistic about.

The Black & Brown debate on Saturday night was uneventful. It was only telecast on HD Net, which we did not get in the campaign office, so our finance staff found a nearby donor who did; he and his wife graciously opened up their home, ordered food for everyone, and went out for the evening, allowing us to turn the apartment into our rapid-response war room. About twenty staffers gathered around the TV; the HDNet feed went out once or twice so we had to listen over streaming audio on a laptop. It was a pretty bush-league moment for a major campaign.

The debate was sleepy, but just as it was ending, the *Register* poll posted online: Edwards, 23 percent; Clinton, 25; Obama, 28.

"We've taken the lead!" yelled Bill Burton, our press secretary, and all of our press and research staff roared at the news.

This result was a bit rosier than our internal polling, which showed us even more closely bunched together, but it captured what would happen if turnout was high and more independents and Republicans showed. More than any other poll, the *Register*'s closely matched our field data and the voter ID work we were doing, which was far more voluminous than any poll's sample size.

This was a trend throughout the campaign. While our conventional polling always showed a tight race, our field data would suggest that if we turned out our supporters, we might be heading to a terrific outcome.

When I walked out of the donors' apartment that night in December, encased in the glow of the favorable *Register* poll, it was snowing lightly, just a gorgeous midwestern night. I decided to walk the forty-five minutes back to our apartment, enjoying the snow, the city, and the fact that, finally, we were getting out of the penalty box.

We were less than a month out from the caucuses when we finally deployed our ace in the hole—the big O.

Oprah Winfrey publicly indicated her support for Obama early in 2007 and had opened her Santa Barbara home in the fall for our largest fund-raiser to date; we raised over $4 million in one evening.

There was a lot of intrigue about how else we might use her, and a lot of back and forth in the press over whether she would help or hurt. While she was a popular figure, endorsements rarely cause people to support a candidate. There was also the question of whether Winfrey's endorsement would feed into the notion that Obama was more celebrity than serious contender. *Time*'s political analysis was typical of the doubts that many pundits shared about her impact. Its story before the trip was titled "Why Oprah Won't Help Obama."

"[D]on't expect [the Oprah] events to do anything productive to allow Obama to get over the biggest hurdle standing between him and the White House," the article read. "American voters are not looking for a celebrity or talk show sidekick to lead them. Obama is an intelligent and thoughtful potential president, but Winfrey's imprimatur is unlikely to convey those traits to many undecided voters.

"In that respect, Winfrey's events might even be—dare it be said—counterproductive."

These were not unimportant concerns to us. We wrestled with the question of celebrity and stature, but decided to plow forward with an aggressive Oprah plan for two main reasons.

First, her numbers among noncore caucus-goers and primary voters in the early states were even higher than among the general population. We tested this thoroughly before deploying her. We thought some high-profile campaigning with Oprah could reach some of these voters in a more compelling way than the traditional messengers and methods would.

Second, we thought it would simply be a great way to gather huge numbers of people, many of whom would otherwise never come to a political event. We would be able to collect their contact information and also get to make a direct pitch—always the most effective form of communication—to a mass of important voters. To reach an unorthodox electorate I thought we needed to try unorthodox tactics.

We decided to devote a whole weekend in early December to campaigning with Oprah. Barack, Michelle, and Oprah would do two events in Iowa, one in New Hampshire, and one in South Carolina.

While much of the national commentary focused on images, we became increasingly focused on raw numbers. About thirty thousand people attended the two Iowa events, in Des Moines and Cedar Rapids. That's almost 25 percent of the total turnout for the 2004 Iowa caucuses!

The South Carolina event was also a huge lift. We drew an enormous crowd to a football field, over thirty thousand people. A huge percentage of the crowd was African American women, a demographic in which Hillary was clobbering us in South Carolina. Not after Oprah. We never trailed in that cohort again.

Some ugliness broke out right after that, which provided real drama for the last and by far the most important debate before the Iowa caucuses.

The *Des Moines Register* debate is a hallowed event that has a history of being a difference maker in the caucuses. John Edwards gave his best debate performance of 2004 in this debate, and Dick Gephardt, probably his worst; Edwards's ascendancy and Gephardt's decline in the closing weeks of the primary campaign can be at least partly attributed to how they fared here.

Bottom line: Iowa caucus-goers pay attention to this one. It would take place on December 13, just twenty-one days before the caucuses.

Two days before the debate, Bill Shaheen, husband of former New Hampshire governor Jeanne Shaheen and cochair of Hillary's New Hampshire campaign, was quoted in the *Washington Post* talking about the vulnerability Obama's admitted teenage drug use would present in a general election. Shaheen wondered if Obama's candor on the subject would "open the door" to further questions. "It'll be, 'When was the last time? Did you ever give drugs to anyone? Did you sell them to anyone?'" Shaheen told the *Post*.

These comments created a furor, and it was clear as soon as this broke that Shaheen would have to go. Rather than aggressively distancing themselves from the comments, the Clinton campaign simply let Shaheen resign, saying he didn't want to be a distraction. They said he was not speaking for the campaign and that they did not authorize these comments. It was a very conventional way of handling a situation like this, almost giving the appearance of a wink and a nod. From a strategic viewpoint, I thought they should have more forcefully criticized Shaheen's comments.

Both Clinton and Obama were in Washington casting a vote the morning of the *Register* debate, a rarity in the closing months of the campaign. They were both needed on what was thought to be a close and important vote, so both broke campaign schedules, traveled to D.C., and then headed back to Iowa for the debate.

In a tableau that might seem excessive to many, both candidates had large private planes idling at Washington's National Airport ready to take them to the debate. Our caravan got there first, and Obama, Axelrod, Gibbs (who had traveled back to D.C. with Obama to do some last-minute rolling debate prep), and our traveling team boarded the plane. Hillary's motorcade pulled up to her plane a couple of minutes later, and her traveling aide came over to speak to us. Reggie Love went down the steps to see what was up and was told Clinton wanted a moment with Obama.

He reported that back, and a minute later Obama bounded down the steps. The two rivals met on the tarmac between the planes.

I was sitting on a plane at Chicago O'Hare, about to fly to Iowa to join up with the traveling team when Axelrod called me. He didn't even say hello. "Barack and Hillary are talking on the tarmac," he said breathlessly. "Hillary's arms are waving wildly and it looks heated."

"Sir?"

I looked up to find a flight attendant standing in the aisle next to me. "Sir, we're taking off. Please turn off your phone."

Unbelievable. But I did as she said. "I'll call you with more," said Ax just before he hung up. And then my plane was taxiing down the runway and we were off. For me it was the longest hour of the whole campaign.

When I landed, they were still in the air, so I stayed on tenterhooks until they got to our greenroom at the debate site. When the traveling party barged in, it was storytelling time. Obama came up to me immediately. "You won't believe it," he said.

"I want to hear it all," I told him.

Obama re-created the conversation, with Axelrod and Gibbs piping in and Ax helpfully performing pantomime as appropriate.

The guts of the encounter were this: Hillary began by graciously apologizing for Shaheen's comments and saying they were not authorized by her or her campaign.

"I appreciate that, Hillary," Barack replied, "and I don't believe you encouraged that behavior. But we all have to take responsibility for the tone of the campaign and the signals that we send."

And with that, Clinton began gesticulating wildly and even shaking a bit (which Axelrod role-played while Obama was recounting the conversation) and said that it was not *her* campaign that put out the D-Punjab memo, or that was talking about trust and character. Obama gently put his hand on her arm to calm things down and said, "I said we all have responsibility, not just you. Let's both tell our campaigns to try to be more careful."

Then it was over, and both candidates headed for their planes.

"For the first time, I saw a glimpse of recognition and deep concern in her eyes," said Obama, bringing the recap to a close. "I think she may finally realize that this could be a battle and that Iowa is a jump ball. I'd still rather be her than us, but we're in their heads for the first time."

Hillary's trepidation had a strong effect on Obama. Clinton was a smart, tenacious candidate who was quick on her feet and highly knowledgeable. And she was the only one in the race with a margin for error. He'd always been deeply impressed by her political skills, but I believe the tarmac exchange gave Obama a real boost of confidence. It might have been the first time he saw her as beatable.

We were minutes before our most important debate to date, but the atmosphere in the greenroom was light and jocular. One bonus in the *Register* debate: they assign the biggest greenroom to the candidate in first place in the last *Register* poll. So we had some fairly spacious digs. It sounds completely dumb, but the competitive juices were flowing so aggressively that even having a bigger greenroom was something to be celebrated. "Screw 'em and their small-ass rooms," you'd say of your rivals. "Serves them right for sucking wind in the polls." Stupid stuff, but it carried a charge.

When Obama left for the stage, Ax, Gibbs, and I huddled and agreed he was in a great frame of mind. We thought we'd have a very good debate.

We did. The key moment of the debate, shown repeatedly on the news, was a smart question the moderator asked Obama about how he could be trusted to deliver on change when many of his foreign policy advisers had played key roles in the Clinton administration.

Before Obama answered, Hillary could be heard laughing very loudly and saying, "I want to hear that."

Obama didn't miss a beat. "Hillary, I'm looking forward to you advising me, as well," he said, smiling.

Fucking home run.

After the debate, all the campaign advisers made the usual media rounds to explain why their candidate won. This is usually a complete waste of time, but if your opponents are out there you always feel you need to make your pitch as well. It's a fairly rote exercise, and usually the key reporters are already off writing their stories and putting together their TV packages, so you end up spinning to Swedish TV and other, even more minor outlets.

Right after the debate, Mark Penn was being interviewed on MSNBC along with Edwards strategist Joe Trippi, and he was asked about Bill Shaheen's comments. As he parroted the line that their New Hampshire chair was not speaking for the campaign, he managed to slip in the word "cocaine," as in "I think we've made clear that the issue related to cocaine use is not something that the campaign was in any way raising."

It was breathtaking, even for Penn. Trippi was standing next to Penn and when he heard this, he interrupted Penn. "I think he just did it again. He just did it again," Trippi piped in. "Unbelievable. This guy has been filibustering on this. He just said 'cocaine' again."

It wasn't Trippi's axe to grind but he seemed genuinely outraged. This exchange was also looped on cable news, making our banner news cycle even sweeter and piling more grief on camp Clinton.

As we were leaving the debate site (word of the Penn cocaine comments had already spread like wildfire), I told Axelrod, "If we needed any more incentive to win, we just got it. What Penn did is despicable and he's got to be beat."

"He's everything we are running against," Ax replied.

———

We were now in two-minute-warning time. After a year of preparing, caucus day was nearly upon us. Our internal numbers told us we had momentum and Clinton was stagnant. Signs were that they now thought so, too, but their execution left a lot to be desired. Two instances of their getting tough ended up backfiring on them and landing right in our message wheelhouse.

Obama kept returning to the idea that he was not running because he thought this was owed to him or because he harbored a lifelong ambition to be president. He was in the race because he thought at this moment he might have something unique to offer the country in terms of leadership; there was no master political game plan at work. And then unexpectedly we got two Christmas gifts from the Clinton campaign.

The Clinton people decided to send out a memo—written quite seriously—which highlighted a remark made by one of Obama's grade school teachers in Indonesia, to the effect that while in kindergarten Obama had written an essay stating he wanted to be president. The point, apparently, was that Obama was being disingenuous about his lack of ambition, because he had clearly harbored dreams of being president dating back to when he was five years old.

I've always wondered what the conversations must have been about this within the Clinton campaign. The fallout was easy to predict: the gambit was universally ridiculed and prompted a great line that Barack started using at every event: "Now, I know some have been rooting around my kindergarten papers, trying to dig up dirt . . ."

It was a consistent crowd-pleaser.

The second Clinton misfire was the unveiling of what they billed as a tough new contrast speech Hillary was going to start giving in Iowa in the closing weeks. In it, she challenged Obama's experience, his ability to bring about change, and our campaign's ability to take on the Republican machine. But she prefaced her new lines by saying, "Now the fun part starts," referring to the speech's switch into attack mode.

We leapt all over this as a prime example of what was wrong with Washington and the current state of politics. No matter the response of her supporters, the American people en masse do not think attacks should be the fun part of politics, and this statement fed into the belief of many Iowa voters that Clinton would not change the political warfare mentality that had dominated recent affairs—if anything, it seemed, she would enjoy it.

In the weeks and even months to come we often deflected political attacks with a blanket statement along the lines of, "What else would you expect from a campaign that thinks political attacks are fun and that what happened in Barack Obama's kindergarten class is more important than what's happening to you and your family right now?" It was brutally effective.

Right before Christmas, about two weeks before the caucuses, I joined Obama on a swing though the eastern and northeastern parts of the state. I wanted to spend an extended time with the road show in Iowa and evaluate how effective our events were in the closing days. You can often get a sense of things beyond the numbers based on the energy, crowd makeup, and dynamic at events this close to an election.

We were primarily in mid- and smaller-sized counties—Jones, Delaware, and Benton in the eastern part of the state—and the crowds were swelling. Even more important than the raw numbers was who, specifically, was show- ing up. Our Iowa staff would run the names of those in attendance against our voter file and find that the majority of people in the crowds were unde- cided; many had no prior caucus history. This was a tremendously important yardstick in our quest to expand the electorate. While it made for good press to have buoyant crowds that conveyed our momentum, what was most im- portant to us was whether our events were preaching beyond the converted.

Iowa caucus-goers could spend a year casually shopping for a candidate, and many did. Now they had to step up to the register—and we had to close the sale. Iowa staff reported that many of the attendees were either signing up to support us at the end of events or shortly thereafter in follow-up conversa- tions. Our conversion rate was very high.

Obama was lighting it up on the road, and he wasn't alone. Michelle Obama was another road warrior, lighting it up around the state. She had become a secret weapon for us in Iowa. Her nickname was "The Closer," because the conversion rate at her events was very high—people just responded very positively to her—and she also was terrific in private conversation about gently putting the arm on folks to sign up. She was directly responsible for thousands of people pledging to support us, which is not an insignificant percentage of our turnout. Just as we had planned, both Obamas were clicking on all cyl- inders as we headed into the stretch. I was not, though. One Saturday morning in December while I was traveling with the road show, I slept through two alarms and had to dash out to the bus, unshowered. As Obama entered his first event, I tried with only marginal success to clean up using the sink and washcloths in the bus. It was a pretty sad sight, and it reminded me that campaigns are best suited for the very young. Gibbs couldn't resist rubbing it in as he witnessed my morning escapade: "Pretty hard out here on the road these days, huh?" He was right.

I had not been able to travel as much recently; leaving HQ was becoming increasingly difficult as the race got more intense. And the road show was exhausting—five or six events a day, early mornings and late nights. Even as hard as I was working from my desk in Chicago, life at HQ paled in comparison to the grueling pace of the road.

Years ago the Iowa caucuses were held in February; lately they had been in mid- to late January. Due to unfortunate calendar chaos in the 2008 election cycle, the caucuses were to be held on January 3, just nine days after Christmas and three days into the New Year. To say that this complicated things would be a gross understatement. Many Iowans would be traveling out of state during the holidays, making it harder to contact them. We urged our precinct captains to change their own holiday plans or shorten them if they planned to go away—we needed them on the job. As a matter of campaign policy, our poor staff in Iowa was forbidden to leave the state or their posts for the holidays. They would spend the time together as a campaign family. For many of them, it was the first time they would not spend Christmas at home. The rest of the campaign staff was permitted to leave on Christmas Eve but had to be back to work the morning of the 26th. For those celebrating Hanukkah, the same strict regimen was in place. We asked for it because we needed it. There was no time to spare.

Barack knew I was attending church services with my wife and son at 5:00 p.m. on Christmas Eve, so when I saw him calling shortly before 5:00, I knew something was up. I excused myself and went into the vestibule.

"Sorry to bother you," Obama said, "but I just got word from someone I trust, someone close to him, that Al Sharpton is planning to come to Iowa for the closing days." He paused a moment to let it sink in. "This person thought maybe he could influence Sharpton's plans, but wanted our take on it."

Sharpton had not endorsed anyone in the primary, but it was clear that his presence in Iowa would not be helpful. We had polled him, as we did many political figures that could potentially endorse one of the candidates, and his

ratings in Iowa were less than 20 percent positive and over 60 percent negative. Our research showed that voters were always interested in whom Obama
would surround himself with in the White House. Based on that finding, we
tried to highlight his advisers in both foreign and domestic policy through
ads, mailings, policy summits, press events, and surrogate speeches. Given
Sharpton's rating, it was clear that having him come out for us—if that's what
he was planning—might raise more questions than support.

"Was there any more detail about what he planned to do or say?" I asked.

"No," said Obama. "The person speculated that he might be going to endorse Hillary. Or even that he might try and engineer a last-minute debate on
urban issues in the final days before the caucus."

My assessment was that even with his negative numbers in Iowa, if he
endorsed Hillary it would have no downside for her. The only negative effect
he could have would be if he endorsed us or hijacked campaign coverage for
the closing week. This was an instance where race, which had been largely a
nonfactor to date, could enter into the equation. If undecided voters got the
impression that Sharpton was an influential adviser for us, it could undermine
their willingness to take a chance on Obama.

"I think we should say that if he's coming to endorse Hillary, of course
there's nothing we can do," I told Obama. "Have at it. But if somehow he thinks
coming there will be helpful to us, the last thing he should do is come to Iowa.
This race is razor-thin and we do not need a press sideshow. We just need to
keep doing our blocking and tackling."

Obama sent this message back to the Sharpton source and we never heard
back one way or the other. But he did not come to Iowa. And throughout the
rest of the campaign, I found Sharpton to be a reasonable and constructive
force.

After church, my wife and I took our three-year-old son on a carriage ride
through wintry downtown Chicago, stopping for hot chocolate. The next day
was wonderful: we unwrapped presents and played with new toys at our
leisure, without the interruption of a single conference call. I think that was
the first day of the whole campaign—nearly a year—without a call. It was
surreal. The Iowa caucuses were moments away but the political world largely
came to a stop. It was like the movie *The Perfect Storm*. There were gale force
winds and turbulent seas behind us and in front of us. But for a brief window,
everything was amazingly, blissfully calm.

In a way, the brief respite was cruel. Back in the trenches the next day, many of us talked about having forgotten what these simple pleasures could mean, especially the joy of being fully present with family and friends. After the election, my son reminded me of that day-after-Christmas epiphany. He pointed something out to me and I responded, perhaps a bit absently, "Oh yeah."

"Daddy, you weren't listening," he said.

"Yes I was, buddy," I replied.

His response cut me to the core. "No, Daddy," he told me. "You said, 'Oh yeah' like you used to in Chicago whenever I tried to talk to you and you were on your BlackBerry and you weren't really listening and just said, 'Oh yeah.'"

He was right. For a lot of us, that strange holiday reminded us of the distracted, isolated lives we had been leading. After going to New Hampshire just before Christmas, we had made the decision to spend the final eight days leading up to the caucuses exclusively in Iowa. We were surprised to see that Clinton was going to spend one day during the closing stretch in New Hampshire but shocked to see Edwards doing the same. We all had a lot riding on Iowa, and their decision to leave the state, even for a day, seemed at odds with that. For us, it was not much of a decision. We had to win Iowa, so that's where we bunkered in.

Between December 26 and caucus day, our daily internal poll showed Hillary winning most nights, us leading narrowly a couple of times, and Edwards gaining ground and decidedly still in the hunt. Conversely, our field data suggested that we were picking up support each day and, just as important, not losing any ground. (Field data comes from a huge number of conversations between our staff and volunteers and actual voters. It hits a lot more broadly than polling, which takes a small representative sample and extrapolates a bigger picture). At this point, we were talking to all of our confirmed supporters to ensure they knew where to caucus, make sure they could still attend, and simply to reconfirm their support. We were able to undertake such massive voter contact only because of the sheer scale and enthusiasm of our volunteers. They opened up a world of possibility for us because of their commitment. Call every confirmed supporter? Check. Call and knock on the door of every undecided or leaning Obama supporter? Check. It was a rare and remarkable thing to witness. Thanks to the grassroots network we had built, we could communicate through any means and have a conversation with any voter, no matter how unlikely they would be to caucus.

Our better than expected fund-raising and early organization building in Iowa were a huge bonus for us at the end—there was very little, if anything, I wished we could be doing that we weren't already. I was in our Iowa HQ full time at this point, and throughout the day I would wander into the office of Mitch Stewart and Anne Filipic to talk to them about the data they were getting back from the field, what their staff was saying, and what the other campaigns were up to. Their office was like a temple to me in those closing days, a no-bullshit zone. No spin, no polls, no pundits. Just the numbers. It gave me guarded confidence every time I checked in.

One day Paul Tewes, our creative and obsessive Iowa state director, was out conducting some last-minute political business. He was finagling Dennis Kucinich to put out a statement encouraging his supporters to back Obama in areas where Kucinich would not hit the 15 percent viability threshold. Tewes was also working with the Richardson camp to come up with a tacit agreement that in places where neither of us was viable we would make it clear to our supporters that each candidate preferred the other on the second run-through. The press always makes too much of these "deals." Voters are going to do what they want to do, regardless of instructions from their first-choice candidate. But every vote counts, and Tewes's approach summed up how we tried to operate during the whole campaign—no margin for error, assume the outcome will be razor-thin, and try to do everything humanly possible to give us any edge on our opponents.

While Tewes was out, I was using his office for a phone call with Obama. Mitch, who was overseeing the organizational side of the Iowa campaign, walked in looking for Tewes. Seeing him, I said into the phone to Barack, "Listen, it's out of all of our hands now. It's in Mitch Stewart's hands. If his organization delivers what he says it will, we are going to win." I looked up to acknowledge Mitch's presence in front of me. "Oh, here he is," I told Obama. "Why don't you say hi."

When I told Mitch the candidate wanted to say hello, his face turned ash white. Mitch was already a jumble of nerves, his hair was falling out, and he was sleeping about two hours a night. This about sent him over the edge. He took the phone from me warily and put it to his ear. "Hello, sir?" He listened a bit, and then said, "I keep looking over the numbers and I think we'll get to where we need to be. Or we'll die trying."

A moment later, Mitch hung up and gave me back the phone. "I think I am going to throw up," he said.

"You'll be okay," I told him. "Sorry to put you on the spot, but he just wanted to say thanks and tell you he appreciates all you're doing.

Mitch managed a queasy smile. "I still want to throw up." It was a lot of pressure for a twenty-eight-year-old.

The last *Des Moines Register* poll was scheduled to come out on New Year's Day, two days before the caucus. As I've mentioned, all the *Register* polls are important, but this trial can build or destroy a candidate's momentum. This poll had boosted Kerry and Edwards four years earlier and was devastating to Gephardt and Dean. It was the only *Register* poll Kerry ever led; no doubt it convinced some late-breaking voters to jump on board with the momentum candidate. The poll would likely be posted at 9:30 or 10:00 p.m. central time, New Year's Eve. We were far too busy to obsess about it, but it was clearly on everyone's mind. Even Obama, who was terrific about not paying too much attention to outside numbers, was on pins and needles waiting for it to come out.

All of us in Iowa were manning phone banks. Call time ended at 8:00 p.m. because it was New Year's Eve and we did not want to harass people too late. I jumped into a car with Pete Giangreco, our lead direct-mail vendor and a key strategist for us in Iowa, and we drove down to Dahl's grocery store to buy a bunch of champagne for the staff. They wouldn't be drinking much that night, but they deserved a little free booze to ring in the New Year. We spent the whole ride chewing over what the fallout would be based on different outcomes of the poll. How far behind would be acceptable for us? The *Register* had endorsed Clinton—was there any way that could impact their polling? What if Edwards was in first? What if we were all tied? "Fuck it," Pete said eventually. "We'll know soon enough and there's not a damn thing we can do about it."

Back at the office, our press staff kept refreshing the *Register* website. The *Register* poll never, ever leaks—which is very rare with polls—nor does the paper's staff send it out to the campaigns a few minutes before they post it on their site. Everyone gets the results at the same time. I was told later that throughout the evening hundreds of thousands of people across the country were frantically hitting refresh on their browsers to update the *Des Moines Register* website. People were becoming obsessed with this race. The poll finally popped up: Obama 32. Clinton 25. Edwards 24.

Our campaign office erupted. People were hugging and screaming at the top of their lungs. The results were better than we could have hoped for. This would give us a huge jolt heading into the last forty-eight hours. The reason for the big lead, according to Ann Selzer, the *Register*'s longtime and respected pollster, was that Democrats were heading to a historic, astronomical turnout, and many younger voters, independents, and Republicans were planning to participate. And they were giving the lion's share of their support to Obama.

Barack was driving to a late-Saturday-night event in Ames, home of Iowa State University, when I got him on the phone. Gibbs had just given him the news of the *Register* poll, and Obama was jubilant. "Things feel great out here on the trail," he told me. "The events are packed, huge energy, and the precinct captains all report good momentum. This *Register* poll ought to kick things into even higher gear, don't you think?"

"It should," I said. "But even if all it does is motivate our staff and volunteers to work even harder and believe we can win, it's still a help."

Obama touted the poll at the event in Ames as a sign that our campaign was gaining momentum, though he cautioned the crowd not to believe in polls, but in their own ability to shape the future.

Within the hour, the Clinton and Edwards campaigns released unusually tough memos taking dead aim at the poll. It was deeply flawed, they said. Too many independents and Republicans. Not enough older voters in the sample. The numbers suggested a total voter turnout approaching two hundred thousand and that's just not possible. Mark Penn was famous for memos throughout the campaign disparaging the methodology of unfavorable polls and extolling the dubious findings of polls that treated Hillary Clinton kindly. It was an all-out assault on Selzer and to some degree it worked. Most reporters I talked to that night thought the *Register* poll was an outlier. And perhaps it was. But on the ground in Iowa, I knew it was going to be a big asset.

Once again the *Register* poll turned out to be rosier than our own polling numbers. But it closely tracked our field data. On the phone with Obama that night, I told him that the poll captured what would happen if a healthy enough number of our confirmed supporters turned out. Our goal was to get confirmation from sixty thousand "1's"—rock-solid confirmed supporters—and thirty thousand "2's"—people who were strongly leaning in our direction. Remarkably, we thought we would hit that by the morning of the caucuses. We would also pick up support from people outside this universe; many voters would not discuss their candidate preference, preferring to keep it secret until caucus night, and there were some people with whom we were never able to connect. The *Register* poll modeled our best outcome. But it was plausible.

The closing days in Iowa were frigid. I don't know what the actual wind chill factor was, but I can tell you it was friggin' cold, and yet our volunteers knocked on more than fifty thousand doors a day. They showed remarkable dedication. It was brutal out in that cold, but we all believed that a last-minute door-knocking assault would pay huge dividends. Our volunteers reported back that they saw comparatively less door-knocking activity from Clinton or Edwards, which surprised us—our data analysis made it clear that door knocking had become much more effective than phone calling. By this point, people had been called so many times that they would often answer the phone rudely, which was unusual in preternaturally polite Iowa. The voters had had enough calling. But when someone came to their door in frigid weather, they were more likely to engage in conversation (out of sympathy if nothing else), and many voters would even invite our volunteers in.

Obama's first event on New Year's Day was in Des Moines, and it was billed as a canvass kickoff. We asked our volunteers to gather at a local high school, where they would hear Barack and Michelle speak before going out into neighborhoods with their canvass materials. There was electricity in the air. The caucuses were only two days out, so that was part of it, but the *Register* poll had clearly sent a surge through our organization. People could smell both the finish line and victory.

We had made big buttons for our precinct captains to help identify them, so I wandered through the crowd before the event and asked these folks where things stood. Some I had met before, many I had not. I was impressed with their grasp of the numbers in their precincts—how many more confirmed supporters we needed to get an extra delegate, how they thought the Richardson or Biden supporters would break on the second ballot, how they were dealing with the challenge of producing a high turnout. It was a confidence-inspiring half hour. These people were so committed. They were on top of it. And I think they realized how much we appreciated them, that we thought *they* were the campaign. It was true—we would rise or fall in two days based on their work. Mitch Henry, a precinct captain and talented community organizer in East Des Moines with whom I had first worked way back in 1991 at the Iowa Democratic Party, went so far as to tell me, "David, you are going to win on Thursday night. I can feel it on the streets. I don't even think it is going to be close." I would take a one-point victory, but a landslide was a fun scenario to contemplate.

One of the last critical moments of the Iowa campaign occurred at this Des

Moines event and involved a decision that would've been a no-brainer at just about any other time. John Kerry had almost endorsed us in late December, which we thought at the time would have given us a real boost. As the Democratic Party's most recent nominee, whose Iowa win four years ago had propelled him to that nomination, his endorsement would have a big media footprint and provide a surge of late momentum. In Iowa, our estimate was that around ten thousand of his supporters from 2004 were still saying they were undecided. We thought his support could tip a lot of these people into our column.

But Kerry got cold feet on December 28 when a public poll came out from a polling firm with little Iowa experience that showed us in third place and trailing badly. Kerry told Jim Margolis, who had helped him win the caucuses in 2004, that he really wanted to support Barack. He had made that decision. But there would be a huge price to pay if Hillary won after he came out publicly. He decided to wait and see how things played out. We were disappointed but moved on.

The morning of January 1, Margolis got a call on his cell phone from Kerry. So did Marvin Nicholson, who had served as trip director for Kerry and was still very close to him. Kerry had seen the *Register* poll. He was ready to come in later that day and endorse us and campaign through caucus night. Margolis called me to relay this—we were all at the Des Moines event but not all together. I told him I would send an e-mail to everyone.

Five minutes later we all gathered under the high school gym's bleachers. Along with me, there was Margolis and Nicholson, Axelrod and Gibbs, Tewes and Mitch Stewart, and John Norris, Kerry's former Iowa state director who was supporting us and providing a lot of strategic guidance. It was pitch dark under the bleachers. Even huddled in a circle it was hard to make out people's faces. We held our cell phones up so some blue light would be emitted and we could see at least the outlines of one another's faces. I've always wished we had a picture of that; we must have looked ridiculous. The setting was humorous, the discussion deadly serious—this was a decision with major consequences.

I started by laying out my view. A Kerry endorsement would be the dominant story all the way through caucus night. We would black out the other candidates and be the only press story in town. It would no doubt push some old Kerry supporters into our camp. But we appeared to have momentum now, not reflected in our polling but in our field data, from what we were hearing from our staff around the state and from the crowds coming to hear Barack and Michelle. We were running as the outsider candidate, severely dependent on new and younger voters, independents, and Republicans. In some ways a Kerry endorsement, the establishment laying hands on us, would fly counter to that message. I feared it could sap some of our momentum and turnout with the harder to reach voters whom we so desperately needed. I was opposed.

Tewes was even more adamant in his opposition. "It just doesn't feel right," he kept saying. "A few days ago, yes. But now, done this late it would essentially serve as our closing argument, a political endorsement. That's not who we are. We can't do this."

Others disagreed—especially those who had worked with Kerry. They felt it would provide a burst of momentum like the one Kerry had received four years ago when the crewmate he saved in Vietnam—and to whom he had not spoken since—showed up out of nowhere the last weekend of the caucuses and dominated the press coverage. This had been a big factor in Kerry's winning Iowa so strongly.

We went back and forth for some time. Eventually there was consensus. We would recommend to Obama no endorsement. There is an oft-published photograph of a few of us sitting in a circle talking to Obama in a locker room in Iowa. That picture captures us discussing this decision. I started by laying out for him the pros and cons and then our recommendation. Axelrod and a few others also offered their take. But Obama was rightly not as interested in what the national staff had to say. He wanted to know what the Iowa guys thought. Tewes and Mitch made a strong case against.

"It's a big roll of the dice," Obama said finally. "But we've come this far and the whole thing was a roll of the dice. I'll call John and tell him thanks, but it will be more important down the road."

And in the end it was. After Kerry did endorse us on January 10, he turned out to be a real trouper, one of our most effective surrogates on the trail and on TV. He never pulled the "I did this four years ago, I know best" routine. He was there for the right reasons and always took a constructive approach, giving us wise but respectful counsel. "This is not my race four years ago, it's your race now," he said to me at one point, "and I've found that unless you're living and breathing it every day, you should be careful giving sweeping advice and pontifications. So take any advice I offer with that grain of salt."

Our handling of the Kerry endorsement illuminates one of the real strengths of our campaign. The political playbook certainly would have suggested the endorsement take place that day. And most campaigns I believe would have taken that route. But we looked deeper than just the tactical benefits and tried to look around the corner strategically. I would often refer to that day when we faced tough decisions down the line and were tentatively leaning in the less predictable direction. It almost became a reference point and rallying cry: "This is a 'tell Kerry no endorsement' moment." In the end, the tough decision we made was unquestionably the correct one. Just about every time we took the road less traveled, we benefited.

On caucus day, I woke up in the Des Moines Holiday Inn for the eighth day in a row, feeling cautiously confident and struck by the fact that this would be our last night in Iowa, perhaps forever. That night we would be flying out to New Hampshire, win or lose. A year of our lives was coming to a close. I thought that if all those young voters, non-caucus-goers, independents, and Republicans turned out in decent numbers, we should be heading to New Hampshire as a winner. I knew our organization in Iowa—both staff and volunteers—had done everything humanly possible to put us in a position to win. And if we did, their work would go down in political history as one of the greatest accomplishments in a presidential campaign.

I felt more sanguine than nervous. We had spent the better part of the year on Iowa, and while we sometimes made mistakes and went through our share of ups and downs, this was one of those rare moments in life when we rightly felt that there was nothing left to be done. We weren't leaving anything on the field.

When I talked to Obama that morning, he felt the same way. "I am at peace," he told me. "We gave it our all. Win or lose, I won't have regrets about what we did here in Iowa."

That afternoon I was in the Des Moines headquarters, preparing to hold a conference call with Nevada reporters, when my cell phone rang. It was my insurance company, calling to ask me a couple of follow-up questions about the accident.

Accident? "What accident?" I asked.

"The accident on Interstate 80 with the tractor-trailer earlier today," the agent replied.

I immediately hung up and called my wife's cell phone, in a mild panic. She answered and I exhaled. "I just got a call from Geico," I said, "Are you okay?"

She sounded a bit shaken but said she was all right. My family knew how much was riding on that night's outcome, and my sister had flown into Chicago to watch our son so my wife could drive to Des Moines for the caucuses. She and a friend from the campaign's policy team had left Chicago before daylight in order to spend the day in our Des Moines field office making calls. Outside of Iowa City, their car had been rear-ended by a semi and the police had driven her to a rest stop, where she was still waiting for a tow.

As I was about to launch into questions, she cut me off. "I'm so sorry you heard about this from the insurance company!" she said. "I didn't want to tell you because you have enough on your mind. But we're fine. I'll see you in a few hours." Then she hopped off the phone to coordinate her rescue.

I felt terrible—my wife was dealing with a serious accident without me because I was so consumed with this infernal campaign. The only upside to losing would be that I could rejoin my family's life. But I had to snap back to campaign reality. In a few moments, I needed to get on the phone with the Nevada press to stress how much time we would be spending there after Iowa and New Hampshire. I was also hoping to drive up the expectations for Clinton, saying we just hoped to keep it close, given the thirty-point lead she had there. And that's how it was: one foot in Iowa, one already creeping out.

After the call I was driven out to the Obama hotel camp west of Des Moines. The traveling party was not staying at our old standby the Hampton Inn because we needed many more rooms than usual; a lot of family and friends of the Obamas had decided to come for the last week.

At a little before 6:00 p.m., the Iowa staff requested that Barack make an unscheduled stop—no press in tow—to greet arriving caucus-goers at a site in Ankeny, Iowa, about twenty minutes away, where multiple precincts were holding their events. "We've left no stone unturned up to now," said Tewes. "Let's not switch gears in the minutes before the caucus. It probably won't make a difference in the math, but if it swings one delegate, why not?" He was right.

Barack and I rode out with the Secret Service, Marvin, Reggie, and Valerie Jarrett. This was as light as we had traveled in months. We pulled up to the suburban high school in Ankeny at 6:15 p.m. The caucuses started at 7:00 p.m. Already the parking lot was beyond jammed. They were parking on the sidewalk, on the grass, just leaving their cars wherever they could find space. Obama and I looked at each other and smiled.

No one was expecting him, so as he climbed the steps and entered the lobby of the school, people gasped and he was quickly surrounded. Some people he spoke with said they were still undecided, so he spent a little time answering their questions and urging them to caucus for him. Most of the people who came up to him, dozens and dozens, said they were supporting him. It almost brought me to tears. Right there, in front of our eyes on caucus night, we were seeing the coalition of voters we had set out to build: high school kids; Republicans who said they were switching their registration to caucus for Barack; Iowa residents attending Michigan and Wisconsin colleges who had stayed home a few extra days to caucus; an older couple who said they had not participated since 1968, when they volunteered for Bobby Kennedy. And my favorite, a man dressed like Gandalf from *The Lord of the Rings*, holding a staff with an iPod attached at the top and a little speaker playing Obama's speeches on repeat.

A few minutes later, when the Secret Service closed the doors of our SUV and we were pulling out, Obama and I shared a fist-bump, more common in our operation than a high-five. "No matter what happens tonight, I'll always treasure that scene," he said. "That's what we tried to build. And at least in that school, on this night, it happened."

We got back to the hotel around 7:15 p.m. and turnout estimates and anecdotes were starting to come in over the e-mail transom. At first, the news was good. Then it was great. We were getting reports of shockingly high turnout everywhere. The only concern was that facilities and caucus officials might not be able to handle the volume, and that some people—especially our less rabid supporters—would leave out of frustration or confusion. We had nothing to worry about. People were dead set on participating that night. A few caucuses were even held outside in the bitter cold because the site ran out of room indoors. But few people were complaining or leaving.

The entrance polls—a reverse exit poll—had Clinton up early, narrowly ahead of us, with Edwards trailing. I paid no attention—with turnout like this, entrance polls would be of even less predictive value than normal, which is close to zero.

Obama was at dinner with his family and friends at a steak house down the road. He told me he did not want frequent updates. "Just call me when you know something," he said.

I kept a post in our conference room with Gibbs and my assistant, Katie, who was staying abreast of updates in our internal tracking. Our data team was crunching every precinct that reported in, comparing it with our projections for each one in terms of turnout and delegate allocation. After only a handful of precincts, they upped our internal turnout estimate to over 200,000, which blew our minds. We thought 175,000 was likely—Clinton and Edwards in particular thought turnout would be lower than that—and that 200,000 was the outer edge. But it appeared now that 200,000 would be the floor. It was nothing but good news for us. Our band of ragtag supporters was turning out en masse.

At some point shortly after 9:00 p.m., I giddily took out my phone and called Obama, who was still at dinner. "Hello?"

"Congratulations, Senator," I said. "You have won the Iowa caucuses." In his calm Obama way, Barack replied, "Are we sure?"

"Yes," I told him. "We hear the networks will be calling it soon, too."

"I'll be back shortly," he said. I envisioned him turning back to cutting his steak and chatting with his friends and family members, saying, "Oh by the way, we just won Iowa." The mood fit the man: not too high and not too low, even as he took a decisive step toward the presidency.

After a short celebration and several rounds of high-fives and hugs with the few people gathered in the conference room, Gibbs and I headed down the hall to Obama's room. He had just arrived and threw open the door to greet us. There was some fist-bumping and backslapping, but no champagne or screaming. Yes, this was a huge step. But after all, it was still just the first step in our plan. And with this triumph we all felt the press of some additional weight that had not been there a day ago—we could actually win this whole thing. In many ways the moment held more gravity than levity.

After the networks called it for us, we loaded into the caravan and headed to our event site in downtown Des Moines. Reggie and I rode with the Obamas, and Barack spent the entire ride fielding congratulatory calls from his vanquished rivals. Biden and Dodd said they were pulling out. Richardson said he might. Edwards was gracious and said he would see him in New Hampshire. Hillary was polite but cool. After hanging up from the last call, he turned to me and said, "I imagine it's a lot more enjoyable to take these calls than make them." I laughed. "Well, then let's make this a tradition over the next few weeks."

The final margin grew to a stunning eight points by the time we arrived at the event site. And it looked like Hillary would finish narrowly behind Edwards. While this might have been a source of extra glee, I was in fact rooting for Hillary to pull into second. If Edwards finished third, his vote share in

New Hampshire would likely fall into the low double digits from the mid-high double digits. And we thought almost all of those votes would go to us.

When we got to the victory party I finally saw my wife, who'd been rescued on the road by one of our traveling teams. The room was a sea of smiling, tear-stained faces, and hers was no exception. Her wet cheek pressed against mine as she gave me a huge hug. "I'm so proud of you," she said.

"Are you sure you're okay?" I asked. "How are you going to get back to Chicago?"

"Forget the car," she said. "We're about to change the world."

After all the speeches and celebrations, right before the motorcade to the airport pulled out, Obama spent some private time with our senior Iowa staff. I didn't go in because I wanted it to be their moment, and theirs alone. They had just made history. I was told it was highly emotional on both sides. Obama emerged from the room red-eyed and said quietly, "I love those kids." He wasn't exaggerating, about his feelings or their age—other than Tewes, they were all under thirty, like so many of the voters who had delivered this win.

We had to swing by the motel to get some bags, and I plopped down in the business center and started to print out all the official results, internal tabulations, and entrance polls I could get my hands on. Turnout had dwarfed even our fantasies—more than 240,000 people came to caucus. Twice I was warned by our advance staff to get up and get moving, but I couldn't pull myself away. We had devoted our lives to this day, and I wanted to spend some of the plane ride really poring over the data to see exactly what had happened. Iowa was done, but I was not ready to be done with Iowa. Finally Axelrod, usually the late one, came up to me and barked, "Plouffe! Get your head out of Iowa! Into New Hampshire!" With a sigh, I reluctantly peeled myself away.

From inception to election our campaign lasted a total of two years. Half of that was essentially spent on Iowa. The state became our laboratory, and much of what we would do and try later in the campaign was a direct result of the lessons learned there.

Those lessons were many. A homegrown, committed grassroots organization was a mighty weapon when properly motivated and trusted to take initiative. Young voters would indeed turn out for Barack Obama. In Iowa, defying all history, voters under thirty turned out at the same rate as those over sixty-five; older voters traditionally had shown up in double the numbers. Our unwavering commitment to an electoral strategy and message made us a more solid and disciplined campaign. With the "big" things settled, we could focus on creative and relentless execution, not casting about for new messages and strategies every few weeks. We had also confirmed an old axiom: money matters. In the last days before Iowa, Clinton and Edwards both had huge outside money spent on their behalf by private groups and individuals. On our side, we started alone on the airwaves and in the mail. Yet we were able to fight back, close to dollar for dollar. The power of our fund-raising and our growing donor base gave us the financial flexibility to ensure that we could match our opponents and their outside help combined.

Directly exposing voters to Obama had been key for us, but we would never again be able to spend as much time doing that as we had in Iowa. From here on, advertising and strong person-to-person communication would be even more important—deficient but important substitutes for the candidate himself. Our core message of change trumped experience. And perhaps the low road that voters thought Clinton was traveling more often than we were might lead her campaign to less success than they expected. We were rewarded in our belief that technology would help us organize and grow the campaign. Many in Iowa organized online for us and even more first made contact with us through the Web. And we found that we could use the Internet to drive our message, in some cases circumventing the mainstream media filter. It also allowed us to provide basic voting info—like where to caucus—that was crucial when trying to expand the electorate beyond habitual voters.

Our campaign team, once considered deficient to the vaunted Clinton juggernaut, not only hung with them but also beat them. We might be unknown and unconventional in approach, but we pulled together and did what we set out to do. And far more important than the rest of the lessons was what we learned from the performance of our candidate. Meandering, unmotivated, and hesitant in the early going, he buckled down and turned in one of the best performances of any candidate in recent memory during the close in Iowa. He was forceful, passionate, clear, and motivational, all without making any major mistakes under the harshest of spotlights. No matter what happened in the coming weeks, the result in Iowa was a testament to him, to his performance under pressure, to his authentic call for change, and the connection he developed with thousands of Iowans who gave all they had to the campaign. The numbers on caucus night reflected their commitment and dedication.

As we drove down Fleur Drive, the last leg to the Des Moines airport, I was flush with memories and thoughts. We passed the apartment building where

I had lived nineteen years before, making $600 a month working for Tom Harkin at the bottom of the campaign totem pole. Now I was leaving as the manager for the first African American ever to win the Iowa caucuses and the first to have a real shot at the presidency.

We did not know if or when we'd be back in Iowa. It had defined our lives for a year. But this, I thought, has to be one of the best feelings in American politics—to be pulling up to the Des Moines airport, your charter waiting, taking off into the early-morning skies as the winner of the Iowa caucuses, heading to New Hampshire with momentum at your back.

As we pulled up, though, we had a bit of a surprise: we had to wait before proceeding to the tarmac because the Clinton plane was taking off. As we cooled our heels I had a delicious thought: this will be the last time she's ever in front of us again.

The first phase of Plan A had gone perfectly. The second phase was New Hampshire, and we were all much more confident than we had been just a few hours before that we would strike a mortal blow to Hillary in the New England snows. As we lifted into the air and the skyline of Des Moines receded behind us, I was still energized. "I don't just want to win New Hampshire," I blustered to Ax, "I want to pound them into submission, win it by double digits."

"Greedy, now?" he asked, smiling. "But yeah, it could happen. Essentially we're tied now. We could be up ten by Saturday and then momentum from the win here settles in. It sets up perfectly."

As we reached cruising altitude I settled back into my seat. "Hope they enjoy that charter up ahead of us. She could be flying commercial sooner than she thinks."

6

Roller-Coaster Time

On Friday, January 4, we landed in New Hampshire after 4:00 a.m. As we got to the hotel, it was nearly time for the day's first conference call, so I skipped sleep altogether. Instead I checked our online fund-raising numbers; they were through the roof, with over $6 million raised in the hours since we were declared the winner of the Iowa caucuses.It was like a lit match had been dropped in gasoline. New donors and fund-raisers were showing up everywhere, wanting to help a potential winner, and our previous donors and fund-raisers were digging deeper as their initial investment was rewarded in Iowa.

Obama made it clear from the beginning that he did not want to be left shouldering a big debt. I had always managed campaigns that way, so we had prepared for the worst and had hoped for the best, budgeting conservatively post-Iowa and projecting only $10 million raised for all of January. We assumed that even with a loss we could cobble together enough money through our diehard supporters to execute our game plan in the remaining early states. Now, we almost certainly would raise over $10 million in the first eight days of January alone and might raise over $30 million in January, giving us what we believed would be a huge financial advantage for Super Tuesday. In the space of a few hours, we had not just won Iowa but also considerably strengthened our ability to compete against Clinton in a drawn-out slugfest.

Friday morning, sleep deprived but showered, Gibbs, Axelrod, and I climbed into the motorcade idling outside our hotel and thumbed through the morning's stories on our BlackBerrys while we waited for Obama to emerge. We were working our way through the standard road show campaign breakfast—coffee and Dunkin' Donuts to go. I was tired but enjoying the moment of peace when Ax erupted from the backseat.

"Shit!" he yelled out. "I don't believe it." Well, I thought, I guess the good times can't last forever.

I turned around to face him in the backseat. "What is it?" I asked. "What a shitty story? Is it bad?"

He looked up at me with a mixture of despair and incredulity. "I got glazed doughnut in the trackwheel of my BlackBerry and it's stuck," he replied. "I can't get the thing to work."

I stared at him for a second before bursting into laughter. In another second the whole van had joined in. Ax looked beleaguered but then finally cracked a smile. For all his brilliance as a communicator and strategist, Ax was legendary within the campaign for spilling food and mishaps with electronic gadgets. But this was the pièce de résistance. It had to be a first in the history of smartphones—death by glazed doughnut. If we had lost Iowa, it would have been just another pain in the ass. But we were on cloud nine, so it was part of the adventure. Glazegate.

I was happy to see Ax bask in the post-Iowa glow. This was Obama's campaign, of course. But after him, the DNA of the organization was mostly David Axelrod's. Over the years he and Obama had become more friends than business associates, and Ax had been instrumental to Obama throughout his career. Without David, I'm not sure Obama would have won his 2004 Senate race and made it to the national stage. Many of us who were working on the campaign at senior levels were there because of an Axelrod connection. David's career was very successful by any measure, but I always got the sense that he was yearning for one last ride. Though Ax was a street fighter when he needed to be, at heart he was an idealist. This campaign, fueled by average people and appealing to their best aspirations rather than their darkest fears, was in many ways his ideal. He had come full circle, having started in politics as a young boy handing out leaflets for Bobby Kennedy in Stuyvesant Town, a housing development on Manhattan's Lower East Side. Whatever happened from here on out, I felt that Ax would feel satisfied that he had experienced the campaign he had long yearned for.

Historically, the period between New Hampshire and Iowa was often the most turbulent seven days of campaigning in American politics—and the longest. Working a New Hampshire campaign, you could pack a couple of lifetimes into that short period. For us, New Hampshire came only five days after Iowa—four campaigning days. It could be a ferocious beast, but we thought we could use it to our advantage. The fallout from Iowa would dominate the first couple of days of press coverage. Most observers, if they had to bet their mortgage, would have put their money on Clinton to win the caucuses. Our Iowa victory in itself was not an earthquake, but when you threw in the eight-point margin, Clinton's third-place finish, and the demographic successes we had, it was seismic. We would be riding the crest of a wave of media coverage about everything we had done right while Clinton was eviscerated for what she had done wrong.

Then, just as the rosy reviews from Iowa began to subside, there would be a major debate on Saturday night that would dominate coverage until Primary Day. People would be voting just as our momentum reached its peak. Or so we thought. Our schedule in New Hampshire was a good mix of retail campaigning—drop-ins at coffee shops and diners—plus scheduled events. We did tons of ground-level, one-on-one campaigning; we wanted to generate pictures of Obama hustling for votes, connecting with average voters, not taking anything for granted. But the press take on the campaign was like those stops never happened. The shots were all of the enormous crowds we were drawing. Granted, it was true—our events brought together some of the biggest crowds ever seen in the New Hampshire primary. But the relentless attention the media gave these events told a different story than the one we were trying to get across. For five days the coverage was predictable and consistent— Obama has huge momentum, he's drawing rock-star crowds, he's gaining and surpassing Clinton in the polls. The only question is how big his margin of victory will be.

All this made us a little uneasy. But it squared with reality. We were surging in every poll, ours included. The fieldwork on the ground was picking up similar momentum. We had every volunteer shift for the last four days filled well ahead of time. We were making every phone call, waving every sign, knocking on every door. We were actually telling people from out of state who inquired about helping that there was no need—the inn was full in New Hampshire. This never happens in campaigns. You always need more help.

Our New Hampshire operation was not as big, to scale, as Iowa, but we had invested early, and our staff was embedded in communities right from the start. We were also fighting a different kind of battle than we had in Iowa, with a strategy geared toward winning a different type of contest. Field and volunteer work can have a decisive impact on a single caucus, where the turnout is much smaller than a state- or countywide primary; theoretically it's easier to adjust the electorate. If ten people normally turn out for a precinct caucus, and you bring two new people, you've significantly changed the math. But when five hundred people turn out in a precinct to vote in a primary, adding two people is tinkering at the margins. And New Hampshire traditionally had sky-high turnout in their primary. There was no way to replicate the near doubling of participants we had effected in Iowa's caucuses—there just weren't that many new voters to find. We would have had to gain support among those who were already likely to attend. The entire Clinton campaign seemed to have a better grounding and comfort level in New Hampshire, from the candidate on down. Iowa had been foreign turf for many of them, Hillary included. New Hampshire was like a comfortable old sweater for her. We had maintained a laserlike focus on Iowa leading up to the caucuses, and the fit in New Hampshire was not as good.

Still, we were hitting all our internal field metrics in terms of doors knocked, calls made, and volunteers recruited. We assumed the Clinton campaign was, too, but we viewed being at rough parity organizationally a plus, given that the Clintons had such strong and deep ties going back to 1991 in the state.

On Saturday we had one big-crowd event scheduled before an afternoon of light prep for the debate. The event was a rally at Nashua North High School, a huge school in an important suburban community where Clinton was strong. As our road show drew near the school, over an hour after the event had begun, there were still people streaming toward the doors. We couldn't believe our eyes: a line of people literally a mile long stood in the snow outside, breath visible above grinning faces, cheerfully waiting to get in. Our hard count—the number of people that had told our staff and volunteers they were coming—was over a thousand, which would have been a huge event by New Hampshire standards. Now it was clear we were going to have four or five times that many. And a great number of those additional people must have decided to go on their own in the final hours before the event, which was an even more important factor than the high turnout.

Obama waved to people as we drove by. "This is unbelievable," he whispered, shaking his head. We were all speechless at the sight in front of us—a huge outpouring of optimism in tough, hardened, flinty New Hampshire.

I told him there was no way everyone could fit in the main gym. The advance teams would have to scramble to put people in at least one if not two overflow areas, which meant he would have to give extra speeches. We were still tired from two sleepless nights and had a big debate looming, so I half expected Barack to meet this announcement with mild complaint. Not today.

"Of course," he agreed, without hesitation. "They've been standing out in the cold, we need to take care of them."

Most of our events in this five-day window were bursting at the seams, so we switched from our normal New Hampshire town-hall format, where Obama took questions from the audience, to a straight stump speech. We had learned that once crowds got over a thousand, question-and-answer did not work well. With the odd exception of one or two smaller, invite-only events at people's homes, we closed our New Hampshire campaigning with large rallies.

When the Nashua event finally wrapped up, overflow speeches and all, we found we couldn't leave. There was one long driveway from the school to the main road, and it was clogged with exiting traffic. If we departed, it would keep everyone waiting as the Secret Service and police cleared the driveway and surrounding road to let us pass. That was a no-no in New Hampshire; it would come off as too self-important, especially since we were trying to attract the support of everyone who had just attended the event. And they had already been forced to cool their heels after waiting a long time to get in. So we waited. And waited. And waited. This was just fine with our candidate, who was never eager to spend hours in debate prep. We spent the wait in the emptied-out gym, shooting hoops, throwing a baseball around, and generally feeling very loose. Gibbs was teaching Obama how to throw a football in a spiral—while Barack was a natural athlete, he had never played football as a kid, so throwing a tight spiral bedeviled him; he was determined to master it. I had seen this routine often and noted his halting progress. His throws were now a little straighter but still lacked rotation. We tried to get him to do a debate prep session by phone with the team back at the hotel, but he brushed this aside. We were not overly concerned, because he was relaxed and feeling confident, which is half the battle.

I called Axelrod, who was back at the hotel working on questions for the prep session, and reported in. "We'd better win this primary," I told him. "And big, because every reporter at this event seemed to think it was the breaking point for Hillary—that the dam broke in Iowa and now we're going to sweep to an easy victory." I thought back on the gym and two overflow rooms packed with people. "And I guess it *was* something to see. But it all seems a little too easy, especially after the slog Iowa was."

Ax was trying to reconcile the facts of our ascendance with his inner anxiety. "I don't know. It just doesn't feel right," he replied. "It almost seems like the New Hampshire primary has become a pro forma exercise in our march to the nomination. But I suspect New Hampshire voters don't see it that way, just like Iowa voters didn't see Hillary as inevitable when we were thirty points down nationally." He let out a sigh. "I just hope we keep gaining ground because I don't like this dynamic now, the rock star gallivanting across the snows of New Hampshire."

Some of this worry I attributed to Ax's tendency to see the glass half empty. But I, too, was concerned that things simply couldn't be as rosy as they appeared.

The debate was at Saint Anselm College in Manchester, and it was our first with a thinned-down field. Only four candidates were left in the race. Richardson had decided to stay in after Iowa, and he joined Obama, Clinton, and Edwards onstage.

The narrower field played to Obama's strengths. He was a good counterpuncher and didn't instinctively try to dominate a debate; as one among eight, his performance hadn't always come across as forceful. With fewer debaters, he was more frequently in the action, and as the hot candidate he was on the griddle, which worked better for him; he could mix it up and be a major presence without forcing it.

We thought Obama gave one of his strongest debate performances thus far and most of the critics agreed. He had one cringe-inducing moment. One of the moderators asked Hillary Clinton if she thought Obama was winning because he was generally considered more likable. Clinton's response was pitch-perfect. "Well, that hurts my feelings," she joked. "But I'll try to go on."

She had started to elaborate when Barack piped in, "You're likable enough, Hillary." Those of us who knew him recognized Obama's dry sense of humor. The Clinton team spun hard that his response offended women, and that it was a significant faux pas; this spin became part of the New Hampshire narrative. It certainly was not the chief takeaway from the debate. At one point, Hillary lost her temper at Edwards, responding sharply to his assertion that she could not bring about change. This moment received more postdebate analysis than Barack's throwaway line. Several national reporters e-mailed me after her outburst with the same message: "She just cost herself the New Hampshire primary."

I asked Obama on the ride back to our hotel if the "likable enough" comment had come out the way he hoped. He was annoyed that it was even an issue. I explained what the other side was pushing.

"I was actually trying to be nice there," he said exasperatedly. "Maybe not too nice. But nice. Maybe I should've said that it was a ridiculous question. I serve with Hillary, she gets a bum rap for not being likable. But it wasn't my question, so I just said something quickly I thought conveyed that." He shook his head. "What a process. A long debate about Iraq, health care, and the economy and this is what they focus on."

Obama generally maintained an attitude of bemusement toward the coverage and how often it could be trivial and banal, obsessed with meaningless detail. I shared this mentality, and frequently we swapped observations on its absurdity as a way of building motivation and releasing the pressure valve. Jon Stewart had a segment most nights during the primary called "Clusterf*&k to the White House" that we thought summed up nicely much of the campaign experience. They key to surviving, we found, was just to fight through the nonsense, keep a true and steady course, and have faith in our strategy. For the first time our internal polls that weekend showed us ahead in New Hampshire, outside the margin for error. Almost every public poll did as well. It was hard to see how we could be stopped.

As our car wound through the streets of Nashua from the debate site to our hotel, Obama raised for the first time the possibility we had so rarely acknowledged: victory in November. "Just think, we might actually win this thing, Plouffe," he said. "Then we'd really have our work cut out for us."

I flew to Chicago Sunday night so I could spend Monday in the office nailing down our post–New Hampshire schedule and budget plans, with a special emphasis on Super Tuesday and allocating our new surplus financial resources throughout those twenty-two states. I had not been in the office in almost two weeks and was struck by the change in atmosphere. Everyone was still boneweary and working around the clock, but I noticed the mood was lighter; almost every staffer was moving with a bounce in his or her step. Headquarters had a different, much more confident feel. It was clear our staff had joined the rest of the political community in thinking that Tuesday's vote was a mere formality. Then Hillary Clinton threw a monkey wrench into the entire primary.

On Monday afternoon, news began to spread that Hillary had broken down on the campaign trail. We all gathered in the press bullpen, where we had six TVs tuned to different channels, to await the video we knew would come any minute. Reporters had described the moment to our press staff as Hillary having "just lost it." When the video aired, my heart sank. At a roundtable conversation with a dozen or so voters in a local coffee shop, a woman asked Hillary a personal question about how she managed even to get out the door every day with all she had on her plate—work, family, doing her hair. Clinton responded by moving the focus away from herself and onto the American people. Her eyes welled up as she spoke. "Some people think elections are a game, lots of who's up or who's down. It's about our country. It's about our kids' future, and it's really about all of us together. Some of us put ourselves out there and do this against pretty difficult odds. . . . We do it . . . because we care about our country, but some of us are right, and some of us are wrong. Some of us are ready, and some of us are not. Some of us know what we will do on Day One, and some of us haven't thought that through enough." Her emotion hadn't knocked her off her talking points, I noticed, but it guaranteed that this moment would dominate the news Monday night and all day Tuesday. I thought immediately it could play well for her. It was a very human moment (though in the heat of the campaign I assumed it must have been deviously contrived and staged) and would appeal especially to female voters. Women had supported Clinton in huge numbers through most of the New Hampshire primary, and though they backed away a bit after our win in Iowa, they still liked her and might conceivably return to her camp in the final hours.

Aside from how the clip would be perceived, the mere fact that a curveball had been thrown into our plans while we were on a great trajectory was deeply concerning. We'd had things right where we wanted them. Now we couldn't be too sure. I called Axelrod, who was on the road with Obama in New Hampshire, to get his take. He shared my unease. "The press will be analyzing this incessantly, some commentators saying she's hurt herself," he mused. "There could be a real backlash effect with women voters. Maybe it's a blip but it could also be a disaster for us."

Monday also brought fresh reports of Clinton robocalls—automated phone messages left on answering machines and voice-mail—and direct-mail pieces attacking Obama. She was accusing us of being hypocritical on our pledge to cleanse D.C. of lobbyist influence, criticizing us for not being able to stand up to the Republican attack machine, and questioning Obama's pro-choice record. To top it off, Bill Clinton was telling crowds that our attempt to differentiate Obama's Iraq position from his wife's was a "fairy tale."

They were lashing out hard. We should have shined a spotlight on these attacks, as we had done so effectively in Iowa. Putting the character of her campaign on trial before voters would have been the smart thing to do and would have dovetailed nicely with the change-versus-status-quo argument that had exploded coming out of Iowa.

Instead we decided to deal with these attacks tactically—and traditionally—by sending out our own automated calls, e-mails, and fliers, rebutting her claims and trying to set the facts straight, rather than getting into a pissing match. Looking back on it, I'm not sure we even had a lengthy debate about whether to turn the negative energy of the attacks back on her. I still kick myself for this overconfidence.

Dixville Notch, a tiny town in New Hampshire, kicks off every primary by casting the first votes at midnight. All the cable networks carry it live and the morning shows highlight the result. I was at home by this point and watched it unfold on TV. We had actually worked pretty hard to convince voters here, hoping for even the small boost a win in Dixville might provide. It paid off: we won overwhelmingly, receiving a whopping seven votes to Edwards's two. Hillary was frozen out. Everyone now seemed to expect a double-digit Obama win; the Clinton people were already spinning that anything less than that would be a "Clinton victory." I went to bed as confident as I have ever been about anything in politics.

Tuesday was a glorious day in New Hampshire, with record highs in the sixties—perfect weather for a trip to the polls. We were thrilled, because we believed a large turnout would help us. It felt like fortune was smiling on us.

The one disturbing piece of anecdotal evidence we received was that some of the independent voters who had pledged to support us (independents can choose to vote in either the Democratic or Republican primary) were showing up at polling locations saying they were voting for McCain in the GOP primary because "he needs the help more." McCain and Mitt Romney were very close in most of the New Hampshire polls while Obama was seen as a lock. When I got to the hotel, Obama was out doing last-minute campaign stops. Axelrod had stayed behind to work on that night's speech, and we decided to grab lunch. On our way we ran into Mark Halperin, a reporter for *Time,* who asked if he could join us. He was working on a cover story about "how Obama did it," and was hoping to get some time with the two of us. We were uneasy at the prospect of talking about how we won before it actually happened, but Halperin persisted. "Listen, you guys are going to win big today," he said. "If a miracle happens and you don't, I won't use any of what you tell me."

We grudgingly went along and tried to carefully talk about how we had pulled off Iowa and New Hampshire. But the whole thing felt uncomfortable and ill advised. As I was leaving the restaurant at the hotel, I stopped by Michelle Obama's table, where she was having lunch with some of her family. She asked me if things were as good as they seemed. "They are," I said. "Hillary's moment yesterday concerns me, but all the numbers suggest we should be fine. Even if we shed some support, we should still win by a margin that would've seemed inconceivable a week ago." I hesitated for a moment and then went on. "But it feels odd to be so confident. It doesn't square with who we are."

Michelle smiled. "No, it doesn't," she said. This rocket ride we were on was something none of us had adjusted to.

As Ax and I walked down the hall to the elevator bank, he seemed increasingly nervous. "I have a sinking feeling in my stomach," he told me. "My head says everything is all right. But something is gnawing at me inside that says our world may get turned upside down tonight."

I hoped this was just run-of-the-mill Ax neurosis.

As evening approached we bunkered down in our makeshift boiler room in the hotel's basement. The first exit polls from the press had us up six. Exits proved woefully inaccurate throughout the primary, and even early on we took them with a grain of salt, but still this margin was troublingly close. Clinton could salvage things by suggesting she was on an upswing. Her husband had used this tactic successfully here in 1992. Losing badly to Paul Tsongas, Bill Clinton proclaimed himself the "Comeback Kid" because he finished a better-than-expected second place while fighting off multiple scandals. I feared we could have another Comeback Kid on our hands. I started e-mailing our press staff, telling them to keep working the reporters: a win was a win. New Hampshire was a must-win for Clinton after losing Iowa. A week ago she had been the inevitable, sure-thing winner. No amount of spin could fudge losing the first two contests; the wheels had come off the inevitability express.

And then suddenly we were falling. The last round of exits had our lead down to two. Actual results started coming in and our New Hampshire staff immediately said the exits were not going to be too far off—it would be close. As town after town reported, we were falling just short of many of our vote goals (we were modeling off getting 42 percent of the vote statewide). I was pacing and pacing and peering over our staff's shoulders to look at results and growing increasingly frustrated. With about a quarter of the vote in, our New Hampshire state director, Matt Rodriguez, who knew the numbers backward and forward, came up to Ax and me. "We're going to lose," he told us.

"What? Are you serious?" I asked.

"Yeah," he said. "Unless turnout is unusually high in some of our base areas yet to come in and low in hers, we'll lose by a couple thousand votes."

This was hard to get my brain around. I was still struggling with how to manage a narrower-than-expected victory. But a loss? It would certainly narrow our already perilous path. It could crush any credible hope we had of winning the nomination.

I told Ax we had better break the news to Obama. We grabbed Gibbs and the three of us rode in silence up to our floor and trudged down the hallway to his room. Gibbs knocked. Obama opened the door and stepped out in the hallway. "What do we know?" he asked.

I grimaced. "Our New Hampshire staff thinks we are going to lose narrowly."

"Lose?" he repeated.

"Lose," Ax confirmed. "Something funky clearly happened here."

"How could everyone be so wrong, us included?" Obama asked, resignation already visible in the slight droop of his shoulders.

"That's going to take a lot of work to figure out," I replied.

Obama leaned back against the wall and exhaled. Then he looked at us and smiled. "This is going to take a while, isn't it?"

Taking charge, he immediately moved to the speech; the current draft built on our victory address in Iowa and was a clarion call for change. "Yes We Can" was a refrain throughout, in answer to the many challenges cynics said could not be overcome. Ultimately, we decided to leave much of the speech intact— "No head hanging," Obama instructed everyone—with the painful exception of adding a line of congratulations to Clinton on her win.

Obama really kept us going that night. He quickly processed the abrupt reversal of fortune and moved on to the practical, immediate questions in front of us. At some point in the future there would be time to analyze, bemoan, and maybe even wallow, but right now we had to plow forward, and he was the one who stepped up and pulled the wagon.

I think had we lost under a different scenario, we would have had a tougher time recovering. If we had lost by a couple points after going into primary day in a dead heat, it would have been devastating. But because we were surprised, because some combination of unknown factors had converged to produce a result in defiance of all the evidence leading up to the primary, it was in some ways easier to deal with. The loss was more of a head-scratcher than a table-pounder, and our reaction more quizzical than heartbroken.

Obama muscled up and delivered a terrific speech. A casual observer would not have known that he had just lost a primary in one of the biggest surprises in modern campaign memory. Moments later, I forced myself to watch Clinton's speech. It was excruciatingly painful. We had heard that Hillary's team had considered having her leave New Hampshire before the polls closed so she would not have to deliver a concession speech in-state. Now, there she was, defiantly victorious and back in the driver's seat as the prohibitive front-runner. The media commentary that night along with the e-mails and calls I received made it clear that most onlookers thought order had been restored. Many seemed to think it would be impossible for us to recover from this devastating blow. I thought this was a very simplistic view and was not grounded in the reality of how the race was likely to unfold. We were no longer a plucky upstart but a fully formed campaign machine, with a stellar candidate who could go the distance. And we were likely to be better organized and funded than Hillary at least through early February.

Winning Iowa had been the lift that allowed us to get on even ground with her, but even still, a victory in New Hampshire was not optional in our scenario. Now the momentum had swung away from us and decisively to Clinton. The question was whether the race would now stabilize in her favor. Any hopes we'd had of a quick end to the primaries were over. As Obama had said, it was going to take a while. And we would need it to.

After midnight we held a conference call for all of our staff around the country. I was concerned that they would have a tough time rebounding. My message was simple, pounding home that we were better organized and funded going forward, and that we clearly had the better candidate, one who brought to the moment exactly what our party and country needed. "This was never going to be easy," I summed up. "Easy is not what you signed up for. But I've never been more confident in a group of people than I am in you and I am still very confident we will prevail. So let's go win this fucking thing."

I believed most of what I said. But after the call I kept working through how we might still pull this off. I had always thought, privately, that New Hampshire was the key to the nomination. Win it, and the odds would be heavily stacked in our favor. Winning Iowa was our entry into the finals, winning

New Hampshire could give us a close to insurmountable advantage after just two contests. But lose it, and the momentum from our win in Iowa could quickly dissipate and we'd be back to staring up at a strong Hillary Clinton, dinged in Iowa, but having righted her battleship.

At about 2:00 a.m., I sat down to check our online money, expecting the worst. When I saw the numbers, I caught my breath. At first I thought I had made a mistake and pulled up the reports for post-Iowa. But I hadn't. I was looking at the numbers for late January 8 and early January 9, and the numbers weren't lying: the money was just pouring in. Even more amazing, a lot of people were giving for the first time. Remarkably, for these folks, our win in Iowa did not prompt them to give, but the loss in New Hampshire did. For the first time since Matt Rodriguez had called the loss a few hours ago, I took a deep breath. Our supporters were not going to be swayed by one setback. They were in it for the long haul.

Obama was planning to do the national morning shows on Wednesday so it would not look like we were hiding in defeat. I decided to travel with him for a few days, so I had to be up early to meet him at the tapings. Sometime after 3:00 a.m. I had finally dozed off, and I was suffering through some fitful sleep when the hotel fire alarm started blaring. Dazed, I lurched into the hallway, where I ran into North Dakota senator Kent Conrad, who had endorsed Obama right before Iowa (our first senator outside of Illinois) and had been in New Hampshire campaigning for us. Standing in my boxers in a hotel hallway in the middle of the night with Kent Conrad, I suddenly experienced an overwhelming urge to get the hell out of New Hampshire.

———

To put New Hampshire to bed we needed to understand what happened. We lost by a few thousand votes. Any number of factors could have been altered to produce our expected win. After much reflection, I reached some conclusions as to what brought about the shift at the end. Let's call it "Plouffe's Primer on How to Lose a Sure Thing."

First, there was Hillary's moment of emotion. Remember, she started out with support well in the range of 40 to 45 percent and maintained that level until the last couple of months. And even those who went to Obama or were undecided at the end still viewed her favorably. There was a very fertile group of New Hampshire voters who had always liked her, and this raw moment brought them home.

Next, we lost too many of those pesky independents. The data showed definitively that a healthy number of the independents we identified as both supporting Obama and intending to vote in the Democratic primary had switched to McCain at the end. In fact, there were numerous reports of these voters telling our staff and volunteers, "Your guy is going to win. I think McCain is the best Republican, it will give us a good choice. But don't worry, I'm voting Obama in November." Third, we suffered the attacks in silence. Had we called out the Clinton attack strategy, we would have profited by it. We were too confident in our position and treated her attacks as discrete issues to be addressed in the context of a limited number of voters and not as the broad opportunity they presented.

Finally, we were guilty—or seemed to be guilty, which is just as bad—of hoisting the icon. This was a term Axelrod used often to describe a dynamic we needed to avoid. The press coverage suggested Obama was taking a victory tour while Hillary fought for her life. New Hampshire loves underdogs and punishes overconfident front-runners. The voters had not been ready to call the race over. Perhaps they felt it shouldn't be so easy for a political phenomenon who had barely seen combat to carry the Democratic torch.

"I actually think this is for the best," Obama said. We were driving down to Boston the day after the primary. "Sure, if we had won New Hampshire, we'd be in the driver's seat. But I'd be like a comet streaking across the sky. White hot. And comets eventually burn up. Now people can see how I deal with adversity, whether we can bounce back." He paused for a second, thinking. "And they want me to earn this. They don't want it to be so easy for someone like me and it probably shouldn't be."

Rather than engaging in a lot of second-guessing—though he did want an analysis of how our polling was off and what we thought happened—he was in a remarkably sanguine place.

I looked at him with raised eyebrows. My first thought was, You are in serious denial, dude. We are royally screwed. But I got the sense that he wasn't rationalizing. It was what he believed, convenient or not. I still wasn't sure if or how we could win the nomination having lost New Hampshire, but I knew our candidate's reaction and state of mind gave us a fighting chance.

Super Tuesday was staring us in the face. Twenty-two states would be voting in less than four weeks—in states with early vote, like California and Arizona, voting was under way. We were trailing in many of these February 5 states by over twenty points. And our internal numbers told us we were likely to lose the next contest in Nevada. We would need to fend off a furious Clinton onslaught aimed at ending the race. The next few weeks were likely to be about survival.

Weeks earlier, we had scheduled fund-raisers in Boston and New York for the day after New Hampshire, which was January 8. After our big win in Iowa, these events sold out immediately. Many donors had thought they would be coming to see the Democratic nominee. Now we were no longer a sure thing, and I wondered if the energy at the fund-raisers would be muted as a result. I needn't have worried. Both events were packed to the rafters with excited donors and great energy. Our longtime financial supporters were particularly energized, and none were hanging crepe. Very few pursued the "How did you guys screw that up?" conversation. They could tell some funky things had happened at the end in New Hampshire—some in our control, many not.

If any guests felt shaky, Obama worked to steady them. "This is not going to be easy," he reminded the crowd. "Change never is. We will have more setbacks like last night in New Hampshire along the way. But if you really believe in the campaign—not in me, but what we are trying to collectively change in Washington and in our world—then it is after the setbacks that we need you most. I still believe with all my heart that we can win this race. But I need you not to get discouraged, to get more energized and go the distance with us."

For many donors, seeing his confidence brought into relief by his realism and self-awareness was a powerful reassurance that their dedication to the cause would be honored and matched. Meanwhile, our Internet money continued to fly in, setting a record for our biggest twenty-four-hour period to date. Some of this was in response to fund-raising e-mails sent to our online list, but much of the growth was organic, as new donors sought us out. Our field offices around the country reported that new volunteers were pouring in. It became clear that this setback had emboldened our supporters rather than discouraged them.

We also had a series of high-profile political endorsements lined up right after New Hampshire. While endorsements were not core to our strategy, we had thought that after winning New Hampshire, it would be important to demonstrate the party uniting behind Barack, in hopes of bringing the primary race to an early close. After the loss, we feared some people who had committed would get cold feet. Obama spent much of Wednesday in between events calling these folks, and to a person they all stuck with us. John Kerry was scheduled to go out Thursday, January 10, in South Carolina, and he was still raring to go. Governor Janet Napolitano of Arizona and Senator Claire Mc-Caskill of Missouri also reaffirmed their commitment, as did countless other members of Congress and local elected officials.

These endorsements, in addition to their political and organizational value, sent a strong message that we would not fade away after one setback. Our robust rebound must have been somewhat demoralizing to the Clinton campaign. With some justification, they likely thought they had regained control of the race. But now they could see that we were still growing in strength organizationally and politically. The endorsements also signaled that more and more politicos were not merely comfortable with Obama on the top of the ticket, but thought he would be the stronger standard-bearer.

Our Wednesday-night fund-raiser in New York City ended just after nine, and Gibbs and I wearily made our way to our hotel, the W in Midtown. Shuffling through the lobby, we could see the bar was hopping. Gibbs and I looked at each other gloomily. After losing New Hampshire, and never even properly celebrating Iowa, a belt or two and a good meal in a lively spot were just what the doctor ordered. But we had hours of conference calls ahead of us. ABC News was planning to give us the front-runner treatment, doing a proctologic piece on *Good Morning America, Nightline,* and *World News.* They were delving into Obama's relationship with Tony Rezko, a political supporter with whom Obama had engaged in a real estate deal, which Barack had subsequently acknowledged as an instance of poor judgment. We had to war-game out how we were going to minimize the damage.

In the throes of a campaign, it's better never to glimpse an oasis like the W bar, or even pay too much attention to normal people going through their daily lives. A campaign is a constant pressure cooker and the only exit is if the top blows. Keep your head down, work around the clock, and don't reflect for a minute on what you're missing—that's the survival mantra.

Gibbs and I grabbed apples from the front desk for dinner that night and grumbled our way to our rooms. Maybe ABC needed some reminding as to which candidate had just lost New Hampshire and which was now more deserving of the "front-runner" scrutiny, I thought.

Nevada, on Saturday, January 19, was the next contest, and we never had a poll showing us in real striking distance. The only way we could win was through staggeringly superior organization. Clinton had the bulk of the establishment support, and as far as we could tell, her team was much better organized than they had been in Iowa. We had put together a deeper campaign, but it probably wouldn't be enough to put us over the top.

We never thought Nevada would mean much in terms of its impact on subsequent primaries; we anticipated it as a blip on the screen. But after Clinton's upset comeback in New Hampshire, the state took on new importance: if she won Nevada she would shout from the hills that the race had turned. So we threw all we could into winning it. Obama campaigned hard, as did some of our new high-profile endorsers, like Kerry and Napolitano. It was a valiant effort, but not enough to overcome Hillary's big lead in the raw vote. She ended up with 51 percent to our 45 percent. Edwards completely flamed out, getting only 4 percent.

About an hour after the race was officially called for Clinton by the news organizations—well before all the results were officially in—our canny delegate director, Jeff Berman, burst into my office looking happier than I expected. "I think we might have won more delegates than Clinton," he said.

"Why, because we were more balanced statewide?" I asked.

"Yep," Berman answered. "I think we'll win more delegates than her in the rural districts. If everything holds as the last numbers come in, we'll take thirteen pledged delegates overall and she'll get twelve."

This was huge news. We could certainly use it to steal some of their thunder. Since Iowa, the Clinton campaign had stuck to the same mantra day after day: "This is a race about delegates." In my view, they took this tack because they thought they would dominate us on February 5, and at this point they still had a huge lead among superdelegates: the party leaders and officials who have a vote at the Democratic convention. But given how much they had hammered at this argument, it would be hard for them to deny the importance of our Nevada coup. Our press staff suggested that Berman and I do a conference call with the press to put our usual spin on the results with the added twist that we would announce that we had won more delegates, to throw our own little monkey wrench into the Clinton celebration.

Berman and the Associated Press delegate tracker, who is considered the authority on all matters regarding delegates, actually got into a colloquy on the phone. At first the tracker disputed Berman's assertion. But then they went through the results, district by district and delegate by delegate, and finally the AP tracker pronounced to the entire national political press corps that, in fact, we did seem to have a split verdict—Clinton had won the raw vote but Obama edged her in delegates.

Many of the stories that ran that night and the next day called it a split verdict. The AP headline that ran across the country read, "Clinton, Obama Split Nevada Spoils." It must have infuriated the Clinton folks to no end. This gave us great satisfaction, though it did not change the fact that Hillary was on a roll.

Nevada also had the effect of beginning to shift the national narrative from raw votes to the question of delegates. As more of the press corps became convinced the race was going to go on for a while—meaning it could turn into a battle for delegates—they started to bone up on the selection process. They already knew that close contests produced essentially split-delegate results—we netted one more than Clinton in Iowa when defeating her by nine points, and tied in New Hampshire despite her raw-vote win. But Nevada illustrated for them that delegate results did not necessarily track the statewide popular vote. This was a critical lesson for us to press upon the media before February 5.

Next came South Carolina, on January 26, and here we had to do more than win. We had to have a victory that somehow produced enough momentum for us to survive Super Tuesday. A close or modest win would likely be insufficient. We needed divine intervention.

It arrived in the form of Bill Clinton.

———

We had recently worried that, as in a forward-thinking chess strategy, the Clinton campaign might decide to cede South Carolina. Sacrificing this piece would essentially render any win there meaningless and would free up Hillary, Bill, and all their surrogates to get a head start campaigning in the February 5 states, where she already held comfortable leads.

Much has been written about the internal debates in the Clinton camp over whether and how to contest South Carolina. According to numerous reports, we had Bill to thank for their decision to go in whole hog. He apparently argued strenuously that they had a chance to win there and should compete hard. The week leading into the South Carolina primary was the most intense week of the campaign to date, as both Bill and Hillary spent a great deal of time in-state; Bill campaigned there almost full time. It really felt like two on one.

The Clinton attack machine had kicked into full gear, going so far as to assert based on a contorted reading of an interview that Obama believed

Ronald Reagan had better ideas than the Democrats. Bill Clinton was especially aggressive during this period. Every time he launched a broadside, it got outsized attention.

We had learned something from New Hampshire, when we did not respond to the attacks effectively. We returned to our approach in Iowa, utilizing what Axelrod would call jujitsu, trying to shine a spotlight on their attacks, not ignore them, and use their negative energy against them.

We set up an in-state "truth squad" of some of our most prominent South Carolina supporters, who would shadow everything Bill Clinton, Hillary Clinton, and their campaign surrogates said that could be construed as an attack and would hold press conferences, make calls, and post on the Web our criticism of the fusillade and their tactics and put out the truth, as we saw it.

We put the Clinton attacks front and center as rationale to vote for change.

I believe they thought their attacks in New Hampshire and Nevada had worked and that they saw no reason not to keep going back to the well.

At the one debate in South Carolina, five days before the primary in Myrtle Beach, things turned ugly fast. Obama and Clinton got into a seven-minute slugfest, leaving John Edwards and the rest of the viewers to watch in amazement as the gloves finally came off. Obama was not going to turn the other cheek in this debate. Accusations flew, with each candidate accusing the other of selling out American workers, and every subsequent claim ratcheted up the intensity level onstage. The details were less important than Obama's display of mettle and willingness to get into a slugfest with Hillary, a champion pugilist. Showing that spine and willingness to fight toe-to-toe was energizing for our supporters and served to shine a spotlight on the Clinton camp's negative and distorted attacks. It was a tactical detour from our standard debate approach and one that we felt paid real dividends.

We had led in South Carolina for some time, but many of the public polls now showed a tightening of the race. So in addition to serving as the venue for a battle royale, South Carolina was starting to look like a possible upset. And if Clinton won here she would almost certainly be the nominee.

John Edwards was still in the race. Publicly, his team insisted they could resuscitate his campaign in South Carolina. But privately, it soon became clear they knew otherwise, and some time after the debate, I got a call from a senior Edwards adviser. This was the pitch:

"Listen. It's clear unless the race is shaken up, Hillary is going to win. You guys might not even win South Carolina. What would shake the race up is John ending his campaign, but not to simply endorse another candidate. All things being equal, John prefers Barack. They should announce they are joining forces and will run as a ticket. Edwards can vouch for Obama with blue-collar and Southern whites and is running on a change message. "It's a perfect fit. And it has to be something that big to slow down Hillary. You need a big shakeup in the race and this could be it."

I listened intently and replied that obviously this was something I would need to discuss with my boss. "Am I authorized to raise this offer with him?" I asked.

"Yes" came the reply. But then right at the end of the conversation, the Edwards rep added a new wrinkle: "Just to be clear, we're going to talk to the Clinton people, too. That's not where John's heart is, but he is at a point of maximum leverage now. We want to see what each of you is thinking."

My initial reaction was that this was a nonstarter. Of course, we wanted Edwards's support and his message was certainly closer in spirit to ours than it was to Hillary's. But political deals like this rarely work; people see right through them. Plus, I couldn't imagine Obama agreeing this far out to lock in his running mate without going through any process or even being certain that we would be the ones making a selection.

Obama's answer was quick and firm: he would cut no deals. If he won, he did not want to be locked in to any personnel matters, and he had little interest in deciding on a vice presidential pick in the heat of the primary campaign.

We decided he would talk to Edwards personally and make clear there could be no promises. During that conversation, Obama reiterated that we wanted John's support and thought it would make a difference, and clearly there could be a potential role for him down the line. But if he endorsed us now, there could be no hint of something concrete in the future.

Shortly after this I checked in with my Edwards contact. Clearly Edwards had already downloaded his conversation with Obama. The contact said that while John's inclination was to be with Obama, it seemed the Clinton folks were more intent on gaining his support. He did not allude to specifics, but the message was that Hillary might offer specific commitments. "Well," I said, "we have made clear that we would value your support and think it would be very meaningful. I hope this is where you decide to hang your hat."

I strongly doubted that Clinton was offering Edwards anything concrete, and certainly not the VP slot. She knew better than most how important decisions like this were, and I had a hard time believing that even a crucial endorsement on this level, days before South Carolina, would warrant much more than a thank-you and a promise to talk further down the line.

I don't know if Edwards sanctioned these diplomacy missions or the level of specificity and brazenness that was presented to us. The Edwards saga petered out after that; he stayed in the race through South Carolina, finished third, and dropped out several days later. Eventually he endorsed us; it came at an important time, and we were grateful to have his support. On Friday morning, the day before the South Carolina vote, NBC released a poll that showed our lead over Clinton narrowing to eight points. More significant from the press's perspective, the poll showed our support among white voters at only 10 percent.

This created a political firestorm heading into the primary. First, it fueled the big question: could Hillary actually pull off an upset? And even if she could not, the consensus was that a single-digit win for Obama would not meet expectations; the thunderbolt we needed out of South Carolina would end up little more than a fizzle.

Second, the cable networks started obsessing over the "racial polarization" that seemed to be taking hold in South Carolina. The pundits ventured that even if Obama won South Carolina, it would now be almost entirely with black voters. This would raise real questions about his electability in the general election, questions that Clinton could use against him as part of her strategy to deny him the Democratic nomination.

While this perception was frustrating to an extent, it was also quite useful to our strategy. Our own polling data and, more important, our field data, showed our lead stable in the mid-high double digits and our white support still over 20 percent. If those numbers held, we would benefit from exceeding expectations in both the overall margin and our support level from white voters. We began to realize that perhaps we could gain outsized momentum from a South Carolina victory after all—if we created a wide enough gap between the expectations produced by conventional wisdom about the race "tightening" and the actual results. To this end, it actually worked to our advantage to have the press see momentum swinging toward Clinton. So when Ron Fournier, a respected AP reporter, went so far as to tell the press heading into primary day that he thought Clinton could pull an upset, it was music to our ears.

Just about every day we heard criticism about our organization-building in South Carolina. Staying true to our plan, we had rejected the idea of vying for the support of local kingmakers and focused on building from the ground up, just as we had in Iowa. We had to expand the electorate. To win, we needed to turn out younger whites, independents, newly registered African American voters, and African Americans who in the past had voted only sporadically. Getting these people involved required a massive ground effort. We held thousands of local house parties in the state; launched a barbershop and beauty-salon outreach program to find African American voters; organized people of faith and held hundreds of small faith-based gatherings; and worked the colleges relentlessly.

We ran a ground campaign in South Carolina the likes of which had never before been seen. And it was widely believed by many old hands to be a colossal mistake. Our South Carolina staff deserved medals for staying focused amid the torrent of criticism from the local establishment. They were ridiculed, mocked, and harassed. But we knew we had energy on the ground and the ability to expand our share of the electoral pie. Obama deserved an enormous amount of credit for sticking by our strategy; every time he was down there, someone pulled him aside to tell him we didn't know what the hell we were doing. But belief in the grass roots was embedded in him as a candidate—and Iowa had shown him how powerful a force it could become.

The sun rose on Election Day and our fate settled into the hands of a few hundred thousand South Carolina voters. The day also brought a new mishap from Bill Clinton. While speaking to the press shortly before the polls closed, he was asked what it said about Obama that "it takes two of you to beat him." Bill chuckled, and replied, "That's just bait too. Jesse Jackson won South Carolina twice, in '84 and '88. . . ."

This response immediately caused a minor furor on the cable shows and blogs. Since it was already primary day in South Carolina, the fallout did not affect the voting, but the radioactivity spread wildly in the days to come. Many saw it as Clinton's way of suggesting that an Obama win in South Carolina could be discounted because of the heavy African American population—that, in essence, he would win because he was black.

Bill Clinton took a lot of heat from the press over the course of the campaign, and from time to time I thought he got a raw deal. But this gaffe was hard to explain away. Empirical evidence showed voters throughout the country had a strong reaction to it. They thought it was low-road politics and certainly not a statement befitting a former president. Field reports throughout the day showed turnout would be through the roof, and we liked the details of who was voting. The first exit polls put us up thirty points, which seemed unrealistically high but suggested we would exceed expectations. Coupled with our own analysis of the turnout, it pointed to the dominant win we desperately needed.

For once the exits were just about dead-on. When the dust settled, we had won South Carolina by a stunning twenty-eight points, earning 55 percent of the electorate, a clear majority. We won a quarter of the white vote, sailing past the media expectations and generating a very positive story line about our broad appeal. We also won white voters under forty, besting Clinton by over ten points. Our expectations strategy had paid off: it was clear this was going to be covered as a very significant win and a big blow to the Clinton campaign. They had competed vigorously and been walloped. Right away, we spun the lopsided margin as a repudiation of the kind of attack politics they had engaged in. Voters appeared to recoil from both their negative tactics and the media obsession with race. Bill Clinton's Jesse Jackson comment, though not a factor in the vote, only served to add fuel to that narrative. We could not have dreamed up a better scenario: an authoritative victory coupled with a postvote analysis that amplified our overall message. I was in the Chicago HQ, where staffers were popping beers, high-fiving, and whooping it up. There would be no long night waiting for results this time—we had doled out an old-fashioned ass-whupping and, boy, did it feel good. Leaving aside our delegate-count coup in Nevada, it had been twenty-three days since our last win.

I talked to Obama on the phone before he gave his victory speech, and he was as ebullient as I had ever heard him, much more so than after Iowa. "Plouffe, we thumped them," he said, with uncharacteristic relish. "I feel so good for the people down here—they rejected all the story lines and decided to write their own."

I went through some of the numbers with him so he could appreciate how deep the win was and how demographically broad. We lost only two of South Carolina's forty-six counties. And for the first time, one candidate had dominated the delegate yield, too. In the first three contests, we had netted a whopping two delegates more than Hillary. But in South Carolina it looked like we would get twenty-five delegates and Hillary only twelve. This was another important moment of education for the press and political community—the only way to net delegates in large quantities was to win by landslides. A net of thirteen delegates in a state that had only fifty-one was a big deal.

Despite the significance of this factor, I could sense that Obama felt relief at the mere fact of the victory. "It feels good to get another W," he said. "And to win the right way."

For both Obama and the campaign, the South Carolina victory offered a chance to exhale. Had we lost the contest or won it narrowly in a racially polarized vote, it would have left us limping. Instead the blowout put fresh gas in our tank and galvanized the whole campaign. Winning contested primaries by twenty-eight points just doesn't happen very often. We had also smashed all turnout records, which was a testament to our organization and a tantalizing glimpse of what might be possible in other states. And to top it off, we had muzzled the naysayers who told us that our plan would never work in South Carolina. It had, and powerfully so. The win was an affirmation of our conviction that the rules could be rewritten.

As Obama took the stage at our victory party a spontaneous chant broke out: "Race doesn't matter. Race doesn't matter. Race doesn't matter." It felt liberating—South Carolina voters had exorcised, at least for one election, the notion that their state could not move beyond race. In the state capital, Columbia, just down the street from where a Confederate flag still waves, a broad and diverse coalition of South Carolinians responded to the skeptics and the cynics with our powerful refrain "Yes we can."

In his speech, Obama shifted focus from his usual message and issues and wandered into what the win meant politically. We needed to tie a bow on our success in the first four states, a goal that had been our North Star for a year. "Tonight," he told the crowd, "the cynics who believed that what began in the snows of Iowa was just an illusion were told a different story by the good people of South Carolina.

"After four great contests in every corner of this country, we have the most votes, the most delegates, and the most diverse coalition of Americans we've seen in a long, long time."

For the first time in eighteen days, I believed once more that we could win the nomination. We just had to find a way to scale the mountain looming ominously in front of us: Super Tuesday.

7

Super Tuesday

The glow from South Carolina lasted only a matter of hours. Twenty-two states would vote on one day; we trailed in most of them and the few leads we held outside of Illinois were narrow. Given the outsized role momentum plays in the primary process, Super Tuesday had developed into a day meant to kill off pesky insurgents and ratify front-runners. We had ten days to prepare.

There were eleven contests in February after Super Tuesday, and we liked our chances in those states based on the demographics and our organizational strength. We thought we could win many of them and perhaps seize the upper hand in the race. But if we lost too badly on February 5, all bets were off.

We had settled on our approach to this quasi-national primary in early January. Pulling out the map, we had methodically laid out where Barack and all of our surrogates would campaign and how we thought we could piece together enough wins and collect enough delegates to survive. It appeared that the two campaigns were pursuing diametrically opposed approaches to this day. The Clinton camp focused their resources on the contests held in big states—California, Massachusetts, New York, and New Jersey. They argued that the big prizes mattered most and whoever won them would be in the driver's seat for the nomination. This was how they spun their strategy to the press.

Our approach was very different. Unless we got clobbered on February 5, we thought the race would be a war of attrition, a delegate-by-delegate battle. There were 1,681 delegates up for grabs on Super Tuesday alone; when the dust cleared the morning of February 6 the results would provide a useful tale of the tape. Anyone who won a large majority of the delegates that day would surely be in the driver's seat. If the tally was close, the race would simply move on. We thought of February 5 not as a chance to triumph but as a bullet to dodge; if we could mitigate their likely raw-vote wins by keeping them from netting too many delegates, we'd stay alive. The Clinton campaign saw Super Tuesday as their crowning moment, the day on which they'd post big-ticket wins in marquee states and decisively consign us to the campaign dustbin. On one point we agreed: if they won big with delegates, we'd be bowing out before long. But if we emerged relatively unscathed, we believed the campaign would enter a new strategic phase. This was our guiding principle and our decisions flowed from it. We reached out to the press with our perspective on these upcoming contests, explaining why it was a mistake to focus on a narrow set of states as the ones that "really" mattered. Our efforts met with little success. Much of the media discussion in the lead-up to Super Tuesday centered on the big states. This was another instance—and certainly not the last—where I felt we were running one campaign and the press was covering another. We had gotten used to the discrepancy by this point and made sure we communicated our strategy internally to our staff and supporters so they understood how we viewed and approached this critical day. Even if they weren't sure our plans were sound, we wanted our supporters to understand our decisions flowed from strategy.

On January 28 we unleashed what became a political earthquake. Senator Ted Kennedy, after assiduous courting from both Obama and Clinton, had privately committed to endorse us. Bolstered now by our South Carolina momentum, we knew we could reveal the endorsement in a big moment that would receive a lot of attention just as voters in many of the Super Tuesday states were tuning in to the contest for the first time.

Kennedy's endorsement would not have been so defining a moment if not for two factors. First, Caroline Kennedy was publishing an op-ed in the *New York Times* the day before her uncle's endorsement, also pledging her support to Barack Obama. She had never before actively campaigned for a candidate outside her family, so her words carried real weight. And it was not lost on people that she was a prominent woman from New York, Hillary's base. I found out later it was not lost on Caroline, either. She knew she was kicking a hornet's nest, but because her children were so taken by Obama, she felt compelled to speak out, damn the consequences.

Her op-ed grabbed headlines around the nation that Sunday and featured some very memorable lines: "I have never had a president," she wrote, "who inspired me the way people tell me that my father inspired them. But for the first time, I believe I have found the man who could be that president—not just for me, but for a new generation of Americans."

I'm not generally given to sentimentality, but I must have read her essay five times. Like many in Democratic politics, I had consumed just about everything produced by and about the Kennedy family. And with these words, the daughter and only surviving child of President John F. Kennedy not only endorsed Obama but connected him to the legacy and spirit of the era of Camelot. It was one of the few times in the campaign when I stepped back and fully appreciated that we were part of something special, win or lose.

Another of the reasons Caroline's statement was so powerful was that she wrote it herself. It wasn't marred by any campaign talking points. Throughout the campaign people's own words and feelings about why they supported Barack were always most effective, whether they came from grassroots volunteers or as significant a national figure as Caroline.

Senator Kennedy took the same approach, and this was the second factor that made his endorsement so significant to the overall arc of the campaign. We did not see his speech until shortly before he and Barack took the stage (joined by Caroline and Congressman Patrick Kennedy, the senator's son), but we wouldn't have changed a word of it. It was an eloquent and forceful speech, offered by a man with a deep understanding of the past half-century of American politics, and rebutting every attack that the Clinton campaign and the media had leveled at Obama. Several times Senator Kennedy linked the criticisms visited upon Obama to those made about his brother John during the 1960 campaign, most importantly on the question of experience. "There was another time," he told the crowd at American University, "when another young candidate was running for president and challenging America to cross a New Frontier. He faced public criticism from the preceding Democratic president, who was widely respected in the party. Harry Truman said we needed 'someone with greater experience'—and added: 'May I urge you to be patient.' And John Kennedy replied: 'The world is changing. The old ways will not do. It is time for a new generation of leadership.'

"So it is with Barack Obama."

By pugnaciously dismissing the argument that Obama lacked experience and by linking Obama's vision and ability to unify and inspire to those of his slain brother—which in forty years he had never before done—Kennedy created a political upheaval. Coupled with our strong tailwind out of South Carolina, it might, we hoped, provide just enough electoral magic to see us through Super Tuesday.

Paid staff had been on the ground organizing in many of the February 5 states since September, and most of our people from Iowa, New Hampshire, Nevada, and even South Carolina had already been dispatched to new states. By the end of the primary, many of our organizers had pulled tours of duty in five or six different places. They'd pack up their meager belongings, jump in their cars, and head for the next contest. It was a brutal life but a great learning experience. Every state's voters and politics are different, and the learning curve from such diverse exposure in a short period of time was something no textbook or standard campaign experience could replicate. People like Paul Tewes and Mitch Stewart, fresh off their Iowa win, ended up pulling leadership duty for us in a number of states. Hundreds of our early-state staffers became a mobile Obama army and ended up being deployed around the country wherever we needed them.

Thanks to our social-networking site and all the organizing done by our volunteers on the ground, we often had an in-state presence well before the first Obama staffer arrived. We felt we had a meaningful organizational advantage in most of the February 5 states, particularly in the caucus states, where organizing could provide the most acute advantages.

Our January fund-raising boom continued, and we ended up raising over $32 million for the month, $28 million of it online. We were now up to 650,000 total donors; perhaps most important, 170,000 new donors joined the campaign in January alone. The windfall allowed us to run advertising in most of the February 5 states. This was critical because Obama would not be a constant presence on the ground in any of these states. Advertising could help fill the void. Clinton's advertising was meager in comparison, a strong signal that they were having a very rough fund-raising month in January. We had thought their money would suffer once the sheen of inevitability wore off, and that appeared to be the case. Our unexpectedly strong January allowed us to run ads in the prohibitively expensive Los Angeles and New York markets. Though we assumed we'd lose New Jersey, New York, and California overwhelmingly, the closer we kept the margin, the fewer delegates Clinton would net. We wanted to avoid getting blown out wherever possible, and we hoped to create a few blowouts of our own. We had money; what we did not have was enough time. Obama would be a fleeting presence in these states over the final ten days. So we let our overall approach to the race define how we would use his time and the time of our surrogates—we would try to harvest votes and delegates everywhere. Rather than concentrating on a handful of states, we set out to blitzkrieg the country.

Obama initially embraced this approach. As some public poll numbers showed California tightening, though, he raised a question about our time allocation, for which I was responsible. He called me from California, where he was spending only half a day before the 5th. "Are you sure we should not come back to California?" he asked. "You have me going to Idaho, but in California for only half a day. If we win California, we could finish this thing off and it seems like we might want to hit more media markets than just two."

I was already getting this question internally, so I was well prepared. "First, we do not think we can win California," I told him. "Yes, it is closing, but over a third of the voters voted early by mail in the previous weeks. And even though we ran an exhaustive early-ballot program, these votes were mostly cast after New Hampshire, when Hillary was riding high. We think she won that portion of the vote convincingly." I could almost hear him thinking along with me. "So while it's conceivable we could win Election Day voting," I continued, "we'll still lose overall. Moving your vote share from forty-three percent to forty-six percent doesn't alter the delegate math very much. And a trip to Idaho or other small states has an outsized reward—you dominate media coverage for days. We just get more bang for a buck going to Idaho than California."

"Okay," he replied without hesitating, "that make sense." And that was that. If he thought you made a reasoned argument, he accepted it, even if he had started on the opposite side of the fence. Our schedule that week was a whirlwind. Obama campaigned in Alabama, Missouri (twice), Arizona, New Mexico, California, Idaho, Colorado, Kansas, Minnesota, Illinois, Georgia, Connecticut, New Jersey, Massachusetts, and Delaware. We even thought of going to Alaska but couldn't pull it off, and we were scheduled to go to Utah but had to cancel when the head of the Church of Jesus Christ of Latter-day Saints passed away.

Idaho and Delaware are terrific examples of our approach. We expected to win Idaho comfortably—the Clinton campaign was largely writing it off—and thought a visit there could potentially push our winning margin so high that we could net over ten delegates, a real blowout in such a low-delegate state. With that in mind, we did an event in Boise at 8:00 on the Saturday morning before Super Tuesday. It was hardly the ideal time of day to fill a big basketball arena, but fill it we did and then some: over thirteen thousand people showed up. This was well over half the number of people who ended up attending the caucuses statewide. Our press coverage lasted for five days.

Delaware offered a more geographically strategic target. We knew we had to get some visibility in South Jersey because there was a healthy delegate yield. But rather than hold an event in New Jersey, we decided to go to Delaware, where we would still get voluminous Philadelphia TV coverage (South Jersey is also part of this market) but would again have an outsized impact in a small state. The rally in Delaware was on Super Bowl Sunday and drew the biggest crowd in Delaware political history. As in Idaho, a healthy percentage of the ultimate electorate attended our event—we reached our target audience with the most direct and effective communication possible.

I am a Delaware native and my parents and two of my siblings live in Wilmington. Before the rally, Obama graciously took photos with a large collection of Plouffes, including my young son, who was in town while my wife worked on the Delaware primary. This was the first time my son had met Senator Obama.

I called him from Chicago as he left the rally for the Wilmington airport, asked him how the event had gone, and started to fill him on the latest numbers. He cut me off with a laugh. "Plouffe, man, I just met your family," he said. "Let's talk about that. Leave the politics aside for a minute."

"Right," I said. "Of course. How are they?"

He filled me in on the bonding experience he and my son had shared over SpongeBob SquarePants and said that my parents seemed like nice, grounded people. "I see where you get that level head and common sense."

I appreciated his graciousness and his real interest in them. Ours is a close family, but I saw my parents only twice in twenty-four months and most of my siblings only once, fleetingly. It was nice to have our worlds collide, if only momentarily.

Every day, Jeff Berman, Jon Carson, and I adjusted our projections for each of the states based on new field data and polling information. Right after South Carolina, our projections suggested Hillary would net one hundred more delegates than we would on February 5. We could survive that, but it meant that our best-case scenario at the end of the primaries in early June would be a pledged-delegate lead for Obama of only fifty or so. As the days passed in this period, our projections kept improving, until we finally had some scenarios that had us netting delegates on February 5. It was astonishing movement after essentially one week and spoke to the huge and surprising momentum that both our South Carolina win and the Kennedy endorsement provided, as well as the power of our financial and organizational strength across Super Tuesday and the fact that Clinton had not yet sealed the deal with more than half of the primary electorate in the majority of states.

The projections kept getting rosier because in the large states where we expected Clinton to win, we were having success eating away at her margin of victory. "Unless something really surprising happens, we will at worst break even," declared Berman, who was not one to engage in hyperbole. "It's amazing. Every hour, I update the delegate projections based on polling and voter-contact reports and they seem to get more positive."

To our amazement, other than Colorado, the Clinton campaign was essentially ceding caucus states. We also thought that in Georgia, a big primary state with a lot of delegates, we could produce a much bigger margin than she would get in places like California. All we could surmise is that they really thought the outcome on February 5 would be so decisive in their favor that they did not have to worry about each and every delegate in all the states. Of course, that's exactly what we were doing. And when it all shook out, one of us would be right and one of us would be wrong; we'd know soon enough who was which.

We were able to game these contests so efficiently because we were fortunate enough to have recruited a Super Tuesday dream team, headed up by Berman and Carson. Berman was an old delegate hand. Every four years he would try to take leave from his law firm and work on a primary campaign, and in 2008 he found ours. Delegate experts are like typewriter repairmen—a scarce and dying breed. I had worked closely with Berman on the Gephardt campaign and was impressed with his mastery of the proportional delegate allocation rules. In most states delegates are awarded through a blend of congressional district and statewide results. A true delegate focus required mounting many mini-campaigns; this way, even if you lost a state's popular vote, you could grab an extra delegate here and there by overperforming in a congressional district or two, minimizing your opponent's delegate yield and possibly even wiping it out completely. Berman had an encyclopedic knowledge of the demographics and past voting histories of the nation's congressional districts. Coupled with my work managing House races throughout the country, the two of us could really go district by district, assessing strengths and weaknesses to determine which ones provided opportunity to us and where we might be in danger. Carson was an experienced operative who had worked throughout the country and was a fanatical believer in the value of organizing—a rarity in modern politics. Back at the start of the campaign, he had set up our Illinois operation to send supporters in that state over the border into Iowa to volunteer and make calls to other early states. Seeing his bang-up job there, Steve Hildebrand and I had decided to ask him to head up our February 5 team. The choice was clearly paying off. Carson had done a great job determining what type of operation to put in place in each state, in consultation first with me and then with Berman for a delegate scrub. Compared with the four early states, our operations in these states were sparse, practically living off the land, but Carson got the most out of them. Watching our projections of Hillary's diminishing delegate pile, we could see his ragtag army was running circles around the competition.

One thing Carson, Berman, and I followed carefully was the battle between the candidates' home states. New York had a whopping seventy-nine more delegates at stake than Illinois, but we were organizing aggressively in New York and were now on the air with TV ads, solely for the purpose of trying to keep Hillary's net delegate number down. We thought that we would likely get to 40 percent in her state and she would not surpass 35 percent in ours. If that happened, we would net more delegates out of Illinois than she would out of New York. Call us stats nerds if you will, but in our world of delegate machinations, this was seismic and sexy stuff. I walked around day after day holding our latest delegate prediction spreadsheet in my hand—it was my bible.

The landslide margins in the caucus states, Illinois, and Georgia, if produced, would yield delegate allocations of about two to one in these states, meaning we could net more delegates from victories in smaller states than Clinton would from her bigger state victories.

We invited many of our big national donors and local elected officials to our election night event in Chicago at the Hyatt. The hotel was connected by underground tunnels to our HQ, and all the reporters who were traveling with us were in town, so throughout the night as results came in I made frequent trips to the press room in the hotel's bowels to put our interpretation on the numbers.

It was clear from the reporters' questions and the general tenor of the TV chatter that the initial press coverage was going to be challenging for us. First, there was a smattering of public polls suggesting that New Jersey, California, and Massachusetts were all going to be very close. Some poll analysis even left the impression that we might produce upsets in these states. This wasn't our view. Barring an Obama tidal wave, we didn't think we had a chance to win any of them and were simply hoping to hold down her margins.

The exit polls also were horribly off. They had us tied in Massachusetts and leading in New Jersey, and generally were too rosy for us everywhere, which had become a common phenomenon. One theory was that our supporters were more enthusiastic about their selection than Clinton's and were more willing to talk to the exit poll workers, skewing the results.

Regardless, over the course of the primaries, the average margin of error on exit polls was eight points. They were meaningless.

But now the press spent a couple of hours marinating in these very positive numbers. So, perversely, Clinton ended up benefiting simply from beating the bogus exit polls. Talk about a clusterfuck to the White House.

It was a night of peaks and valleys as we traded wins. Many of Hillary's big victories came at the beginning of the night, when she held off the threat in states like Massachusetts and New Jersey, winning by bigger margins than predicted by some pundits and a few public (and clearly flawed!) polls. So the early part of the coverage had a very positive Clinton slant to it.

Primaries also report much more quickly than caucuses, meaning a lot of our better news would be aired much later, in some cases after midnight. I kept telling our press staff not to get too wound up about the coverage—what mattered was where the numbers stood at the end of the night. If they turned out as positive as we thought they might, even the most unsophisticated reporters would get their import.

As the night dragged on, what we had hoped could happen began to play out. We won some close primary contests that were important, less from a delegate perspective than from the demonstration of broad electoral viability: battleground state Missouri, Connecticut in Clinton's backyard, and my home state of Delaware, where my wife and family were hooting and hollering as the win was broadcast.

We won Georgia with almost 70 percent of the vote, producing a bushel full of delegates, and to our great satisfaction, we netted more delegates out of Illinois than Hillary did out of New York.

And our effort to create some landslides paid off handsomely. The tale of New Jersey and Idaho is my favorite mathematical example from the entire primary.

New Jersey offered a total of 107 delegates in the primary, Idaho only 18.

Hillary won New Jersey comfortably by 10 points but netted only 11 delegates: the delegate margin was 59 to 48. We won Idaho with over 80 percent of the vote, winning 15 of the 18 total delegates, netting 12. The result was we netted 1 more delegate out of tiny Idaho than Hillary did out of big New Jersey. That's the real story of Super Tuesday.

We ended up losing California by under 9 points, a result we were very pleased with. Our sense was that we actually won primary day but already faced such a huge deficit in the absentee voting that all we could do was narrow the overall margin. California was the biggest delegate prize of the whole primary, with 370 delegates at stake. Hillary netted 38 as a result of her win. But we netted 38 delegates from our blowout wins in Kansas and Minnesota, erasing her gains in California.

Though Hillary's camp achieved their goal of winning the popular vote in big states, we felt we came away from Super Tuesday with a decided advantage. We won 14 of the 22 states to hold contests that day, and netted a total of 15 delegates, besting our rosiest projection. On a day with over 1,600 delegates at stake, a difference of only 15 was essentially a split decision, which for us was an unqualified success. Bullet dodged.

I was talking to Obama throughout the night, including several times after his evening wrap-up speech. On his drive home during the wee hours, I told him we had just been declared the winner in Missouri. "How come all the states we're winning are being called after most people have gone to bed?" he joked. It was true—many we won were out west or caucus states, which take longer to count and report. Some, as in Missouri's case, were just too close to call for hours. "Luckily, we are not in the 1970s anymore," I told him. "People won't have to wait until tomorrow night's evening news to find out what happened. They'll turn their computers and TVs on in the morning, and see what a terrific night we had." Even though we had an early start the next day, Obama wanted to stay up until we had a more complete picture of what had actually happened. We last talked about 1:30 a.m., when I told him definitively we would end the day with more delegates. This pleased him, but after having watched a bunch of coverage at home he was still somewhat annoyed at the way the pundits were scoring the day. "These results are better for us than we or anyone expected," he said. "The question is, will the press cover it that way or will they keep obsessing about California and New Jersey?"

"I think the numbers here will be hard to ignore," I replied. "We'll do a briefing for the press tomorrow and walk through where the race stands, state by state. Then we'll give them a look ahead at the next eleven contests, which we project winning ten to one, and stress that our delegate lead, which now stands at twenty-eight, should grow significantly." I rarely defended the press's coverage of the race, but this was a case in which I thought the enormity of what happened in terms of the broader impact would settle in and be properly captured in the coverage.

I took a deep breath and offered my summation. "Barack, for the first time I feel confident telling you that if we play our cards right in the coming weeks, you should win the Democratic nomination."

He was quiet for a moment before replying. "Tell everybody they did a great job. Talk to you tomorrow morning."

Our boiler room team was still gathering final results and crunching numbers straight through until the morning. I stayed at the office until four or so and went home to shower and start work on the outline of my presentation to the press, which would happen in several hours. Looking out over Lake Michigan, I thought that maybe this whole crazy ordeal would be worth it.

It felt strange to think it, but I knew we should actually win this thing now. And I felt very good about the type of campaign we had run. As I reflected on the Super Tuesday results, I was filled with admiration for our staff and volunteers. They had expertly, creatively, and relentlessly executed our plan. We had outwitted the inevitable Clinton juggernaut. And without our grassroots supporters organizing on their own in states like Georgia, Missouri, Colorado, and Minnesota long before the campaign had any official presence on the ground, there is no way we would have prevailed. This was their victory in many ways. These folks believed when very few people did. They saw what was possible, even more quickly and clearly than we did in Chicago. Our campaign was really becoming the art of the possible, lifted by this grassroots movement that was growing like a gathering storm throughout the country. I think even now about people like Cheryl Jewel, an Atlanta housewife new to politics who became involved after watching Obama at an Atlanta rally in April 2007. She dedicated herself to the campaign for the next ten months, getting trained in organizing by our staff and setting up meetings for supporters in her area, to build our campaign list. When campaign staff finally came to town, she became the office manager. And like Jerry Riley, who was not new to political volunteerism; he had worked on tons of local campaigns over the years. He attended Camp Obama, a training program we had established in Chicago and a few other cities, where volunteers from around the country could receive additional training on organizing—how we did it and why we did it. Jerry decided to dedicate himself whole-heartedly to the campaign, becoming known through the volunteer circle as "Mr. Fix-It"—because of his political connections, he was able to get anything that the campaign needed at a moment's notice (rally permits, sound systems, and so on).

Or like our St. Louis for Obama group, led by Jennifer Haro, Crystal Lovett-Tibbs, and Patrick and Angela Green. They formed the group using My.BarackObama.com and Facebook very early in the campaign and eventually attended organizing training together—though by that point they could have trained many of our staff. They were making it happen on the ground, with no resources, just creativity and passion. The group relentlessly grew the Obama community in St. Louis. When staff arrived in September 2007, the group was asked to focus some of its energy on Iowa, which bordered Missouri. They started weekly van trips from St. Louis to Ottumwa, Iowa, over five hours each way on small, bad roads. They met in a Target parking lot at 5:00 a.m. each week, in order to get to Ottumwa before 11:00 a.m., train walkers, knock on doors, get back in the bus in the early evening, and return to the St. Louis Target after 10:00 p.m. Jennifer, Patrick, Angela, and Crystal would then return the rented vans to the airport, getting home at about midnight. After Iowa, they moved all their energy into the Missouri primary, just a month away. They filled phone banks with the volunteers from the Iowa bus trips to keep the lines filled 100 percent of the time. Our state director, Mike Dorsey, said without their early efforts, all done on their own, and the hard push across the finish line, there is no way we would have won Missouri by the narrow eleven thousand votes that we did.

They were the heartbeat of our campaign.

———

At age forty, sleepless nights were far rougher than when I was a twenty-one-year-old field organizer, but as the dawn broke on February 6, I was filled with energy.

We had some great states in the next weeks and were likely headed for a winning streak. I thought the race was close to reaching a turning point, in our direction.

In fact, the next two weeks would probably be the most fun of the whole two years. But that exhilaration would soon turn to despair, as we faced the greatest threats to Obama's candidacy we would experience in the entire campaign.

8

Ecstasy. Agony.

We rolled out of February 5 feeling strong and surveyed the road ahead. The next two weeks held eleven contests: Washington State; Nebraska; Louisiana; Maine; the Virgin Islands; Virginia; Maryland; Washington, D.C.; Democrats Abroad; Hawaii; and Wisconsin. Total delegates at stake, 537.

Demographically this was a terrific group of states for us, filled with progressive white voters, significant African American populations, and independents who would be allowed to participate. And caucuses. Lots of caucuses.

Our organization and grassroots supporters understood how to win caucuses. The Clinton campaign had performed so poorly in them they took to maligning them. Wolfson and the rest of the Clinton team argued that caucuses catered to a more liberal-activist slice of the electorate and discriminated against working-class voters who didn't have the flexibility to attend a caucus during the scheduled one- or two-hour window.

This argument was total bullshit. The caucus base—those who had consistently attended previous caucuses—in just about every state we polled favored Clinton, in some cases by a healthy margin. She was the establishment candidate, after all, and the establishment attended caucuses, so she started with an advantage. As in Iowa, we had to expand the electorate to win, and our current lead in these states reflected all the hard work we had already put in on the ground. My view was they should shut up and start organizing.

In the wake of February 5, Maine, which had never seemed winnable, began to look more like a toss-up, and we believed our projected margins of victory in the rest of the February states could grow, producing more delegates, maybe even pushing us over 100, which would give us a virtually insurmountable lead in the count of so-called pledged delegates—those awarded based on primary and caucus results.

This was a strange period, filled with two- or three-day mini-campaigns and little on-the-ground stumping by Obama due to time constraints. We had been organizing in all these states for at least the month since the Iowa caucuses (Clinton had almost no presence) and had already been advertising. On February 6, we upped our media buys; we thought our performance the day before, coupled with what should be a nice little run of wins, would make February our strongest fund-raising month to date, so we could gamble a bit financially and pour it on.

We ended up raising $55 million in February, shattering records and surpassing our next-highest fund-raising month by over $20 million. Our list of donors also continued to explode. By the beginning of March we had over a million of them, more than double Clinton's total. In fact, during this period her money situation became so dire that she very publicly lent her campaign $5 million of her own money. This was tactically smart—it roused some of her supporters from the reverie that she needed no financial help, and her fund-raising spiked for a bit. We read it as a sign that she was having serious difficulty reloading month to month.

The days after Super Tuesday also marked the point when the dam began to break open for us with superdelegates: the approximately eight hundred party leaders and elected officials around the country who were given a vote to decide who the Democratic Party's nominee should be.

The Democratic Party established superdelegates during a wave of reform after the 1972 election. McGovern had lost in a landslide, carrying just one state, and the party felt it needed some kind of mechanism to guard against the voters nominating another unelectable candidate. The large number of superdelegates means that in a close race, it is possible (though not likely) that if a mass of them voted together, they could actually tip the nomination to the candidate who came in second with pledged delegates.

The supers had never decided the nomination; voters always delivered a breakaway selection. Even in 1980 with Carter and Kennedy and 1984 with Hart and Mondale—when the race went all the way to the convention—the prevailing candidates both won a clear plurality of the delegates awarded by primaries and caucuses. So far the supers had not affected the outcome.

The body of supers is made up of elected officials (governors and members of Congress are all automatic superdelegates), all the members of the Democratic National Committee, and a smattering of esteemed former party leaders—Speakers, former presidents, among others. They are not bound when voting by their state's or district's election results; they can make an independent judgment—though some do make their choice based on who wins in their area.

On the whole, giving so much power to the supers was not a very democratic approach for the Democratic Party. But those were the rules and we had to play by them, even if it meant taking some time away from convincing voters to work on politicians.

"I had no idea this race could come down to me groveling to party insiders for support," Obama told me after making an hour's worth of calls to superdelegates. "If we win, we need to look at making sure the voice of the voters carries more sway." This kind of obvious unfairness particularly frustrated him. "Half the superdelegates I talk to don't want the obligation anyway—they think it looks bad that party insiders have this role. Some didn't even know they had a delegate vote that could affect the race."

"I agree, it needs to be changed," I told him. "But ironically, to be in a position to fix it in the future we need their support now. If it's any consolation, I'm spending some of my day calling supers too."

"Really?" he asked. "How many have you got to commit so far?"

"One," I said. "But he won't commit until May."

Obama boasted, "I have you beat. Three so far."

"Well, we'll see," I countered, egging him on. "Some of your hard commits might be less firm when we circle back to ask them to announce their support."

Many of the superdelegates possessed their power only because Bill Clinton had appointed them to party positions in the 1990s, and almost all had deep ties to the former first family. But Hillary's lead among this group was not as large as we had expected it to be. We attributed this gap to apathy as well as some real concern about her electability and potential effect on down-ballot races. Because quite a few of them had not committed early to Clinton when she was the odds-on favorite, we thought the whole universe of undeclared supers was up for grabs. The Clinton campaign was notoriously unsubtle; we considered fair game anyone who had managed to resist its entreaties so far.

Before Iowa, she had led us in superdelegates by well over 100, but on February 6, our internal review showed that the count stood at 250 to 179 in her favor. Encouraged by our progress, we set an internal goal of erasing her superdelegate lead by March 4.

———

This two-week period was my favorite of the entire campaign. We scored win after decisive win. Our closest margin of victory was in Wisconsin at seventeen points. We won "toss-up" Maine by nineteen. In the process we racked up an enormous number of delegates, opening a real and sustainable lead for the first time.

The Clinton campaign went through a long-anticipated management shakeup in this period, replacing the campaign manager, Patti Solis Doyle, and her deputy. Thankfully the real culprit behind their underperformance (in our view), Mark Penn, was left in place.

By now many news reports had emerged describing acrimony and huge disagreements in the Clinton camp. These reports suggested Penn was responsible for pushing the message of inevitability and was fighting suggestions that Clinton should be humanized more in their message and ads. Some articles even speculated that Penn did not properly understand how the delegate system worked, and that late in 2007 he still thought delegates were awarded winner take all, not proportionally. I found accusations of such ignorance hard to believe, but it was the first explanation I saw of how they might have developed their flawed strategy for Super Tuesday.

All in all, it was a fun time to be Barack Obama's campaign manager. He was invariably on the road on election nights, usually in a state where the vote was drawing near; there was no sense making a victory speech in a media market where the polls had already closed. The calendar was so aggressive that we needed to be on to the next state as quickly as possible.

Every few days, I got to have the following conversation:

"Well, the press is going to call the race at poll closing. It looks like we blew her out again. We will net at least X delegates, more than we projected."

"This never gets old."

You've heard of baseball fantasy camp? This was like campaign fantasy camp. We were in a highly competitive presidential election that had been tighter than a tick since Iowa and now we were winning contest after contest by laughably big margins against Hillary "Inevitable" Clinton and her massive political machine. Here's a breakdown with raw vote percentages and delegate margins:

State/Contest	Obama %	Clinton %	Delegates Netted
February 9			
Washington State	68	31	26
Virgin Islands	90	8	3
Nebraska	68	32	8
Louisiana	57	36	12
February 10			
Maine	59	40	6
February 12			
Maryland	61	36	14
Washington, D.C.	75	24	9
Virginia	64	35	25
February 19			
Wisconsin	58	41	10
Hawaii	76	24	8
Multiday voting			
Democrats Abroad	67	33	2

I'm not sure any candidate in the modern era has had a run like that in a very competitive overall race. Our average margin of victory was 34—34!—points. We also netted 125 delegates in the period alone, pushing our overall pledged-delegate lead to over 150.

A variety of factors were behind our success. Once again, it seemed like we had outplanned the Clinton campaign. They must have assumed they would clinch the nomination on February 5 and did not concern themselves with states that would come later. Conversely, we had been salivating about this two-week period as far back as the summer of 2007. Carson, Berman, and I were convinced we could dominate this run if we were at relatively full strength coming out of Super Tuesday, though even we couldn't have predicted such whopping margins. Clinton barely had a presence in these states and, for the first time, seemed a little aimless. Their schedule did not always make strategic sense to us, and they seemed unsure of their footing. This was a far cry from the Clinton juggernaut we had feared for over a year. Our respect for their political history and acumen was monumental at the beginning of the race; even now it was hard to believe we were hanging loss after loss on them.

We were able to execute so well because we had long ago put into place in these states what we thought we needed to win. The added boost of resources in the last month allowed us to communicate at an even higher level, but I don't think this extra money made the real difference. Yes, we outspent the Clinton campaign in this period and on February 5. But up to that point both campaigns had about the same amount of money available. We just spent and planned more carefully, following our rigid internal rules of the road on budget matters.

Throughout our organization, it was known that trying to get an idea funded required an airtight pitch, and even that was no guarantee of a check. Staffers were challenged aggressively if they had a new budget request or if their projects came in over budget. Culturally, that was important. Our staff was conditioned to think first about how we could do without and to budget accordingly before looking for more money. This conservative approach gave us a big strategic advantage after our opponent had burned through her money.

Our grassroots supporters again deserve the lion's share of credit. The farther we got from Iowa, the more important our volunteers were. The campaigns in these states were shorter and we had fewer staffers on the ground. The volunteers built our campaigns in the February states and executed incredibly well in the closing weeks. They recruited more help, identified supporters, and made sure people knew where to vote and caucus (an unsexy but critical step when dealing with untraditional voters; if they don't actually vote, their support means nothing).

Huskers for Obama, Virginians for Obama, Badgers for Obama—the groups that emerged very early in the primary and organized for a year while the spotlight was elsewhere are the real heroes of February. When staff arrived bearing more resources and focused goals, followed by advertising and some candidate time, the foundational work of our supporters on the ground paid huge dividends.

Yet throughout the campaign, we never stopped running into people who thought we were going about things the wrong way. During the general election, on a conference call we held with labor leaders, one of Clinton's big labor supporters who had spent millions on her behalf in the primary derided our belief and trust in volunteers. He insisted that we needed to pay people to do things like door-knocking and phone calls, and that we should rely more on local elected official organizations.

"Well, our volunteers certainly did a number on you in the primary," I reminded him.

He was one of many who, even after witnessing the endgame, discounted our grassroots strategy in favor of the old dusty playbook. The way I saw it, we were able to run such a disciplined campaign because most party leaders did not jump on the Obama bandwagon in the early going, and those that did were open to change. We were able to make decisions without a lot of guff from our leading political supporters because they were not in the driver's seat. We had a clear message and strategy to push forward, and volunteers were our engine. Groups and political leaders who supported us were the caboose.

———

Many candidates would have thrown in the towel after eleven straight beat-downs. Not Hillary Clinton. And while I resented it at the time, I had to admire her remarkable resilience. She must have known the odds now were very steep—our delegate count was going up while her bank account was going down—but she also knew, as we did, that she could rely on some pretty big wins in the upcoming primaries, and that in politics anything can happen.

While the Clinton people complained that the press was trying to run her out of the race, we thought the opposite was true. Any other candidate would have been long gone. But reporters and Democratic leaders alike kept telling us that, after all, these were the Clintons. "They're like Houdini," said one Democratic superdelegate I was courting. "It looks hopeless but somehow they find a way to survive. Anyone else, this thing would be over. But in the back of your mind, you're wondering what they may have up their sleeve. So, we let the race play out."

On February 10, the *New York Post* said we were "locked in a dead heat"—after eleven consecutive wins. The race was now all about the pursuit of delegates, and we had opened up a meaningful lead, one we did not think we could lose. The moment marked a critical juncture in our strategy: at this point we needed to shed the mantle of underdog and explain to the political community and press where the race really stood.

Most important, we needed to explain the state of play to the superdelegates.

They made up roughly 20 percent of the total of 4,049 delegates at stake. The magic number to clinch the nomination was half of that plus one, or 2,025. That number became a mantra inside our campaign, just as Iowa had been for all of 2007. It was our new North Star.

By now we could see in our projections that if Clinton stayed in until the end, neither of us would get to 2,025 delegates through pledged delegates alone. We would have more than Hillary but still would need the added support of roughly 200 supers to claim the nomination.

Our operating philosophy, going all the way back to my first plan drafted at the end of 2006, was that the supers would ultimately follow the voters. We did not prioritize their endorsements as a core imperative of the campaign. We communicated with them frequently and certainly celebrated when we got an endorsement, but we assumed that if we did well at the polls, the supers would follow, and if we stumbled early, it wouldn't matter.

Since supers had never come into play before, the media was all over the map trying to present the delegate race to the public. Most news organizations had their own delegate count, and while these were roughly in the same ballpark, there were some significant distinctions from outlet to outlet. Many cable and TV networks started off counting supers and pledged delegates together, a measure that benefited Clinton and misrepresented the real status of the race. Supers, unlike pledges, were not bound by their initial pick, and the pledged number alone reflected the outcomes of the primaries and caucuses, the true measuring stick at this point in the campaign.

We worked over the networks and cable stations very hard on this point, and finally they started showing two graphics, one each for counting pledges and supers. It was a small victory, but we tended to be obsessive about even small things that could affect the outcome.

The *New York Times*, however, was in a category all by itself. In their calculation of delegates won to date, they did not count caucus delegates, where we had an enormous advantage. Their rationale was that caucus states employed a multilayered process: after being elected through precincts, caucus delegates must attend further caucuses at the county and district levels before being officially selected at state conventions. Therefore, the *Times* did not consider these delegates locked up until their selection was set in stone at the state level. Technically this was true, but as a practical matter, the initial caucus results always reflected the final allocation, with only two exceptions: when a candidate dropped out or if one of the candidates did such a poor job organizing for the later rounds that their number of delegates slipped because the other candidate thoroughly skunked them in organizing and attendance.

I thought our campaign had made it quite clear that if we knew nothing else, we knew how to organize for caucuses. It simply wasn't credible to suggest we might end up with fewer pledged delegates than we earned on the initial caucus day; if anything, we might stand to gain a few through better organizing.

Despite the erosion of the mainstream media's once all-encompassing footprint and the ascendance of highly visited political websites and blogs, we were still concerned with how the race was interpreted by leading national outlets. What the *New York Times* said still mattered a lot, especially given the shifting nature of the race: just about every superdelegate read it. When the Gray Lady offered a take on the campaign, either through straight news coverage or frequent political analysis columns, it had outsized impact on audiences we increasingly had to be concerned with. And the paper's distortion of the delegate situation was driving me crazy.

I finally called Adam Nagourney on February 11, after we had won Nebraska, Louisiana, Washington, and Maine by wide margins and opened up our first significant delegate lead. Adam was the leading political reporter for the *Times* and perhaps held more influence than any reporter in the country. I told him that his paper was completely screwing up.

For the next twenty minutes or so, I walked him through the flaw of their delegate-counting process (a frequent topic between us—he actually agreed with me but said it wasn't his decision) and took issue with the fact that they were still writing about the race as a dead heat, even after our run of victories.

"The point is we now have a definitive front-runner for the Democratic nomination," I argued. "We have reached a tipping point. Yet reading the *Times*, which is supposed to be the leading referee and voice on issues like this, you'd never know it." Then I offered an incentive. "You can be the first to explain that the race has taken a dramatic turn. And this is not spin. It is the facts."

What I really wanted out of this conversation was not just a correction of their delegate-counting process but a real affirmation of our advantage in the race. "Of course there's still hope for Clinton, however slim," I told him. "But it lies solely in supers. Obama has almost assuredly wrapped up the pledged-delegate victory. If you believe the supers will not overturn the verdict of the voters—that the winner of the most pledged delegates will persevere—then he's almost certainly the nominee."

Adam was quiet for a minute. "I hear you," he said. "If I can get them to agree, would you be willing to get on the phone with our polling unit, which manages our internal delegate-counting operation, and our political editor and walk through all this?"

"Sure," I said. "Anytime."

The next day, Bill Burton, our press secretary, gathered us in a paper-strewn conference room overlooking the frozen Chicago River for what would be one of our most important conference calls in the primary. It was an unusual gambit—part advocacy, part education, with the nation's most important newspaper. I felt like we were sharing the secret recipe for Coke. Taking this stand carried a risk; for the first time, we were suggesting we were no longer the plucky underdog but the front-runner, based on the math. And being the front-runner had its own set of negatives. Hillary would have a field day with our argument. But it was a price we had to pay.

On the call, I once again walked through our view of where the delegate race stood and how it would unfold, as well as the disservice I felt they were doing their readers by not accounting for caucus delegates. The *Times* folks took it all in and seemed to accept that, if the caucus delegates stayed roughly the same, we had, in fact, reached a turning point. What was a little unsettling was that this seemed to be dawning on them all, except Adam, for the first time.

One of their polling unit members kept coming back to caucuses. "But you're not disputing that those delegate allocations could change through the caucus process, right?"

"No, we're not," I said. "But pledged primary delegates could change as well under certain scenarios. If we both stay in the race, then the estimates of delegates won at caucuses will largely stay the same. Somehow, you have to account for these delegates in your coverage of the race."

They said they would discuss our arguments. And shortly thereafter, we had our victory, of sorts: Adam reported back that they had decided to start counting caucus delegates, but with some caveat included—essentially an asterisk—to indicate that the results were not "final."

This interlude doubtless lacks the drama of the campaign's more adrenaline-filled moments. But our mission was simple—to win. We had reached a point in the campaign where it made the most strategic sense to have our advantaged position in the race reflected in the media.

The *Times* conference call was soon followed by a lengthy Adam Nagourney political column on February 14 that had a deep impact on the superdelegate battle and the conventional wisdom of the race. Talk about an unexpected Valentine's Day gift.

The column was titled "Obama's Lead in Delegates Shifts Focus of Campaign." One of the key sections read:

> A delegate count by *The New York Times,* including projections from caucuses where delegates have not yet been chosen, showed Mr. Obama with a 113-delegate lead over Mrs. Clinton: 1,095 to 982. . . .
>
> By any measure, Mr. Obama is in a much stronger position on Wednesday than he was just a few days ago and in a significantly stronger position than Mrs. Clinton thought he would be at this point. That is because Mr. Obama not only won a series of states, but also won them by large margins—over 20 percentage points—so that he began picking up extra delegates and opening a lead on Mrs. Clinton.
>
> And that is the problem for Mrs. Clinton going forward. If these were winner-take-all states, Mrs. Clinton could pick up 389 delegates in Texas and Ohio on March 4. Now she would have to beat Mr. Obama by more than 20 percentage points in order to pick up a majority of delegates in both states.

From then on, the paper's coverage of the race showed a whole new flavor. We shared this story with every superdelegate (most had read it already) as well as with our entire organization and fund-raisers so they understood how we were approaching the rest of the race strategically, and so, once again, they would have context for the decisions we made.

We heard from supporters on Capitol Hill that this story was an eye-opener for their colleagues, many of whom were undecided superdelegates. One of our key people in the Senate called me that morning: "I know you guys kept preaching the delegate message to us, but until it was in print like this, it didn't hit home," he told me. "Our Hill supporters are fired up, and newly motivated to get their colleagues to join the winning campaign. And a couple of senators supporting Hillary told me they had no idea she was in such a tough position—they felt like the campaign wasn't being honest with them about how they could win."

Motivation and clarity for our team, dissent and confusion for theirs. It was a great way to start the day, kind of like getting an air purifier for our headquarters and rolling a stink bomb into theirs.

There was one other key passage in the *Times* story, which reflected a new gambit for the Clinton campaign. Needing to reassure their supporters and convince superdelegates that there were metrics other than pledged delegates to evaluate in backing a candidate, they developed their own criteria:

Mrs. Clinton's aides said they would also argue to superdelegates that they should give less deference to a lead from Mr. Obama because much of that had been built up in states where there were caucuses, which tend to attract far fewer voters than primaries, where Mrs. Clinton has tended to do better than she has done in caucuses.

"I think for superdelegates, the quality of where the win comes from should matter in terms of making a judgment about who might be the best general-election candidate," said Mark Penn, Mrs. Clinton's senior campaign adviser.

They were now constantly redefining success, and the measurements they invented got more creative over time. I viewed it as their alternate reality. As the Clinton campaign's rationales became more and more desperate, our message remained clear and consistent: whoever wins more pledged delegates will and should be the nominee.

We issued memos, held conference calls, and sent e-mails nearly daily to our entire universe stressing this point. Barack, Michelle, our senior staff, and I called all the superdelegates individually. There was no room for compromise on our part, and supers had to factor that in; left unsaid but not missed by anyone was that if they awarded Clinton the victory after we had won more pledged delegates, the party could be torn apart. None of our supporters would abide a coup without a fight.

I wanted to have this message amplified throughout the press corps, so I decided to do a conference call with all the national press to walk through the delegate situation as we had done for the *Times*. I ran this by Barack, who had loved the *Times* story; it made our position in the race feel more real to him, too. He was gung-ho for the new education project but asked me to be cautious. "Just don't gloat or make firm predictions for the future," he advised. "Lay out the facts and your math."

I agreed, and he seemed satisfied. "It'll be a pleasure to see the race we're running reflected in the coverage," he mused. "It's been a while."

"I would still advise you not to pay attention to most of the commentary," I said. "We've come this far playing our own game, let's not switch gears now."

"I'll leave the TV on the bus tuned to ESPN," he joked. And he did, for pretty much the entire campaign. It might seem funny, but I thought this worked to our advantage; had he regularly watched cable news, we probably wouldn't have run so strong a campaign. A candidate can't help but be affected by constant criticism and second-guessing, so basketball on the bus was a godsend.

Breaking with our campaign's operating philosophy—which was not to talk about the political process—bred another rarity: Ax and me disagreeing. He understood why we needed to make sure the supers knew where the race stood. But he was concerned that to voters, we would come across as cocky and arrogant.

As we were plotting this out, he dropped into a chair in my office and sighed. "I don't like it. This is going to backfire big-time with voters."

He was absolutely right that there would be some downside to the move. Even though Obama would not talk about it on the stump, and we would not engage directly with voters on any of these process issues, naturally the default press shorthand would be "Obama says he has taken a commanding lead." No fool, Hillary would quickly feed off the coverage in the remaining primary states, claiming that we were trying to make an end-run around the voters by appealing to superdelegates.

Axelrod was fairly despondent. "She's going to be out there like Joan of Arc and this will be just like New Hampshire," he moaned. "She's the feisty underdog and we're the big bully trying to prematurely end the race."

"No doubt," I said. "This will cost us with some voters—and she'll use it as a rallying cry. But we have to land this plane. And the pathway to victory now is winning the primaries that we can, but it's also managing the atmospherics so that the insiders don't steal this from us. She's still leading superdelegates today, even after we just won eleven straight."

This last bit seemed to resonate with him, so I went on. "Look," I said, "you and I both know we're going to get thumped in some states down the line. We need the measuring stick to be the race in totality, not a reassessment after every primary. She's going to win more states than we do from here on out; it's much friendlier terrain for her."

Ax put down his sword. We were partners, but on these types of strategic electoral matters, it was my call, just as in matters of message and advertising, I generally gave him the benefit of the doubt. If I had a concern about an approach or language and he felt very strongly about it, I often relented. And he was usually right.

Our new attitude had already produced some cringe-inducing headlines: "Plouffe: She Can't Catch Us"—Politico.com, February 13, 2009.

All of this heat was a necessary side effect of achieving our objective: change the framework for media coverage of the race. The correct frame acknowledged that the race was no longer in a dead heat, that we were going to win the pledged delegates, the only question was by how many, and that supers should support the winner of the pledged delegates as the only relevant metric that mattered. We had to put our heads down and get some beer spilled on us as we ran through the tunnel, confident that at game's end, if we achieved our goal of positioning the race properly, we would be holding up the trophy.

Next up, on March 4, were four states; 370 pledged delegates would be awarded that day. The only friendly territory at the outset was Vermont.

Rhode Island, also on the bill, was small like Vermont and offered a modest amount of delegates. We believed Clinton would win here comfortably and aimed to minimize her margin and delegate haul.

The two big prizes were Ohio and Texas. Two weeks out we trailed in both by double digits, though we had made up some ground from the twenty-point deficits the polls had shown a few weeks prior. These were big states in which Obama had spent no time and where Hillary's numbers were very strong. She had been tattooing us with older voters and Hispanic voters, two groups that would play key roles in these states, respectively.

We had started advertising in all four March 4 states in mid-February. Staff and organization had long been plowing away on the ground. Our most valuable resource, Obama's time, we planned to split between Texas and Ohio, with a possible trip to Rhode Island. Our plan was, first and foremost, to maintain our commitment to a delegate strategy. If we also managed to win one of the two big states, then perhaps Clinton would think about ending her campaign. I explained this strategy to Obama, and he was on board.

Meanwhile, the political pressure for Hillary to abandon her quest was growing. In a *New York Times* article titled "For Clinton, Bid Hinges on Texas and Ohio," a Clinton superdelegate told the paper, "She has to win both Ohio and Texas comfortably, or she's out." No less an authority and interested party than Bill Clinton said shortly thereafter while campaigning in Texas: "If she wins Texas and Ohio I think she will be the nominee; if you don't deliver for her, I don't think she can be."

Texas presented a very unusual situation as it related to delegates. It was the only state to hold a hybrid contest—a primary and a caucus on the same date, the caucus at night. Two-thirds of the delegates would be awarded in the primary and a third in the caucus.

When we alerted the press to this idiosyncrasy early in February (Texas had not had a competitive primary since 1992, so it was new to out-of-state media), their responses and the reaction from the Clinton camp tipped us off that the Clintonites did not have a handle on Texas's unusual way of selecting delegates (it's the only state with a hybrid caucus and primary system). This was hard to believe, especially since Bill Clinton had gone through it in 1992. Regardless, we were already planning ahead and sent our Iowa caucus director, Mitch Stewart, to Texas to manage the caucus side of the operation. We never saw much organizing there from the Clinton campaign.

The delegates in the Texas primary were also distributed a bit unusually: they were awarded by state senate district, and districts with very high Democratic turnout in past statewide elections were awarded proportionally more delegates. This benefited us tremendously, because some of our stronger areas—progressive cities like Austin and African American areas like Houston—were advantaged under this allocation formula. For example, a state senate district in West Texas where Clinton was strong might offer only three delegates total, while a district in the middle of Austin would offer nine, even though both had the same population.

We built our strategy accordingly, focusing on gaining extra primary delegates in our base areas and winning the caucus portion of the contest. If we succeeded, we could win the overall delegate battle in Texas even if Clinton won the popular vote. This delegate-oriented approach had been our bible to date, and we saw no reason to change it.

We were outspending Clinton by enormous sums in both Texas and Ohio. Our fund-raising was on fire, particularly online, and since we were trying to win one of the two big states, we decided to pour it on. I went down to Larry Grisolano's office right after the Wisconsin primary and told him he had another $15 million on top of our already robust budgets in Texas and Ohio. "Let's finish this thing off," I told him. "Let's bury her."

We bought everything imaginable—our TV and radio levels were strato-spheric; we actually bought five days' worth of full-page newspaper ads in all the major dailies in both states. Our Internet advertising was omnipresent. It was like playing with Monopoly money for two weeks.

As well as the campaign was going, I was ready for it to be over. Everyone was. We were dog-tired and sick of the fight with Hillary Clinton. We had been in the trenches for over a year now, with virtually no respite. It was all but impossible to see light at the end of the tunnel.

One Sunday night during this period as I paced around our tiny Chicago apartment on the phone, my wife intercepted me at the conclusion of a confer-ence call and suggested we sit together for a few minutes of companionship and a pep talk. Smiling, she presented me with a small bag filled with tissue-wrapped gifts. "No matter how this all ends," she said, "you have a wonderful life waiting for you. Here are some reminders of what you have to look forward to."

First out was a car air freshener in the shape of a palm tree. It smelled like the beach. Next came a bookmark; it had been a long time since I'd spent an evening with a good book. I unwrapped a wiffle ball, a promise of afternoons at the park with my son. Finally, a white plastic stick, which confused me at first. Slowly I realized I was holding a pregnancy test—and in the little window was a big pink plus sign.

"Wow. Seriously?" I asked. Her smile had grown and a few tears ran down her cheek. "When are we due?"

"We won't know for sure till I see the OB," she said, "but I think we're in the clear." She had already done the math, matching our due date to the elec-tion calendar.

She was almost right. Our baby was due November 2. Two days before the general election. I was over the moon. Win or lose, a baby would assure a quick return to reality and our family life.

———

Our first head-to-head debate with Clinton—a much-anticipated encounter—had occurred back at the end of January in California, at the Kodak Theater in Hollywood, where the Oscars are held. Obama had done quite well; as expected, his style was better suited to fewer combatants. Each candidate spoke for about two minutes at a time, and the rhythm was steady: punch, counterpunch. He gained a lot of confidence after that first debate; "Now I know I can hang with her for ninety minutes," he told me.

In the run-up to the March 4 primaries, Clinton and Obama had two more head-to-head debates, one in each major state. By this point it felt like we'd been going through the same exchanges since the dawn of time. Barack could give Hillary's answers and vice versa. On a conference call shortly before the Texas debate, he gave voice to what we all were feeling. "More than winning, the thing I'm most looking forward to is having no more Democratic primary debates," he said, prompting a rousing chorus of assent. "We've now been debating for a year. And I bet the voters feel the same way we do—they're sick and tired of us." Given this malaise, we simply wanted to survive the encounters with no self-inflicted wounds and get on with the ground campaign.

There were two notable moments in these debates, one in each. In the first debate in Texas, Clinton offered a comment that was immediately read by the press as valedictory and wistful, suggesting that perhaps the end was near.

"No matter what happens in this contest," she told the crowd and the audience watching at home, "I am honored to be here with Barack Obama. I am absolutely honored."

We thought it was quite meaningful ourselves; it was unlike Clinton to display any sort of political weakness, and this seemed to be a window into her personal thinking. Obama also reported that their stage interactions were friendlier than usual, and he thought perhaps she was coming to grips with the reality of the race. But the Clinton camp pushed back hard; they insisted she was simply being polite and that this was yet another example of the press trying to shove her out of the race.

Any illusion that Clinton was preparing a graceful exit went out the window at the Ohio debate, which was moderated by Brian Williams with Tim Russert, who would die a few months later. Throughout the proceedings, Clinton seemed determined to show she was not going anywhere. She made frequent attacks but saved her most meaningful jab for something that played off a *Saturday Night Live* skit.

The previous weekend's show had included a sketch lampooning the media as gaga over Obama, picking up on a message the Clinton camp had been pushing. The skit featured a mock debate at which the faux moderator leads with a pampering question to candidate Obama: "Senator Obama, are you comfortable? Is there anything we can get for you?"

At the outset of the Ohio debate, Clinton was asked the first few questions. Clearly using some rehearsed lines, she tried to make the media's supposed treatment of Obama the story, asking rhetorically why she always seemed to get the first question in debates (which she hadn't). Then she referred to the *SNL* skit, saying, "Maybe we should ask Barack if he's comfortable and needs another pillow."

The press ate it up. For the next twenty-four hours Hillary's answer and the skit played nonstop in the coverage.

I found preposterous the notion that Obama was being carried across the finish line by the press. We were winning the race, and generally candidates who are winning receive more positive coverage. In the fall of 2007 when we were given up for dead, was the Clinton campaign complaining about our coverage? Or after we lost New Hampshire? Of course not.

In fact, if anything, the press seemed to be giving her a much more important pass. The most damaging media scrutiny when it comes to campaigns is of the investigative variety. And from Day One, reporters had been putting us through those paces, examining every episode and era of Obama's life.

Odd though it seems, Clinton had gone through little such scrutiny. We asked reporters and their bosses why they didn't pursue investigative pieces on her. The answers were variations on a theme. "All that's old news," we were told. "It was covered in the '90s." This sounded almost irresponsible. In our view, all the issues from the 1980s and '90s—the travel office, the Rose law firm, and so forth—merited fresh attention, even if only as a bearing to gauge her electability; certainly the GOP would use these episodes against her. And what about the seven years since the Clintons had left the White House?

Personally, I thought many of the Clintons' travails were irrelevant when the Republicans and press went after them in the '90s. But fair is fair. What burned me the most was the Clinton campaign's insistence that Obama was a risky nominee because he had not been adequately vetted. Surely the Republicans would push every possible attack on Clinton in a general election, at which point each node of controversy would once again be newsworthy because it was "new," having not been raised in the primary.

There wasn't much we could do about this—Obama forbade our pushing these kinds of stories after Punjabgate—but I found it frustrating nonetheless.

Our polling in Texas and Ohio improved dramatically over the first ten days of the two-week period. We were essentially tied in Texas and narrowly behind in Ohio. Maybe the eternal primary campaign would finally be over.

Just as we prepared to exhale, the Clinton effort to work the referees in the media began to have an effect. Relentlessly, day after day, they pushed the idea that the press was taking it easy on us. At the start they whispered it in private conversations with reporters but eventually they started openly asserting it in conference calls with the media. Over and over they charged that we were not receiving the kind of scrutiny and challenging coverage befitting a front-runner.

Two gifts materialized for the Clinton campaign, one a self-inflicted wound, the other a mistake from the past coming back to haunt us. These hits caused us to limp, if not bleed, into the crucial voting on March 4.

Austan Goolsbee, an economist who had helped Obama in his 2004 Senate race, was on leave from the University of Chicago and part of the campaign's economic policy team. He was not on payroll and was not quite a staff member, but he was deeply involved in some of our policy development, and Obama trusted him. He was an affable guy but like most college professors, naive to the ways of hardball politics.

Shortly before primary day, one of our press staff got a call from a reporter who said he understood Goolsbee had held "secret discussions" with the Canadian government to assure them that our rhetoric on trade was just that—political talk, not principled beliefs.

Obama had been campaigning vigorously in Ohio against unfair trade deals, promising that as president he would renegotiate NAFTA to make it fairer to workers and protect the environment. Manufacturing jobs fleeing to countries like Mexico and China had decimated Ohio, and Obama believed that NAFTA was a flawed trade deal. But he also believed strongly in trade and had supported trade deals in the Senate that included labor and environmental protections.

The campaign's message on trade at this point was admittedly simplistic; a witness to the Ohio campaign might have been left with the impression that our position was no different than that of Dennis Kucinich, an ardent anti-trader. Our message lacked nuance; our TV ads and mail pieces were stridently critical of NAFTA and offered little evidence of Obama's more complex take on trade.

Meanwhile, Hillary was shortcutting her own trade record, trying to suggest that although NAFTA passed in her husband's first term, she had been neutral in its passage and now was an avowed opponent of such trade deals. This claim was soon shown to be preposterous. Several quotes emerged capturing her in full-throated support of NAFTA, and we quickly disseminated the relevant passages to mailboxes and answering machines. As the mini-debate over NAFTA positions swirled, participants from a 1993 White House meeting on the trade agreement came forward and recalled her as offering strong support for the deal.

She was caught red-handed and we should have had an opening. Instead we were caught in our own bumbling response to Goolsbee's Canadian adventure. When first questioned about the reporter's claim, Goolsbee explained he had been invited to the Canadian consulate in Chicago not in his capacity as an Obama adviser but as a University of Chicago professor. He was given a tour of the embassy and engaged in some chitchat but never got into any official or even memorable discussions about Obama's policies.

Armed with this information, we forcefully pushed back the notion of back-door discussions. We thought there might be some dirty tricks at play on the part of the conservative government north of the border but brushed it off as a tempest in a teapot.

Shortly after this I held a press call, trying to set expectations for March 4, and found myself asked repeatedly about the Canada situation. I fully denied any merit to the story, asserting confidently that Goolsbee had not been visiting on behalf of the campaign or even with the campaign's knowledge. It was truly a social visit, I insisted; certainly we did not offer a wink and a nod to the Canadian government that our trade position was hollow politics.

Then a memo surfaced, leaked by someone in the Canadian government, and suddenly the NAFTA saga went from burning embers to a full-scale firestorm. The memo was from a Canadian embassy employee in Chicago, reporting to Ottawa on our adviser's visit and stating flatly that Goolsbee had reassured the Canadian government that their trade rhetoric was just politics and would be softened once we were out of Ohio and had secured the nomination.

It looked like we had lied about the interaction. The press was in full lather and Clinton struck hard on the campaign trail in Ohio, asserting that workers couldn't trust Obama because he was not being straight about trade; he was saying one thing to them and another to the Canadians.

The story was a direct hit on Obama's character and took an immediate toll. It also dominated the press coverage for a few days, sapping all of our momentum and rolling back the gains we'd made in Ohio. I still maintain that we got sucker punched here; maybe the worst thing our adviser said—and we put him under intense interrogation to get the facts—was that our position was more nuanced than its presentation on the campaign trail. It didn't matter. Our protests were no match for a leaked memo.

Still reeling from the trade blow-up, we were further damaged by a bomb from the Clinton campaign. On the Friday before the primary, they released a new Texas ad titled "3 a.m." Using ominous images of defenseless children sleeping in the dead of night, the ad implied that Obama could not be trusted to keep the country, or its families, safe in a crisis.

The press nearly soiled themselves from excitement over the ad's drama and continued to obsess about it throughout the remaining months of primaries. At times it seemed like they wanted more blood on the floor in our race and embraced explosive tactics to produce it.

Within hours we had a response ad out, making the point that Hillary's judgment had already been tested on Iraq and proved unsound. On a call with national reporters, I pushed back on the ad.

"Senator Clinton has already had her red phone moment," I told them. "It was a decision whether to allow George Bush to invade Iraq, and she answered affirmatively. She didn't read the national intelligence estimate; she didn't even do her homework."

Our response was largely lost in the shuffle. Reason is no match for bloodlust when it comes to making good TV. The press played her ad over and over, always noting that it came on the heels of our NAFTA blunder. This coverage eventually bled beyond cable punditry to straight reporting and analysis on all three national networks, with heavy local coverage in Ohio and Texas.

And like that, we were on our heels heading into Tuesday's crucial primaries. Our field numbers did not suggest a freefall, but we were certainly trending down. Then on Monday, twenty-four hours before the contests that we'd once hoped could end the primary, things got even worse.

In the last year, Tony Rezko, a real estate investor and deal maker of all kinds, had grown into a persistent problem for Obama. The Obamas had bought a new house in 2005 and the sellers were selling a vacant, developable lot as well as the house and would not sell the house without simultaneously selling the lot. The Obamas were not interested in the lot but mentioned it to Rezko, who was interested.

The *Chicago Tribune* broke this story, suggesting that Rezko was doing Obama a favor and pointing out that the lot sold for full price but the house below the asking price. The sellers—who had no connection to Obama— strongly disputed this and said the Obamas' bid was the highest one they had received. Nonetheless, the suggestion of something shady persisted and the reporting was woefully inaccurate. Reporters stated that "Rezko subsidized the Obama purchase," "Rezko enabled Obama to get a sweetheart deal." Flat out false. Obama copped to poor judgment in the initial *Tribune* story, saying it was a "boneheaded move."

Rezko was one of Obama's key fund-raisers throughout his career. As hard as the press and our opponents looked, we looked harder to find any favors Obama might have done for Rezko. And we found nothing. Zip, zilch, nada. Rezko raised money for Obama but got nothing in return.

But things grew more complicated in October 2006, when Rezko was indicted and charged with multiple counts of fraud and bribery related to Illinois state government. None of the business involved Obama. Yet in what had to be some of the worst timing ever for our campaign, his trial was set to begin on March 3—the day before the primaries.

The start of Rezko's trial offered a perfect chance for the news media—and the Clinton campaign—to revisit him and fully explore his connection to Obama. Rezko was the lead story that night on all three networks, and while they were all careful to say that this was a political problem for Obama and not a legal one, the presumed guilt-by-association did damage enough.

We decided to have Obama hold a press conference that day in hopes that taking on some of this stuff directly might defuse it. Interestingly, Obama's instinct was not to talk to the media. This was unusual for him; he generally thought we did not schedule enough full-blown press conferences. But we pushed him because we thought it was important, and he acquiesced. The press coverage was going to be horrible no matter what, we reasoned, so perhaps by standing there and taking questions, he would at least get credit for not ducking this rough period.

Wrong. The press conference was a disaster. The reporters were hostile, their questions accusatory, and his answers weak. Obama was visibly perturbed to be there. Press reports even kicked him on the way he went out the door, noting that Obama "fled" the press conference after finding himself besieged by a fusillade of tough questions.

He called me afterward. "Plouffe, you guys threw me to the wolves!" he said. He was laughing, but I could tell he was rattled.

"We screwed up," I acknowledged. "Apparently, nothing is going to go right in the close. It's one shit sandwich after another."

We hobbled into voting day about as lamely as possible. Our momentum had not just stalled; it was pretty clear from our data and public polling that it had shifted in Hillary's favor. That meant Ohio was gone, though we still thought we could keep the delegates close there. In Texas the question was not whether we would win the delegates—we felt very confident about that—but whether our turnout operation could make up for the loss of support with swing voters enough to eke out a popular-vote win.

The day before the vote, I drafted a memo that attempted to put into proper perspective what we thought would happen the next day. We sent it to the press and to our key supporters, and posted it on our website. The memo reviewed the probable results through the prism of the overall race, not the overheated conclusions we felt sure would be drawn that night. I wrote it assuming we would lose both big states—and that this infernal primary would go on for a long time.

Fearful that too much significance would be placed on Hillary's likely wins, we strove to remind the political community where the race stood broadly. The math was still the math. It was called "The Real Meaning of March 4th," addressed to "Interested Parties." After reviewing various recent Clinton pronouncements about momentum, I summed up these points.

By their own clear definition of where they expected and believed they needed to be after Ohio and Texas, the Clinton campaign will fall terribly short on March 4th. The Obama-pledged delegate lead stands at 162. The question for the Clinton campaign if they do not significantly erode that lead on Tuesday is what plausible path they have to even up the pledged delegates in the remaining contests. There are 611 pledged delegates left after March 4th's contests. They would need to win at least 62 percent of all remaining pledged delegates to get back to even. And while they have often talked about Pennsylvania—where public polls show their lead deteriorating rapidly—the Wyoming caucuses on March 8th and the Mississippi primary on March 11th could potentially result in more pledged delegates netted to the winner than on March 4th. So it is clear that narrow popular vote wins in Texas and Ohio will do very little to improve their nearly impossible path to the nomination—they will be facing almost impossible odds to reverse the delegate math. While the Clinton campaign gamely continues to try to move the goal posts, at some point there has to be a reckoning. It is a very simple question: what is their path to secure the nomination? No amount of spin can change the math. We look forward to their tortured answers on Wednesday morning.

Tuesday, I flew down to San Antonio, where we were holding our event on Election Day. Obama was playing his traditional primary day basketball game when I got to the hotel, so I went for a run. I ran by the Alamo, fervently wishing Hillary would face hers that night.

After all the problems with exit polls, you'd think we would have completely ignored them on primary night. They were like counterfeit money. But we were just desperate enough for good news that we couldn't put them down. March 4's exits showed us tied in Rhode Island, ahead slightly in Ohio, and tied in Texas.

Much as we liked them, these numbers made no sense. The only possible explanation was that our turnout was much stronger than Clinton's. And while we thought that might be possible in Texas, where there were a lot of new younger voters and a surge of African Americans, in Ohio our ability to expand the electorate was fairly limited.

Axelrod, Margolis, and I sat with Joel Benenson, our lead pollster, in a conference room at the San Antonio hotel chewing on results as they came in. Our boiler room in Chicago was updating numbers in real time, running and rerunning the models that told us whether we were ahead of or behind projections. We were also obsessively refreshing the media sites that were posting votes.

It was clear early in the tallying that the Ohio exits were woefully off (as were Rhode Island's; we lost by 18 percent). We'd be lucky to hold the margin under 10 in Ohio. The press waited to call it until well after it was clear to us we had been hammered. When they did, and Hillary emerged to give her victory speech, I wanted to throw the TV through the hotel window.

We also got news around that time that John McCain had wrapped up his nomination that night. His general-election campaign would begin the next morning. I sighed heavily just thinking about it: ours could be three wearying months off.

In the conference room we had now turned our prayers to a split decision. Muttering turned to something just below a yell, "C'mon, Texas! Don't fuck us."

Obama gave his speech before Texas was called. It was a pretty desultory crowd (many people were still at the caucuses) and his energy level was low. He was off his game and disappointed in the results. Before he took the stage, I gave him the latest update: though we led in early voting, we would probably lose Texas unless turnout in the remaining Hillary areas was unusually low and ours was very high. After the speech, I called him with confirmation: we were going down. The media wasn't calling it yet but they would soon.

"It goes on," he said quietly. "I'll see you tomorrow."

Our conference room was a den of gloom. Half-eaten sandwiches and soggy coffee cups were scattered across tables. We all did a lot of cursing and sighing. It didn't matter that two weeks earlier we'd had no chance to win either big state. In the intervening days, we had moved so quickly that the prize was in our sights. Now we had blown it.

Once the media called Texas, we packed up our laptops and left somberly for a short night of restless sleep. Without the final delegate data (there were some caucuses in addition to the direct voting), we found it hard to put the proper frame on how fundamentally unchanged the situation was.

It wouldn't have mattered. The press was not interested in delegates. There was only one story: Hillary Clinton had staved off elimination, and Barack Obama had failed to close the deal. The commentators also quickly moved to what the results could mean to superdelegates; Obama had done poorly with working-class older whites in Ohio and Hispanics in Texas; did that indicate a looming electoral problem that Clinton could use against him? So began a fierce debate about electability in the general election.

The Clinton campaign maintained that we would struggle in the general election with blue-collar voters, seniors, and Hispanic voters, and that the Republicans would find ways to make their swiftboating of John Kerry look like child's play. They rejected our claim that we could change the electoral map, asserting that the question would really come down to which of us could flip Ohio and Florida to the Democratic column on November 4, not who could put new states in play. Their argument got a lot of attention from the press and political community. Obama's "electability problems" became a new narrative for us to fight through, less in terms of how voters processed the argument than how it was received by the few hundred superdelegates who now held our fate in their hands.

For trail-weary campaigners, it felt like unnecessary misery, largely because the fundamentals of the race had not changed—our pledged-delegate lead remained close to insurmountable, we had almost caught Clinton in superdelegates, and we simply saw no avenue for her to win. In fact, the numbers had gotten much worse for Clinton.

There had been 370 delegates at stake on March 4, a sizable haul. Despite all the significance granted to her Texas and Ohio victories, the final delegate breakdown of that day was Clinton 187, Obama 183. She netted only 4 delegates! Meanwhile, a big chunk of real estate was taken off the board. It was now virtually impossible for her to get our pledged-delegate lead below 100, much less erase it.

I was certain that eventually the reality of the delegate math would reemerge as the dominant story line: yes, she had extended the campaign, but in fact her position had grown only more tenuous.

I planned to discuss this the next day with Barack and Michelle as we drove from the hotel to the San Antonio airport. We were all headed back to Chicago for a meeting to assess what had happened and how we would handle the seven weeks before Pennsylvania.

As the motorcade idled in the bowels of the San Antonio Marriott the next morning, I mentally reviewed the points I wanted to make from the third-row seat of our SUV. A few moments later the Obamas emerged from the elevator bank and climbed in.

"Morning," I said, aiming for cheerfulness.

"Hey, Plouffe," replied Barack. He seemed fine. But Michelle was not in a good place. Her quiet "Good morning" seemed clipped and distant.

Barack and I talked about the results, where the delegates stood, and what the press coverage was like. I tried to get a laugh out of him, saying, "Well, at least we won Vermont." He ran with it. "See, Mich," he said to his wife, "at least we won something last night." No response. Barack tried another time or two to lighten the mood, as did I, in the spirit of helping a friend with his spouse, but all we got were uninterested, monosyllabic responses. Michelle was giving us both the cold shoulder and it continued on the plane ride home.

I stewed in her tacit criticism. Sure, we had stumbled at the end. But our position in the race was fundamentally unchanged. And, hey, look at where we had come from. Nine times out of ten Hillary Clinton should have won the nomination. Yet here we were, still in the catbird seat, set to assume the Democratic mantle. Hillary Clinton *was* the Democratic establishment. Things never go as planned on campaigns.

The loss seemed easily papered over. But as the plane made its way back to Chicago, and I spent the hours staring out the window at nothing, I began to see that Michelle had a very valid point. While we were pinching ourselves at having come so far, the undeniable fact was that we had missed our chance to close out the race.

This primary would now go at least another two months, maybe three, because of our failure. If we had closed out the primary, Barack and the rest of us would have had more time to spend with our families as we ramped up to the general election; everyone could have recharged a bit. Instead of spending more interminable weeks fending off Hillary Clinton, we could have planned more methodically for the general election.

We had also delivered our Republican opponent a rare gift in politics—three extra months of practically unopposed campaigning. It occurred to me that we might have just cost ourselves—and our party—the presidency.

As I reflected on this and thought harder about our March 4 losses, I tried to go beyond the surface explanation that these were tough states for us and we had closed poorly. I bolted upright in my seat when it finally dawned on me: for the first time in the campaign our strategy had been off. We should have put aside our delegate chase for these contests and gone in for the kill in Texas, trying to win the popular vote. We should have focused at least two-thirds of our effort there instead of splitting our resources with Ohio. Thinking back through our efforts, I realized we hadn't even campaigned vigorously in the Hispanic areas of Texas or in many of the rural and small-town areas, where Clinton annihilated us. We focused our time and attention only on the areas where we could net more delegates.

If we had gone all-in, we would have had more time to campaign all over the state. If our schedule and other activities had been based on a statewide vote goal, we just might have pulled out a win in Texas. We lost by only 4 percent statewide; more time and focus might easily have changed 2 percent of the electorate.

Maybe it wouldn't have worked. But it hadn't even been considered. And that mistake rested on only one set of shoulders—mine. I was responsible for our electoral strategy, from making the decisions on our direction all the way down to design and execution. And I had not even considered adjusting to a Texas-focused popular-vote scenario until that moment on the plane.

The close in Texas also hearkened back to the finish in New Hampshire, where we wound up on the defensive. Michelle was right to be upset about the outcome. This was our race to win, and we had just coughed up our best chance to close it out. My head had been deep in the sand.

The consequences were severe, especially when I thought about how we had just given John McCain, a formidable general-election opponent, a significant leg up. What if we lost the presidency, and my lack of judgment and foresight resulted in the continuation of Bush economic policies; of an abysmal war in Iraq; of fraying international relations? Those were the stakes.

On our ride in from Midway Airport to our HQ in Chicago, I shared my thoughts with Obama, sparing him the drama but trying to explain how I thought I had failed to adjust our strategy to meet the moment.

"I hadn't thought about that either, but it makes complete sense," he responded. "I did feel like we were going through the motions a bit, that we were just moving forward after Wisconsin without asking the tough questions about whether our strategy was correct for the next challenge.

"In any case, we can't let it happen again," he continued. "This is your job. Maybe you need more time to think—whatever it takes, you need to figure out how to stay ahead of the game on electoral matters like that. But we all played a part in coming up short."

Our meeting at HQ included Obama and our senior staff, a group of about fifteen. We met like this infrequently but had scheduled this gathering before we knew the outcome of March 4, hoping to discuss how we would segue from the primary to the general election. Instead we had a discussion about mistakes, changes, and the challenges ahead. There was a lot to talk about.

Obama started the meeting with a critique of his own performance. To have a boss willing not just to shoulder blame but to do so first established an indescribably healthy dynamic. It made people less defensive and more open with their own critiques, of themselves, him, and the campaign as a whole.

His major point was that during those last two weeks, he had not been driving toward the finish line. He wanted the race to be over more than he wanted to win it, and it showed in his day-to-day performance, most notably at the disastrous Rezko press conference the day before the vote. We had become too predictable and stale. He felt he needed to regain the pre-Iowa mentality and suggested we all did. And he needed to regain the bounce in his step and the sense of mission that had seemed to abandon him in the last two weeks.

Moving on, we discussed the two small contests coming up, Wyoming and Mississippi. We thought we would win both, and probably comfortably.

Looming after Mississippi was a seven-week stretch before the next primary, Pennsylvania, a contest we were already dreading. Unless something very surprising developed, we had next to no chance of winning. Demographically, it was one of the worst states for us in the whole country—older and more blue collar—and independents were not allowed to participate. Hillary had the support of Governor Rendell and most of the in-state Democratic machine. And Pennsylvania was one of the few states where the machine was still formidable.

We decided at this meeting that we would campaign hard in Pennsylvania but not exclusively. Indiana and North Carolina were two weeks after Pennsylvania, so we would spend time there as well and potentially in some of the states holding contests even later. Michelle had already told Barack she was all-in for the run in North Carolina and Indiana and would find a way to devote close to full-time campaigning for these two weeks. She knew the stakes and wanted to finish out the race now. We wanted the race to be viewed by the press—and ultimately the supers—as in its last stages. To take some of the focus away from Pennsylvania, our mantra would be that Pennsylvania was just one of thirteen states remaining. There were 607 delegates to be awarded in these states, and we looked at them as a body of contests; all that mattered was whether Hillary could dramatically cut into our delegate lead.

The Clinton campaign was already calling Pennsylvania the "New Iowa," trying to move the coverage and analysis of the race from our broad advantage to the narrow question of who would win Pennsylvania. We were determined to avoid playing into the all-or-nothing trap that was being set for us.

It was a sound strategy. But soon, a reverend from Chicago would explode on the scene, upending our best-laid plans. Electoral strategy took a backseat, as we were quickly engaged in a desperate fight for political survival.

9

Agony. Ecstasy.

Had the Clinton campaign approached the entire primary as they did Wyoming, it probably would not have changed the ultimate outcome. But it might have.

It was clear to both campaigns that Obama would win the Wyoming caucuses. We had been organizing for months and built up a solid lead. In a change from their approach to prior caucuses, however, the new Clinton regime decided to compete in Wyoming in an effort to hold down our delegate yields. They placed staff—albeit late—and both Hillary and Bill campaigned there in the closing days with other surrogates. It paid off for them in delegates.

We still won by a big margin, 61–38. But if the Clintons had not made that late effort, we almost assuredly would have gotten over 62 percent, which would have grown the delegate spread from 7–5 to 8–4 in our favor. Whether the Clinton campaign fully appreciated this lesson, I don't know. "It's a good thing they wised up so late in the process," I told Jon Carson that afternoon. "Super Tuesday could have been a different ball game entirely."

We also won Mississippi, as expected, netting a total of nine delegates in the two contests and erasing Clinton's gains from March 4. That's all it took.

There were now just 611 pledged delegates left to be allocated in the remaining contests, and our lead was just over 160. It was impossible—barring cataclysmic collapse—for Clinton to get within 100 pledged delegates of us. She had zero chance. Too little real estate left on the board.

We fixated on 100 as the magic number based on conversations with undeclared and undecided superdelegates. If our pledged-delegate lead never slipped below 100, there was virtually no chance that the supers would do anything but break en masse to us and deliver the nomination officially.

Meanwhile, we remained in a frustrating limbo. Obama's eventual nomination was all but assured, but we had to play out the remaining contests. McCain was already gallivanting around the country, running for president as the Republican nominee. Our race dragged on and on and on, with Clinton grasping on to faint hope that we would self-destruct in some way that would cause the supers to determine Obama was not electable, voters be damned.

That hope grew stronger when the Reverend Jeremiah Wright burst back onto the scene as we headed into the seven-week death march toward Pennsylvania, which voted on April 22. Those who missed him the first time around with his quotable zingers in *Rolling Stone* surely got a full dose of him now.

Wright was Obama's longtime pastor at Trinity United Church of Christ. He married Michelle and Barack, and baptized the adult Obama and his children. In Obama's early years at Trinity, the two men were quite close.

After their girls were born, the Obamas attended Trinity less frequently. Barack was traveling a lot, further cutting down his attendance, and his relationship with Wright was not as close as it had been. But Trinity was the Obamas' faith home, and Wright was the flamboyant and forceful leader of the congregation and parish.

Of course, we knew as early as Obama's announcement speech that Wright would be a problem. Our research team had reviewed some of his sermons but not all. Many of them were available from the church for purchase. Researching them was as easy as buying them all and screening for problems. This was not brain surgery.

We didn't do it. But one of our opponents or their allies apparently did. Wright's extreme views had been bubbling just below the surface for months, but they finally burst through into mainstream consciousness on March 12 when ABC News and then Fox News began playing excerpts of his most inflammatory sermons on constant, endless loop.

The snippets that were being played on Fox were real doozies:

"Not God Bless America. God Damn America!"

"The USA of KKK."

"We have supported state terrorism against the Palestinians and black South Africans, and now we are indignant because stuff we have done overseas is now brought back into our own backyard. America's chickens are coming home to roost." (This right after 9/11.)

Within hours these tapes were running on all the other cables and the networks and flooding the Internet. They were inescapable. It felt like being in a madhouse.

And the worst part? We were seeing the clips for the first time. The lapse was unforgivable, and ultimately it was my failure. I knew how explosive the tapes could be and should have confirmed that every frame of the greatest threat to Obama's candidacy had been thoroughly assessed. The press and our opponents would unquestionably go through them in detail, and throw the worst moments at us, and now it was finally happening.

We had also failed to discuss the various options we might explore vis-à-vis Wright. We never raised with Obama the idea of leaving the church, or discussed with him in any detail how we would respond if inflammatory statements were to emerge. We were in denial. In any competitive enterprise, you need to know everything your opponent knows about you and limit the number of surprises by getting out damaging information yourself before it can be used to sucker punch you. We knew this, but acted like novices.

Hour after hour, the wall of TVs in the campaign press office featured all Wright, all the time. He filled every screen, his purple robe billowing, eyes ablaze, ranting and spewing invective. I had to stop looking up at the TVs. It grew too painful.

HQ was morose. Ax and I sat in my office and tried to think of the best way to deal with this. "Maybe we just have to ride it out," I suggested. "Be calm, make clear he disagrees with the statements and try our best to create a distance."

"It would have been easier to distance ourselves last year," Ax rightly replied. He was fuming that we had got caught with our pants down on this one. "But we didn't do the damn research, so now it looks reactive. Honestly, I don't know if we can survive this. But maybe I'm just having trouble seeing with a ton of bricks sitting on my head."

"So far, the superdelegates are holding," I reported. "But they're nervous. They want to see how we handle this and if we can dig ourselves out. Before this, I thought we were a one-hundred-percent lock to get the nomination. Now I think it's dropped to eighty percent—we could hemorrhage."

"Really?" responded Ax, droll as always. "Because right now it feels like I'm hemorrhaging plenty."

Our initial response to the controversy was formulaic and consistent with what we had said when asked about Wright previously.

"Let me say at the outset that I vehemently disagree and strongly condemn the statements that have been the subject of this controversy," Obama said. "I categorically denounce any statement that disparages our great country or serves to divide us from our allies. I also believe that words that degrade individuals have no place in our public dialogue, whether it's on the campaign stump or in the pulpit. In sum, I reject outright the statements by Reverend Wright that are at issue."

We also made clear Obama had not been in church when Wright made the statements being circulated. Altogether, though, it was a woefully inadequate response. We were doing due diligence and making pro forma responses, but Wright's statements were filled with bile and hatred for America, and required a stronger comeback. Many of us have heard things from the pulpit we disagreed with, but this was far beyond the pale. It threatened to undermine the profile we had spent fifteen months building: Obama was someone who sought to and would bridge divides, a man of deep faith, a steady leader and pragmatic problem solver.

These tapes raised grave doubts in voters' minds about that portrayal. They were hungering for more information about Obama and Wright. Did Obama hear these sermons? If so, how could he not walk out? Were these snippets par for the course for Wright or rare moments of departure? Was Wright an adviser now and someone Obama would rely on for advice?

On a call, Axelrod, Gibbs, and I pressed Obama for what he knew.

"I don't recall any of these parts of these sermons," he said with not a little exasperation. "From time to time—and it was fairly rare—Wright would say something I thought crossed the line or was even in poor taste. I would often come up to him after and say so, and he and I would sometimes have heated disagreements. But I'm positive I never heard anything like this."

I had assumed this was the case, but it was still relieving to hear it from him.

"I went much less frequently in recent years," Obama continued. "And if you talk to people who attend Trinity, they will tell you he has gotten more erratic over time. But these excerpts simplify Wright. Most of his talks are about love and support and fairness. It's a wonderful church community with a pastor who is mostly positive but can draw outside the lines sometimes."

Armed with this information, we had to face a barrage of questions from the press. Had he been in the pew for any of these excerpts? No, we said definitively. But that raised another set of questions. Can you tell us the dates of all the services he did attend? Would he have quit the church had he heard them? What sermons had he found objectionable?

And of course rumors were flying that tapes would emerge any minute showing Obama nodding, applauding, and generally whooping it up to Wright's inflammatory statements. This was a Grade-A shitstorm.

Our press staff could not answer these questions. Obama would have to, and pronto.

The Wright story broke on a Wednesday and exploded across the media landscape the next day. We decided Obama had to take questions about this head-on on Friday, in a series of lengthy national cable interviews.

There was one not so minor complication. He was already scheduled to do editorial boards that Friday afternoon with both Chicago papers about Tony Rezko, two hours each, no holds barred. Given no choice but to address Wright as soon as possible, we decided we would do a round of TV interviews on him directly after the Rezko boards. It shaped into quite a day, like having your legs amputated in the morning and your arms at night. The question was whether we would still have a heartbeat at the end of the day.

The Chicago papers would be loaded for bear at their sit-downs with Obama. Even though they had asked him plenty of questions about Rezko through the last year and a half, we had not given them an opportunity to poke, prod, and look for inconsistencies at length. They would put him through the paces and then some.

And we had tactically mishandled questions about Rezko, adding fuel to the fire. Because Obama had nothing to hide, we should have done this session right at the start of the campaign to lance the boil. But we stubbornly refused, too concerned about creating a negative story line. It was myopic and a mistake. Some in the press felt we were being cagey and thought, with some justification, that we must be hiding something or afraid of a full airing-out.

Obama finally got fed up and demanded we schedule the Rezko interviews, so we did. Now the Wright interviews would immediately follow. It was like asking someone to scale Mount Everest and then saying, "Nicely done, now on to Mount Kilimanjaro." But we had no choice.

Obama came into our HQ that Friday a couple of hours before the first editorial board to prep with Ax, Gibbs, me, and Bob Bauer, our invaluable campaign attorney. We ended up doing only about fifteen minutes of Rezko prep before deciding we needed to release a fuller statement on Wright, one that might soften the blows he would get that night on CNN, MSNBC, and Fox. Obama looked at our draft statement and decided he needed to rewrite it. So as we were peppering him with the likely questions he would receive on Rezko, he was redrafting our comments on Wright.

It was chaos and, quite frankly, frightening. I felt like the wheels could easily spin off our whole venture. Still, Obama was the pillar of reassurance. "Don't worry, guys," he told us while making some notes on a stack of pages, "I can do more than one thing at a time. We are taking the trash out today. It won't be fun but we'll be stronger for it."

A little while later, Barack and Gibbs left for the first editorial stop at the *Tribune*. Bauer, Ax, and I looked at each other with trepidation. If there had been thought bubbles above our heads they would have read "We are screwed."

But Obama handled everything with brilliance. The editorial boards, though grueling, went well. They resulted in positive editorials from both papers, which were rightly seen as the official judgment on the Rezko matter. The Rezko problem never went away completely but eventually faded in importance because Obama had faced the toughest jury on the matter and satisfied them of his innocence. His success in putting the Rezko matter to bed only underscores our error in delaying the reckoning. Clearing the air up front would have mitigated a lot of heartburn, especially in the days before the Texas and Ohio primaries.

He also handled well the additional questions the boards threw at him on Wright, partially because in Chicago the reverend was known and understood in fuller context, whereas the rest of the country knew him only from the looped snippets of venom. The hometown papers were familiar with the great ministry at Trinity and the church's work with kids and the disadvantaged, and to them, Wright wasn't the monster he had become across the country.

Obama went on to do a terrific job in the Wright interviews on CNN, Fox, and MSNBC. But as we watched from the office, Ax and I knew that while Obama's assurances might staunch the flow, we would continue to bleed.

Obama called me after eleven that night, while my wife and son were sleeping. As with almost every call I took, made, or participated in from home during the campaign, I spoke with him while shut into our bathroom. We had a small apartment, and it was the only room in the place where my talking would not wake my family.

All campaigners know there's no glamour in our work; perhaps the best example of this from the Obama story is that significant parts of his presidential campaign were run or hashed out in that small, spartan bathroom. For two years, when I was not on the road, I led just about every crack-of-dawn conference call from that bathroom. When I think back on the campaign, this is the first image that comes to mind: me sitting on the lid of a commode, or pacing back and forth two steps each way, in front of the tiny bathroom mirror in that awful echo chamber. Another important lesson: if you ever run a presidential campaign, spring for an apartment with an extra room.

On this night Obama got straight to the point. "I thought the interviews went well," he said. "What did you think?" I concurred. We both let out a breath. "So we survived," he went on. "But it feels really unsatisfying—to me and I'm sure to voters. Wright will consume our campaign if I can't put it into broader context. This is a moment where conventional politics needs to take a backseat. I think I need to give a speech on race and how Wright fits into that. Whether people will accept it or not, I don't know. But I don't think we can move forward until I try. I know you guys may disagree."

Obama had raised giving a race speech back in the fall. At the time, Axelrod and I strenuously disagreed, believing that we should not inject into the campaign an issue that for the most part was not on voters' minds. Now we were in a much different situation. I agreed that a traditional political move—the damage-control interviews we had done that night—would not be enough. But a speech was fraught with peril. If it was off-key it could compound our problems.

"I think that makes sense," I told him, "but we have to work through a lot before we pull the trigger."

He said he was calling Axelrod and that after they spoke he wanted me to call Ax and then conference him in; the three of us would make a decision. "I don't want a big meeting or conference call on this," he told me. "You and Ax and I will arbitrate this. But know this is what I think I need to do, so I'll need an awfully compelling argument not to give this speech. And I think it needs to be delivered in the early part of next week and I need to write most of it."

The logistics of pulling off the speech in a matter of days were daunting, especially considering he had very little time to work on it—his schedule was jammed, and we agreed we could not break it without generating campaign-in-freefall stories.

First, though, we had to hash through the concept. Axelrod and I spoke a few minutes later and quickly decided we were in uncharted waters. There was no playbook for how to handle something like this. It had never been done.

"He really wants to give this speech," I concluded. "And I don't have a better idea. Do you?"

"Nope," said Ax. "And since he has the majority of the voting shares, we should tell him we think he should proceed. And pray that somehow we can survive."

Ax began to fret about the real-world problems of constructing the most important speech of our candidacy largely on the fly, when I interrupted. "Look, let's call him and walk through it," I said. "We'll do the speech but he has to own the reality of the time constraints."

We conferenced Barack in. "So?" he asked. "What's the deal?" We told him we agreed with the speech but that it was going to be hard to put it together.

"Tonight is Friday—well, Saturday morning," I said. "We have to give this speech no later than Tuesday. You have a full schedule in Pennsylvania the next three days. It has already been publicized. If we start canceling events it will fuel the impression that we're panicked and our candidacy is on the rocks."

"No, we can't cancel anything," Obama interjected, "but I already know what I want to say in this speech. I've been thinking about it for almost thirty years. I'll call Favs in the morning and give him some initial guidance. And I'll work on this during downtime in the hotel room each night. Don't worry. Even if I have to pull all-nighters, I can make this work."

We were flying by the seat of our pants. Somehow we had to keep faith that it would come together.

Obama asked if he should come home to Chicago to give the speech. I said no, we shouldn't break stride, and raised the prospect of giving it at the National Constitution Center in Philadelphia, which I had visited with my wife shortly after it opened in 2003. "I assume you'll talk about race from a historical context, and the Constitution Center sets that tone," I argued. "It's as good a backdrop as we're going to get for addressing the weaving of our racial history."

Obama and Ax liked this idea, and we decided to move forward. Tuesday morning. Philadelphia. An as-yet-unwritten speech that would likely determine the future of our candidacy.

Monday morning, Michelle called me. It was very rare for her to express an opinion on something like a venue, but she had some concerns regarding the location we had picked. "I think Barack needs to be in a bigger setting for the speech," she told me. "He needs to see supportive faces and to be boosted. The Constitutional Center sounds great in theory, but it can only fit about a hundred people after the press is accounted for. We need energy and fight and passion, not something that will come across as a dry lecture."

I understood where she was coming from. This was going to be the most raw and important moment of her husband's political life. Of course the instinct would be to seek as hospitable and uplifting a setting as possible.

But we thought setting this speech at a rally, where people would be applauding and boisterous, could create an unwanted sense of distance from his real audience, the American people, when he needed more than ever for them to feel personally his sincerity and desire to connect. This needed to be a sober speech, and we needed a crowd to match.

I double-checked with Alyssa and with Anita Dunn, who by now had taken on an über role overseeing communications planning and research, to see if they thought we were making a mistake going with the Constitution Center. They strongly thought we needed to stick with the plan. So I went back to Michelle and laid out why, her reservations notwithstanding, we thought the NCC made the most sense in terms of location and size.

Michelle was very good in moments like this. She didn't raise many questions about the campaign broadly, but when she did, it was with good reason. Once she determined we had worked things through thoroughly, she was generally satisfied, and that was the case now. We were on for the Constitution Center.

I did not see the speech until Obama e-mailed it to Ax, Favs, and me very early the day it was to be given. It was stirring, and while I doubted it would put Wright to rest entirely, I thought it should be received very well in all quarters and give us some room to move forward with the campaign. Ax wrote Obama a one-line e-mail response: "This is why you should be President."

Whatever the reaction of the rest of the country, our campaign staff agreed with Ax. As we watched the speech from Chicago HQ, all other activity ceased; our bus depot of an office fell totally silent. Many on our team were crying. We had varied backgrounds but were all deeply proud to be working for this man. Though most of us over twenty-five, and certainty those over thirty, had worked on many campaigns and had become hardened operatives, we still shared a certain idealism. Our candidate was living up to our expectations not just for him, but for any leader. Instead of talking down to the country, or ducking one of our nation's toughest issues, he wrapped himself in it, took a step back, and tried to give us all some context. His goal was not simply to mitigate political damage, but to try and raise our discourse.

The speech received rave reviews from political commentators and spawned hundreds of positive editorials. The *Dallas Morning News* put it this way: "Has

214 The Audacity to Win

any major U.S. politician in modern times ever given a speech about race in America as unflinching, human and ultimately hopeful as the one Barack Obama delivered yesterday? Whether or not the speech satisfies critics of Mr. Obama's close relationship with the Rev. Jeremiah Wright, this remarkable address was one for the history books."

"[T]he most articulate and profound speech on race in America," added the *Sacramento Bee*, "since the Rev. Martin Luther King Jr. proclaimed, 'I have a dream,' in 1963."

More important, voters also responded very well to it. Wright still bothered them—but they respected how Obama dealt with the issue.

As was the case throughout the campaign, most people did not watch the speech on TV. It was delivered on a Tuesday morning, when just about everyone was at work. Instead, people watched it online, most of them on YouTube, either as it was happening or at their leisure later that day or in the days to come. Eventually, tens of millions of voters saw the speech through various outlets.

This marked a fundamental change in political coverage and message consumption, and one that will only continue as technology rolls forward: big moments, political or otherwise, will no longer be remembered by people as times when everyone gathered around TVs to watch a speech, press conference, or other event. Increasingly, most of us will recall firing up the computer, searching for a video, and watching it at home or at the office—or even on our cell phones.

As a result of Obama's race speech and our subsequent ability to start working other message points, our numbers finally began to bounce back a bit. But we had no chance to win Pennsylvania. Our best hope was to keep it relatively close, minimize the Clinton delegate haul, and try to mitigate the overheated political analysis suggesting we could not close Hillary out.

Both candidates had strong bases in every state, and even though we had taken the upper hand mathematically in the campaign, Hillary was still a formidable candidate. Very few voters cast their ballots based on the delegate tallies. They made individual determinations. Some states were jump balls, with the outcome unclear. But in most we could predict with a high level of accuracy what would happen based on the makeup of the electorate.

Pennsylvania was one of the best states in the entire primary for Clinton, with its older electorate, closed primary system, and a sympathetic state party apparatus. Despite that, we campaigned hard to cut down her lead. Obama

Barack Obama announced his candidacy in Springfield, Illinois, on February 10, 2007.

The road show. Much of the campaign was spent on planes. Here Obama confers with his body man, Reggie Love, and Eugene Kang.

David Axelrod, our master strategist.

In the bumper cars at the Iowa State Fair in 2007, the Obamas enjoyed a moment away from the campaign.

Flashing a few dance moves, Barack and Michelle led a parade of supporters to the site of Iowa's 2007 Jefferson–Jackson Day dinner.

Obama on the soapbox in Iowa.

The brain trust shared a moment before a debate in Nashville, Tennessee: Axelrod, me, and Robert Gibbs.

Democracy in action: a crowded Iowa precinct on caucus day.

Hillary Clinton's surprise win in New Hampshire delivered one of the greater setbacks to our campaign. Her victory swung momentum back in her direction.

The support of Senator Edward Kennedy and Caroline Kennedy provided Obama with a huge boost heading into Super Tuesday. Congressman Patrick Kennedy is at the left.

Bill Clinton was a major presence, with mixed results, on the campaign trail for his wife.

Our local campaign offices weren't glamorous but they were effective. Here a volunteer plows through another day of phone banking.

Obama loved speaking directly to supporters. Here he made a personal call to a voter.

A lighter moment on the campaign plane: David Axelrod with our dedicated press and advance staff.

Obama enjoyed shooting hoops on the trail whenever possible. Here he played with the members of the University of North Carolina Tar Heels.

The controversial speeches of longtime Obama pastor Jeremiah Wright caused much grief for the campaign, especially in the weeks leading up to the Pennsylvania primary.

Obama on the trail in southwest Virginia, the much more conservative region in what the campaign saw as a must-win state.

No one expected the massive turnout for Obama's public event in Berlin, Germany, in June 2008.

After the brutal primary, it was time to bury the hatchet: Obama and Hillary campaigned together in Unity, New Hampshire.

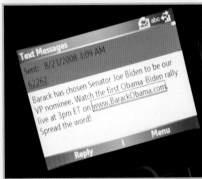

Those who shared cell phone numbers with the campaign received a text informing them that Obama had picked Joe Biden for the number-two spot on the ticket.

Back in Springfield where it all began: Obama and Biden at the official announcement of Biden's selection.

I gave a speech to a modest crowd at the Democratic National Convention in Denver. "I hope you have pictures to prove to your kids that you actually spoke," Obama joked with me.

Sarah Palin became a political sensation when John McCain made her a surprise selection as his vice presidential nominee.

Obama's convention speech at Mile Hile Stadium drew nearly eighty thousand people and was the first to be held outdoors since JFK's in Los Angeles in 1960.

I stood in for John McCain during a debate walk-through.

The emergence of questions about Obama's relationship with former radical Bill Ayers dominated coverage for several weeks in October.

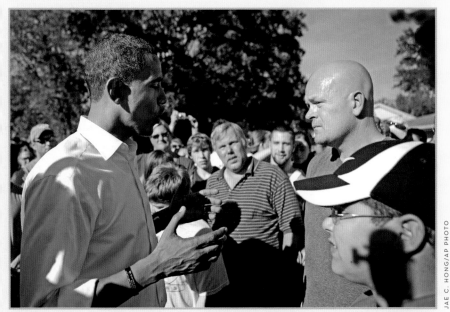

Joe the Plumber became a minor campaign celebrity after his conversation on taxes with Obama. At the final debate, his name was mentioned twenty-five times.

Obama won all three debates with McCain, including the town-hall–style debate at which McCain was favored.

Watching election night returns.

Networks called the election for Obama at 11 p.m., EST, unleashing a wave of jubilation among supporters across the country.

went on a six-day bus tour, crossing the state from west to east. He shook hands and did retail politics in small communities, visiting sports bars (during NCAA college basketball's March Madness) and even infamously bowling a few frames, during which he threw more gutter balls than strikes.

The bowling session was read by most reporters as a gaffe—he only rolled a 37, and they said he was trying too hard to fit in and look less "elitist." But voters viewed it differently. Many voters saw Obama as a gifted figure, very calm and collected, who made few mistakes. His willingness to try something he was not good at, under a withering media spotlight, was refreshing to them.

The incident hadn't been scripted. He and our great supporter in the Keystone State, Senator Bob Casey, were supposed to shake hands with bowlers and leave it at that. But Casey and Obama decided it would be fun to throw a few frames, much to the chagrin of Dan Pfeiffer, our message policeman on that trip.

"The bowling I don't mind," I told Obama that night. "But at least you could have taken off your tie. In the pictures you and Casey look like accountants going office-bowling."

He laughed. "Just make sure the press staff makes it known I did not bowl a thirty-seven," he said. "I bowled a thirty-seven in six or seven frames. Sure, I was bad, but at least let the record show I would have broken fifty."

Throughout the rest of the campaign Obama occasionally pined to go bowling again; he wanted to expunge his record with a better performance. I found this both amusing and insightful. Despite his calm demeanor, Obama was prideful and competitive, and hated that he had failed so utterly at something.

Things had stabilized in Pennsylvania until Obama made his biggest unforced error of the entire campaign. I happened to be in western Pennsylvania, doing a round of interviews about the primary and meeting with some of our volunteer team leaders, when all hell broke loose.

The popular blog *Huffington Post* ran a story from a woman named Mayhill Fowler. Fowler, who had actually contributed to our campaign and was part of Huffpost's citizen journalist brigade, had attended a recent San Francisco fund-raiser featuring Obama and surreptitiously made an audio recording of Barack's speech.

In it, Obama made some cringe-worthy remarks: "You go into these small towns in Pennsylvania, and like a lot of small towns in the Midwest, the jobs have been gone now for twenty years and nothing's replaced them. And they fell through the Clinton administration, and the Bush administration, and each successive administration has said that somehow these communities are gonna regenerate and they have not.

"And it's not surprising then they get bitter, they cling to guns or religion or antipathy to people who aren't like them or anti-immigrant sentiment or anti-trade sentiment as a way to explain their frustrations."

Fowler reportedly agonized for days about whether to post and release the comments. She knew it would cause us major problems. Finally she talked to an editor who told her she had an obligation to make them public. Fowler agreed, and suddenly we were back in major damage-control mode.

The first problem was that once again we were blindsided. None of us knew he had made the comments. The event staff hadn't flagged it. We normally recorded everything Obama said, but, inexplicably, we had failed to do so at this event. We never made that mistake again.

I couldn't imagine a worse context for him to have made such boneheaded comments: standing in a room full of wealthy donors in San Francisco—to much of the country a culturally extreme and elitist city with far-out views—speaking in anthropological terms about the middle of the country; describing the setting, it really couldn't sound much worse.

I called Obama immediately. He began to make a somewhat halfhearted effort to explain what had happened. First, he focused on the fact that he did not know he was being taped.

"C'mon," I said to him, "in the world we live in, you know there's a terrific chance that anything you say anywhere could be captured."

He quickly shifted gears. "It should be clear what I was trying to say," he argued. "But I really did mangle the words. It didn't dawn on me at the time that I had misspoken, but looking at the transcript now, I really don't know how the hell I constructed my point like that."

I told him we would just have to fight through this. We'd say that the words were chosen poorly but the point is valid—economically stressed voters feel like their voices aren't heard, that their struggles take a backseat in D.C., and that all too often efforts are made to distract and divide on social issues.

He was very quiet. A moment later he was going into an event and we had to wrap up. "I felt like we were really beginning to hit our stride again," he said. "And this will set us back again. I can't blame anyone but me for this. I'm sorry."

That might be the only time in twenty years in politics I saw a candidate confront a setback so honestly. In my experience, politicians almost always look to blame someone else, circumstances, being tired—anything but accepting responsibility. And it's not just politicians. It's human nature.

With as light a heart as I could muster, I said, "Well, I'm just glad this broke after I left the meeting in rural western Pennsylvania. Most of the discussion was about how to convince people you weren't going to take their guns away. Had this come out while I was there, I might have been bitter. At you."

The incident was in many ways an updated version of George Allen's Macaca moment from 2006, when he was caught on video making racially insensitive comments. In the world we live in, nothing is private. At any time, someone could have a small video camera, audio recorder, or cell phone camera. No room was safe; anything the candidate said could be captured and launched on the Internet and then taken up by the mainstream media, ginning up a first-class crisis.

When I was coming up in politics, the saying was, Don't put anything on paper you don't want to see on the front page of the *New York Times*. The new adage should be, Don't say anything you don't want posted on YouTube and whipped around the Internet at warp speed. We were spared to an extent in that there was no video of his comments in California, and the audio recording was not great quality. The words were still replayed incessantly, but because online video is now king, the clip didn't get the play it might have.

My flight back to Chicago was delayed several hours. Once all the conference calls wrapped, I wandered over to the airport Chili's for some comfort food and a beer. It was crowded, the Pittsburgh Penguins game was on, and in between some cheers and boos I picked up a conversation about "Bittergate," which was just in its infancy. The gist of it went like this:

"So maybe this is who he is after all," a guy at the bar said to his buddy sitting next to him. "He hid it for a while, but now we see he looks down on us if we hunt, go to church, lead normal lives. Just like the rest of the Democrats."

"Maybe, but maybe he just messed up," his friend replied. "It doesn't sound like him. I'm going to put him on probation."

That was music to my ears. Eyes lifted to the hockey game, I thought maybe we'd get put in the penalty box but not thrown out of the game. If the bitter comment had happened the previous fall, before he was as well known, we might not have recovered. But people now had enough of a sense of Obama to know that the statement was discordant with his whole approach and demeanor.

As I was leaving the bar I passed a full-size replica of Franco Harris (who was supporting us) of the Pittsburgh Steelers making the Immaculate Reception back in 1972, the most famous catch in Pittsburgh sports and perhaps in NFL history.

I thought to myself, "Franco, could we just get one friggin' break here, and not have to keep catching balls right before they hit the turf? How about a nice slant route where the ball is thrown perfectly and we get a clean run, like back in February?"

The Pennsylvania primary was never going to be easy for us and there was nothing immaculate about our performance. We fought through the "bitter" comments and actually had some success turning Clinton's inevitable attacks on the issue against her. She lost no time calling us "elitist" and "divisive," and began making the assertion that we were now damaged goods with rural and small-town voters in the general election.

Obama struck back immediately, ridiculing her as the new tribune for hunters and the working class. A line he completely ad-libbed, "She's running around like Annie Oakley," was my personal favorite.

The Clinton campaign returned fire—wrongly, in my view. In politics you have to know what issues to lean into and when to leave your opponent punching into the wind. By trying to capitalize on it politically, they gave us an opening and we took it. Our response ad called out their attacks as more of the divisive politics that have let our country down. These comments will do nothing, we told voters, to create jobs or lower the price of gas. It was reminiscent of a tack Bill Clinton took against George Bush in 1992 when he declared, to great effect, that political attacks have never educated a child. It worked for Clinton in 1992, and it also worked for us.

Pennsylvania was a roller coaster. We started way down. Climbed to within shouting distance after our bus tour. Plummeted after Wright but then began to bounce back after Obama's speech on race. We dropped again after Bittergate, but as we pivoted off the Clinton attacks, we began to see some positive movement again. Hillary would still win, but it seemed we might keep her margin to five or six percentage points and minimize her net delegate yield.

Two events in the closing days stopped any momentum we had and handed Clinton the big win she desperately needed.

Our lone Pennsylvania debate took place six days before the primary in

Philadelphia, on April 16. This was our twenty-second primary debate, and Obama had won or tied the three previous one-on-one meetings with Clinton.

Not this one. Our prep was a disaster. I wasn't there, but I received constant e-mail updates from Ax. Obama was arriving late and leaving the sessions early. He was unfocused and generally annoyed by the types of questions he knew were coming: Wright, bitter, his viability with white voters. He fiddled with his BlackBerry constantly, e-mailing Valerie Jarrett concerning various rumors about Wright: whether he was going to start speaking again, what those close to him were saying his next move would be, and other distracting chatter.

He called me before taking the debate stage. I said I had heard debate prep was spotty and that this match promised to be brutal; he needed to pull himself together and have a strong ninety minutes. We had not made our decision public yet but had determined internally that this would be our final primary debate.

That's the card I played to get him to focus. "If nothing else," I urged Obama, "get excited that this will be your last primary debate. One year, twenty-two debates, and dozens of forums later the nightmare has finally come to an end. You will never have to debate Hillary Clinton again. Never."

He chuckled wearily. "I'll get my game face on but this one's not going to be fun."

His prediction was more accurate than we imagined. Moderators George Stephanopoulos and Charlie Gibson spent the entire first half of the debate pummeling him. Sidestepping substantive issues, they led a cook's tour of all our campaign controversies: Wright. Bitter. Flag pin. They even introduced Bill Ayers, a former domestic terrorist and acquaintance of Obama's who would later assume a starring role in the campaign.

At first Obama handled the interrogation with characteristic poise. But as it ground on and on, he grew increasingly on edge and stopped trying to segue back to our message. The barrage of questions forced him to play defense, and he got pounded.

The debate halted our momentum and particularly hurt us with women in the suburbs of Philadelphia, still a prime battleground at that late date. I was furious at the moderators and was not alone; they received a torrent of criticism for their handling of the debate. The relentless negativity exemplified why people get disengaged from politics. Yes, Barack needed to address in a public forum his relationship with Wright and the sentiments he expressed on bitter Americans. But with all the other issues facing the next president, these subjects did not merit half of the debate between the two Democratic contenders.

On shaky footing already, we mishandled the close of the Pennsylvania primary. Rather than turning Clinton's negativity against her, we got down in the muck again. On the last weekend of the primary we addressed a bogus Clinton TV ad tying us to Dick Cheney on energy with an overheated response of our own claiming Clinton was in the pocket of big oil. We even attacked her for misrepresenting the particulars of her trip to Bosnia as first lady; she said she had come under sniper fire when pictures from the trip showed her in a calm setting receiving flowers from schoolchildren. The Bosnia episode hurt her, because it struck at her credibility and received an enormous amount of coverage, but adding fuel to the fire was unnecessary and discordant with Barack's message of a new politics. We were thinking small and forgetting who we were.

We paid for it on primary day. Clinton beat us by nine points in Pennsylvania. It wasn't a shock but it was painful. The national narrative quickly centered on two questions: Why couldn't Obama close the deal? Did he have a lasting problem with seniors and working-class whites?

Looking at the larger, long-term picture, there were some rays of sunshine poking through the storm clouds of the moment. Amazingly, after Bittergate, Wright, bowling, and a terrible debate, we left the Pennsylvania primary with generally high favorability ratings across all spectrums of voters. They didn't vote for us in large enough numbers, but we had actually improved our standing over the six weeks. Obama campaigned hard, and these voters saw us fight wave after wave of adversity. Despite its outcome, and the scars it left, our primary battle in Pennsylvania significantly strengthened our chances of winning the state in November. We had spent more time there than in any state but Iowa, with the same eventual outcome: even voters who did not participate in the primary got a heavy dose of Obama. Ultimately it gave us a big leg up against McCain.

There was another long-term payoff as well. We registered a lot of independents (and some Republicans!) so they could participate in the primary. It didn't help us much then, but it did help our cause greatly in November.

Many voters who liked both candidates simply chose Hillary in the primary. That did not mean they would not vote for Obama in November. The suggestion that primary results predicted general-election outcomes was silly, but that was the narrative of the moment. I was absolutely confident that, come November 4, the Democratic nominee would get 90 percent of the Democratic vote. The desire for a change from Bush and his policies was so great that just about everyone would come home to their party nominee. The deciding factor in the general election would be independents; McCain held real appeal to those voters. We also believed we could peel off over 10 percent of the Republican vote in select battleground states and drive historic voter turnout among young voters and African Americans.

That's how we saw it. And fortunately most superdelegates agreed. But the margin of our Pennsylvania loss guaranteed another six long weeks of fighting through the fog of Clinton's opposing view.

The only silver lining the night of the Pennsylvania primary was that I had promised that if we finished within four points I would jump into the Chicago River. The first exit polls were woefully off and had the race a dead heat. I wasn't checking water temperatures just yet but there was buzz in the office that I might be getting wet. Unfortunately, I stayed dry.

10

Closing the Door

We had a meeting of the campaign's senior staff at the Obamas' house the night after our brutal loss in Pennsylvania. After the girls were in bed, ten of the senior staff gathered around the dining room table with Michelle and Barack. Bowls of nuts laid out for us to munch on served as dinner, though few of us had any appetite. The room was tense.

Obama started by laying out what he could have done better in Pennsylvania. He did not spare himself and was particularly critical of his debate performance and having allowed us to get sucked into a tit-for-tat with Hillary.

"I want us to get our mojo back," he said. "We've got to remember who we are."

Then we went around the table and took turns suggesting ways we could improve our performance. Soon our discussion moved to the critical primaries thirteen days away, May 6, in Indiana and North Carolina. We were up in North Carolina by double digits and trailed slightly in Indiana.

Obama said flatly that he still agreed we were going to win. But he did not want to stumble to the finish line and end up a wounded nominee. Winning Indiana would be hard, but he thought we should try.

"We need to go all-in," he told the table. "We have to try to finish this now. Even if Hillary stays in for another month, if we push hard now we will have won the nomination, not backed into it. And I'll campaign round the clock. I'll do anything you ask. Right now, we're teetering. We need to regain our foothold."

He was right. This meant ceding some margin in North Carolina, both in raw votes and delegates. It marked the first time we approached a set of contests with political victory and not delegate acquisition as the core of our strategy. It was what we should have done in Texas.

No one dissented. We were betting the house on Indiana and would barnstorm the state, campaigning very close to the ground with few rallies. We would not engage with Clinton, at least not on the air.

At Obama's request we also started regular, nightly calls with him and the senior staff at the end of each campaign day. These centered almost exclusively on message as opposed to budget, operations, or political matters. We went on to do these every night until November 3; sometimes they lasted five minutes, sometimes an hour, but they were important for a number of reasons. First, it was good to download the day's events with him as a group. The staff had been in a rolling conference call with each other for eighteen months at that point. Obama talked mainly to Gibbs on the road and to Ax and me on the phone if we weren't traveling with him, for updates, to bounce around new ideas, and to share what our surrogates and opponents were up to. The three of us were the conduit to the rest of the senior staff about Barack's thoughts and concerns.

Now, with all relevant parties on the phone, we could more efficiently adjust remarks planned for the next day and, occasionally, even retool the entire day's message focus. And for those senior staff who so far had had little direct contact with Obama, it helped to give them a better sense of what he was thinking.

These discussions were also efficient in that they allowed Barack the opportunity to raise whatever was on his mind without having to call or e-mail a bunch of us individually. Ax and I still often talked to him after the staff call about more strategic matters, but now he could deal with speech edits, a question about a surrogate he saw on cable who was off-message, and the interview roster for the next day, all in one fell swoop.

It quickly became clear to me we should have been doing these end-of-the-day calls since Iowa. Anita Dunn ran these discussions for the whole campaign and did a fantastic job keeping us on track. They effectively rounded out our other regular staff calls at 7:00 a.m. and 6:15 p.m. as the sound tracks of our lives.

Before we left Obamas' house the night after Pennsylvania, I made one sobering point. The Reverend Wright was reemerging during this crucial two-week period. He was scheduled to do an interview with Bill Moyers in two days, a speech in Detroit that Sunday, April 27, and then, most disturbingly, a speech and a Q&A session the next day.

"Even if we're lucky," I warned the group, "and he doesn't completely blow himself and us up, half the coverage in the next thirteen days will be about Wright. The timing could not be worse. Even if he conducts himself like a Boy Scout, day after day his sermons will be all over TVs and the Internet." Everyone was exhausted, and my observation was greeted with weariness and I think some fear. "His events will be covered like debates," I continued. "They'll be the biggest thing going on. It'll make it that much harder winning Indiana, where Wright has numbers worse than the Ebola virus."

His first two events went off without our getting too wet. In fact, he came across in the Moyers interview as less racial bomb thrower than quiet, studious intellectual. He still led the news and his sermons were once again ubiquitous, but this was as good as we could have hoped for. The campaign had no contact with Wright at this time, so we had no idea what to expect.

Watching his Detroit speech Sunday night, prepared to fold into a fetal position at the slightest provocation, I almost exhaled at the end when I realized we'd made it through unharmed. Certainly not what I would have scripted, but for Wright, it was fairly docile and not inflammatory. Perhaps, miraculously, we were going to dodge a bullet. Two down, one more Wright event to go.

And then, Monday morning, eight days out from primaries that could make or break us, the dam burst. Our worst enemies could not have designed an appearance by Wright that was more damaging. Speaking at the National Press Club, he was divisive, hateful, bombastic, conspiracy-crazy, and just generally repugnant. He said he thought the U.S. government might have deliberately spread HIV in the African American community. He compared American military efforts to terrorism. He said that Obama "does what politicians do," and that Obama's denunciation of some of the language in his sermons was "based on electability, based on sound bytes, based on polls."

I was sitting at my desk in Chicago watching it unfold, on the phone with Obama as he drove to the airport. I tried to describe for him what was happening, but eventually my description broke down into sheer negativity. "This is worse than anything we could have expected," I moaned. "It's like a *Saturday Night Live* sketch, but it's real." I was slumped in my chair, chin planted on one hand, staring at Wright on-screen with a mixture of venom and bewilderment.

Barack was crestfallen. I don't believe he was even thinking about the political damage this would do. Despite their disagreements and the distance that had grown between them over the years, Wright was still his pastor, and, more important, the pastor of a church community Barack loved and respected. In that moment, most of all I think he was hurt.

As the speech wrapped up and I went quiet, Barack was as down as I have ever heard him. He quietly told me he had to go, and he wanted to watch the whole performance for himself that night.

The press smelled blood and it was clear Barack had to say something immediately. We gathered the press traveling with us and he went on record as saying that he disagreed vehemently with Wright's remarks, that they completely went against the grain of all he believed and all his campaign represented.

He wanted to do our nightly call after he had watched the speech on YouTube. That call, which took place well after midnight, was short and to the point. Obama said he needed to go out in the morning and make clear how repugnant he found Wright's comments and that he could no longer stand by him—the reverend had crossed a line and permanent separation was the only acceptable recourse. Obama also raised the possibility of leaving Trinity but could not yet bring himself to do so, mainly because he thought it would be devastating for the community.

I asked if he wanted Favreau to draft some remarks and he quickly said no. "Only I can do this."

The next day, Obama held a press conference and said that Wright's divisive outburst contradicted "everything I am about and who I am." He was particularly outraged that Wright suggested his Philadelphia speech was political posturing. He called the reverend's comments "divisive and destructive," "wrong," and "outrageous." The separation was unequivocal.

Our initial research suggested that voters once again accepted how he handled Wright. There even seemed to be relief that the Band-Aid had finally been ripped off. But Wright had taken a toll on our standing in crucial primary states. In our polling, and confirmed by what we were getting back from the field, Clinton's lead in Indiana had opened way up, by more than ten points. Obama still led in North Carolina but the margin was shrinking.

We desperately needed an assist. And then, amazingly, we got one. Our salvation came jointly from Clinton and McCain, though this wasn't clear at the outset. Once again we found ourselves in a situation where we defied conventional political wisdom, and were rewarded for it.

Gas prices were soaring; in most states it cost $4 a gallon or close to it. The idea of suspending the federal gas tax for the summer, billed as a way to give consumers relief, was gaining traction in Washington. Both Clinton and Mc-Cain jumped on it.

Obama had two major problems with the proposal. First, the relief to drivers was minimal, perhaps a savings of only 30 cents a day. Washington would proclaim it a major fix, pat itself on the back, and call a papered-over problem solved. Barack thought this was a perfect illustration of what was wrong in Washington: short-term political gimmicks trumped tough choices that might put us on the path to energy independence.

Second, suspending the gas tax, which channels revenue to federal and state highway projects, would cause many construction projects to cease for lack of funds, costing tens of thousands jobs and delaying much-needed work.

We did no polling before we made a decision. Obama simply laid out his position on a conference call: "I just can't be for this. It's nuts. It's the opposite of leadership." We had no idea how the politics would play out. But the political playbook certainly suggested we were making the wrong move.

We decided to go whole hog with it in the closing days of the Indiana and North Carolina primaries. We would convert most of our advertising dollars to support an ad spot on the issue, figuring we could just ride the debate all the way in and use it as a proxy for our larger message: political calculations and Washington politics were failing the country.

Clinton clearly thought this fight was working for her, too. She ran ads suggesting we were thumbing our nose at hard-working Americans, and implying that in the real world, a few dollars was a big deal. From her ads' perspective, Obama was an elitist who did not understand the pain higher gas taxes were causing.

At first we were charging uphill. But a fascinating thing happened as the days went by: support for the gas tax repeal began to slip in both states, especially in North Carolina, where college-educated white voters in particular quickly began to move away from the idea.

And as support for the tax fell, support for us rose. Some of the voters we had lost with Wright were returning to our camp. They seemed to be saying, "This is the Obama I remember. Someone different, willing to take tough stands and fight the status quo."

It felt good for us, as well, to wage a lonely fight both against our opponents and conventional Washington thinking. "For the first time in a long time we feel like us," I told Obama.

———

We had one of our semiregular National Finance Committee meetings in Indiana on May 2, the Friday before the state primary. After the October meeting in Iowa, we made a tradition of holding NFC meetings in the war zone, so our fund-raisers could get a better feel for what was going on in key primary states and also spend some time knocking on doors and making phone calls.

Going in we knew this would be our roughest finance meeting so far. Four days out from the primary many pundits were predicting a blowout loss for us in Indiana and suggesting there was an outside chance we could also lose North Carolina.

Already in the state campaigning, Obama swung by the meeting. He chose not to cheerlead. He told the room we were being tested and would come out stronger for it and expressed confidence in the final outcome.

Still the room crackled with a kind of strange paranoia. For the first time in a long time, the financial bedrock of our campaign seemed to believe that we could let the nomination slip away from us. And it was not just them—their anxiety was shared by many of our grassroots supporters across the country. We kept a close read on the mood of our volunteers and found a mixture of frustration and dejection. They, too, wondered if at the eleventh hour we could lose.

I decided to lay it on the line. This group had become like family, had been with us through thick and thin. I owed it to them to speak plainly.

I told them Wright, Round II, was a real threat to our candidacy. It had put us in a deep hole in Indiana and caused real erosion in North Carolina. We thought we were climbing back because of the gas tax fight and also believed our organizations in both states were superior. I thought we would finish better than expected and that our performance would have a very positive impact on superdelegates. We had a good grasp of whom they were going to support and when, and we believed that well over two-thirds of them would come out for us in the next few weeks or right after the final primaries in early June.

We had enough private commitments to get us over the finish line. The only thing that could stop us would be the utter destruction of our candidacy, from external assault.

I hated to see some of our oldest and most fervent supporters in the grip of doubts, feeling we were on a glide path to victory only two months ago and now wondering if we were in an irrecoverable tailspin. Yes, I told them, we were fighting through a tough patch. But the structure of the race was solid. And Barack Obama himself didn't want to limp across the finish line. He was determined to win with strength. I thought we could.

Someone in the audience of two hundred broke in to voice the group's central concern: "But could we lose this?" he asked. "Could it be taken from us? How hard are we prepared to fight?"

"Let me be clear," I responded. "We will have earned this nomination. We have followed the rules and will have won this fairly by all the metrics that matter. If the Clinton campaign and some party leaders try to steal this nomination, to assert their will and judgment in place of the voters', we will burn the house down." My voice began to rise. "It will make Kennedy-Carter and Hart-Mondale look like fairy tales. We will win this ugly if we have to. They are not taking this from us. Barack Obama will be our nominee and he will be our forty-fourth president."

The place exploded. If nothing else it was therapeutic, for me, too. Something very strong welled up inside of me as the question was asked. We had walked the most improbable electoral path perhaps in presidential campaign history. We would not be stopped by what I saw as chicanery.

———

Things started to pick up for us in both states. The word in the political community was that Hillary needed to win North Carolina or lose it narrowly to have any chance to change the dynamics of the race and convince superdelegates we were damaged goods. They had poured everything they could into the state and were expressing real confidence to reporters about their prospects. Once again, the expectations gap could work to our advantage: beating long odds impressively would affect the way the day was analyzed and ensure that publicly undeclared superdelegates remained committed to us.

Monday night after 11:00 I got a scary e-mail from Ax: "Red alert. Call me." He had left me a voice-mail, too. My stomach instantly went to knots, and I called Ax from my normal bathroom posting. "The bottom fell out in the Indiana track," he said worriedly. Each night our pollsters sent out the numbers to a small group of us by e-mail, but Ax often pestered them for advance notice. "We were down twelve in tonight's calling."

It was a huge gap, and a serious departure from our previous few nights of polling. "That just doesn't make any sense," I said, racking my brain for an explanation. "We're on a good run here. We know the gas tax argument is working. The only possibility is a bunch of people at the last minute decided they couldn't swallow us because of Wright. But this seems like a screwy poll to me."

Ax concurred. But he was still a wreck. I tried to calm him down, though I felt just as nauseated. I didn't sleep at all that night. I doubt Ax did either.

The next day was all pins and needles until it slowly resolved into a portrait of pure elation. The moment the polls closed in North Carolina, the networks declared us the winner; we won in a blowout, by fourteen points. As the returns came in we could see the traces of our strategy's design: by registering over one hundred thousand new voters, producing strong turnout among African Americans and young voters, and winning college-educated whites thanks to our stand against the gas tax, we had made ourselves unbeatable in North Carolina.

Indiana produced its own drama. As usual, the exit polls were way off— they had Clinton winning by eight points. As the votes were actually counted, we began to think the gap would be a lot closer than eight points. We were hitting or coming just shy of our vote goals in many smaller and rural areas where Clinton was winning but not blowing us out. In Indianapolis and its suburbs, we were actually exceeding our vote goals in some areas. Slowly it became clear the margin would be razor-thin, either way.

Then the networks changed their position on the Indiana race: it was now "too close to call." This subtle shift in language had an enormous effect. Even if Hillary ended up winning Indiana, the perception would be that she had failed to meet expectations, especially considering the hammering we gave her in North Carolina. Pressing doubts about our staying power were the Clinton lifeline in the face of their mathematically dubious position, and now we had taken a huge step toward emphatically quashing those doubts. Finally, we had taken some of their best punches and come away unscratched.

That night, and in the following days, the top-line analysis recast the race just as we hoped: Hillary had failed to get the "game changer" she needed in Indiana and North Carolina, we had weathered the storm, and Obama would now almost certainly sew up the nomination. The question was no longer if but when.

Tim Russert, whose voice on these matters carried enormous weight, made the pronouncement on air that night, even before Indiana was called. "We now know who the Democratic nominee will be," he said. The Clinton campaign was furious.

In the end, we just missed winning Indiana. Jon Carson and our Indiana staff down in the boiler room thought that unless there were some really funky late results, we would lose by about fifteen thousand votes out of over 1.2 million. Such a close loss would normally be hard to bear, but in the current situation we would take those results in a New York minute.

We ended up losing by fourteen thousand; once again our data team was spot on. If Rush Limbaugh had not encouraged Republicans to vote in the Indiana primary for Hillary as a way of extending our race, we would have won outright. Since Mississippi, in states where Republicans could participate in our primaries, Limbaugh had encouraged them to vote for Hillary. We had once welcomed Republican participation; those who participated in our primaries had voted our way overwhelmingly. Not anymore. Now Hillary was winning the Republican vote, and it wasn't because they had suddenly fallen in love. Over 12 percent of the Indiana primary vote was Republican and Hillary carried it, despite her through-the-roof unfavorable numbers with these voters. Limbaugh's project worked in Indiana—it cost us that victory—but it didn't matter. The die was cast.

Beer and laughter flowed freely at HQ that night. We were back in the saddle.

I talked to Obama by phone throughout the night. He was in North Carolina and our last conversation was very late, around 2:00 a.m. I was still at Chicago HQ and the relief in both of our voices was palpable. We were having a senior staff meeting at HQ the next day to take stock and talk about the next phase. I told him I felt strongly that we had nearly closed the book on the primary. We needed to execute well on our remaining tasks—locking in and announcing superdelegates, winning the few remaining states where the numbers favored us, and making sure that the Florida and Michigan situation was resolved properly. The Clinton campaign was ferociously pushing for new contests in both of those states, as well as trying to count the results of the beauty contests—meaningless straw polls—that neither one of us competed in. We needed to put this issue to bed so it didn't linger like a mirage to which they could cling in hopes of keeping the race going.

"We should do some modest campaigning in the rest of the states," I said, "but we have to get going on the general election. We have an obligation to the party—and the country—not to get too far behind." I felt like I was tearing away a heavily marked-up sheet to reveal a fresh map on which to sketch the race anew. "We've been doing a lot of planning and that'll continue," I went on, "but I think you need to start campaigning in some nonprimary, battleground states—especially Florida and Michigan where we're behind organizationally— and start quietly sending some staff into these states so we're not scrambling a month from now. And I think we should largely ignore Hillary's attacks—it's time we turned the page."

Obama agreed. He was anxious for the next phase and felt an enormous obligation to win in November. He had told me in the middle of the Wright episode during the Pennsylvania primary that he would end his candidacy if he honestly thought Hillary had a better chance of winning and that he really was damaged electoral goods.

There were some lessons from Indiana and North Carolina that would inform us going forward. We registered many thousands of new voters in both states, and these voters participated at high rates, defying the conventional view that new registrants turn out in very low numbers. A strong showing from African Americans and younger voters might put both these states in play in the general election. We had done very well with independents in North Carolina, and with independents and non-Limbaugh Republicans in Indiana. That also boded well for the fall.

And the gas tax debate reminded us that whenever we played it safe and conventional, we were punished. As the likely Democratic nominee, we would have to remember who we were. The coat of conventionality was a poor fit.

———

There were only six primaries left after May 6: West Virginia, Kentucky, Oregon, Puerto Rico, South Dakota, and Montana. We knew we would get slaughtered in West Virginia, Kentucky, and Puerto Rico (and we did), but we thought we'd win Oregon and Montana comfortably, and that South Dakota would be competitive. Looking forward to the general election, we decided to do a minimal amount of campaigning in all these states and instead start spending a lot of time in battlegrounds like Ohio and Iowa, and building some start-up machinery in Michigan and Florida.

We were endorsed by Edwards and Al Gore in May, and held both of those announcements at large rallies in Michigan. We also did large events in Florida. It was important that we quickly build up our organization in these two states, and attracting people to events and then asking them to help was the best and quickest route. Thirteen thousand people showed up in relatively small Grand Rapids, which was a very good sign that we could put together a formidable organization in a historically tough part of the state for Democrats.

The Clinton campaign continued to attack us on electability but they were largely shouting into the wind. The superdelegates were not buying it, so we increasingly ignored these attacks. We were locking down superdelegate support at a ratio of 5 or 6 to 1.

The Clinton campaign also was spending a lot of time trying to gin up attention and press coverage of the Florida and Michigan situation.

The DNC Rules and Bylaws Committee would meet on May 31, just four days before the last primary, to decide what to do about allocating delegates from the two states. Neither state held do-over elections, so the decision was now solely in the hands of these thirty committee members. Our position was clear: the delegates should be split 50–50 since no contest was waged and, according to the DNC rules, no delegates were at stake. The Clinton position was that they should net the full amount of delegates based on the voting that had taken place. This suggestion was a complete nonstarter for us, and it rubbed me raw that we had played by the rules only to see them try to move the goal line when we were about to cross it.

I flew into Washington for the committee meeting. Checking into the hotel, I was surrounded by Clinton supporters. Her campaign had organized a protest of the meeting the next day, to demand that Florida's and Michigan's votes be "counted." We had asked our grassroots supporters in the D.C. area not to show up, to avoid creating an ugly scene.

I wanted our approach to "Florigan" as it was popularly called, to be focused on our preferred outcome, not on playing the PR war. Our goal was simply to make sure that when the DNC meeting was over, no new door to the nomination had been opened by so much as a crack. I planned to keep my head down, work strategically, and shut Clinton down quietly but effectively.

Even though I was not a publicly recognizable figure like Ax or Gibbs, who were on TV a lot, this group of die-hard Clinton supporters knew my face. I ducked angry glares the whole way through the check-in line and as I walked through the hotel. I didn't understand how people could truly believe that Clinton was being wronged. Rules are rules. And really, who should have been more adept at playing by the DNC rules—the outsider candidate or the one who put most of the people on the DNC in the first place?

The day of the meeting was pure chaos, though the protesting Clinton hordes never materialized. Testimony and debate dragged on for hours. During a break from the deliberations, one of our leaders on the committee huddled with Berman, Matt Nugen, our political director who handled superdelegates, and me. He said we had the votes—by one or two—to win the 50–50 distribution. But there was another proposal to yield five additional delegates to Clinton as some acknowledgment of her performance in the beauty contest. He said that this plan would even get some votes from the Clinton side, so it would be seen as a much more legitimate outcome.

This was a hard one to swallow. But we wanted peace with her supporters, so I assented. Nugen was despondent because that meant he'd have to round up an additional five supers to fill the hole. "After this door is closed, it won't be a problem," I reassured him. "They won't have any credible argument for how they can win." Still, I felt for him. We were getting to the bottom of the barrel.

When the Rules and Bylaws Committee announced their decisions, the Clinton supporters in the crowd erupted. "Denver, Denver, Denver!" they shouted. They wanted to take it all the way to the convention floor, I guess. From what I heard, they also said very disparaging things about Obama. Some even started chanting "McCain." It dawned on me then that by building up the importance of this meeting and not being honest about how it would turn out (nothing that happened here was going to change the outcome of the election), the Clinton campaign had raised false expectations for their most rabid supporters.

I smiled as the chanting continued. The second to last chapter of this epic book was now closed. All that remained was for us to nail down a few more superdelegates before next Tuesday. We had removed the last possible barrier to our primary victory.

———

I headed back to Chicago the next morning, happy to leave the circus behind and excited just thinking that in three days the unending primary race would finally be over.

After counting the delegates we knew we would earn from Montana and South Dakota, we started June 3, the last day of primary voting, a few dozen superdelegates shy of clinching the nomination. We had more than that in commitments and fully expected that by evening, we'd cross the new magic threshold of 2,118 delegates (the Florigan decision pushed it up from 2,025).

As the day rolled on, more and more previously undeclared superdelegates agreed to come out for us. Some superdelegates never wanted to declare their support publically—they were generally afraid of offending the Clintons, and some just didn't like the new spotlight on their role in the nomination process. Out of principle, a block of them wanted to wait until the polls closed in the last primary state, Montana, before declaring their support. This was a relatively sizable group, and at the start of the day we thought that their announcement would likely put us over the top.

But now many supers were coming out of the woodwork without waiting. They wanted to play a part in our clinching the nomination—and probably to get some "credit" for their support. It now looked likely that we would cross the delegate threshold before polls closed, with a conservative allocation of pledged delegates from our anticipated victories in Montana and South Dakota.

The networks and news organizations were all doing their own counting and calling around to superdelegates. Each wanted to break the news that we had clinched the nomination.

ABC was the first to do so. Charles Gibson led off the news on June 3rd with these words: "*Historic* may be a word thrown around too loosely in our times. Less than 150 years ago, black men and women were held in involuntary servitude. Slavery was the law of the land. And now, the Democratic Party will nominate a black man to be president of the United States. And that is historic by any definition. Historic in any age."

It might seem strange, but we didn't think very often about the historic nature of what we were doing. I watched the ABC newscast from my office and was momentarily overwhelmed by what we had accomplished. This was an important moment in American history, though it was hard to appreciate that when you were still stewing in the middle of a cauldron.

All through May we had been discussing where to acknowledge surpassing the delegate threshold. Chicago? Iowa? Florida or Michigan? Steve Hildebrand, our deputy manager, suggested doing it in the city where the GOP would be having their convention; in the same building, in fact, where in three months the GOP would be delivering their own vision for America's future. Bingo, I thought. Right away, we could use the opportunity to frame the stark choice voters would face in November: Obama was going to claim the Democratic nomination in Minneapolis–St. Paul.

For the last several days, different staffers had asked if I was going to the event and suggested strongly that I should; they said it was important for me to be there at the end of this first leg of our journey. I preferred to be in Chicago HQ to make sure we had everything buttoned up on the superdelegate front, and just generally to make sure we brought the plane in for a smooth landing. I also wanted to be in Chicago that night with the staff who couldn't go up to Minnesota—this was going to be a special moment and I thought I should share it with them.

But people kept asking why I wasn't going to Minneapolis. It got ridiculous. Even Obama started in on it. Clearly something was up. Finally Alyssa told me that Barack wanted to bring me up on stage with him and was disappointed I didn't agree to go. The subterfuge wasn't his style, but he knew that if I found out what he was planning, there was no way I would set foot in Minnesota. And of course he was right.

Not that I wasn't moved. It was a remarkably kind and unusual gesture; candidates rarely think to praise their staff, never publicly, and certainly not on the biggest night of their political life to date. But aside from being mortified by the attention, I also thought this was a strategically important night, the first time the nation would be tuning in to see the Democratic standard-bearer. We couldn't afford to waste any precious words or time on staff like me.

We rented out a bar in Chicago where staff and their families could celebrate after the speech. Several hundred people showed up, all of our HQ staff and some folks who had been out in the states and wanted to share this moment with their colleagues.

It seemed appropriate for me to say a few words. I wanted to convey to the campaign staff that night that it was time to put the primary behind us. To win, we would need Hillary and all of her staff and supporters. We had to let go of whatever venom we had built up—only with a unified party could we win the election.

Then I watched her speech in New York. All of the networks by that point had declared us the winner. The race was over. Yet Terry McAuliffe, her campaign chairman, introduced her as "The Next President of the United States." I blinked; for a moment I thought I was in the Twilight Zone. I watched with disbelief as Hillary gave a defiant speech and suggested that despite the fact that we had just won—won!—her fight would go on.

It sucked the generosity right out of me. I started my speech to our fired-up staff by returning full circle to the beginning of the campaign eighteen months ago, mocking our opponent's opening message. "Well," I said, "it looks like one of us was in it to win it!"

The staff went crazy. Reconciliation would have to wait for another day.

Obama and I talked by phone when he landed in Chicago. I went out into the street and paced up and down the block for about half an hour as we chatted. He was already moving on to the general election. After his speech, he had met with Clinton's most prominent supporters in Minnesota and was surprised that to a person they all said they would do whatever we asked. They even seemed excited about it. This happened over and over again in the coming days.

We started talking about what we thought the McCain strategy would be in the coming days and weeks. We naturally assumed they would have one. I feared that the first days after we won the nomination would be reminiscent of storming the beach at Normandy. They'd had three months to get ready for this moment, and I figured they'd have all sorts of surprises waiting for us. It could be ugly.

McCain had given a terrible speech that night, trying to counter our grand achievement. Standing between an ugly backdrop and a desultory crowd, and sporting a new bizarre slogan that played off ours—"A Leader We Can Believe In"—he had delivered an awkward screed. "We have to assume these guys will pick up their game," I told Obama. "But watching McCain tonight reminded me that the team we just beat was a hell of a lot more formidable."

––––––

As we leave the primary—that long, historic, heated primary—it is important to step back and understand some of the core reasons why we won.

In politics, your two main pillars are your message and electoral strategy. What are you offering voters in terms of vision, issues, and biography? What is your most accessible path to a winning vote margin? (This is much more complicated in a presidential nominating race—in the primaries we had fifty-four different primaries and caucuses, not to mention the superdelegates.) We were willing to adjust tactics but not deviate very often from our core message and strategy, even as both came under fierce criticism from the political community (not to mention our opponents).

We had one slogan. Clinton had too many to count. We made decisions about allocation of resources and time strictly through the prism of electoral strategy. It made decision making less eventful—we had a clear road map about what was important and served our strategic interests and what didn't.

And we attracted more resources than our opponent had—or than we ever thought was remotely possible. Money still matters in politics.

Obama said at one point in the fall of 2007, when conventional wisdom dismissed us, "People will either accept me and my message or they won't. But we are not going to cast about for a political identity. We just need to ride this out."

I felt the same about our electoral strategy. Mark McKinnon, George W. Bush's chief campaign ad guy, said something in a documentary after the 2004 election I found very compelling: "I'd rather have one flawed strategy than seven different strategies." In any organization, you have to determine your pathway to success and commit to it. There will inevitably be highs and lows. But you have to give your theory and strategy time to work. Maybe it won't. Many endeavors fail. But without a clear sense of where you are headed, you will almost certainly fail.

Technology was core to our campaign from Day One and it only grew in importance as the primary went on. We started with fewer than ten thousand e-mail addresses, and by June 3, 2008, our list had grown to over 5 million. A huge portion of that group—almost 40 percent—had either volunteered or contributed.

At the campaign's outset, our goal was to have the dominant Internet presence in the field and try to fund-raise, organize, and move message using digital tools. We exceeded even our most optimistic goals in all three. We raised over $200 million online in the primary. Our volunteers and staff had used our social-networking site as a primary weapon to outorganize the Clinton campaign. We were able to move message—on both issues and political-electoral matters—directly to our entire list and subsets of that list, avoiding the media filter. I saw it as augmenting the political coverage and providing more depth and understanding to our supporters. We had also built a balanced relationship with our supporters. The hundreds of e-mails we sent out in the primary were a healthy mix of pure information, requests for organizational help, local and statewide e-mails, and fund-raising asks.

And our data about voters—the radar of the campaign—was constantly improving.

We were blessed to have a terrifically talented staff, who were smart, driven, creative, and perhaps most important, in it for the right reasons. They created a terrific esprit de corps. The culture of our campaign was very healthy. We had a real sense of mission, and everyone knew we were working our hearts out for Barack and the country, not ourselves. We tried to be fearless while also being disciplined and committed to our plan. It sounds corny, but we had become a family.

We simply would not have won without the historic level of participation from our volunteers. They made changing the electorate in Iowa possible (and in every place where we made the electorate more Obama friendly) and did what was considered impossible in South Carolina. They were the major reason that we not only survived but thrived on Super Tuesday. They delivered eleven victories in a row. And even when we were losing primaries at the end, they never lost faith and made sure we kept earning enough delegates to stay on track. They registered hundreds of thousands of new voters. And the growing power of this grassroots movement also had a deep effect on the superdelegates—they could not overturn the work of these millions of committed Americans who were breathing fresh life into our party.

Our supporters also played an invaluable role in motivating and inspiring Barack and all of his staff. Dozens of times Barack and I marveled at the commitment and talent of our grassroots supporters and pledged not to let them down. "I feel such an obligation to them," he would say. "They believe in me. In us. In themselves. What keeps me going day after day? Besides a clear sense of why I am running for president, it's them, our volunteers. It is a special thing we've built here and I don't want to let them down."

Of course, by far the most important factor in our success was our candidate. He had the right change message in a change election. But his steady performance, his growth over time, the way he dealt with setbacks, his integrity with all he dealt with throughout the campaign, including all of us, and the personal bond of trust he built with voters all over the country ranks right at the top in terms of presidential candidates. He began the race as a national political novice, having never had a negative ad run against him. He had no organization, and no real knowledge of many of the states he would campaign in. From such a start, he defeated the strongest front-runner and best political machine our party has seen in modern times.

We had very good electoral strategy and stuck with it in tough times. We executed at the highest levels and innovated throughout the campaign. But staff are replaceable. A mass of dedicated volunteers is not. Our grassroots supporters did not become involved because they liked our backroom strategy or tactical brilliance. They got interested and involved for one reason—Barack Obama. He kept the faith with them, and they dug in harder and deeper because they believed in him so much. That may have been his greatest accomplishment—in this cynical age, he built a grassroots movement that believed in its own ability to effect change, and which grew to become more powerful than anything witnessed to date in primaries of either party.

The morning of June 4, after maybe two hours of sleep, Katie Johnson, my assistant, tracked me down and said Rick Davis, McCain's manager, was urgently trying to find me. I called him, and after perfunctory congratulations on both sides, he said they were going to issue a challenge to us to do ten joint town halls in addition to the presidential debates, starting as soon as possible.

Well, I thought, game on.

11

Reloading for the General

Before we could plunge full force into the general election, we had to engage in a delicate dance with Hillary Clinton and the remnants of her campaign. Success in November demanded full party unity, and it fell to us to welcome all her political supporters, volunteers, and contributors with open and grateful arms.

The day after Barack clinched the nomination, Clinton held conference calls with many of her key political supporters. According to press reports that surfaced right after that, her supporters made clear they thought she needed to withdraw from the race and enthusiastically get behind Obama, to avoid any hint that she might, symbolically or otherwise, take her battle to the convention. Her campaign quickly sent out word that she would be holding an event in Washington, D.C., that coming Saturday, June 7, at which she would end her campaign and formally endorse Barack. Relief washed over us. After eighteen months of combat, there would be no more attacks from our fiercest opponent.

Clinton and Obama met on June 5, two days after we formally clinched the nomination and two days before Clinton's formal concession. Hillary suggested to Barack—they personally handled much of the logistics around the meeting—that they meet at California senator Dianne Feinstein's house in Washington. I was not wild about having it at the home of someone who had supported Clinton so vigorously, but Feinstein was Barack's colleague as well, and we wanted to tread very carefully. My view—and Barack probably felt more strongly about this than I did—was that we should say yes to anything that was relatively easy and was not clearly against our strategic interests. Given that, we agreed to the setting.

By this point we had a press pool with us around the clock, following

Obama's every move. I did not want the meeting to become a media circus and certainly didn't want news of it to break before it even started. The day of the meeting, we were on our maiden general-election campaign trip in Virginia, and at my direction, we sent the press covering Obama to Dulles Airport and had them fly back to Chicago, where Obama would be spending the night. They assumed he was in the motorcade and would be flying back with them. He had actually peeled off after the last campaign event and was en route to Feinstein's house. We chartered another plane to take him back to Chicago.

Once they were on board, the press could see from the empty seat up front that Obama was not present. Poor Robert Gibbs. He was on the plane and knew he was going to be drawn and quartered by a gaggle of reporters. But he understood the strategic value of keeping this meeting under wraps and agreed that it was worth the cost to maintain discretion.

Still, I was happy not to be his seatmate on this particular flight. A little while after Obama took off for Feinstein's, Gibbs sent a small group of us an e-mail: "They now know he's not on the plane and it's mutiny. When should I talk to them?"

I e-mailed back: "After you take off."

Gibbs later described to me the relentless and very personal pummeling he received on the flight to Chicago. "Robert, Robert, Robert," they barked at him, their voices running together when he went back to face them. His name was perhaps the only polite term employed.

Put plainly, the press were furious. In the days after, we received many strongly worded e-mails and letters complaining about "an unprecedented breach of trust." I understood their frustration. They had been hijacked and misled. Despite some deep frustrations with how the campaign was covered, the press plays an invaluable role in the process that must be respected by those of us on the other side of the fence. But there is almost no escaping the ever-present media and its microscopic coverage of modern presidential politics. Occasionally a campaign has to have space to breathe.

News of the Clinton-Obama "summit" broke as the meeting got under way, as our abducted press contingent deduced the reason for the deception and elicited confirmation from the Clinton camp. Details such as venue and exact participants were not yet public. Later the two campaigns issued a joint statement confirming the meeting that simply said, "Senator Clinton and Senator Obama met tonight and had a productive discussion about the important work that needs to be done to succeed in November." That alone was heralded as big news: a joint statement from former enemy combatants was further proof that the primary was indeed over.

Barack called me to report on the meeting as he was en route to the airport. "No blood?" I inquired. He laughed. "Actually, we had a nice conversation. Some reminiscing about funny moments along the way, none of the tough ones. She said all the right things and I think she meant them. She's established a committee of three people from her campaign to sit down with us and work through issues. I told her you would be our point person. She asked that you call Cheryl Mills to set up a meeting."

"A committee?" I responded incredulously. "We're not negotiating a hostage release here. The general election is in less than five months. I don't have time for the Yalta peace talks."

Obama laughed but was firm. "I know you don't have the time," he said. "But I need you to deal with this first. Try to make progress and hopefully you can delegate a lot of it on the back end. We need to work out a lot of things quickly, so we can move on. My sense in talking to Hillary is the only big sticking point will be the debt. It sounds bigger than we knew and they clearly want our help on it."

I told Obama I would call Cheryl and rope in Bob Bauer, our attorney, as my wing man.

Cheryl Mills had worked in the White House counsel's office during Bill Clinton's impeachment trial, and she was heading up the Clinton delegation. Also involved were Bob Barnett, a leading Washington lawyer who was very close to Hillary, and Minyon Moore, a longtime Democratic operative and former White House political director.

I sent Cheryl a meeting agenda that ran the gamut: how to get the Clinton donors and volunteers involved; when and where Hillary and Barack should first campaign together; the Democratic Convention, which would necessitate its own set of complex discussions; Bill Clinton's role; how much time Hillary could give us for surrogate campaigning; and, finally, the debt. She easily agreed to the schedule, which came as a surprise. I was conditioned from the last year and a half to believe all interactions going forward would be like pulling teeth.

In many ways, watching Hillary concede that weekend made our victory more real to me than did the speech Obama had given in the Twin Cities. The race had been conducted at such a breakneck pace for months and months, and she had hung on so long and so defiantly that it was difficult to believe it was truly over.

Our entire HQ gathered on Saturday to watch. There was unanimous agreement that her speech was phenomenal. She thanked her supporters and famously said, "Although we weren't able to shatter that highest, hardest glass ceiling this time, thanks to you, it's got about eighteen million cracks in it," a reference to the number of votes she received in the Democratic primary. They had a lot to be proud of.

Her endorsement of Barack—and more important, her call for all those who supported her to follow suit—was unambiguous, clear, and compelling. We couldn't have asked for anything more. Under what must have been painful circumstances, she delivered a ten-strike.

Bauer and I met with her committee for several hours, and the discussion went swimmingly, with the exception of one topic—the topic that dwarfed all others.

Their debt was well over $30 million. Hillary had loaned her campaign over $10 million, which she gallantly wrote off, but they still owed more than $20 million to campaign vendors large and small, and that money had to come from somewhere. It was clear they expected us to take responsibility for erasing all or most of this figure. I thought this was preposterous. Given that our fund-raising would have to stay competitive with the entire Republican machine and all its offshoots as we headed toward the general election, we simply could not take on the Clinton debt.

This was going to be thorny, if not downright toxic. I think they believed we could send out a couple of e-mails and generate enough money to erase their debt. They clearly did not understand our supporters, or divine the extent of the hard feelings still lingering in the ranks of the victors.

We knew our supporters would respond very poorly to a request for Clinton debt assistance. First, it was just too soon after eighteen months of pitched battle. It would take some time for things to cool off. Second, and more important, many of our small donors were making a real sacrifice to give us twenty-five or fifty dollars every once in a while, and they did so because they believed fervently in our unique candidate and message. They would consider debt assistance a "politics as usual" ask and not part of our core mission. And many of our supporters who were new to politics would be downright disgusted by this political deal making.

As I saw it, it had been their choice alone to keep racking up debt, and, in fact, their continued spending had forced us to do the same, making it more urgent that we focus on rebuilding our own coffers. At this point, McCain had more money than we did.

We agreed that we would ask the members of our National Finance Committee, our strongest fund-raisers, to write checks to pay down the Clinton debt and to raise money from others to do so. Ultimately we raised almost $2 million for them in the aftermath of the primary. The Clinton folks were not pleased by this figure and likely believed we were only going through the motions. But we tried hard. Obama made some calls himself, and even he ran into fierce resistance. I had numerous conversations with people who had previously come through on everything I asked of them. To this they said, "David, I simply can't do it. I can't ask people whom we need to give money to Obama for America and the DNC to write a check for Clinton debt."

On every other score, the two camps worked very well together, and Hillary campaigned her heart out for us through the fall. For both groups, the suspicions toward the other waned over time, as it became clear we could work together, resolve issues, and listen. But it did take time. Obama took the lead on our side when it came to fence-mending, sending a clear signal within the campaign that he wanted no dancing in the end zone; the message was, work smart and welcome Clinton staff and supporters with open arms. When I occasionally complained about the words or deeds of someone in the Clinton camp, he reminded me to take it easy. "Put down the sword, Plouffe," he would say. "It's over."

Primaries are like family disputes—the wounds can be deep and long-lasting. The 2008 primary was fierce; at times it got downright nasty and personal. For most of a year and a half I woke up wanting nothing else but to destroy the Clinton campaign (I'm sure they felt the same way about us), and I believed passionately that we needed to turn the page, not only on George Bush but within our party.

Still, when you go through an experience like we did, you also develop a grudging respect for what your opponents do well. You actually start to feel a certain connection with the enemy with whom you shared the arena; after all, they're the only other people who truly understand the battle just waged.

Barack Obama was a better candidate than his campaign. Almost all successful candidates are. Some days the gulf was wide (see D-Punjab, Texas, Wright) other times his campaign played a complementary role in his victory (our electoral strategy and discipline, harnessing the grassroots energy he inspired, innovating campaign use of technology and message tools).

In Hillary's case, I believe the gulf was consistently wide. Ultimately candidates have to take responsibility for their campaigns, but they need to have strong staff to handle a lot of strategy and planning details. And it was clear that Hillary's staff did not understand delegates as well as they should have, did not appreciate the role Iowa could play in resetting the race, and made a host of other strategic and tactical miscalculations that opened the door for us.

No candidate should be expected to be the lead strategist on those matters. Hillary was first and foremost responsible for going out every day and making the best possible case for her candidacy. And she performed at a very high level. She won most of the primary debates; as the campaign dragged on and she became the underdog, she really hit her stride. She got to a compelling economic message before we did. As we started playing more of an inside game to lock down superdelegates, she skillfully took on the underdog role and got enormous mileage out of it.

She had to know for months that her odds of winning were absurdly low. Yet day after day she campaigned effectively and with gusto, only rarely betraying her political position in the race and becoming a real voice for economically struggling voters. Very few human beings could pull off what she did. It was a remarkable and often frustrating dynamic to watch from the front row, and I couldn't wait to have her out campaigning for us; I thought she could be a terrific advocate, particularly in making an economic case for Obama's candidacy. But for this to work, we'd first have to earn each other's trust, no small feat after everything we'd just been through.

―――――

The primaries took us to forty-eight states and six territories. In that respect, the length of the contest served us well. By the time we crossed the delegate threshold, we had built organizations in every battleground state except Michigan and Florida, and Obama had campaigned in them all.

As we plowed into the general election, core principles developed during the primary helped guide us. We had no time to come up with new approaches, even had we wanted to. We were three months behind John McCain.

First, as in the primary, we studied our opponent. We thought about his campaign as carefully as we thought about our own.

We had enormous respect for McCain's potential strength as a Republican nominee. He was their only possible nominee with existing and perhaps even majority support among independent voters, the group that often decides the presidency. He had a history of supporting some reforms, most notably the campaign finance legislation that bears his name, and was celebrated by the press for being a "maverick" willing to buck his party. This reputation made him very dangerous to us and our stance as the true change and reform candidate. However, in pursuit of his party's nomination, McCain had embraced the Bush agenda whole hog, including items like the Bush tax cuts, which he had originally opposed as too large and irresponsible. We assumed he would now try to unwind much of that during the general election, to try to reclaim the mantle of independence.

McCain's camp was also asserting that they could peel off a healthy percentage of Democrats, especially the so-called Hillary Democrats: older, downscale whites. While we never believed this claim was valid, based on historical voting patterns, it was something we had to watch carefully. McCain also was unique among Republicans in his standing and potential strength with Latino voters, who could make the difference in battlegrounds like Florida, New Mexico, Nevada, and Colorado. Bush received 44 percent of the Hispanic vote in 2004, and we could ill afford to have McCain match that number. This was another narrative the press sank their teeth into; because we lost Hispanic voters decisively to Hillary in the primaries, the conventional wisdom was we would struggle mightily to earn their votes in the general.

While Latino voters bore watching, the notion that primary trends carried over into the general rested on flawed logic, and defied history. In fact, our initial general-election research showed that some of the groups we struggled with in the primary—older women, Latino voters, union households—would be bulwarks for us in the run for the White House. And some of our bases in the primary—upper-income voters, male independents—would prove a much tougher slog. Forests were destroyed with all the stories about our potential problems with Hillary's primary voters.

Presidential races are often covered as if they are a national race. This is far from true. In the 2008 election, much of the media focused on national polls, paying far too little attention to what was unfolding on the ground in the battleground states. When the new Gallup poll came out each day, for example, the cable networks treated it as breaking news. But in actuality the national polls had little to say about the real story of the race.

Winning the presidency requires piecing together a combination of states to reach 270 electoral votes. That is all that matters. In 2000, for the second time, a presidential candidate lost the popular vote and won the presidency—and George W. Bush lost the raw vote by a healthy margin. We now turned to Electoral College votes with the same laser focus we had trained on delegates during the primary. "Two-seventy" was our new mantra.

Our plan was to attempt to run the most muscular state campaigns ever assembled in battleground states. If we were successful, the campaigns in those states would have a deep impact, potentially creating a clear departure from the national polls. TV and radio ads, Internet advertising, historically large grassroots campaigns focused on turnout, voter registration, and aggressive in-state press operations—all these would create their own dynamic, one that didn't necessarily track with conventional polling techniques. Of course, national news would still matter and things like the conventions and the debates would break through battlegrounds and nonbattlegrounds alike.

Most of the country—those who lived in safely red or blue states—did not truly witness the 2008 presidential campaign. The real contest occurred in only about sixteen states, in which swing voters in particular bumped up against the campaign at every turn— at their doors; on their phones; on their local news, TV shows, and radio programs; and on their computers on the Internet. In these states, we trotted out the candidate and our surrogates, built large staffs and budgets to support our organizational work, and mounted ferocious and diversified advertising campaigns. They were the canvas on which we sketched the election.

From an electoral perspective, nothing was more important to us strategically than having a wide playing field. This was my goal from Day One. We did not want to wake up on the morning of November 4 dependent on one state, as Kerry was on Ohio in 2004 and to a lesser extent Gore was on Florida in 2000. We wanted to have a wide set of targets so that we could lose some and still win the presidency.

We believed Barack Obama would have unique and strong appeal out West in states like Nevada and Colorado, in Mid-Atlantic states like North Carolina and Virginia, and throughout the Midwest, including unlikely targets like Indiana. In these states, he was polling very well with independents in suburban areas like northern Virginia, the suburbs outside of Denver, and the research triangle in North Carolina. We thought registration activity and turnout boosting here could make the electorate more favorable. But Obama's appeal would not be enough. We needed to be able to mount individual state campaigns hearty enough to meet our vote goals. Ample funding was a piece of that puzzle, but far more important was the strength and growth of our grassroots movement in these states as we got closer to the election.

To figure out which states we should target, we focused our analysis on determining where we could credibly get to a win number, 49 or 50 percent in most cases (third-party candidates would skim a few votes in some states). We modeled many different scenarios, playing with various turnouts among certain demographics, different scenarios for how undecided voters could break, and the effect of increased voter registration. Our calculus took into account patterns in each state's voting history, demographic analysis, our own research, and some old-fashioned gut instinct. We put states through the paces under various scenarios to see how they held up and if they gave us a reasonable path to victory.

This was one of the most important and enjoyable exercises in the campaign. Our data team, led by Hildebrand, Carson, and Jen O'Malley (our battleground-states director, whom we brought in from Edwards's campaign during the spring), developed a range of scenarios in each state that ran the gamut from optimistic to pessimistic.

I met with this group every couple of days in May, as we were still winding down from the primary, to review where we stood in the general. My strategic outlook was that we needed to play on the widest map possible in terms of targeted states. In 2000 and 2004, our party was forced to have its fate rest on the outcome of one state. That would not happen in 2008.

Consistent with the philosophy of the campaign, we eschewed head fakes. We wouldn't target a state we couldn't win solely to draw McCain into additional contests, forcing him to spend what would likely be his thinner resources more diffusely. Where that occurred, it would simply be a derivative benefit. If a state went through our obstacle course and came out looking good, it meant we believed we could win it.

I also didn't want to play it safe. We were likely to be rolling through a fairly favorable climate politically and financially once we got into the fall, and we knew we would have a more robust grassroots presence. Rather than spend a lot of resources defending every state won by John Kerry in 2004, we gambled that most of these states would likely stay the course without much push from us; if we ran into trouble, we could always swoop in and correct our difficulty with a rush of time and money. I wanted our orientation to be almost exclusively offensive. This would increase our ability to win tougher red states and could potentially prevent McCain from playing offense himself. His campaign was prattling on to the press about how he could win states like Connecticut, New Jersey, and California. We didn't take the bait. Our goal was to force them to defend Bush states, and we saw little to no evidence that they could add to the Bush Electoral College margin. If our plan worked, we would wake up the morning of November 4 with many different winning combinations, giving us greater margin for error. We could lose many of our targets but still get to 270. McCain, on the other hand, would have to run the whole table.

The states John Kerry won yielded 252 electoral votes. While some would unquestionably fall in our column, others looked likely but not certain. There was no doubt Michigan and Pennsylvania would be fiercely contested, and we could not afford to lose either. If we did, it would force us to win a much higher percentage of our targets than we felt comfortable with. Given this, those two big states would get the full treatment: we would spare no expense and they would get a lot of Obama time (and Pennsylvania already had in the primary).

Four additional Kerry states were critical strategically: First, in the Northwest, Oregon and Washington. These two states are always key battlegrounds and were very close in 2000 and 2004. The Democratic nominees spent a lot of time and money ensuring they went blue on Election Day. This year they looked to be tilting heavily Democratic, and even more important, they were states where Obama performed unusually strongly with independents. We also had very strong organizations built up during the primary in both Oregon and Washington.

With these factors in mind, we decided to gamble a bit and not fully target these states—no media budget, very modest staff presence, and no candidate visits. As the race unfolded, McCain gave us a big advantage by not fully engaging in either state—keeping them out of play took a couple of his potential moves off the table. We were delighted. Having Oregon and Washington in our column from the start let us devote resources to fighting McCain on his turf.

In the Midwest, Minnesota and Wisconsin were also traditionally fierce battlegrounds. Wisconsin was decided by less than one percentage point in both 2000 and 2004. It was clear McCain was going to go all-in on these states, but we took a more conservative approach. We planned a more rigorous presence than in Oregon and Washington, but less so than in the Bush states we were trying to convert. These states possessed two of our most muscular grassroots organizations in the country, and we brought in talented staff to work with an army of volunteers, who would make up for the absence of a live candidate and media buys.

Obama's strength in the Northwest and upper Midwest was never properly appreciated during the primary, when electability was being debated as a criterion for winning the nomination. In the Midwest, Obama had regional appeal, and in both geographic areas, he was overperforming with independents. For a Democrat running in any of these states, combining a solid and energized base with a lead among independents was game, set, match. Perhaps other Democratic nominees would have won all four of these states in 2008, but I believe they would have had to fight much harder than we did. And money, time, and focus are zero-sum factors; any spent in your own backyard is unavailable for launching an assault on your opponents.

The list of Bush states we were putting through the paces went as follows, west to east: Nevada, Montana, New Mexico, Colorado, Texas, North Dakota, South Dakota, Iowa, Missouri, Indiana, Florida, Georgia, North Carolina, South Carolina, Virginia, and New Hampshire. This is a big list and once again flowed from our belief that we should not follow a conventional playbook. We looked at the Electoral College with fresh eyes, ran the traps, and based our strategy on our analysis, not on preconceived notions about what a Democrat could win.

We believed Iowa and New Mexico presented the most solid opportunities for takeaways. McCain did not compete seriously in Iowa during the 2000 or 2008 caucuses, choosing to start his primary campaign in New Hampshire. Conversely, we had spent more time in Iowa than anywhere else so far and had a huge organization on the ground. New Mexico was strongly trending Democratic, and even though it neighbored McCain's home state of Arizona, we saw no sign that he would have outsized appeal to the Hispanic voters that made up a hefty percentage of New Mexico's electorate.

If we held on to all the Kerry states and won Iowa and New Mexico, we were sitting at 264 electoral votes, just 6 away from victory. With no remaining slam dunks, though, we needed a broad set of targets for those last votes. We could lose almost every other state if we won just one state with five or more electoral votes (a 269–269 tie would be decided by the U.S. House of Representatives, which the Democratic Party would almost assuredly control).

All things being equal, New Hampshire would have joined Iowa and New

Mexico on the list of Bush states leaning toward Obama. The Democrats were in ascendance there, having won just about all there was to win in 2006. But McCain had a special relationship with voters in New Hampshire—they had given him a huge win in each of his runs, and we were a little gun-shy after Hillary had the rug pulled out from under us in the primary.

Virginia was a cornerstone to our strategy. Consequently, it was the first state Obama visited after having formally secured the nomination. We went to southwestern Virginia, the rural, more conservative area; a Democrat has to avoid being routed here in order to win the state. Soldiering into historically unfriendly territory sent a very important message both in Virginia and nationally: we were going to fight for votes in every corner of every battleground state. We also thought our early endorser, Governor Tim Kaine, would help us develop a solid road map and execute our game plan.

Virginia had changed enormously through the decade; after years of Republican dominance, Democrats now routinely won statewide office. It was also a relatively large state, offering thirteen Electoral College votes. Wresting Virginia from McCain would severely limit his options. He would have to win a large Kerry state or the race was over. We thought Virginia was prime real estate for us, and fortunately, the McCain camp did not believe they could lose there until it was too late.

McCain met several of our other targets with similar indifference. His campaign told the press we could not win North Carolina, Montana, Indiana, or, remarkably, Florida, so they would not compete there. This gave us a huge head start in states we believed were certainly in play. All in all, it was a huge gift.

My personal favorite target was the 2nd Congressional District of Nebraska. Nebraska and Maine are the two states that do not award all their Electoral College votes based on statewide results. Instead, the winner of the raw vote in each congressional district receives one Electoral College vote. We felt confident we would carry all of Maine's (though McCain made an ill-considered play for the northern congressional district), and it was clear McCain would carry two of Nebraska's three districts comfortably. But we thought we could steal the 2nd District, around Omaha, where our organization was strong, and we already had ads on the air to reach Iowa voters.

The political history nerd in me would have loved to win 270–268, through a combination of all the Kerry states, Iowa, New Mexico, Nevada, and one vote from Nebraska's 2nd Congressional District to put us over the top. I mused to

Obama about this scenario, remarking how unusual and historic it would be. In some ways it would resemble our primary win, where we stitched together an unlikely electoral path. "Plouffe, that's interesting daydreaming," he said, laughing. "Let's try not to have it all come down to Nebraska 2."

We knew both campaigns would compete aggressively in Missouri, Ohio, Colorado, and Nevada. We thought Ohio would be close no matter what; it was one of the few states where we did not think we could fundamentally alter the electorate, a top strategic goal in all battleground states. Because it had been ground zero in the Bush-Kerry race, turnout and registration levels were already exceedingly high. Even if our enthusiasm levels were higher than McCain's, and he had some drop-off from Bush's turnout (a distinct possibility), we would still need to win the persuasion war with swing voters on the economy.

We believed Missouri, usually considered a bellwether, was an outlier in 2008 and trending a bit against us. If we won there, it would be by the thinnest of margins. The state had eleven electoral votes, though, and McCain was investing heavily, suggesting to us that they saw something that concerned them. In the end, Missouri was a bridge too far, but we hung in there, and forced McCain to as well.

Colorado and Nevada were great takeaway opportunities. Neither state broke Democratic or was particularly close in 2000 or 2004, but the growing influence of Latino voters and Obama's appeal with western independents gave us a great shot to pick them both up. Expanding the electorate through voter registration could have a meaningful effect in both states, and we thought younger voters could really help juice turnout favorably.

As I played with the map, a dozen times a day, I kept coming back to a scenario in which we won the White House by holding all the Kerry states and winning Iowa, New Mexico, and either Colorado or Nevada. This was our most conservative win formula. Of course, we would have liked the biggest margin possible, but we all tried to keep our appetites focused on what we had to have, not what we wanted to devour. "I'm not really interested in spending my time dreaming up landslide scenarios," Obama told us. "Let's just make sure we hit 270. I don't want to get 260 wishing for 360."

Perhaps wishing for 360, we initially targeted Georgia, North Dakota, and Alaska. We actually never had a credible path to 50 percent in these states but thought that if the two third-party candidates could get a few points—and Bob Barr, the libertarian candidate, was from Georgia—we might be able to eke out a win with 47 or 46 percent. We ended up pulling back from all three states, though we jumped back into Georgia and North Dakota. Ultimately we received 45 percent in both states—a very high number for a Democratic nominee—but we made a mistake including them on the original target list. It was just plain greedy, and target states we were unlikely to win wasted money and focus we could have used in the core battlegrounds.

This was the playing field. It was critical to keep all these states in play throughout the race, ideally taking the lead in some. But we built our campaign to do everything possible to win close battleground states. That's what we assumed would decide the outcome.

On a trip to Washington in June, I outlined this approach for the press. We had put together a presentation that laid out our electoral strategy, where we saw the race message-wise, and some of our perhaps underappreciated assets: our grassroots operations, the ability to register voters, and so forth. We played it straight, no hyperbole. After struggling during the primary to get the press and the political community to understand our electoral strategy, we wanted to lay it out as clearly and as simply as possible. This way, as we were making moves, they could understand why and evaluate them through the prism of our strategy.

Right away, I could tell by the reporters' facial expressions and questions that they were deeply skeptical. I resigned myself to another round of the primary dynamic: our strategy and theory of the race would be neither properly understood nor believed. The press was conditioned to focus on a few key battlegrounds as the prism through which to see the race, usually Ohio, Florida, and Pennsylvania. Virginia, Indiana, and North Carolina were not in their vocabulary.

Headlines after this press event read, "Obama Camp: We Can Win Without Ohio, Florida." Damn right, I thought. But this wasn't arrogance, foolishness, or spinning a poor hand. And it wasn't meant to suggest that we planned to ignore these. Quite the contrary: we would vigorously contest both of them. A win in either would doom McCain, and we thought we had credible, if uphill, paths in each. But some in the press suggested that (1) our strategy was flawed for being too broad, and (2) we would hurt our prospects in Ohio and Florida by suggesting they weren't the be-all and end-all of the race.

The last point was nonsense. Real voters aren't influenced by political process arguments. They vote based on issues, character, and leadership qualities. To say that voters in Ohio and Florida might be less likely to support us because we had suggested their states didn't hold the key to the election, and that this had somehow hurt their feelings, was just silly. As to the first point, we were used to outsiders finding fault with our strategy.

Writing in an op-ed in the *Los Angeles Times,* one prominent commentator suggested our strategy of widening the playing field could doom us and that investing in states like Virginia, Colorado, North Carolina, and Indiana was too risky a proposition. "If McCain pulls off a victory in November," the piece opined, "there will be a lot of postmortem scrutiny about the prudence of playing it safe versus the dream of shooting for the moon."

In retrospect, I should have offered the press a simpler visual technique for understanding our plan. We would hold all the Kerry states and flip Iowa and New Mexico. That puts us on the threshold. McCain at that point would be like a hockey goalie, and we would pepper him with an onslaught of shots. He might stop Ohio, Florida, Missouri, Indiana, Montana, New Hampshire, Nebraska 2, Nevada, North Carolina, and Colorado. But if Virginia slipped past him into the goal? Game over. His margin for error would be close to zero. That's what we were setting out to do.

We could do it only by growing and strengthening our powerful grassroots movement. We ended the primary with over 2 million contributors and more than 7 million people on our e-mail list. Almost all the contributors were volunteers (highly unusual in politics), and we had many more volunteers who had not yet contributed. Our record on that front was promising. We had what businesses call a high conversion rate. I referred to it as the enthusiasm gap. In the primary, our supporters were more committed and passionate than Hillary's had been. She drew plenty of diehards, and they hung some big losses on us. As a percentage, though, a greater number of Barack's supporters were willing to work ten or twenty hours a week, make multiple contributions, and convince others to climb aboard.

We thought the enthusiasm gap would be even more pronounced in the general election. Democrats were wild about replacing Bush. Republicans were less excited about a third GOP term. Bush's performance had left even some hard-core Republican activists disillusioned and unmotivated, further depressing enthusiasm. And though McCain had a core of passionate support- ers, he had a very thin base of hypermotivated voters. Many on the right were still skeptical of him; they found him too willing to oppose the party in the past and distrusted him on some social issues. Of course, this dynamic had an upside for him as well; it explained why he was attractive to many independent voters and why we thought he was the strongest GOP candidate of the 2008 field. Independents would play a huge role in this race, and more-extreme candidates, like Mitt Romney and Mike Huckabee, surely would have been busts with these voters.

But the tension and lack of enthusiasm within his party could cause him real problems. In 2004 Bush won Ohio largely due to off-the-charts GOP turnout; McCain might have trouble matching this. And having fewer super-motivated supporters could also leave McCain facing an organizational deficit that would have real impact on the outcome in battleground states.

Even with this leg up, we had to grow our numbers. Much of the work would be similar to the primary at the ground level, but voter registration would take on a greater focus. We would need a persuasion army to convince Republicans and independents to support Barack. The sheer scale of the electorate in a general election dictated that we continue to amp up our recruiting.

With this in mind, I told Joe Rospars, whose new media team had already built an unpredictably successful online campaign, that we needed to come close to doubling its size in five months—we had to have at least 3.75 million contributors and the e-mail list needed to surpass 12 million names. Our volunteer numbers would also have to jump considerably. Joe sighed. "We'll do our best," he said. "But we'll need more resources, both staff and external spending, to get it done."

This was a daunting task and not one that could be achieved simply by ticking off points on a plan. Of course, we would buy more Internet advertising to capture people and then hopefully convert them. On the event side, we'd hold a lot of large rallies, which were always a great source of thousands of new names. We also hoped a high percentage of Hillary Clinton's most active supporters would eventually decide to get involved. But this effort alone would not grow our ranks sufficiently. We had to hope that the excitement of the general election, the stark Democrat-versus-Republican issue matchup, and the intensity of the campaign's "big" moments—conventions, debates, and unscripted incidents—would help spike the number of people coming to our site and signing on.

Central to this effort to grow was our supporters' continued use of social-networking sites like MyBO.com and Facebook to build the campaign and organize themselves. We wanted to make it easy for these self-starters to connect with our huge staff in the battleground states, most often our young, talented, and fearless field organizers. And always we made sure to stress to volunteers that they had standing behind them a national HQ—and most important, a candidate—that believed in them and would make sure their work was strategically sound and received adequate resources.

We made some of our key strategic and targeting decisions based on the belief that we could grow the grassroots movement to this level and that we would get maximum productivity from this engorged group of supporters. Without them, we could not have targeted states like North Carolina and Indiana. For one, we would not have had the money. But most important were the volunteers on the ground; we could not convert enough Indiana Republicans unless we had their neighbors talking to them about why they were supporting Obama, explaining his positions and defending him against McCain's attacks.

If we did not register enough African Americans and young voters in North Carolina and then turn them out on Election Day, we could not win. Facing a traditional electorate meant we shouldn't even bother with a state like North Carolina, no matter how much money we spent. Quite simply, money was no substitute for committed volunteers. Without question, we had to grow the campaigns in these states enough to shoulder the massive workload. Without our volunteer army, our strategy of a wide electoral map and multiple avenues to victory would have been the fantasy many people believed it to be.

One decision we had to make quickly as we formally entered the general election was whether to participate in the public funding of federal elections. Candidates who agree to accept federal taxpayer funding—in 2008 it was $85 million per candidate—get a check from the government in return for ceasing their campaign's fund-raising after their party convention. The government put this system into place after Watergate, and since then all presidential candidates have agreed to public funding.

In 2004 this cap especially harmed Kerry because the Democratic convention was held a month earlier than the Republicans'. Both campaigns received the same amount to spend, but Bush had to pay for only eight weeks compared to Kerry's twelve, a huge advantage. Kerry later told me that staying within the system was one of the biggest mistakes they made.

Axelrod and I saw what happened in 2004 from a unique vantage. The DNC hired our firm to produce ads for the so-called independent expenditure, or IE, unit of the committee. Since Kerry would not be raising money for his campaign after the convention, he asked his contributors and other supporters to give money to the DNC instead. The idea was to have the DNC supplement the campaign's activities.

As it turned out, largely because there was so much energy in our party to defeat Bush, the DNC raised far more than had been predicted. In fact, we ended up spending more on advertising alone that fall than Kerry did on his whole campaign, well over $100 million. But there was one big catch: to honor the public financing agreement, campaign finance laws make it illegal for the party to communicate with the campaign. So nothing we did could be coordinated with Kerry or any of his people.

As a result, while we spent over $100 million, we did so inefficiently and with many tools not at our disposal. We had no access to the candidate, and so believed our role should be to run negative and comparative ads, allowing the campaign itself to run more positive ads since they could actually film Kerry. That roughly worked. But we spent as much time trying to figure out what we should do as we did actually doing it once we figured it out. Our first rule was "Do No Harm." We wanted to make sure everything we were doing was strategically aligned with the Kerry campaign, but since we couldn't talk to them, this was a dilemma.

We looked for smoke signals every day to determine if we were on the right course. Was the campaign sending us messages through the press about an issue we should hop on? Their television point levels went down in the St. Louis media market—is that because they're preparing to throw in the towel or feeling more confident? They're not buying radio heavily but Bush is—does that reflect a lack of resources or a belief that there aren't many available voters in those markets? We were playing second chair at best, just trying to divine their cues and strategy and act accordingly.

Kerry also could not afford to support a field and organizing campaign, so almost all his groundwork was done by the DNC, state Democratic parties, and outside groups. This situation offered a clear lesson, one that stuck with me—if you believed in running a strong ground game based on people leading the charge in their own communities, nothing could be more problematic than having zero control over that operation.

The 2004 experience carried a lot of weight with me as we worked through the 2008 funding decision. It gave me a deeper understanding of the system's drawbacks as they would relate to our campaign. So important was this election that I believed we owed it to our party and country to have a very clear view of how the funding decision might affect our chances of winning.

Complicating the decision making were statements we had made earlier in the campaign suggesting we would "aggressively pursue" an agreement with the Republican nominee to stay within public funding. We never should have set down so bright a marker that early in the campaign, when we barely had the lights in our office turned on, but we were overly concerned with making sure the reform community and elites like the *New York Times* editorial board, which care deeply about these issues, would look favorably on our approach. And honestly, we weren't doing much thinking in February 2007 about our general-election campaign. We could hardly see past Iowa into New Hampshire then.

If we opted out, we knew we would be heavily criticized by the media, campaign finance watchdogs, and, most important, McCain, who had made it very clear he was staying in the system and would consider it an outright lie and a breach of public faith if we did not.

Then an issue questionnaire from the obscure Midwest Democracy Network popped up. Our policy staff had filled out hundreds of these questionnaires throughout the campaign, but this one, completed in the fall of 2007, really came back to bite us. When asked whether we would commit to being in the federal system, our team had responded, "Yes. . . . We will aggressively pursue an agreement. . . ." We had never before or since used that one word—"yes." It was declarative, and it unquestionably stated we'd be in no matter what the GOP nominee did.

The answer blindsided all of us at the senior level of the campaign. It was an unforced error and would make a decision to opt out of the federal system extra painful.

We had to look at this decision through two lenses. First, Barack Obama had been a reformer in practice, accomplishment, and outlook since he was elected to the Illinois state senate in 1996. He had championed tough ethics and campaign finance reforms in Illinois, the first in a generation. After arriving in Washington, he led the fight for tough new lobbying restrictions, drawing the wrath of insiders and colleagues from both parties. "You are going to cost us the majority!" one prominent Democratic senator had yelled. "We are in power now and you're going to take away some of the advantages that allow us to stay there."

Reform was in Obama's DNA. We knew McCain would try to make us pay a price, but that was of less concern than making sure whatever we did squared with Obama's reformer credentials and instincts.

The second lens focused on the practical considerations. Which path gave the campaign the best chance of success? I felt we had a searing obligation to win this race—not just for Barack or on behalf of the staff, but from an absolute belief that we could not afford another four years of George Bush's domestic and foreign policies. To my mind, we needed to look through this second lens first, before we got to the harder question of principle.

If we decided to stay within the system, the DNC would be the major spender on our side—we would have our $85 million in federal funds, and I figured the party would raise at least $250 million, almost all from the existing Obama donor base. But a healthy percentage of our contributors were Republicans, independents, and nonpartisan types who would not give money to the DNC, even if they were asked to by Obama.

If we opted out, I thought it was safe to assume the campaign would raise $350 million and the DNC $100 million. The party's portion could be spent in coordination with our money; it would not be an independent expenditure with all the legal barriers prohibiting communication. DNC chairman Howard Dean and his senior staff had prepared well for the moment our party chose its nominee; they were ready to "hand the keys over," as Dean put it. We could essentially subsume the DNC into the campaign and gain control of all their resources as well as of our own.

The overall difference in funding would be around $100 million, not chump change. Sacrificing this added cash would mean we either had to pare our list of target battlegrounds or run less rigorous campaigns in each. These were highly unappetizing options.

More important than the dollar discrepancy was the control that would be ceded in the campaign. With only $85 million, we would find ourselves in Kerry's position, unable to afford a field organization or a broad range of advertising. Instead, the DNC and outside groups, with their far larger financial resources, would be forced to take the field and airwaves for us.

And all their decisions would be made without our input. They would invariably be running a negative health care ad in a market where we would have preferred a tax cut comparative. And since tone was so important to our campaign—we did not want traditional low-blow negative ads run on our behalf—this factor took on added weight.

Most painfully, taking the federal funds meant losing control of our secret weapon: we would have to largely outsource our entire grassroots ground campaign to the DNC. As with fund-raising, there were many people volunteering for us who would offer their help in the name of Obama. If these people were forced to volunteer through the Democratic Party, no matter how clearly the mission was stated, we feared we could lose up to 20 percent of our volunteers.

Finally, nothing would be under one roof. One of the central tenets of our campaign was to look at everything together, not stack them into individual silos labeled media, press, field, and so on. We wanted everything synched up so we could keep our communications tight and coordinated, and maximize the value of all possible data points when making decisions.

I wanted a campaign in every battleground state with a robust enough field and advertising budget to address all our needs and to deal with whatever attacks McCain and his outside henchmen threw our way. Staying in the federal system would seriously impede our ability to mount the kind of campaign that left no stone unturned. We needed to be clear-eyed about that.

I thought if we opted out of the system, we would also enjoy a significant financial advantage over McCain. Our sense was that his campaign would feel they could not raise enough money to justify opting out. McCain lacked a powerful online fund-raising program, and he would have to do a lot more traditional fund-raising events than we did. This would take up a lot of his time, pulling him out of battleground states. From this perspective, it would make more sense to stick with the devil you know and let the RNC raise the money.

I thought this would be a grave mistake for them. The decision was not just about total dollars. More important than resource disparity would be a "control gap." If we were out and he was in, he would be at the mercy of the RNC and outside groups, while we controlled our own destiny.

For example, in October, it would be likely that in Cleveland, Ohio, McCain could afford to run only one ad a week. To supplement this, the RNC would then need to run their own ad (or two), and several outside groups would also have to get on the air for him. And all this would happen with the threat of felony prosecution guaranteeing that no communication beyond smoke signals was taking place between the candidate and his outside help.

Conversely, if we opted out, we would be able to run the positive ad we thought was in our best interest, a comparative or negative ad, and other ads geared to different demographics, like seniors or middle-aged women. We would also have the resources—and more important, a fully coordinated strategy—to deal with any attacks, no matter where they were coming from.

So from a practical perspective, opting out seemed like the right move. With that settled, we turned to the principle questions. As far as how opting out of the federal system squared with our claim that Obama had been and would be a reformer, there was quite a lot to recommend it. First of all, we all felt very, very good about how we were raising our money. Obama was the first presidential nominee to ban contributions to his campaign and the national party (DNC) from PACs and lobbyists. Despite McCain's talk and record on reform, his campaign was scooping up all the insider money they could find.

We had achieved what many consider the ideal of campaign reform—receiving a lot of small contributions from a lot of people. Our average contribution was under $100, and our donor base composed a diverse portrait of America: teachers, retirees, small-business owners, farmers, students. I certainly felt that our present fund-raising method was a lot cleaner than what we would be forced to do if we stayed in the system.

The maximum allowable contribution to the campaign was $2,300. If we opted in, and had to turn our attention to raising money for the DNC (though we could have no knowledge or say in their spending), the limit would be just over $30,000. The McCain campaign had already done numerous RNC fund-raising events with lobbyists, where each attendee was asked for $30,000. And shadowy outside groups would have almost no limits. If we stayed in the federal system, these groups on our side would kick into high gear. Very wealthy individuals and interest groups would write, in some cases, multimillion-dollar checks, with little outside accountability when it came to how that money would be spent. It was clear to me which of these pathways was the more questionable.

Whatever we decided, I was determined not to make a decision out of fear of some hypocritical lectures from John McCain about breaking our word. There is also a federal financing system in the primaries, and when McCain's campaign foundered in the middle of 2007, he signaled that he would take the money. Before that point, they had sent the clear message that they would not be bound by limits. McCain signed his own name to loan documents in

December of 2007, using the promise of federal money as collateral. Without the loan, McCain might well have lost to Mitt Romney in New Hampshire, ending his campaign.

Yet once McCain wrapped up his nomination in March 2008, he reversed course and said he would not be participating in the federal primary system. The reason was politically transparent: our primary would still be dragging on for some time and they wanted to have maximum financial flexibility to wage what was in essence a general-election campaign for those five months before the GOP convention. This reversal undercut any moral authority he might claim on campaign finance reform.

Obama and I talked about this issue a lot through the late spring and into early June. In the beginning he was genuinely torn—all things being equal, he was an instinctive reformer who was determined to win. Ax also played a part in these discussions. Like me, he was determined we not enter the general with one arm tied behind our back. But Ax is more sensitive to press criticism than I am and wondered if we could have our cake and eat it, too. He suggested opting out of the federal system but limiting contributions to, say, under $250.

The idea sounded appealing. But when our finance staff ran the numbers, it became clear this option would produce the worst of both worlds: we would not raise enough money to justify the pummeling we would take. Meanwhile, Ax had shared this idea with Obama, who mused about it in a press interview. I immediately sent them both an e-mail banning further trial balloons.

More than any of us, Obama was living the way we raised our money; maybe it wasn't pure, but it was as close to the ideal as had been achieved in presidential politics. Out on the trail, he met our grassroots donors all the time and even called up some of them unprompted, to try to stay connected with the ground.

The largest two categories of donors to our campaign were retirees and students. I doubt that has ever before been the case in American politics, and it's all the more remarkable that these are two groups filled with members who are often living on very fixed budgets. But their dedication was unwavering and inspiring. After the campaign, we got an e-mail from a college student named Brandon Humble, who described how he found the money to make several donations to us. "I didn't eat out, grabbed some ramen on the weekends instead, and kicked in ten to Barack's campaign," he wrote. "Didn't take the girl to a movie, just had drinks together, kicked in another ten. Small things.

But it was my belief that there were millions of us, scraping what we could together, and through the small things and the small people, headed by the campaign, a movement was created."

We also had some wildly successful online promotions, including one that was fittingly called "Dinner with Barack," where we would select a group of donors to have a meal with Obama. Other contest winners got to spend time with us on the trail. Barack loved these. He got to meet donors like Michael Wilson of Cocoa Beach, Florida, an Air Force veteran of Operation Iraqi Freedom who disagreed with the reasons for our going to war. A registered Republican, Mike believed Barack reflected "what America is and what America needs." As Obama pondered the finance decision, these were the people he visualized.

———

On the phone late one night I laid out for him the different campaigns we would have to run in the two scenarios. "I've made up my mind," he said when I finished speaking. "We'll get out of the system. Let's execute it right away. No reason to delay."

The most important component of our decision was sharing it first directly with our supporters. We had done this from time to time, though never on something this significant, and learned that it held real value to our supporters—it made them feel very connected to the campaign. They loved getting information directly from us, rather than seeing it reported elsewhere.

Obama filmed a short video explaining his decision. "It's not an easy decision," he said, "especially because I support a robust system of public financing of elections. But the public financing of presidential elections as it exists today is broken, and we face opponents who've become masters at gaming this broken system."

We sent the video out by e-mail to our entire list on June 19, and that's how the press and John McCain learned of our decision. As predicted, the press hammered us and editorialized against our decision, saying that we had dealt "a body blow both to the system of campaign finance and to [Obama's] own reputation as a reform candidate." McCain, perhaps prizing media opinion over voters', spent days denigrating our choice. But we thought voters had bigger concerns and that he wasted precious time making a process argument when his own hands weren't clean.

Next we had to lock in how we planned to spend the revenue. We had quietly begun planning and budgeting in April and May, so we would be prepared when the general election began in earnest. Hildebrand, Jen O'Malley, Grisolano, Carson, CFO Marianne Markowitz, and Henry Desio, our chief operating officer, and their teams began a very arduous process to lay out our state and national budgets for the final five months.

I gave them a figure of $475 million to work with. Our fund-raising staff was very nervous about these numbers—their projections had us raising under $400 million. But I expected the grassroots funding to explode after the two conventions and throughout debate season, and did not want to budget too conservatively. It was a leap of faith but one I thought was justified given our trajectory. Campaigns often spend money haphazardly at the end because they did not accurately budget for the inevitable surge in contributions as the country's interest waxes in the days before the election.

Budgeting is an art, not a science. I wanted us to have an approach of high growth and risk, because I actually believed that $475 million would just be our floor. Some of this was based on incessant calculations I did on my own. Pure gut instinct was a factor as well. This race was so intense and our supporters so passionate that I thought we had to plan as if the additional money would come.

As I expected, the budget team came back with a much larger budget than $475 million. Their first cut was $611 million. This was brazen but laughable, and my response was short. "Right now there is no play in the $475 million," I told them. "This is not a negotiating exercise."

Despite Herculean efforts, their next budget was still over $500 million. To get to $475 million we cut even more paid media, which is usually the sacred cow of campaign budgets. Media gets funded first and fully, and other departments make do with whatever is left.

This time I believed that our state campaigns should be the driving factor. Registering voters, person-to-person persuasion, building strong local organizations, boosting turnout where we needed to, and gathering as big an e-mail list as possible would be more important than advertising to our ultimate success. It is much more effective to throw late-stage surplus funds on TV than to field operations, which need time and infrastructure to grow.

Advertising would be critical, though, and we would do plenty of it. We still needed to educate voters about the basics of Barack's biography and values, as well as his positions; many of the general-election voters did not pay close attention to the primary, and McCain had already spent decades on the public stage; he was a much more known quantity.

Our paid media team was nervous. For all the McCain campaign's belly-aching, our ad spending and theirs were roughly equal through July and August in the states where we both advertised. But I was comfortable with the risk inherent in our de-emphasizing paid-media funding. First, there are some races where advertising is the central driver, but these tend to be Senate and House races, which don't dominate local news coverage or voter attention. Voters follow presidential races carefully. They watch the conventions and debates. Thanks to the explosion of the Internet, following the contest had never been easier. The personalities and stakes of the 2008 race promised to deliver a highly engaged electorate, which alleviated the need, at least early, to have monstrously large media buys. Second, with McCain staying in federal funding limits, we could develop quite a gap in our media spending at the most critical time—the last two months of the campaign—even working within our $475 million budget.

With so many factors in play it often felt like throwing a dart at a moving bull's-eye. We developed a good system to help us stay within budget, assess why we were exceeding it in certain areas, and make strategic adjustments. We never dipped into the red; only once did we have cash-flow issues—as projected, right before the Democratic convention when our spending was ramping up and the dog days of August made for sluggish fund-raising.

While the budget team was initially in Fantasyland, the final budget was far from spartan. It funded every state at muscular levels and represented the most expensive presidential campaign effort in battleground states in history, by several factors. Our Florida budget was $38 million; our Virginia budget, $22 million; and our Colorado budget, $10 million. We built budgets that we thought could produce wins and did not tier the states by importance. We were all-in.

As we transitioned into the general, we needed to make some staff additions and changes. Most pressing was building our senior team in all the battle-ground states. Many state leaders were drawn from our staff in the primary, but we had ample holes and filling them was harder than we expected. For starters, we had a salary cap, and some folks balked at it because they could make more in other campaigns. That was an easy one for us. No negotiating, no looking back. See you later.

Second, our approach in the states was very different from previous Democratic presidential campaigns. In many elections, state directors handled their local politics, made sure the candidate's trips into the state went well, and helped spread the campaign's message when the candidate and other princi-pals were not there. Our state staff leadership would have these responsibili-ties, but we asked much more of them. We valued above all their ability to build a state campaign that worked day in and day out toward our voter-turnout goals, constantly measuring their performance against established metrics, and prioritizing volunteers above party leaders.

Those with experience in the Kerry, Gore, and Clinton campaigns were not necessarily the best fit. Not everyone we talked to grasped this concept or agreed with it. It took some time to fill out the roster, but we ended up with terrific state staff, a healthy balance of Obama primary warriors and new blood.

We sent Paul Tewes, of Iowa fame, to manage the DNC for the last five months, to make sure we were in alignment and getting the most from that committee. Mitch Stewart was running Virginia. Emily Parcell, another Iowa stalwart, took Indiana. Ray Rivera, who led us to a key win in the Colorado primary, now revamped his team for the general election. These Obama veter-ans were joined by people like Aaron Pickrell, chief of staff to Ohio's governor Ted Strickland, who had worked his heart out for Clinton but now ran the Buckeye state for us. Marc Farinella, a longtime Democratic consultant, went back to his campaign-manager roots and ran North Carolina. Steve Schale, who worked in the Florida statehouse, took a leave to head up our team in the Sunshine State. These folks and their colleagues were some of the strongest state directors in the history of presidential politics.

We also needed to build a staff for our yet-to-be-named vice presidential pick. Our selection for the top job on this team surprised many—we selected our old nemesis, Patti Solis Doyle, who had been Hillary's campaign manager until she was fired after the Maine caucuses. The vice president's campaign chief of staff was a largely organizational figure; key strategic decisions would all come from our core Obama team. We needed a leader who would make sure everything was well managed day to day, someone who could get our VP up to speed quickly on message and electoral strategy, and make sure he (or she, at this point) was briefed properly as breaking news or new attacks surfaced.

After she left Clinton's campaign, Patti came under fierce criticism for how she managed their money, and she was a prominent contestant in the blame game of how they had been outfoxed on electoral strategy. Those may have been valid criticisms. But Patti had been Hillary's scheduler and then her top political person; her skill set matched up very well with the position we needed to fill. As a Chicago native, she was also a known quantity to Axelrod and Obama—Ax in particular—and they felt she would be a good fit.

Many Clinton supporters attacked us for hiring Patti, suggesting we were rubbing salt in a wound and insulting Hillary by bringing on the person they blamed for her defeat. One insider reacted to Patti's hire by saying, "Translated subtitles aren't necessary. There is no other way to interpret this other than '[Expletive] you.'" Wow.

This took me by surprise. Suggesting we had the time or inclination to make important hires based on what would annoy Clinton partisans was nuts. We stuck to our guns and tried to explain to those who asked that we would never be illogical or mean-spirited in making any hire, particularly one so important to the campaign's smooth operations. We brought in other Clinton campaign veterans, including senior people like Clinton's policy director and speechwriter and many of her state staff. There was a lot of talent out there and we needed the help. Secondarily, we thought it would expedite the healing and make Clinton's supporters around the country feel more comfortable getting involved.

Fitting all these new people into the framework of our well-oiled campaign offered its own challenges. Our existing senior staff sent a message to the new additions: We had largely been a collegial campaign with a healthy culture, relatively devoid of drama. If that changes, we asked the newbies, where was the first place we'd look to figure out why? The message was not lost. For the most part, the assimilation went well. Having strong continuity in our campaign made this task easier. We were not making wholesale changes—we simply strengthened and expanded our core, which remained fiercely loyal and like a family.

This unity was highly unusual in Democratic presidential campaigns. Most organizations experience upheaval at some point, as the pros from Dover come in to replace some of the candidate's loyal, local inner circle. Barack did not want that. "We rode into town together, we'll ride out together, win or lose," he often said.

Once we squared all this away, I turned my attention to the one remaining senior position that needed to be filled: mine. In early spring I told Barack that once we had sealed the nomination I would step down as campaign manager.

I pledged to stay heavily involved, but I could no longer run the show in Chicago.

I was not abandoning ship. I fundamentally reject the notion that any member of the staff is irreplaceable. Fathers, however, are. I had been largely absent from my young son's life for over a year. We had a baby due two days before the general election; I wanted to spend some time with my boy before he had to share me with a sister.

My wife had decided to leave Chicago and return to Washington in August, in order to be with family and old friends for the last months of her pregnancy, and to allow our son to settle into a new hometown and start preschool with the rest of his class. Unfortunately the home we would be moving back into was being renovated, meaning my four-year-old and his extremely pregnant mother would spend two months staying with various friends and family, hoping the house would be ready before the baby came. I knew it would be tough and I couldn't stomach not being there to help.

Barack was not happy with my decision. He had come to lean on me and we had developed a solid relationship. There was also a comfort factor; with everything else Obama needed to do, he did not want to have to adjust to a new manager to boot. I thought perhaps Jon Carson, who had masterfully managed our state operations in the primary, could step in. I tried to get Ax's approval on this, and he shrugged his shoulders. "Sure, Carson would be great. But you're not going to leave as manager. Obama simply won't allow it."

Barack told me to hire as many people as I wanted to help ease the load but insisted I stay in place as manager, driving and making big decisions as others handled more execution. "I just want to know you are managing the process," he said, "and ultimately making the big strategic decisions. And I want to keep the relationship you and I have had, talking through everything every day."

This didn't address my central problem, which was a need to be with my family. Our senior staff was terrific—I certainly did not think it wise to make any broad expansions to our existing tight unit. I was also exhausted and thought a fresh and singularly focused manager might serve the campaign in its home stretch.

In early 2008, when I first discussed with my wife my stepping down, she had been supportive. Now, as word leaked within the campaign that I might go, several members of the staff expressed to her their personal alarm at the disruption it would cause. As the primary stretched into June, they pointed out, when the countdown to the VP selection, convention, debates, and Election Day had already begun, there was no time to spare for a leadership transition.

Still, I was not prepared for what my wife told me late one night at the end of the spring. "I think you have to stay," she said. "There will inevitably be a hiccup or two transitioning to a new manager. It's almost summer already; the campaign doesn't have time for growing pains. You just fought like crazy to make Barack the Democratic nominee; we have an obligation to do everything we can to elect him in November. I have no idea how we will manage. But we will."

I was moved but still not convinced. This was not just about what I thought would be best for them. It was about being true to myself. And if I stayed as manager, it would mean that I was choosing not to be the father or husband I aspired to be. This was the kind of choice I had always sworn would be easy. Family first.

It's what wives want their husbands to do, defying history, odds, and tradition. But there would be no surprise announcement of chivalry and commitment. My wife's rationale that it was simply too late to make a change carried the day. I stayed in Chicago.

Having allowed myself something of a fresh start, I took stock of things in my office and found I had a hole organizationally. I needed someone to handle a lot of the day-to-day budget matters, interpersonal and human resource issues, thorny political problems, and some key projects: basically, a campaign chief of staff. I wanted more time to spend on large-scale resource-allocation issues and to chew over the states and our Electoral College paths. On top of that I wanted to be able to spend more time with our advertising team and to start focusing on the debates.

I needed someone with a strong management and campaign background and who would make a good fit into the No Drama Obama culture. Barack's Senate chief of staff, Pete Rouse, suggested I bring in Jim Messina, who was himself chief of staff for Montana senator Max Baucus and a veteran of many successful campaigns. Messina dived right in. He endeared himself to me from the get-go by taking not two weeks to wrap up his affair but drove across the country in two days and got started. He was a terrific addition, quickly earning people's trust and confidence despite being new to our core senior group. I made clear from Day One that he spoke for me, and we made sure there was no daylight between us, which helped. As the weeks passed, I wondered how the hell I had survived the primary without someone like Jim.

One night in June, Axelrod and I were sitting in my office at HQ. Piles of paper were everywhere, and the walls were covered with maps that had not worn well since being tacked up over a year earlier. It was late, and we were taking a moment to catch our breath. "You know," I said to him, "we have four big things in the next five months we have to excel at. If we can nail those, knowing we should be able to win the message war, especially the economy, have more money and a better organization and electoral strategy than McCain, we should win."

Ax immediately rattled them off: "Trip. VP. Convention. Debates."

Translated out of campaign shorthand, this meant a foreign trip we'd decided to embark on in July; the selection and announcement of a vice presidential nominee; the Democratic convention; and the four debates, three between the presidential candidates and one VP debate.

"A gauntlet for sure," I replied. "But if we can beat Hillary, we can handle these."

Ax shot me a look. "A foreign trip where one thing goes wrong and we could implode," he ticked off, "a VP process that is months late and draws from a thin field; a convention that we haven't even gotten our arms around—and don't forget the Clinton drama that could dominate Denver—and debates, not exactly our strong suit, whatever improvement we've made. Thanks, Plouffe, for seeing the bright side."

For all his characteristic gloom, he was right. It is often said presidential campaigns are not won in August but they can be lost there. We would soon find out.

12

Innocents Abroad

A key factor for many voters in 2008 was their belief that America needed to repair its relationship with the rest of the world. Relations had largely been decimated by the Bush years—Iraq, walking away from climate talks, a knee-jerk aversion to diplomacy—and Americans believed that their next president needed to bridge some of these divides. We were surprised to learn that general-election voters across the board felt just as strongly about the need to repair relations abroad as primary voters had. In an increasingly intercon-nected world, they believed we become stronger by cooperating with the rest of the globe while still playing a central leadership role.

Within the campaign, we had been talking as early as the summer of 2007 about making an overseas trip. Obama's unique family background and his time spent living in Indonesia, along with his clear and pronounced differences with Bush and McCain on the need for more rigorous diplomacy, convinced voters from the outset of the general election that Obama would do more to fix our relationships with the rest of the world than McCain, by a healthy margin. This was an important attribute advantage.

A trip overseas could accomplish two different but equally important things: it would show that Obama could operate effectively on the world stage and would also acutely demonstrate how his election would change the nature of our relationship with the rest of the world.

A small group of us—me, Axelrod, Gibbs, Alyssa, Anita Dunn, Dan Pfeiffer, and Denis McDonough, our top foreign policy adviser—hashed out the itiner-ary in a series of meeting and calls. Denis was carefully reaching out to some of our key outside advisers to get their input as well. Ultimately we recom-mended an itinerary of Iraq, Israel, Germany, and Britain; a seven-day trip, including travel back and forth.

We chose each destination to serve a distinct purpose. Iraq would allow him to meet with the commanders and the troops; Israel, to demonstrate once and for all his deep commitment to the Jewish state, as well as his intention to play a leading role in the search for Middle East peace; Germany, to meet with Chancellor Angela Merkel and to hold our one public event; and Britain, to do a quick meeting with Prime Minister Gordon Brown.

Late in June, on our last call before locking in the itinerary, Obama insisted that we add France to the agenda. He said that while it might not add much to this trip, if he was elected president, this perceived slight could start him off on the wrong foot. We fought this but he pulled rank, and that was that. It would now be an eight-day trip, with the addition of a meeting and probable press conference with French president Nicolas Sarkozy.

This may sound like the type of trip presidents take all the time. But Obama was not president. We had to pull this off as a campaign, a private organization with no government or diplomatic resources. It was hard enough to put on a flawless week of campaigning in the States, but doing so overseas would test us as we had never been tested before—from Obama on down.

Any of a million things could go wrong: A diplomatic gaffe. Mishandling substance and questions. Bumbled logistics. As Dan Balz of the *Washington Post,* one of the deans of national political reporters, wrote before we embarked on the trip:

> [T]he tour is fraught with risks. The large media contingent that will follow Obama means that any misstep or misstatement will be magnified and potentially read as evidence of his inexperience, adding to doubts about him. If he successfully navigates his itinerary, however, the political payoffs could be significant enough to affect the outcome of his race against Republican Sen. John McCain this fall.

I thought that just about nailed it. As Ax said to me right before the trip, "This trip—and the idea to do it—will go down in history as either brilliant or colossally stupid."

"Well, for the history books, we'll make sure they knew it was your idea," I replied.

We thought the strategic upside was huge, and as a bonus we would get real coverage, not just pundit chatter, that would reach voters right before they began to check out through the dog days of summer.

I also believed that by pushing ourselves, the trip could help pull us closer together internally and force us to execute at the highest possible level—it stretched us organizationally, made us grow, and would strengthen us for the next impossible task. We all knew the risks: a mistake on this stage could cause serious, lasting damage to our candidacy. But each time we did something really hard in the campaign, the result was that we benefited—voters began to put a value on our ability to execute. Our boldness reminded them that we were not cut from the same typical Washington cloth. No one had ever before attempted a trip like this in presidential campaign history.

During the planning phase, our most important decision was where to hold the one public event we thought the trip required. We immediately ruled out Paris and London, believing that American voters would not assign great value to our ability to draw a big crowd and communicate with the populations of those countries. It would be a little too expected. But we thought Berlin would mean a great deal more to people. Germany was perceived as less socialist than France and a less reliable ally than Britain; our relationship, while strong, had weathered recent ups and down. In a rare instance, we did not poll this. We based our decision on gut and instinct.

The Berlin gamble was truly audacious. We planned an outdoor rally, speaking directly to the citizens of Germany as well as to all of Europe. We believed this would visually demonstrate an important premise: the world was still hungry for American leadership, but of a different, more cooperative kind that only Barack Obama could deliver.

The size of the crowd he drew was less important than the text of the speech, but we certainly wanted a strong showing. Both Alyssa, whose team would be responsible for building the site and generating a crowd, and Denis, who had been consulting with outside advisers on what kind of crowd we could expect, offered no guarantees. They said it could range from a few thousand to a hundred thousand people; we wouldn't know which until showtime. Unlike at our domestic events, where we had a very good sense based on pre-event online sign-ups and a good local feel on the ground, here we were essentially flying blind. When I reminded Alyssa that we needed a large, pulsating crowd, she offered a sober response. "A rally in Berlin, New Hampshire? No problem," she said. "In Berlin, Germany? We're so far out of our comfort zone, I have no idea what will happen. Everybody better keep their expectations in check."

Even still, I could tell she and her team were animated by the challenge.

This event was an advance person's dream—and potential nightmare. The lights would never shine brighter. I thought we would rise to the occasion. A big day in Berlin provided a nice interruption from the eighteen months of events and rallies we had been doing just about daily in the States, and that had become somewhat routine.

President John Kennedy had spoken before the famous Brandenburg Gate in Berlin in 1963. We were mindful of comparisons and did not want to encourage them. There was a big difference between a president speaking to a divided Germany during the Cold War and a presidential candidate speaking to a unified Germany nearly half a century later. With this in mind, we scouted other locations.

A couple of days before the trip, I was fund-raising in California when Katie Johnson, my assistant, called me with urgent news. "Denis is in the hospital," she said. "He suddenly became disoriented and couldn't remember what day it was or what he was doing. He's undergoing tests."

Denis had come to me from time to time in the previous weeks expressing great anxiety about the trip. He was clearly shouldering much of the pressure and felt our success hinged largely on his planning and briefings for each leg of the trip. To a large degree, he was right. He and Alyssa were the star performers on this high wire. I had tried to tell him that he was not up there alone, that we had decided as a group to go and we would rise or fall in that way. "Denis," I had assured him, grasping at every metaphor within reach, "this trip is going to be a home run. And if isn't it won't be because of anything you'll have done but because we made a bad call to do it in the first place."

Denis was tough as nails, a former college defensive back, not one to let a physical illness stand in his way. I assumed his poor health was due to anxiety. He and Gibbs had been working closely, so I called Robert to get his take. The conversation quickly confirmed my suspicions. "The trip is just eating Denis up," Gibbs told me. "He hasn't slept for days. Night after night, he's been lying awake thinking about everything and making sure he hasn't missed anything."

It turned out he was just having an allergic reaction to Ambien and was temporarily disoriented. They kept him under observation long enough to ensure he had not had a stroke or developed a brain tumor. The whole episode was unsettling, not the least for Denis. Mercifully and happily, he made a lightning quick recovery. The next morning, he sent us an e-mail saying he was leaving the hospital and would be back at his desk shortly. We discussed whether he should stand down, but he would have none of it. But the incident only underscored the tremendous pressure we all worked under to get this right.

———

The first leg of the trip took Obama to Iraq and briefly to Afghanistan. He had been to Iraq once before in his official capacity as senator, in 2006. We felt it critical that he return on this trip, since the war represented the policy area of perhaps greatest disagreement with McCain. We had pledged to bring combat troops out of Iraq within sixteen months of being elected president, while McCain had suggested—out of context, they claimed, but it sounded pretty clear to us—that we could be in Iraq "for maybe a hundred years."

Very few Americans were interested in another five years in Iraq, much less one hundred, so highlighting that difference was an important component of Obama's visit. But he also wanted to spend time with the commanders and troops on the ground, making clear that while their mission would change when he was elected president, he deeply valued their judgment and heroic work.

Though for the rest of the trip Obama would be traveling as a private citizen, he went to Iraq and Afghanistan in his official capacity as a senator and member of the Senate Foreign Relations Committee. He was joined by Senators Jack Reed of Rhode Island and, in a coup for us, Republican Chuck Hagel of Nebraska. Hagel had become a fierce critic of the Bush-McCain Iraq strategy, or lack thereof. He never gave Obama an official endorsement but joining him in Iraq sent all the right signals.

Because this was a diplomatic, government-sanctioned trip, no campaign staff or resources could be made available for this leg of the journey. Obama was assisted only by Mark Lippert, a Navy reservist who had been his foreign policy adviser in the Senate and who had been absent for much of the campaign while on an intelligence assignment in Iraq. Tony Blinken, who was the staff director for the Senate Foreign Relations Committee, also traveled with the delegation. I stayed behind in Chicago while Ax, Gibbs, Denis, and Alyssa flew to Amman, Jordan, where they would eventually meet up with Obama.

After eighteen months of instantaneous contact and zero-delay feedback, we were suddenly inside a black hole. E-mail was spotty in this portion of the trip, and there was no one other than Obama and Lippert to send updates. "It's only our most important day of the campaign so far and we're completely in the dark," I joked to Dunn and Pfeiffer. "It feels like we're back in the dark ages."

Lippert finally sent word by e-mail that the meeting with the troops had gone very well and that Obama had played a little basketball with some of the soldiers. Before photos from the meeting were aired on TV, Obama called me to check in. It wasn't long before he brought the conversation around to his preferred talking point.

"Did you hear about my shot?" he asked.

"I heard you shot some hoops," I replied.

"Well," he said with characteristic understated confidence, "you guys are going to have to get me back into a bowling alley soon. I was with the troops in the gym, someone threw me a basketball, and I swished the first three-pointer I tried. Money. Let me out on that bowling alley and the first ball I roll will be a strike."

When I saw the pictures, I understood why he was crowing. It was a pretty awesome scene: Barack in dress shirt and pants, casually knocking down a three on his first attempt while the troops went nuts. A pretty good first day, I thought.

The next day he would meet with General David Petraeus, who had publicly stated his disagreement with our plan for a phased withdrawal of combat troops; he thought it would bind the hands of the commanders on the ground. One clear objective for the meeting, then, was to not back down one iota on Obama's commitment to having the bulk of combat troops out of Iraq in sixteen months.

Barack's take on the meeting, confirmed by Lippert, was that he and Petraeus established a very good rapport and that they had a healthy debate about timetables for winding down the U.S. presence in Iraq. Obama had stood firm on his position, while simultaneously making clear he would pay heed to the commanders on the ground in terms of execution.

The two men also undertook a helicopter tour of parts of Iraq, which generated terrific front-page photos of Obama in sunglasses and radio gear talking to Petraeus. He looked like a leader. Some in the media captioned the picture "Senator Bad-ass."

I received one of our periodic gifts, this one visual, from McCain that day. He was doing some fund-raising in the Northeast and paid a visit to George

H. W. Bush at his compound in Kennebunkport, Maine. The pictures from this get-together showed Bush and McCain driving around in a golf cart, dressed in country club attire (McCain in a turtleneck). The differences between these images and our helicopter shots could not have been starker. Obama looked young and strong, McCain looked old and silly. Obama looked like the future; McCain, the past.

The impact of McCain's golf cart photos was nearly equivalent to that of seeing Mike Dukakis in a tank in 1988 or John Kerry windsurfing in 2004—indelible. The side-by-side pictures of the candidates' respective field days were shown over and over and had to be a real low point for the McCain campaign. I could not get enough of the footage of Bush and McCain tooling around the compound and encouraged us to use it in every ad we could. "Bring back the cart!" I'd say.

The visit to Iraq could not have gone better for us. Israel was next and promised to be trickier. Obama held a high-stakes outdoor press conference in Sderot, near Gaza, where he handled a multitude of tough questions from the press corps without missteps. He spent some time at the Wailing Wall in private prayer. In the previous months there had been a consistent guerrilla e-mail campaign around the country, suggesting that Obama would not be a stalwart friend of Israel. The pictures and news coverage from his time there provided ample evidence to the contrary.

The subsequent meetings with European leaders were judged to have gone well. If there was a problem it was that they went too well—Sarkozy essentially endorsed Obama in glowing language during their joint press availability. This created some blowback in the American press that being the candidate of Europe and France could backfire with voters. We found this thinking dated but, nonetheless, we monitored the story line carefully.

Throughout its duration, the trip dominated coverage in every medium. Demonstrating leadership qualities abroad was a crucial part of our strategy, and for over a week, it was hard to turn on the TV, radio, or computer without catching those qualities on full display in Obama. We also were running foreign policy ads—TV, radio, and Internet—in all the battlegrounds, providing real amplification to the press coverage. Everything was synched up and working in symphonic consonance.

The Berlin speech provided the trip's only real controversy. We knew this would be the obvious target but were surprised by the path McCain chose to try to undercut us. Initially, the media coverage and pundit world largely declared the Berlin event a raging success. At first blush, thanks to the turnout, it was hard not to.

We really had no idea how many people were going to show up. Alyssa kept e-mailing me with crowd updates as the event start time grew closer. She was blown away by the number of people massing at the event site at Tiergarten, a large park close to the Brandenburg Gate. "This is going to look awesome on TV," she wrote. Axelrod chimed in: "There are Germans waving American flags as far as the eye can see."

We were hoping for over fifty thousand but would not have been surprised by half that figure. Instead of a factor, we got a multiple: over two hundred thousand people showed up, most from Germany but many from all across Europe. The scene was breathtaking. Obama strode onto the stage looking out into the historic Berlin streets, and a mass of humanity waving American flags hung on his every word. The hunger for new American leadership was palpable.

Back in my office in Chicago, it was hard for me to focus and not get swept up in the moment. We were a long way from fifty skeptical people at a house in rural Iowa.

In his speech, Obama challenged Europe to play a more engaged and constructive role in Afghanistan, but did so in a spirit of potential cooperation, grounded in our shared past looking with hope toward a shared future.

"Yes, there have been differences between America and Europe," he told the crowd. "No doubt, there will be differences in the future. But the burdens of global citizenship continue to bind us together. . . . Partnership and cooperation among nations is not a choice; it is the one way, the only way, to protect our common security and advance our common humanity. . . ."

The one passage for which we caught flak—some commentators went so far as to call it a major gaffe, and McCain's campaign certainly tried to fan the flames—was the following: "Tonight, I speak to you not as a candidate for president, but as a citizen—a proud citizen of the United States, and a fellow citizen of the world."

It was "a little too post-nationalist for the typical American swing-voter," said one *New Republic* commentator. "I'm not sure you win the presidency without being seen as an unambiguous nationalist." Many in the media shared this reaction. I thought this was another example of the press looking in the rearview mirror instead of seeing the race in front of it.

True, four short years earlier the Bush campaign, with some success, portrayed John Kerry as an effete, European sympathizer. They leveled the most devastating criticism available: he "looked French." But times had changed. Voters wanted a different, more cooperative relationship with the rest of the world. Our research after the speech showed that the vast majority of the American people agreed with that sentiment. They did not want the United States to compromise its values or leadership, but they did not see these two goals as mutually exclusive. Once again, voters proved more sophisticated than the press gave them credit for.

From a morale standpoint, the trip was a real boost to the whole organization. It felt good to stretch and succeed. For the first time, we could also visualize what an Obama victory might mean to the rest of the world. The reaction overseas was very motivational.

Barack praised the team's performance effusively. We talked at length by phone when he landed in Chicago, and he went on and on. "Everybody really lifted their game," he told me. "It went better than I could've ever imagined. It's the hardest thing we've done and the best thing we've done in the whole campaign. I've got to think voters will look at this—how we pulled this off— and it'll be another piece of the puzzle in convincing them we can handle the presidency."

This benefit of the trip hadn't dawned on me, but he was right. According to our research, the campaign itself increasingly became a touchstone for people when describing how they were wrestling with the experience issue. In focus groups, we heard more and more voters saying, "Well, he might not have been an executive or been in Washington long, but he seems to run a hell of a campaign and doesn't play it safe. Beating Hillary Clinton, giving a speech in Berlin, traveling around the world. All that should mean something."

A few days after Barack returned, the McCain camp settled on their next offensive thrust, using Obama's speech in Berlin as the hook. They released an ad using footage of the speech intercut with crowd shots (interestingly, not the Berlin crowd) chanting "Obama! Obama! Obama!" Then came paparazzi pictures of Britney Spears and Paris Hilton. The ad's payoff line: "He's the biggest celebrity in the world. But is he ready to lead?"

Obama found the ad downright silly. "I just can't see any serious person doing anything besides laughing this off and feeling that the McCain campaign is small and irrelevant," he said. "You may not like me or vote for me, but by now I think I've at least made it out of the Britney and Paris category."

"I agree," I told him. "But tell me, how does it feel to be the biggest celebrity in the world?"

Barack laughed for a moment. "I'll try to wear the crown with grace and dignity."

The Paris-Britney ad was a weak shot, but we had gamed out many other possible attacks that might be stronger. Our view was that once the torpedoes came, it'd be better to know with some degree of certainty ahead of time whether we faced a direct hit and how to retaliate rather than scrambling after the fact. Our guiding principle: if something could be known, know it. In the case of attacks, it was best to find out how the jury, the voters, would evaluate the charges against us.

As we exposed voters to McCain's "celebrity" attack and argument, they ratified our belief that he had overreached. Women voters especially considered this ad out of bounds. "Obama may not have enough experience," they told us in focus groups. "But to compare him to Paris Hilton and Britney Spears? It's insulting."

Thus began the erosion of John McCain's reputation as a nontypical politician. People just did not accept the celebrity angle as a credible argument, particularly with the economy getting increasingly worse; they thought it was irrelevant, childish, and off-point.

Still, the attack did work with one audience: the press loved it. It was a very personal attack, and though voters weren't biting, the media seemed convinced that the McCain campaign was on to something. Emboldened by this reaction, the McCain campaign kept pounding. They released new versions of ads suggesting Obama was a substanceless rock star. "[N]ot long ago, a couple hundred thousand of Berliners made a lot of noise for my opponent. I'll take the roar of fifty thousand Harleys any day!" McCain told the crowd at the Sturgis Rally, a huge biker gathering in South Dakota. I thought it strange to see such blatant xenophobia on the airwaves. At times his campaign seemed driven by a consuming need to control the cable-news-cycle war; voter reaction was almost an afterthought.

We felt like we had little to worry about from it all. Events coming down the pike would naturally connote stature: The selection of a VP nominee. The Democratic convention. Three presidential debates. Given the natural course of events in the race, the McCain campaign seemed to be playing checkers, not chess.

Day-to-day operations in their camp were now being run by Steve Schmidt, a legendary war room communications strategist. With that background, he brought to the table the ability to attack creatively and respond in ways that captured the lion's share of attention. This approach has its place, but in many ways, it increasingly came to define their campaign, often at the expense of logic, to my view. Over time I found it more and more difficult to divine consistent and clear strategic decision making in the McCain camp.

When the polls tightened a bit, the McCain folks credited the celebrity attack, but we thought that was bunk. Any slippage in the numbers had little to do with McCain's antics and everything to do with the fact that Barack Obama went on vacation for a week.

Every year Barack and his family returned to Hawaii to see his beloved grandmother, his sister, and other friends and family. He was not able to make the trip in 2007. Now, he was flat out exhausted after twenty-one months of nonstop campaigning and pressure, and he really needed the break. We talked about vacation after securing the nomination. He asked whether I thought it was feasible that he and his family could have some downtime.

To me, this wasn't much of a decision. Even though his being absent from the playing field could cause some temporary erosion in the numbers, it would be just that: temporary. I thought it more important to give Obama some time to recharge. He could work on his convention speech and focus on how to be a better candidate in the fall, when the bright lights were really shining. Plus, his grandmother, who had raised him for periods of his life and to whom he was extraordinarily close, was in poor health. A visit seemed imperative. She was his last link to his childhood and formative years. So, Hawaii it was.

Axelrod and I were convinced that the trip was the cause of any slippage. We were invisible and McCain was everywhere, so they were bound to gain a bit of ground. "It's like a five-on-zero basketball game this week," commented Ax. "Of course they're going to put up some points. But it's garbage time. None of this movement will be permanent."

I agreed. Right or wrong, we had decided to go to Hawaii. There was no point wringing our hands over McCain's dominating the race for a few days. In general, we made a point of refusing to obsess over things we could not control.

We also used the week our candidate was on vacation wisely, internally. We spent most of the week the Obamas were in Hawaii doing final message planning and strategy for the general election and laying out most of the rhythm and priorities for issues and events for the last sixty days of the campaign, from the end of the GOP convention to Election Day. We also did a final scrub of the self-research to make sure we didn't have any nasty surprises still lurking, trying to predict which land mines the McCain campaign would be trying to put in our path and how and when they might deploy them. Spending as much time thinking about what your opponent should or might do was always a critical exercise for us and a discipline we tried to maintain in both primary and general.

Campaigns can be like riding a bucking bronco: you just try to stay upright day to day and are forced all day, every day, to deal with things that have the potential to take you off plan. That being said, we wanted to have the most crucial stretch of the campaign laid out methodically so that we knew why, when, how, and where we would be putting emphasis on certain issues and ideas and what we saw as McCain deficiencies.

The celebrity battle provides a bit of insight into how the two campaigns viewed the race. The McCain camp seemed to approach it as a contest to dominate what insiders were talking about, and they were much more tactical than strategic. We tried to focus exclusively on what voters were concerned about: the economy, health care, Iraq.

Was it fun to read story after story about how smart the McCain campaign was and how we were reacting too slowly and poorly? Did we enjoy hearing that we were making the same mistakes weak Democratic nominees always do, and the suggestion that the celebrity attack was the next iteration of the swiftboat attacks on John Kerry in 2004? Of course not. But we had a game plan and felt we had good radar about what was truly damaging to us. We would stay focused on our own evaluation—the progress we were making in the states—not whether Wolf Blitzer thought McCain was winning the day.

13

Filling Out the Ticket

One item on Obama's plate as he headed to Hawaii involved perhaps the biggest decision he would make before the election. He needed to select his nominee for vice president.

The late finish to our primary really put us behind the eight-ball on a number of issues—the selection of a VP was one. We had quietly assembled a vetting team so that once we clinched the nomination, the process could begin in earnest right away. We trod very carefully, because although by May we were certain we would win, we didn't think it would help cement party unity to get deep into the vice presidential process while Hillary Clinton was still ferociously campaigning.

John Kerry and Al Gore both had several months longer than we did to figure out their picks. Given our limited time, our process had to be tight, well organized, and structured to let us make decisions quickly.

We had our first formal meeting in early June, in the conference room of a hotel around the block from Chicago HQ. Here, for the first time, Obama, Ax, the three members of our vetting team, and I discussed names of potential candidates. We needed an initial list so the vetters could start digging through the candidates' lives and identifying any problems. Likely suspects had already received cursory attention in May, but now we needed to begin to focusing our efforts.

Our vetting team was made up of Jim Johnson, Caroline Kennedy, and Eric Holder. All three had to commit much of their time over the next couple of months to the task. Jim, who helped run Walter Mondale's race in 1984, had managed this vetting job for Kerry and Gore. He endorsed us very early, one of the few quintessential D.C. insiders to do so, and given our short time parameters, he seemed like a good choice to head things up.

The job of the VP-vetting group is largely misunderstood. Jim and his team would not help select the nominee. Their primary role was to manage a network of attorneys, all volunteers, who would work around the clock to complete a thorough examination of potential VP candidates. Jim, Caroline, and Eric would also meet with party leaders to get their confidential ideas on nominees. It was a complex and secretive process and one for which Jim had received high marks in the past for his discretion and competence.

Barack and I did not want just one person tasked with running this show; we wanted multiple sets of eyes looking at information and participating in opinion-gathering exercises. We decided, at Ax's suggestion, to ask one very unconventional choice, Caroline Kennedy, because we had grown to trust her judgment and discretion as she had been out campaigning for us; we also thought it would be good to have an outsider's perspective, and yes, Caroline was probably the only Kennedy who could possibly be described as an "outsider." Eric Holder rounded out the team. A former senior member of the Clinton Justice Department and a prominent attorney, he was a natural fit in terms of helping with rigorous vetting.

History largely suggests that the VP candidate is the most overcovered story in presidential politics. The picks rarely make a big difference in the campaign but are obsessed about ad nauseam for months. This factor defined our central operating philosophy in selecting a nominee. Naturally we did not want to pick someone who could potentially hurt the ticket, and looked for a candidate who ideally would bring some assets. But at that meeting Obama made his priorities very clear. "I am more concerned and interested in how my selection may perform as an actual vice president than whether they will give a boost to the campaign," he told us. "A boost would be fine, of course. But I'm not sure that person exists and I don't want it to infect our thinking."

At that first meeting we talked through every Democratic governor and senator, some House members, prominent mayors, business leaders, and some military leaders; we cast a wide net. Our initial list included about twenty people—a mix of state, local, and federal elected officials; some former elected officials; and a former military person or two.

Hillary Clinton was on the list from the start. During the meeting, Obama filled our vetting team in on what Ax and I already knew from their conversation at Feinstein's house. Clinton said she only wanted to endure the full, formal vetting process if it was a near certainty she would be picked. Because we had already researched her so thoroughly, this was not a big problem. We were light-years ahead in our vetting of her than of anyone else.

What surprised me at this meeting was that Obama was clearly thinking more seriously about picking her than Ax or I had realized. He said if his central criterion measured who could be the best VP, she had to be included in that list. She was competent, could help in Congress, would have international bona fides, and had been through this before, albeit in a different role. He wanted to continue discussing her as we moved forward.

The vetters had their marching orders. They needed their teams to start digging into this initial list—and fast. No one else in the campaign was involved in these discussions, for two reasons: First, we didn't want people spending an inordinate amount of time on it in the early going. We had a general-election campaign to mount and wage, and were late to the ballgame. Second, we did not want to risk any loose lips, even in as tight a campaign as we had. The circle had to be tiny. Ax and I decided to refrain even from offering too many leading opinions. This was the most important, and personal, decision Obama would make. The choice needed to be his alone.

———

We met again a couple of weeks later in mid-June, at Eric Holder's office, and winnowed the list down to about ten names. Obama and I had been talking daily about this, so I had a sense of his general direction, and there was no dissent from the group.

I came to realize during this process that perhaps he was even better suited to the presidency than to the campaign. Only two months remained before our convention, the drop-dead date for having a VP nominee, and rather than agonize about the quick pace and all our lost time, Obama was methodical, calm, and purposeful. Were he to win, I could envision this behavior and approach translating very well to the Oval Office, where steadiness and rigorous thought and questioning would serve him and the country well.

Even still, the process offered its fair share of frustration. Innumerable times, he said to me, "Plouffe, did you find our magic bullet candidate yet? Can we get a Constitutional exception, and not pick anyone?" He joked, but he had a point. None of the potential nominees would make the election much easier, if at all. And we would have to incorporate a new person, team, and set of challenges into our operation in the last weeks of a hotly competitive presidential race.

This dynamic of incorporating vice presidential nominees has received little analysis, but it's a fairly big deal. Sure, the VP lets you cover more ground on the trail and can help on media and fund-raising. But it is an enormous burden to have a major player dropped suddenly into your campaign, often in need of a lot of remedial work, with no time for basic training. The bullets are flying and the nominee needs to take the battlefield right away. As we looked at it, a VP, any VP, could be as much headache as help.

Our process went from the backroom to the front pages when our press staff sent word that the *Wall Street Journal* was about to break a story claiming that Jim Johnson had received what was called a "friends of Angelo" mortgage from Countrywide Financial, a firm he had previously regulated. "Angelo" refers to Angelo Mozilo, Countrywide's CEO. This news produced an immediate Grade-A shitstorm.

We had not vetted Johnson extensively, any more than we had vetted other people playing advisory roles throughout the campaign. Because he was a volunteer, and never officially hired by the campaign, we failed to register that the importance of his role would naturally elicit intense scrutiny. Jim was a Washington insider for sure, one of the reasons we added Kennedy and Holder to the team, but it never occurred to us that his business dealings would be something we would have to own or that they could cause turbulence in the campaign.

But own them we did. The issue quickly started blowing back at us. The day the story broke, we discussed on our nightly call with Obama whether we needed to ask Jim to step down; Barack wanted to think about it overnight. He almost never made rash decisions and didn't want to start doing so now. Most political figures react and make decisions based on someone else's timeline—the media's or their opponents'. Obama had the composure and fortitude to set his own clock. That day, the press had asked him about the Johnson controversy, and he said, "I didn't hire a vetter to vet the vetter," suggesting that the story was perhaps a tempest in a teapot.

By morning, though, it was clear we could be consumed by the Johnson distraction. The press coverage had grown louder and more critical, and raised legitimate questions about our judgment in selecting someone to conduct such an important task without a thorough scrub of their connections. I told Barack we had to do something. He said that as much as he hated to give Johnson up to the mob, we needed to do it.

I made the call to Jim, who handled it like a pro. For someone who had encountered little turbulence in a Washington career that spanned decades, it had to be painful, but he was gracious and understanding. Jim's son also worked for our campaign and turned out to be one of our more talented field organizers. I was glad Jim could still have that connection to the campaign.

———

At our next meeting, again in Holder's nondescript conference room, we narrowed the list down to six. There were no huge surprises. Barack continued to be intrigued by Hillary. "I still think Hillary has a lot of what I am looking for in a VP," he said to us. "Smarts, discipline, steadfastness. I think Bill may be too big a complication. If I picked her, my concern is that there would be more than two of us in the relationship."

Neither Ax nor I were fans of the Hillary option. We saw her obvious strengths, but we thought there were too many complications, both pre-election and post-election, should we be so fortunate as to win. Still, we were very careful not to object too forcefully. This needed to be his call.

Kennedy and Holder also tread carefully, but they raised all the obvious questions we'd have to ask—and that the press would ask—if we got very serious about picking her. Her campaign donor records, Bill's financial information, records from her legal life—these would need to be not just reviewed but most likely released publicly, given our focus on bringing added transparency to government. The vetting team also thought choosing her would look like a very political decision (which was somewhat irrelevant, as Obama was viewing her through the prism of capability in the office), and that many of our supporters would be discouraged by the selection.

We had initially received a lot of advice from many of her supporters to pick her, though this "advice" was perhaps more accurately described as subtle pressure. The constant drumbeat from her donors and political supporters said that the best way to achieve party unity and put forward the strongest ticket in November would be to pair the two primary combatants. Their fervor was abating a bit every day, though, helped by Hillary's comments that this was Obama's decision and that he should be left to make it.

As the vetting continued, we began the difficult task of bringing together Obama and the finalists without revealing the meetings themselves or the identities of the contenders. At this point I brought Alyssa into the loop and gave her the names of the people we needed to meet. Alyssa, though only thirty, was a grizzled veteran of this type of cloak-and-dagger mission, having played a similar role in the Kerry '04 race, with Obama in the Senate. She is the type of person you want on your side in a tough environment—when I asked her to do something, I had no doubt that it would get done, thoroughly and discreetly, without too many extraneous questions. I told her she was the only person outside of Ax and me who knew this list or even that the meetings would take place, so she would need to handle everything herself—making contact with the candidates, arranging the meetings, and bringing in a handful of staff only at the end to facilitate the meetings at the selected locations. Even most of our road show would not know these meetings were taking place, much less who was attending.

The meetings all took place on the road, at hotels Barack happened to be in for the night. The "targets," as we called the VP contenders, were flown in very early, squired to the hotel before Obama and the road show arrived, secreted in through back and basement entrances, bunkered in a room they could not leave, and then furtively evacuated after the meeting through an alternate exit so no press would see them on their way out. We never had a close call—the press made not a single solid inquiry about a meeting taking place on a certain day with a certain person.

Before Obama was scheduled to leave for Hawaii in early August, he narrowed his list down to three names: Senator Joe Biden of Delaware, Senator Evan Bayh of Indiana, and Governor Tim Kaine of Virginia. Hillary did not make the last cut. At the end of the day, Obama decided that there were just too many complications outweighing the potential strengths. But I gave him a lot of credit for so seriously thinking about his fierce former rival. Some in the Clinton orbit thought we gave Hillary short shrift. My view is that any serious consideration was somewhat surprising given all the complications and the toxicity during the primary campaign.

All three of the finalists had much to recommend them as well as their share of warning flares. Biden had loads of foreign policy experience, which could be helpful both in the campaign and, more important, in the vice presidency. He also had some blue-collar appeal as a middle-class kid from Scranton, Pennsylvania, which could be of some value as he campaigned in the fall. His personal story was compelling: Biden lost his wife and infant daughter in car crash at the age of twenty-nine, when he had just been elected to the Senate, and showed immense character both in pulling through that period and raising terrific children with his second wife, Jill. And legislators on both sides of the aisle thought highly of Biden, giving him the ability to potentially transact meaningful business in Congress as VP.

On the cloudy side, Biden had been dogged by plagiarism charges when he ran for president in 1988; these would of course be rehashed. He was also known to test even the Senate's standard for windiness, taking an hour to say something that required ten minutes. He also was prone to making gaffes; it was in his DNA and we couldn't expect that to change. In fact, on Biden's first day as a candidate in 2008, he caused an uproar by praising Obama as, among other things, "clean" and "articulate," leaving the impression that other African Americans were not. Barack took no offense and thought none was intended. But it was clear that if we picked him, we would suffer a few self-inflicted wounds.

Overall, though, we liked what we saw. During the Iowa campaign, we got to watch him fairly carefully, and through our many shared debates we thought he comported himself quite well. Based on his primary-debate performances, I thought he would hold his own in the one VP debate, which is the most critical campaign moment for VP nominees.

Tim Kaine had been elected Virginia governor in 2005, having previously served as the mayor of Richmond and as the state's lieutenant governor. He was the first major elected official outside of Illinois to endorse us, and he and Obama had a great rapport. The two men shared a background and many interests. Kaine's family was from Kansas, as was Obama's mother's family, and Kaine's Catholic faith had shaped the contours of his life, including his missionary work in Honduras. He and Obama also talked often about their shared belief in extreme pragmatism. Of the three finalists, Kaine would clearly present the best initial working relationship and would also allow us to double down on our message of change by enlisting an outsider.

Kaine brought no foreign policy experience to the campaign trail or the VP's office, and his relationships with Congress were tangential at best. We thought he presented perhaps the biggest initial downside but was also probably the candidate with the biggest growth potential, both before November 4 and after. And as a result of his early support and frequent campaigning for us, Barack was closer to him than he was to the others. Through e-mail and conference calls over the course of the campaign, Kaine had often shared his strategic and tactical thoughts, and they were usually dead-on, frequently unconventional, and focused on people, not pundits. He got who we were; his selection would have made for the most comfortable and seamless transition.

Evan Bayh had been on this list before. He had almost run for president in 2008 but ended up campaigning hard for Hillary Clinton in the primaries, which was of little concern to us; it potentially presented a political boost. Bayh was known in the Senate as a cautious moderate, building on his years as a young governor in Indiana, where he led as a centrist and pragmatist. These qualities appealed to Obama, as did his steadiness. One of the raps on Bayh was that he was boring, but in an enterprise like ours, that was no scarlet letter. Both the Obama campaign and a potential Obama administration would welcome Bayh's discipline.

In our view, Bayh was the safest pick. He and Obama had not always voted the same way (which might cause some angst with our base), and he also remained hawkish on Iraq long after most Democrats who had supported the war morphed into critics. We would have to navigate this, but it also wouldn't be the worst thing in the world to demonstrate through our VP pick that Obama was truly committed to governing for results, not by rigid ideology. Dunn and Pfeiffer were both close to Bayh, having worked for him in the past, and confirmed that he could be trusted to stay on message and not make any big mistakes.

Shortly before he took off for Hawaii and his much-needed vacation, Obama asked Axelrod and me to meet with the three finalists. He was going to spend a lot of time thinking about the choices and hoped to have a decision before he came back or soon thereafter; the convention was looming.

I told Katie and Alyssa that Ax and I needed to meet quietly with these three and ideally we'd see them all in one day to cut down on time out of the office. They pieced together a schedule that had us departing Chicago at 5:30 a.m. for Wilmington, Delaware, to meet with Biden; then on to West Virginia, where Bayh was vacationing with his family; and then to Virginia to meet with Kaine.

We boarded a small private plane before the sun was up and were met in Wilmington by Jill and Beau Biden, Joe's oldest son and Delaware's attorney general. They drove us to Biden's sister's place in a small, out-of-the-way area over the state line in Pennsylvania. We met outside, by the pool. Comically, the meeting started with Biden launching into a nearly twenty-minute soliloquy that ranged from the strength of our campaign in Iowa ("I literally wouldn't have run if I knew the steamroller you guys would put together"); to his evolving views of Obama ("I wasn't sure about him in the beginning of the campaign, but I am now"); why he didn't want to be VP ("The last thing I should do is VP, after thirty-six years of being the top dog, it will be hard to be number two"); why he was a good choice ("But I would be a good soldier and could provide real value, domestically and internationally"); and everything else under the sun. Ax and I couldn't get a word in edgewise.

It confirmed what we suspected: this dog could not be taught new tricks. But the conversation also confirmed our positive assumptions: his firm grasp of issues, his blue-collar sensibilities, and the fact that while he would readily accept the VP slot if offered, he was not pining for it.

He also said a couple of things that made an impact with us. First, we asked him how he would answer questions about differences in views or voting record with Obama. We used a bankruptcy bill, where, put simply, Biden had taken the position of the banks, and Obama, of the consumers. Delaware was the state with the largest number of financial corporations, so this was not a small matter in terms of how Biden would approach it.

"I would say Barack was right about that," he said simply. "I was wrong, and his position is the one I will be advocating for as his vice president." It was a surprisingly concise and effective answer.

He also talked at length about John McCain, with whom he was personally quite close; he had actually been present the day McCain met his second wife, Cindy. Biden's insight into McCain—particularly his belief that McCain valued unpredictability above just about everything and that this could affect his decision making—would be useful if he were in the bunker with us.

Biden was driving us back to the airport in his pickup, baseball hat pulled low. Suddenly, Ax startled us with a shout. "Shit!" he said. "I think I left my computer bag at your sister's house." I couldn't help but chuckle a bit as we turned around to retrieve yet another misplaced possession of Ax's. It was a quintessential Ax move: incisively assessing a potential vice president but having trouble remembering a bag. The phones, BlackBerrys, and other equipment he had lost in the years I had known him would fill the back of Biden's pickup. Ax was like a brain surgeon but a little absentminded, so you needed to make sure he was on time for surgery and double-check that he knew where to drill the hole. Once inside, though, he was without peer with a scalpel.

Our meeting with Bayh was also largely confirmatory. We met in his hotel room; his wife and kids were out. He had just showered after playing tennis with his kids and was dressed in a polo shirt and shorts. Despite the laid-back setting, Bayh never really relaxed. His answers to our questions were substantively close to perfect, if cautiously so. This of course is very common in politics, and we thought it would make for headache-free days on the trail—we knew he would hit his marks. Seeing Bayh right after Biden provided some interesting contrasts and comparisons.

Listening to Bayh talk I thought, There's no way this guy will color outside the lines. Biden may cross them with too much frequency. Biden will probably end up having more range—he can reach higher heights but could cause us real pain. Bayh's upside and downside are probably the closest spread of the three.

Bayh was thrilled we were contesting Indiana. "I don't know if you can win," he told us, "but I bet you can make it close. Something is stirring my state—I get the sense that we may be seeing a once-in-a-generational electoral shift." He was modest about his ability to help deliver the state, which we appreciated. "I don't know if I can help push you over the line there. I assume it won't hurt, but I couldn't in good conscience say those eleven Hoosier electoral votes will be in your column if it's Obama-Bayh," he confessed.

Bayh's best moments with us related to family. His wife served on a number of corporate boards, and it was clear that her positions would draw fire if we selected him. He passionately defended his wife's board service, both in terms of her professional qualifications and talent as well as the lengths they both traveled to remove any conflict of interest. We were satisfied he could bat down any questions on that front.

The Bayhs had chosen to raise their young children in Washington instead of Indiana, sending them to private schools, which, fairly or not, would draw some criticism. He was earnest and resolute in explaining their decision. Keeping the kids close allowed their family to spend the most time together; he was clearly committed to real involvement in their lives. He wrapped up this part of the discussion by saying, "I just won't allow anyone to question the decisions we have made as parents and as a family." In these moments, he gave off a humanity and warmth that was very appealing, and showed a dimension that belied his reputation.

As the day grew long, we headed to Richmond, our last stop. We met with Kaine in the governor's mansion. He was like family by then, so the meeting was comfortable from the get-go. Picking Kaine would be the biggest leap, though it was clear in talking with him about issues that he would be a skilled communicator on the trail and in the media. His own outlook dovetailed closely with Obama's, so he was exceedingly comfortable serving as his advocate.

We appreciated his opening remarks. "I'd be honored to be picked," he told us. "But I have to assume I'm at the bottom of the list right now. I'll try to explain why I think I'd be a good pick, both for the campaign and after we win, but just know that I won't have an ounce of hard feelings or disappointment if I don't get picked. I signed on to this team in the beginning—all I want is for Barack to be elected president."

It certainly endeared him to us further, without making it easier to select him. There was no great way to explain putting someone with no foreign policy experience a heartbeat away from the presidency. If we chose him, we would need to rely on some of the same language we had used on this issue as it related to Obama—judgment versus Washington experience, a new foreign policy vision versus the status quo—but doubling down would make it twice as tough for us to roll this boulder uphill. A Kaine pick would entail the roughest entry, but if he availed himself well, we could find our way through. There was no doubt he'd be a trusted ally for Obama.

As our flight took to the skies from Richmond's airport, Ax and I reflected on our day while we ate the boxed dinners Governor Kaine's wife had graciously made for us. At root, little had changed. Biden was the top choice for us, but with reservations. The day had shown both the promise and peril of his selection. Bayh was someone we could both embrace, as he would likely make our lives easier and generate fewer surprises, but it felt like he might be too safe a choice. And we wished Kaine had a little bit more experience, because he had so many of the qualities we knew Obama valued.

"This is a jump ball," Ax declared. "There's no clear choice. Anyway, I'm glad it's up to him and not us. It'll be like the decisions he'll need to make as president—lonely and tough. Should we tell him we oh so slightly favor Biden?"

"I think we owe it to him to put our thumb lightly on the scale for Biden," I replied. "But we really need to play it straight and balance out our critiques of each. I don't want a call from him during a crisis in 2010, where he says, 'Plouffe, now tell me exactly what you were thinking in convincing me to pick Biden?'"

Thinking about that made us both laugh a bit, but gingerly.

"If he does pick Biden though, that will be your account," I warned Ax. "You're going to have to deal with him every day to make sure he stays in the corral. If he picks Bayh or Kaine, I'll take point. Call it manager's prerogative and the penalty for forgetting your damn bag at Biden's place and making us late."

"Me take Biden?" he asked. "Forget it. You're the Delaware guy. He's all you."

"No way. You love talking and he loves talking. It's a perfect match. And what's a couple more hours in the day to you?"

Eventually our barbs petered out and we landed in Chicago. Later that night we held a conference call with Obama to brief him on our day. He mostly listened as we reviewed the bidding. "Well it sounds like you both are for Biden, but barely," he said. "I really haven't settled this yet in my own mind. It's a coin toss now between Bayh and Biden, but Kaine is still a distinct possibility. I know the experience attack people will make if we pick him. But if that really concerned me, I wouldn't have run in the first place.

"My sense is—and you tell me if the research backs this up—that Barack Hussein Obama is change enough for people. I don't have to convince people with my VP selection that I am serious about change. But I think people will grow to really respect and appreciate Tim Kaine. He's the wildcard. We kind of know what we are getting with the other two.

"I'm back to where I was in the beginning," Obama continued. "I'll really think this through over the next few days, trying to visualize various scenarios in the presidency, and whom I'd most like to have by my side."

Obama let out a heavy sigh. "I wish I didn't have this hanging over my vacation."

"Well," I said sarcastically, "if we pull this off, you can just consider it a practice run for all of your vacations over the next eight years. Just remember—when you leave office, you'll be in AARP but not too old. You'll still have a few enjoyable vacations left."

Obama laughed. "Right," he said. "That's why I'm working so hard—so at fifty-five, I can have unquestionably the best job in the whole world. Ex-president."

———

The selection of his vice presidential nominee was his first presidential decision, and shortly after he returned from Hawaii, he finally made it. On the evening of August 17, he called Ax and me with the news, "I've decided," he said. "It's Biden."

The decision had been difficult, but Barack was excited about his pick. More than anything, he felt Biden would be a trusted adviser during tough moments after the election, someone who would always give his unvarnished opinion. And even after all his years in Washington, Biden remained a real advocate for people, which was ultimately what this whole enterprise was about.

Now that Barack had picked him, I felt some exhilaration thinking that Biden would be a nice complement to Obama, in age, background, and style. Once we had things going I thought the mix would work nicely. But at the moment, with the announcement in front of us, I still felt a bit like we were about to take a hard, hairpin turn without being strapped in.

We would formally announce Biden the following Saturday, August 23, in Springfield, Illinois, the site of our campaign launch. Joe Rospars came into my office one afternoon with the idea of telling our supporters first, before the media or politicos. "While our e-mail list is growing exponentially, our mobile numbers could use a big kick start," he explained. "Why don't we ask people to sign up for a text alert? We can tell them that they'll be the first to know who Barack picks as VP."

The idea appealed to me on two levels. First, it was consistent with other key junctures in the campaign—reporting fund-raising numbers, the decision to limit our primary debates, opting out of the public funding system—where we had communicated first directly to our supporters. This was their campaign as much as ours, and they deserved to get a heads-up from us about important decisions. Those previous announcements had all been made by e-mail or Web postings; this would be our first large-scale text-only notification.

Second, this was a great way to grow our text-messaging list. Rospars was right about the increasing gap in our contact figures: our e-mail list was now over 6 million, but our list of mobile numbers was in the low six figures. Making a big announcement by text would ignite a spark and juice the latter number.

It sure did. By August 22, the night before we announced Biden, over 2 million people had signed up to receive the VP announcement by text. Our first communication announcing the "Be the First to Know" campaign had happened on August 10. In less than two weeks, we had grown our list over fifteen-fold.

That the Republican convention was scheduled to begin just a week after ours was terrible in many ways. The dates of both parties' conventions were set back in 2005, when Obama was still figuring out where the bathrooms were in the Senate. The party in control of the White House always gets to go last, but usually there's a buffer period of a few weeks. I remembered thinking when the dates were announced that having the GOP convention right on top of ours was less than ideal, but I figured it would be someone else's problem.

No such luck. And the situation was worsening. It was bad enough getting only a week's lift in the coverage to begin with, but now McCain's camp signaled to the press that his VP selection would be announced the day after our convention. In the very next news cycle our convention would be relegated to the dustbin while all the attention turned to their pick and the lead-in to the GOP convention. Our bounce, if there were one, would be fleeting. We planned to have Obama and Biden campaign together for first time that week, figuring that by having our two nominees out on their maiden trip, we would have something that would, if not rival their VP announcement, at least compete credibly for attention.

But first there was the matter of informing the selection that he'd been selected. Obama called me from the road Thursday after he talked to Biden.

"Even for Joe, he was going a mile a minute," Barack joked. "He also said he was humbled and ready to do anything we ask, the way we ask it. He has a million questions, so I told him you'd call him to give him the overview of the next few days and how we're going to get him and his team integrated."

I called Biden right away. He was driving to Philadelphia with Jill, to take his mother-in-law for some medical tests. She was quite ill at the time. Despite this family situation, I could tell over the phone he was elated. Netting the VP nomination really was a capstone to his storied career, and despite the indifference to being picked he'd shown at our meeting, now that it had actually happened I could hear how much it meant to him.

I told him we were thrilled to have him aboard and took the opportunity to remind him that he'd had some tough competition in the selection process "You know, Senator, we didn't push, but Axelrod and I were rooting for you," I told him. "And Barack knows that. So let's do us all a favor and make sure we reward him with a terrific, focused, and error-free ten weeks." He got the message and eventually proved to be every bit the team player we needed.

We were taking extra precaution to keep the pick secret until our announcement, including flying Ax and Patti Solis Doyle to a West Chester, Pennsylvania, airfield instead of Wilmington so the flight could not be traced by its tail number, and in case the airport was being staked out. Ax and Patti would be briefing Biden in the morning and flying with him to Springfield. When they got to their hotel late that night, Ax sent me an e-mail that said simply: "You cheap bastard." They had been booked at some fleabag motel off I-95. I told him to enjoy the thin sheets and dirty bedspread.

At least he would sleep a couple of hours that night. As it turned out, none of us involved on the press or text-message side of things would sleep a wink. As the hours progressed, it seemed more and more likely that some news outlet might break the story of our selection—hard evidence or not. If so, we'd have to put in motion our text alert right away.

The media was frantic, each outlet in a rush to be the first to break the news of our selection. Shortly after midnight, the Associated Press was the first to name Biden as the pick. Their story was based on one unnamed Democratic source. One. It sounded pretty thin to me. Almost all news organizations—including the AP—usually require one named source or two unnamed sources before going with a story.

I was absolutely convinced they did not have it directly. They might have talked to someone who thought they knew, but not any of the few of us in the campaign who knew for certain, or Biden or his immediate family.

I understood the competition to be first. But I felt this was a real low moment in terms of reporting in the campaign, and I subsequently learned that some of the AP reporters were uncomfortable as well. They knew their story was shaky but their bosses said to go regardless.

We started sending out texts right away. It took a couple of hours to get them all out, but it was late, so most people on the East Coast and in the central part of the country heard from us first when they woke up (or when our arriving message woke them up). Night owls and West Coast supporters might have heard it first from the media, because as soon as the AP went, everyone else jumped in, and within minutes it was breaking news on TV and on the Web. We felt good that it held as long as it did and that most of our supporters heard from us first. The message read, "Barack has chosen Senator Joe Biden to be our VP nominee. Watch the first Obama-Biden rally live at 3 p.m. ET on www.barackobama.com. Spread the word!"

It's important to note that we encouraged people to watch the live stream on our website. We were doing this with greater frequency, and many people were watching major events on our site and then afterward logging on to MyBO.com to discuss what they had just seen with their fellow supporters. We were accomplishing what we set out to create—a website that could be a real "home" for our supporters and a one-stop shopping place for anything campaign related. It was like having our own television returns.

The sun filled the sky in Springfield on the day of our announcement, with temperatures promising to hit the nineties. I flew down from Chicago with Barack and Michelle, and we talked about how the last time we were in Springfield, no one could have credibly predicted we'd be returning on the eve of the Democratic convention to announce Barack Obama's running mate.

"Remember how cold it was?" Michelle asked. "I couldn't feel my toes by the end. Now we'll be lucky not to sweat through the whole event."

We were all in a great mood. Michelle was very happy to have a sidekick for Barack, someone who could shoulder part of the load and defend him against attacks in a way the rest of us couldn't. "I think Joe is going to be a warrior," she said. "A happy warrior. It's good to have some reinforcements."

I joked that last the time we were in Springfield, Gibbs and I had shared a room, and it was not a pretty sight in the morning. "At least this time we aren't overnighting, so I won't have to wake up to the sight of Gibbs in his boxers," I said.

Gibbs piped in from down the aisle of the plane, "Or you in yours. Scary stuff, Plouffe."

The event itself gave us a real boost. Obama and Biden looked great together, and it seemed to be a marriage that worked—the young, inspirational insurgent matched with the experienced Washington hand. Most of the early commentary was favorable, and some of the smarter observers got that Biden was not the safest choice we could have made. Yes, he was a political veteran, but his past controversies and penchant for creating new ones required a small leap of faith on our part.

We also had Obama and Biden film their first video together, in one of the historic rooms at the Old State Capitol, which we sent directly to our supporters. The video introduced Biden and asked viewers to recommit to the campaign by contributing financially, volunteering, and recruiting new supporters. We were trying to include a lot more videos in our e-mail communications—the data suggested that supporters spent more time with these e-mails than with the text-only versions.

Obama usually did these tapings in one or two takes. He was the best I had ever seen at nailing a script, or ad-libbing to produce a more effective product. This video, however, required at least ten takes because Biden kept stumbling over his lines. That was the norm for most political figures. We were just used to Obama's almost effortless performances.

Conventions aren't what they used to be. These days they run short on suspense, and shorter on TV. The networks no longer cover them all evening long; in 2008 only three total hours of each party's convention made the cut. Those hours reached by far the broadest audience, and we needed to spend a lot of time making sure we got them right. But the cable and Internet audience would not be insignificant, and the news coverage would be tremendous, so we also had to think beyond the network hours to create a broader idea of what we needed to accomplish each night.

We had hashed out our goals for the convention during a few conference calls in June. These were pretty straightforward: We needed to put the final nail in the coffin of the bloody-primary/fractured-party story line. In both perception and reality, we needed to come roaring out of the convention a unified, powerful Democratic Party. We needed to introduce Barack's personal story to the millions of Americans who still did not know it—his humble beginnings, strong values, and deep love for this country. We needed to lay out the case against McCain as well. By the time we wrapped up, there could be no doubt in the public mind about the different directions in which these two men would lead the country.

And finally, we wanted to use the convention to bolster our campaign in Colorado, a battleground state where we thought we could break McCain's back if he let things slip away. At the day's end, our plan revolved around taking crucial electoral votes away from McCain wherever possible. If we could use the time and platform of the convention to strengthen our organization and enhance Obama's standing in a pivotal state like Colorado, it was arguably as important as anything that might result at the national level.

Negotiations with the remnants of the Clinton campaign couldn't have gone down easier. Scores of media reports leading up to the convention suggested otherwise, implying that the "Clinton drama" would overshadow our message. First, we were confident that both Clintons, Hillary on Tuesday and Bill on Wednesday, would deliver strong and compelling speeches. Even if we occasionally still questioned her team's motives—and we did less and less of that because Hillary was campaigning her heart out for us—we knew it would be political suicide for either of them to give anything but a full-throated, stirring endorsement of Obama. If we lost in a close race, lackluster support from our former primary opponent would quickly surface as a main culprit of the defeat.

We raised the idea with the Clinton camp that on Wednesday during the traditional roll call of states, Hillary would enter the floor, stride to the New York delegation, and ask that the convention end the roll call and nominate Barack Obama by acclamation. We suggested doing this around 6:30 p.m., right as the network news programs were beginning, for maximum effect.

Clinton readily agreed, and her request unexpectedly turned into a powerful and gripping moment that sent an electric charge through the convention. With poise and confidence, she commanded the microphone in the New York delegation and said, "Let us declare in one voice, right here, right now, that Barack Obama is our candidate, and he will be our president!"

The convention roared its agreement and pandemonium broke out. The song "Peace Train" burst from the speakers, and confetti and balloons rained down. Tears and emotion were flowing throughout the arena, and I imagine in living rooms and offices around the country as well. I watched the scene with the staff at our convention HQ office at a hotel a few blocks from the hall. At that moment, the history, the long battle, and the improbability of it all washed over me; emotion came rushing to the fore. The spectacle grabbed the media, too, whose commentary was very focused on the historic nature of Barack Obama's nomination, as well as the brilliance of Hillary's making it official—and her humility in agreeing to do so.

It's nice to be surprised in this business. And we were, all of us, that when this moment finally arrived, it carried such authentic emotion. Barack watched it from his hotel room; he had just arrived in Denver. He told me it affected him, too. "That was terrific that Hillary agreed to do that," he said. "Seems like it sent a jolt through the whole convention."

The Clinton speeches were all we could have asked for, unambiguous in their enthusiasm for Obama's potential presidency and forceful in their denunciation of McCain's flawed vision for America. Our convention hall staff HQ was right off the floor, and Hillary had to walk through it on the way to her holding room after she spoke. As she entered the room, we all burst out into loud and sustained impromptu applause. We understood better than most the fortitude her public embrace of his candidacy required. After everything we had thrown at each other, she had given us her all.

———

Michelle Obama's speech on the first night of the convention was critical for two reasons. First, it was our best opportunity—better even than Obama's own speech—to show what kind of person Barack was. There were shadowy suggestions floating both virally on the Internet and in the mainstream press that he was un-American, a Muslim, an elitist, a privileged phony.

Michelle's speech would tell the truth about Obama as a son, a husband, a father, and a citizen. Even though voters found Barack quite likeable, too many of them still found him somewhat remote and did not have a grasp of what his life had been like. Helping them understand this would make his promise to try to improve their lives more tangible and real.

The second objective was to showcase Michelle herself in a slightly different and more accurate light. A whisper campaign had been circulating for months, saying that she was hurting our campaign, that she was too angry. A misconstrued statement she made during the primary—"For the first time in my life, I am proud of my country"—left some voters wondering what really made her tick. I wanted America to see and truly understand the real Michelle Obama, someone who profoundly appreciated the generosity and bold spirit of her country.

She delivered an absolute gem. We introduced her with a video narrated by her mother, a beautiful presentation that described Michelle's parents, the sacrifices they made, and her own improbable success. Her speech built on this and also revealed a side of Barack that many voters had not been exposed to, most memorably with a tender line about Barack driving back from the hospital after their first daughter was born.

"And in the end, after all that's happened these past nineteen months," she told the crowd, "the Barack Obama I know today is the same man I fell in love with nineteen years ago. He's the same man who drove me and our new baby daughter home from the hospital ten years ago this summer, inching along at a snail's pace, peering anxiously at us in the rearview mirror, feeling the whole weight of her future in his hands, determined to give her everything he'd struggled so hard for himself, determined to give her what he never had: the affirming embrace of a father's love."

Michelle's favorable numbers jumped eighteen points that night in our tracking, and they never dropped the rest of the campaign.

Preparing for the convention speeches illuminated one interesting contrast between Michelle and Barack. Michelle wanted a draft of her speech more than a month out so she could massage it further, get comfortable with it, and practice the delivery. Barack was always crafting his at the eleventh hour. In this regard, Michelle was a concert pianist—disciplined, regimented, methodical—and Barack was a jazz musician, riffing, improvisational, and playing by ear. Both Obamas, it turned out, were clutch performers when the curtain rose.

We were determined to break Barack's habit of last-minute prep and have his convention speech together well in advance, but we knew he would not dig in until right before showtime. At one of our planning meetings, I raised the idea of taking Barack's acceptance speech outside, so grassroots supporters throughout the country, not just the Democratic delegates inside the arena, could attend the event. We were a grassroots campaign, and it felt wrong that our biggest night so far could not be shared with those who had selflessly given so much time and effort. Plus, many of the additional people—numbering in the tens of thousands at least, depending on the outside venue—would be Colorado voters. Everyone was gung-ho in theory, but execution would be a far more difficult task.

Alyssa and her team looked at every option, including holding the speech outside in the streets of downtown Denver, where there would be no limit on the number of attendees. We thought we could easily draw 250,000 if we did not have space limitations. But for security and other logistical reasons, we needed a confined venue, which left us only one option—Mile High Stadium.

Four of our central operating philosophies came together in one moment. First, the willingness to chuck the old playbook and chart our own course. John Kennedy was the only candidate to have previously given an outdoor acceptance speech, in Los Angeles in 1960. I hadn't remembered that when making the suggestion, but once I found out, I appreciated the historical connection.

Second, testing the organization by consistently reaching to accomplish difficult things. When this idea was first broached with the convention staff in Denver—who technically worked for us now but had been plugging away on the convention for months awaiting a nominee—they told us flat-out there was no way financially, organizationally, or politically it could be done. It would add millions to the cost; we'd have to move all the delegates to another location, which was logistically impossible, they said; there were no hotel rooms anywhere in the Denver area for all the new people an outdoor speech would draw; and the delegates would be upset that the event would be opened up to the public. After all, this was their special night; they were the ones nominating Barack Obama. "We'll find a way to make it happen," we told them. Winning the primary had infused our whole campaign with the sense that anything was possible, which is a great mind-set for any organization to have.

Third, we knew who we were—a grassroots campaign to the core. We started with our supporters on the ground and they led us to victory. It just did not feel right that this important night would exclude the people most responsible for Obama's being the nominee. The fourth principle the decision reflected was our belief that the election came down to winning battleground states. Colorado perhaps trailed only Virginia in my mind in terms of importance. McCain had to have Colorado's nine electoral votes to have any hope of winning, and opening up our convention to the people there could go a long way toward tipping the state into our column.

———

One Saturday shortly before we had to make a final decision, Obama and I were on the phone talking through the pros and cons.

"Tell me again what happens if it rains or if there's lightning?" he asked.

I said we had checked in with our friends at the meteorologists union, who did a study of the last hundred August 28s at 8:00 p.m. mountain time. It had rained on only one occasion, and that was showers, not a drenching rain. Colorado was usually bone dry that time of year.

It sounded reassuring, but he asked the natural follow-up question. "Well, what if this is that one time? Can we look at the most detailed forecast that morning and decide to go back inside?"

"Unfortunately not," I replied. "For Secret Service reasons as well as just logistics of having tens of thousands of people en route, it's lock and load. And that's leaving aside all the money we'd be out. It is costing us a pretty penny to retrofit the stadium. If we decide now to go outside, we have to live with the decision."

He was quiet for a moment. "Okay, let's go for it, as long as we can have some sort of covering on standby so I don't have to give the speech in the pouring rain." He wryly added, "It's only the most important speech I may ever give."

"Uh, that's a no-go," I told him. We had looked into it and found we couldn't have a temporary rain shelter moved into place at the last minute. It just wouldn't work visually. If we did it, the shelter would have to be built into the stage construction, and if it didn't rain, we'd regret having a big overhang.

Barack was a bit incredulous. "So, what, we're just going to go with a wing and a prayer and hope beyond all hope we get lucky on the weather?" he asked.

"First, the odds are with us it won't rain," I said. "Look, I know this isn't the soundest way to make decisions, but this whole enterprise has been a roll of the dice. Every time we've gone up on the high wire, it's worked out. We shouldn't stop now."

I wasn't sure I could get him to buy into it. He had understandable concerns. But I knew the idea of bucking conventional wisdom appealed to him.

Finally, he made his decision. "Okay, we go outside," he said. "But at some point our luck will run out. So if it's raining, I want you and Axelrod out there holding goddamn umbrellas over my head while I give the speech."

I laughed. "Deal."

Strategically, we had decided some time ago that we had three major imperatives for his speech. First, build on what Michelle and some other speakers had done that week by talking about his family and values, and to a lesser extent his experience. This would make his motivation and commitment to help the middle class more authentic and believable—he and Michelle had walked in those shoes for almost their entire lives.

Second, lay out in great detail exactly what he would do as president. We had long faced a chorus of criticism that we were too light on specifics. Too much hope, just give us the dope, said some. In response, we had always planned for a heavy dose of issue specifics in Denver. And, again, because this moment presented the chance to leave a large footprint, we also thought it was important for Obama to lay out a tough critique of John McCain's agenda—how it represented little change from the Bush agenda, domestically and internationally, and that we simply could not afford more of the same for another four years.

The last item surprised a lot of people. Generally, the nominee stays positive while the rest of the convention speakers beat up on the opposition. And our other speakers had certainly laid out compelling arguments against McCain. But we thought it was important that Obama himself not shy away from any of these critiques. A healthy percentage of our ultimate jury would be watching or would hear about the speech; we needed to make our best case to that audience.

Gibbs and I started that Thursday together at the stadium at 4:00 a.m. for rounds of TV interviews. It was eerie being there in the pitch black, with the cool mountain air rushing in and the signage for all the states reaching toward the open sky. The advance team had finally locked everything down just hours before.

We could have fallen asleep standing, but it was hard not to be taken in by the scene. "We've come a long way from Springfield," Gibbs said, looking around the stadium. "But some things are the same—we're exhausted and we still don't have a final speech."

I laughed. "Fixing that would be change I could believe in."

———

Fifteen hours later, Gibbs and I were standing backstage with Barack. He was loose and clearly very comfortable with his speech, which had once again magically come together sometime during the day. I had spoken at the convention earlier that afternoon, giving an organizational pitch and campaign update, and now Obama was razzing me about it.

"Plouffe, how many people were there when you spoke?" he asked.

I flashed a smile. "About two thousand. And none of them were listening."

"Well," he said, "I hope you have pictures of it to prove to your kids that you actually spoke."

Gibbs and I left the holding room along with Axelrod, who was going to watch the speech with some of the media and production folks a short distance away. We had learned Obama liked to spend some time alone before a big moment, to get ready and perhaps just to get in the zone.

That night was remarkable. The weather was perfect, warm and still, and almost eighty thousand people waving American flags filled the stadium. A roar erupted when Obama walked out, and the electricity as he spoke raised the hair on my neck.

Gibbs and I both were speechless. A lot came washing over us at that moment—what it took to get there; the beauty of the decision to go outside; the historic nature of what was happening; and pride in the guy we worked for, who was rising to the occasion, once again, and giving the speech of a lifetime. Gibbs and I looked at each other often during the speech, saying little, but communicating a lot. And for perhaps the first time in the entire campaign, we both went a full hour without looking at our BlackBerrys.

"For eighteen long months," Obama told the masses, "you have stood up, one by one, and said, 'Enough' to the politics of the past. You understand that, in this election, the greatest risk we can take is to try the same old politics with the same old players and expect a different result. You have shown what history teaches us, that at defining moments like this one, the change we need doesn't come from Washington. Change comes to Washington. Change happens—change happens—because the American people demand it, because they rise up and insist on new ideas and new leadership, a new politics for a new time."

As the speech ended, Gibbs and I made our way to Ax and his media team, and there were hugs all around. Obama had just nailed it, and we had nailed the week. This was the third of the four hard things Ax and I had discussed back in my office in June, and so far we thought we were three for three.

Backstage, Obama was more demonstrative than usual, and actually seemed downright giddy. He was still calm, but I could tell he knew he had done well, and how much that mattered. "We all performed well this week," he told us. "Now we only need eight more weeks like this." Put that way, it seemed digestible and doable.

My dad and wife were in Denver, so I told Obama I needed to duck out for dinner with them. I gave him a last fist-bump and was off. It was nice to have an hour free and clear of the tumult. We had a late dinner at our hotel, talking some about the big night but also about family and sports. My dad and I are rabid Philadelphia Phillies fans, so we were likely bemoaning their latest loss or bad move.

We cleared out of the restaurant somewhere around 1:00 a.m. I planned to get up at 5:00 a.m. Colorado time to see my wife off and to start the workday— McCain would be announcing his VP nominee that morning, and I wanted to get a head start.

But my phone and e-mail started going off well before then. Rumors were swirling that McCain was going to make a surprise pick.

14

Hurricane Sarah

"It looks like they picked Sarah goddamn Palin. We have to get moving."

It was early morning, Denver time, and the echoes of Barack Obama's stirring convention speech were still ringing in my ears when my cell phone erupted with calls and the first rumors started flying online. I was in the fog of a couple of hours' sleep. Palin—it took me a moment to place the name. Mitt Romney, Tim Pawlenty, Joe Lieberman—these guys had been filling my brain for weeks now. But in an instant they became also-rans.

My mind strained to remember the pertinent details on Palin. She was on our initial list of about twenty potential McCain picks when we started the process back in May, somewhere near the rear of pack. It had been months since we discussed her at our campaign HQ.

The first thing I did was call Jim Messina, who was managing the day-to-day VP opposition research project. I woke him up, and he sounded like he'd been celebrating until very recently. "Stop screwing with me," he pleaded into the phone.

"This is not a fire drill," I said to him. "It's the real deal. You need to get your team going on Palin. We need a game plan for moving forward, and quickly."

We always knew this day was going to be a pain in the ass. Coming right off the exhaustion and exhilaration of our convention week and VP pick, we would have to jump right in and deal with theirs. But Palin was a bolt of lightning, a true surprise. She was such a long shot, I didn't even have her research file on my computer, as I did for the likely McCain picks. I started Googling her, refreshing my memory while I waited for our research to be sent.

Her story was original: small-town mayor takes on the establishment and wins a governor's race; she was an avid hunter, sportswoman, and athlete, and her husband was a champion snowmobiler; she had just given birth to a child with Down syndrome. A profile out of a novel, I thought.

But here she was, joining our real-life drama. And given her life story, coupled with the surprise nature of her selection, her entrance to the race would be nothing short of a phenomenon. I felt certain that all the oxygen in the campaign would immediately go to the newly minted McCain-Palin ticket.

But I also thought it was a downright bizarre, ill-considered, and deeply puzzling choice. The one thing every voter knew about John McCain's campaign at this point was that it had been shouting from the rooftops that Barack Obama lacked the experience to be president. In fact, the celebrity attack was still going on!

With the Palin pick, he had completely undermined his core argument against us. Worse yet for McCain, he would look inherently political in doing so. His strength—and the threat he posed to us—was rooted in the fact that many independent voters believed in his maverick reputation and believed he did not make his decisions by prioritizing politics over what was right. I guessed people would view this choice more as a political stunt than a sound, reasoned call.

Though VP selections have rarely made the difference in presidential campaigns, voters do put a huge premium on candidates' making wise, responsible choices of running mates who could plausibly serve in high office. After all, historically, about a third of vice presidents have ascended to the top job.

Our campaign did not like surprises. We had established a game plan for the picks we thought were plausible, developing what our top-line response would be and deciding which areas of controversy we'd highlight for the press. Getting Palin right would be a challenge.

———

On our 6:00 a.m. conference call, Anita Dunn, who had worked against Palin in Alaska in the 2006 governor's race, warned us that she was a formidable political talent—clearly not up to this moment, she assured us, but bound to be a compelling player and a real headliner in the weeks ahead.

"All of you on this call should watch video of her debates and speeches," Anita counseled. "The substance is thin but she's a very able performer. And her story is out of Hollywood. She'll be a phenomenon for a while."

Axelrod added that no matter how talented she was, these were rough waters to drop into, especially with no national exposure or scrutiny. "It's like throwing a baby into the ocean and asking it to swim," he said.

Our strategy with the other potential picks would've been to start by saying that choice X subscribed to the same failed George Bush policies as John McCain; all they were doing was doubling down on the same out-of-touch economic policies that had hurt American families.

We should have gone the same way with Palin. But McCain had been haranguing us for months about experience, and we were incredulous that he had picked someone with zero foreign policy experience who had been a governor for less time than Obama had been a senator. Galled by the hypocrisy, we moved in a more aggressive direction.

We decided to call McCain on the experience card directly. The value was in making him look political—essentially, calling him full of shit—and we sent out a release making that clear. "Today, John McCain put the former mayor of a town of 9,000 with zero foreign policy experience a heartbeat away from the presidency," it read. "Governor Palin shares John McCain's commitment to overturning Roe v. Wade, the agenda of Big Oil, and continuing George Bush's failed economic policies—that's not the change we need, it's just more of the same."

Ax and Gibbs were en route the airport with Obama when this went out. Our approach seemed so clear-cut and obvious that we did not run the statement by him before we released it. Ax and Gibbs would brief him on the plane about our conclusions. We advised him not to engage Palin at all when he saw the press later in the day in Pennsylvania and Ohio. Instead, he should welcome her to the race and make the point that Palin, like all McCain supporters, would be defending a discredited economic philosophy. Biden was with Obama for the ticket's first day of campaigning together, and we said the same advice held for him.

Our statement immediately received an enormous amount of attention because it went right at her experience. The press clearly sensed heat and was eager to help drive the fight. Seeing the reaction, I began to think perhaps we had misfired.

Obama clearly thought so. He called me from the air. "Listen, I just told this to Axelrod and Gibbs," he began. "I understand the argument you guys were trying to make. And maybe we should make it someday. But not today.

We shouldn't have put out the first part of that statement. I want to put out another statement that simply welcomes her to the race, and I'll call her and congratulate her when I land."

I didn't disagree, but thought backtracking would only add to the sense in the press that perhaps Palin was a brilliant game-changing pick that had scrambled the race. Even the famously disciplined Obama campaign can't get their story straight—this would be the blowback.

"Look," I told him, "simply say that you're adding your own personal voice, one principal to another." He acknowledged that he understood and would watch his words. "We'll send out a personal statement from you and Biden," I said, "but it's important you not suggest we misfired on the original statement. Don't throw the campaign under the bus."

But when he took a few questions from the press later that day, he inevitably got one about the difference in tone between the two statements, and he proceeded to drive the bus right over us. "I think that, uh, you know, campaigns start getting these, uh, hair triggers and, uh, the statement that Joe and I put out reflects our sentiments," he said. Great, I thought, already imagining the heat we'd take on this. But all in all, I felt solid about our instincts. Despite our clumsiness, I still thought we had nailed, in the predawn hours, what this pick would mean over time.

Obama and I had a long talk late that afternoon to evaluate Palin. I was sitting at the Denver airport, eager to finally get back to Chicago. He was between events, on our campaign bus.

"I just don't understand how this ends up working out for McCain," he said. "In the long term, I mean. The short term will be good for them. But when voters step back and analyze how he made this decision, I think he's going to be in big trouble. You just can't wing something like this—it's too important."

Reports had already begun to surface that McCain picked Palin at the very last minute, only days after his first conversation with her, on the phone. The pick increasingly seemed not just political, but the result of a haphazard, irresponsible process, if you could even call it a process.

"I know this sounds over the top," I replied. "But in my gut I feel like this might have sealed McCain's fate."

"What do you mean?"

"Well, they have a tough hand to begin with, given Bush's numbers and how we see the Electoral College situation," I explained. "You add this in . . .

my guess is that the more we learn about Palin and the lack of process behind the pick, the bloom will come quickly off the rose. No one wins the presidency with stunts. And that's what this smells like—a reckless stunt."

"I think we just need to sit back and play our game," said Obama. "It actually won't be bad to be off Broadway for a few days. We should just leave her out of the equation. This is a race between John McCain and me. To the extent we talk about Palin, I think it should be about the differences in our selection processes—it illuminates differences in how we'd make decisions in the White House."

In moments like this I really appreciated Barack. His predisposition to taking the long view of things and to coolly and rationally examining situations was one of the reasons our campaign made decisions the right way—through the prism of our strategy and message. And for the first time, we used terms like "impulsive" and "erratic" to describe McCain.

———

Within days, rumors about Palin were flying around the Internet. These included some disgraceful claims made about her family based on conjecture and malice, which we wanted nothing to do with. But it was clear watching their response to these wild assertions—and to valid ones, like her history of support for pork-barrel projects and details on the ethics charges she was facing—that the McCain campaign was completely unprepared for the fallout from their pick. They had little to no knowledge of Palin's record, her past statements, details of her time as mayor of Wasilla, or anything else. From where we sat, they seemed to be largely flying blind, scrambling to answer a torrent of questions only nine weeks out from the election. Before we picked Biden, we had sussed out almost every question we'd get about his past and record and how to deal with it. Given a three-month head start on us, our opponents were struggling with the basics. It was no way to run a railroad.

Interestingly, Jim Messina and Anita had struck Palin off their list of top potentials for VP back in May, when their friends in Alaska started sending them all the clips on Troopergate, which seemed to them pretty disqualifying for a position where "first do no harm" was a basic job requirement.

Our campaign had zero interest in family stories becoming part of the political coverage. When Bristol Palin's pregnancy became a news sensation in late August, we actually thought that it might provide a boost to our opponents. The family looked victimized by the extensive coverage and the many talking heads moralizing about the supposed hypocrisy of a family-values candidate having a pregnant teenage daughter. These personal attacks would likely generate sympathy from voters.

Obama thought the topic had no place in the campaign and wanted to send a strong message to all who supported him that they should leave it alone. "I have said before and I will repeat again: People's families are off-limits," Obama said in an interview on the subject. "And people's children are especially off-limits. This shouldn't be part of our politics. It has no relevance to Governor Palin's performance as a governor or her potential performance as a vice president. So I would strongly urge people to back off these kinds of stories. You know my mother had me when she was eighteen. How a family deals with issues and teenage children shouldn't be a topic of our politics."

Controversy or not, it was clear that Sarah Palin was a meteor the likes of which had not crossed the political sky in some time. She was not simply a political candidate; she was an American phenomenon.

We assumed she would give a knockout speech at the GOP convention that week. Tapes of her previous speeches revealed she was a skilled communicator, and we believed the expectations for her were quite low—she had come out of nowhere and immediately found herself beset with controversy. The news media, and perhaps the voters, would likely judge even a decent performance a home run.

As the Republican convention started, we were beginning our prep sessions in advance of the first presidential debate, which would take place at the end of September. These were preliminary strategic discussions, during which we worked through exactly how we wanted to approach various issues likely to come up in the debates. On the night of Palin's much-anticipated convention speech, we held one of our first sessions in a cramped Pennsylvania hotel room after a day of campaigning. Obama's night-owl tendencies were an asset in this regard; even after a long day on the trail, he was unfazed by prepping for another two or three hours at night. He was often at his best and most energetic in the evening, and he liked this part of prep—the development of strategy and messaging around issues—much more than the practicing and critiquing of answers.

Showing discipline that night, we decided not to break for Palin's speech on Thursday night. We worked right through until eleven or so and watched it on YouTube. Some reporters sent us the text of her speech shortly before she gave it, and reading through, I knew it would light up the convention hall.

I wasn't wrong. Palin delivered with gusto and presence. She was utterly undaunted by the national stage, sticking a knife into Obama with a smile. Her demeanor was jaunty and funny; she was clearly a terrific political performer.

But did voters believe Palin had the stature—or the familiarity—to play the role of attack dog? Generally in politics, before candidates can attack their opponent, they needed to build up some credibility with voters. One reason incumbents win so often is that it's easier for them to undercut their opponents; they've already established legitimacy with voters for their opinions and positions. A challenger who attacks an incumbent without first finding solid ground often provokes a "who the hell does he think he is?" reaction. I suspected this might be the case with Palin. She had burst onto the scene and attracted wide media coverage, but public knowledge about her was still skin-deep.

She also made a couple of big mistakes in the convention speech, like belittling "community organizers," almost suggesting they were subversives. I thought this comment insulted the millions of people who volunteer in their community simply trying to do good. The crowd in the hall loved it, but I thought America might see it differently.

Palin's speech also offered very little in the way of substance, serving mainly to attack Obama and praise McCain's biography and character. Our research showed clearly that McCain was already viewed as attacking Obama much more than offering any positive ideas. And voters saw Obama as doing the opposite. If opinions continued to move in this direction, we thought it could give McCain real difficulty, particularly with women independents who were turned off by sleazy ads and attacks. Our research also showed that these women reacted quite negatively to the Palin pick, as did the "Hillary Democrats" that the McCain camp was supposedly courting with her selection.

In Palin's first speech the day she was picked, she had made an overt and fairly clumsy appeal to Hillary voters. By this point, most Clinton Democrats had buried any hesitation and were firmly in our camp. We found that many of them were insulted by the notion that Hillary's supporters would move in droves to the Republican ticket simply because Palin was a woman, even though she was diametrically opposed to Clinton on just about every major issue.

After watching the convention speech, Ax and I stood in the hallway of our nondescript hotel in central Pennsylvania and ruminated. "That speech will only get the critics and the cynics more amped up that we should go after her, to try to destabilize McCain," I observed. "And she's now become the most interesting political figure in decades, so the coverage of her will only intensify."

Ax shook his head. "We just have to hold tight," he said. "I may be wrong. But she's now reached the stratosphere. Political gravity inevitably pulls someone shot this high back to earth. And usually it's not a pretty fall."

I concurred but added that it would test all of our discipline to stay the course and not get dragged into a shooting match. "That's the fight the press and political community wants. We have to avoid it all costs."

I was still pondering about how we'd stay the course when I went to my room at around 1:00 a.m. to check our online fund-raising numbers. Pulling them up onscreen, I couldn't believe what I saw. We had taken in millions of dollars in the three hours since Palin had started speaking. We hadn't even asked for most of it; we had sent out just a single unplanned fund-raising e-mail highlighting her attacks on community organizers, but it was just starting to hit people's in-boxes as I checked the numbers. So the big response from the last three hours meant people were merely venting via contribution.

Her speech might have ginned up their base, but apparently it had sent ours into orbit. The image that came into my mind was of people sitting home with a computer on their laps, watching the Palin speech, and getting angrier and angrier, contributing again and then again. "I hope she keeps this up," I thought. "Sarah Palin has now become our best fund-raiser."

The next day our field staff reported an avalanche of new volunteers calling and e-mailing and showing up at their offices, all with the same message: "We're so angry after the Palin speech—so offended by McCain's choice—that we can't sit on the sidelines anymore. Put us to work." A huge number of former Hillary Clinton volunteers also showed up for the first time, clearly peeved at the implication that they were supposed to abandon their principles because McCain had picked a woman. Despite her stated disdain for community organizers, Sarah Palin had suddenly become one—for us.

She was pretty good at turning out her own party, too. Before the pick, McCain was typically drawing fewer than a thousand people to his events. Now, with Palin at his side, they were drawing Obama-like crowds of fifteen to twenty thousand people with regularity. As a result, his camp announced to the press that McCain and Palin would stay together on the trail for the foreseeable future, doing their events together in battleground states. I understood the thinking behind this—they believed Palin was generating energy that wouldn't be there when McCain was by himself, and at this point the cable news stations would generally cover live any Palin speech—and some of McCain's, too, if she was there.

But I thought it was a fundamentally unsound approach. Just a minuscule fraction of true swing voters watched cable news—its audience was almost all partisans on both sides. What really mattered—and our research was clear as a bell on this—was the local news. True swing voters watched their local TV station and read their regional paper.

By keeping McCain and Palin joined at the hip, they were sacrificing one of the most crucial components of potential electoral success: their reach into battleground markets. On a day when McCain and Palin were together, they did maybe four events, sometimes three. Traveling separately, Obama and Biden would do at least three events each, usually more. So we were doubling our exposure relative to theirs in the battleground markets, dominating local news, and garnering the organizational benefit of having our candidates rally volunteers and test the field operation. By the end of the campaign, our two principals had done almost twice as many events as their Republican counterparts. That differential was priceless.

Palin was a phenomenon all the way through. Cable stations covered at least part of just about every speech she gave. They rarely covered Biden like that. While we complained, citing the need for balance and fairness, we didn't sweat it. In one day Biden would be in, say, Joplin, Missouri; Cedar Rapids, Iowa; Flint, Michigan; and Toledo, Ohio, generating terrific, on-message coverage. So it wasn't hugely important to us that Biden's speech be covered on CNN. Biden and Obama both did a lot of local interviews as well, to amplify and increase the coverage our stops were getting. In the beginning, Palin did much less of that, further eroding their footprint.

———

We misfired tactically in one area at the end of August and beginning of September. While we saw little or no evidence that the celebrity attack was hurting us, we got a bit defensive and decided to start doing fewer rallies, and the ones we did we would hold after the nightly news broadcast. This ensured that the pictures on the news and in many papers, both locally and nationally, would be of Obama in more intimate settings—on a shop floor, in a diner, taking questions from smaller crowds.

We had always diversified our events. The campaign wasn't one long string of rallies, day after day. But during this time period we lost our balance and in many ways our energy. Our instinct—primarily Axelrod's and mine—was off. We let the attacks and press narrative of the moment get into our heads and compensated by changing course, though there was no evidence we should. Our state staffs were especially unhappy with the change-up because rallies were the best way to attract voters in large numbers; we found that previously undecided or lean-Obama voters who attended rallies converted in high percentages.

So for a while in late August, it was like the candidates had reversed roles. McCain, with Palin's assist, generated large crowds and enthusiasm while Obama's energy felt stagnant and produced desultory events. Recognizing this shift led us to rectify our course and resume regular rallies. Our state staffs were thrilled.

We largely stayed away from engaging Palin directly during the fall. Obama slipped up only once. During an interview on CNN, he took the bait on a question comparing his experience to Palin's. He dived right into the résumé game, and within hours it spawned stories everywhere about Obama versus Palin on experience. The last thing we wanted was to be drawn into that battle.

That night on our evening call with him, I started to raise the interview. Obama cut me off. "I messed up and took the bait," he said. "It won't happen again."

Every interview he was doing in this period was about Palin, Palin, Palin. I give him credit for letting it get to him only once.

The week to ten days after the Palin pick were tough externally. National polls showed the race very close, some even giving McCain a slight lead. The public state polls also showed a closer race than they had in August, though if you were to predict the Electoral College based on looking at them cumulatively, we would have won, albeit narrowly.

But as we headed into the second week of September, and things were settling down a bit post-Palin, previously undecided voters began to make up their minds. In state after state, we started winning independents who expressed a preference, and Democratic enthusiasm really started to rear its head. A little less than two months out, our voters showed more excitement about voting for Obama than theirs did for voting for McCain.

By this point we were running a more forceful campaign in the battlegrounds than McCain was. While we had clearly outspent him on the ground in terms of offices and staff in the lead-up to his convention, our advertising spending during that period was about equal. But now that he had entered the federal finance system and we were out, the disparity began to emerge in ad buys as well. In many markets we were running positive ads, others challenging McCain on the issues, a response ad to his attacks, and ads geared toward women, seniors, and younger voters, as well as African American and Latino voters. And these ads blanketed every medium, from TV to radio to the Internet.

The funds at the McCain campaign's disposal would be at best a third of ours because of our respective decisions on public funding. They were generally running a couple of TV ads, but these did not seem targeted to specific demographic groups, and they did very little radio or online. The RNC was spending tens of millions on the air for McCain, but our testing showed these ads were woefully ineffective. The RNC and McCain, exploiting a loophole in the law, were pooling some of their money and running what are called hybrid ads. Since party money was being used, these ads could not be just about McCain and Obama. To meet this legal requirement, McCain-RNC ads featured fifteen seconds of McCain's message before making a tortured turn to attack Democrats generally, usually by showing images of Democratic senators like Chuck Schumer, Harry Reid, and Dick Durbin.

The voters we researched found these ads utterly confusing. They didn't know the featured politicians and kept wondering who they were. Many voters even forgot what the attack on Obama was supposed to be. We almost (but not quite) felt sorry for the McCain high command, saddled with this terrible hybrid construct as the only way of stretching their dollars.

But what satisfied us the most was seeing our advantages in cash and organization finally begin to materialize in the numbers. I thought a superior, historically well-financed series of battleground campaigns could be worth anywhere from one to four points, which would make all the difference in a close race. And that's what ultimately mattered: not snarky ads or manufactured controversies, but how we were doing every day with the voters who would determine the outcome in the battleground states. How many did we register today? How many sporadic-voting Democrats did we contact? What was our support level like with independent women voters between the ages of thirty and fifty in a certain state? By that measure, even in the midst of the turbulent Palin period, we liked what we were seeing.

We were also amazed that McCain had not yet fully engaged in states like Florida, Virginia, North Carolina, and Indiana. In the latter two, they were doing nothing at this point—no staff, offices, advertising, or visits.

Their silence in Virginia puzzled me the most. Virginia had changed demographically during the decade in ways that favored us. Democrats had won two successive governors races and a big Senate upset in 2006. We couldn't have advertised any louder our intention to win Virginia and our belief that it was critical to our strategy. Obama and Biden traveled there constantly, and we had built a massive campaign based out of Richmond that stretched across the state. By my calculations, if McCain lost Virginia's thirteen electoral votes, his chances to win dropped below 10 percent. He'd have to win multiple Kerry states to make up the gap.

What was particularly amazing about the McCain indifference was that they were headquartered in Virginia, right smack in the middle of our ferocious campaign. And John McCain lived in Virginia and was there with some frequency. Yet they didn't hold their first campaign event there until September 10. I marked it down as another instance of gross malpractice on the part of his staff. They must have thought that to lose traditionally Republican states like Virginia and North Carolina meant they were doomed from the start; better, then, to dig their trenches in a narrower set of traditional battlegrounds where they figured the race stood a real chance of being decided. But that looked at the race as a national contest, where individual strategies and campaigns in states were of minimal value. We saw things completely differently.

On a phone conversation with Obama, I was reviewing the state of play across the board and could barely contain my incredulity that in some of our key targets, McCain was still either leaving the playing field to us or not contesting as hard as I thought he should.

Obama laughed. "You know, Plouffe," he said, "most people would be celebrating the fact that their opponent is making bad decisions that could make winning easier. But you seem to be bemoaning it, almost like you're offended by it."

"You know, I hadn't thought of that until now," I replied. "But I think on some level I *am* offended." I tried to find the right words to capture my feelings. "This is for all the marbles," I told Obama, "the presidency of the United States. You can't leave any stone unturned. And making excuses about money, or that ultimately if we lose a state like Virginia, it means we're toast anyway—it just doesn't cut it. This is a war. You cannot leave certain fronts unprotected. They run the risk of losing this race not by losing Ohio, Nevada, or Pennsylvania, but by losing states like Virginia, North Carolina, and Indiana. These states are not linked. What is happening in one does not happen in all. The strategy and effort in each state matters. We could lose what's considered a more favorable state like Colorado and win a harder state like Indiana, simply because we believed we could and the McCain people left it to us and never competed."

Obama concurred. "It's why we have to keep stretching the playing field," he said. "What you just said is the avenue to victory we have to keep in place."

Our agreement on this was part of what made my job easier. But I could tell that the rest of our party was getting restless. Even internally, our media team kept asking me if we shouldn't trim our spending in places like Indiana, North Carolina, and Missouri to concentrate on states like Pennsylvania, Ohio, and Michigan.

But I had never believed more strongly in our game plan. We needed to keep pressing, not play it safe; even if we won states like Pennsylvania and Michigan by smaller margins, the complex puzzle we were trying to piece together would be more doable with more states in play. As the *Los Angeles Times* put it in a September story about our electoral strategy, "If the map were a roulette table, Obama would be dropping chips all over." Well said, I thought. We were not going to start loading up our chips on just a few numbers.

I quickly shut down the internal debate—we were not a democracy in this regard. Still, there was no doubt that if we lost the campaign, I would go down in infamy for spending too much time and money in Virginia and North Carolina.

The *New York Times* was preparing a front-page story on the party's nervousness about our campaign after the GOP convention. The gist was that Democrats thought we were mishandling Palin, she had thrown us off our game, we were not running an aggressive enough campaign, not attacking enough, and were in danger of losing must-win targets because of our pursuit of untraditional states.

It sounded like a classic *Times* story, though this kind of criticism was not surprising. Whenever a campaign in either party goes through perceived turbulence, there is never a shortage of unnamed officials and operatives willing to point fingers. Some even reproached us directly. I had one governor tell me our "tepid" response to Palin had "doomed us to fail"; a Democratic operative said to me, "I never thought you guys would lay down like our previous nominees. But it's the same nightmare and you guys won't wake up and fight back."

The *Times* story would be a headache, but I thought it might also present an opportunity. I told Bill Burton, our press secretary, that I wanted to go on the record for the story, which was a bit unusual; generally I avoided press interviews. But I wanted to send a strong message—externally and internally—that we were confident and would not fall prey to nervous navel gazing. "We're familiar with this," I told the reporters, "and I'm sure between now and November fourth there will be another period of hand-wringing and bed-wetting. It comes with the territory."

They loved the quote but doubted their editors would allow it to run. I said if it got rejected, they could use just "hand-wringing," but I vastly preferred the original. To my surprise and pleasure, they ran the unedited quote. I could tell our staff at HQ loved it—it was defiant without being entirely arrogant—and I wanted to remind them that we never made decisions based on armchair critics and wouldn't start now.

The morning the story ran, I received a very distressed call from a senator who was a loyal and great supporter of the campaign. "David," he said with concern, "my colleagues here think that you're calling them bed wetters."

"Senator, I am," I replied.

No organization can survive flitting from thing to thing, trying to please outside observers. Win or lose, I was not going to allow the second-guessers, who didn't have the facts or numbers to back up their opinions, to take us off our game plan.

Once again, we knew who we were. The two main pillars of the campaign—the message and electoral strategy—were firmly established and not up for debate, which meant we could focus on execution. We made decisions quickly and grounded in clear and consistent principles. That is especially important when there is a chorus of critics hollering at you to change course.

This period was tough personally, too, on everyone in the campaign. The pressure was brutal and the hours beyond what would be considered healthy or tolerable in most situations. Families were largely abandoned, relationships tested, friendships put on ice. We took strength from our bond as a campaign family based on our deep desire to see Barack Obama elected president. We also came together over the common circumstances of campaign life, the personal struggles, and lack of any normalcy.

Though the finish line was in sight, these last two months felt like two years. My wife and son had left Chicago in mid-August. I watched them pull out of the garage of our apartment building and drive off, and for at least ten minutes I just stood there, staring at where the car had been. It broke my heart that they were leaving and would have to navigate without me the last two months of my wife's pregnancy and my son's acclimation to a new home and school.

I planned to visit on my son's birthday in the fall and if possible the weekend before the election, when our baby was due, but that was it. In this early- to mid-September period, when things were more than a little challenging, anytime I began to think the campaign was rough, I thought of my wife and son, who were bouncing between various friends' homes. Our own house was still uninhabitable, and there was no guarantee they'd have a home or a husband and a father in time for the birth of our baby.

The mounting stress of dealing with a difficult time in the campaign finally blew into the open on one of our daily, early-morning conference calls. For the first and last time in a two-year period, Axelrod and I got into a heated shouting match. The point of contention was insignificant, and to this day other members of the staff have different memories about what actually sparked the flare-up. All they remember is that for the first time, we blew up at each other. Ax and I can't recall exactly what it was about, though I vividly remember the heat, if not the light. Most on staff recall it was some kind of dispute over scheduling Obama to meet with an editorial board or group of reporters, which I didn't want to do and Ax did. The conversation went something like this:

"Well, that's fine," he screamed. "We'll just thumb our noses at one of the most powerful papers in the country."

I responded too icily and personally. "I didn't realize discipline was situation dependent. You don't want to let down your buddies in the press. We aren't going to do something in the closing weeks that is not strategic."

"Give me a break," Ax shot back. "It's a couple hours. So is your fucking answer no? Is it?"

"It should be clear it's fucking no," I spat out. "And this conversation is over."

"Fine," Ax yelled back, and got off the call.

When I got to the office that morning, people who had been on the call tiptoed around me. Finally, Messina came into my office and said, "That was horrible. It was like watching your parents have a screaming match at the dinner table."

He was right. That's not how we should have conducted ourselves. I had no idea how we had spiraled out of control so quickly. The pressure must have been mounting inside us both and needed somewhere to escape. Ax and I had worked together for years and generally got along beautifully. There was genuinely no tension simmering between us.

I called him to apologize but he jumped right in. "Sorry," he said. "I don't know where that came from. We should never fight like that, much less in front of all the staff."

"Me, too," I replied. "I can barely even remember what we were arguing about an hour ago. Clearly it was a proxy for other things. Anyway, it was bound to happen once. I just wish the subject had been worthy of the blowup."

Ax laughed. "Yeah. We blew our wad on silly shit."

15

It's the Economy, Stupid

The economy had been worsening throughout the campaign. In early 2007, Iraq and health care were the two dominant issues, with the economy lagging behind in priority. But as the market softened, growth slowed, and jobless numbers began to creep up, economic concerns began crowding out most other issues. By the spring of 2008, the economy was front and center for voters.

As the fall arrived, it had exploded as the dominant issue in the general election. Voters' stock portfolios and retirement savings were taking on serious water, and economists began suggesting the recession could become long and severe, with many more millions of jobs at risk. In August, the investment bank Bear Stearns had collapsed, and there were strong rumblings on Wall Street that other financial institutions could follow.

It was against this backdrop that a group of us met with Barack on Sunday, September 14. He was in Chicago for the afternoon and evening, a rarity those days, and asked us to set up a meeting to go over our advertising strategy for the closing weeks. He wanted to get an overview of how we intended to finish up, and in particular he was concerned that our advertising was not communicating clearly or strongly enough his ideas and solutions for the economy.

Obama did not generally get deeply involved with our advertising, other than rewriting and editing some of the spots he would appear in, and reviewing any negative or contrastive ad. His primary role was to tone them down or ask us to hold off, a role he played when it came to speeches and remarks as well. Barack took seriously the job of tone policeman, and Ax was his partner in this regard. We tried, fairly successfully, to remove the snark from our messaging, to keep the personal out, and to assume that voters were actually hungry to have an adult conversation about the issues. Obama often excised lines he thought were too political, overly simplistic, or intellectually dishonest.

For instance, we were ferociously attacking McCain's health care plan, which had at its centerpiece a proposal to begin taxing workers' health care benefits as income to generate money to cover the uninsured. We started hammering away at this idea in TV and mail, calling it the biggest middle-class tax increase in history. Obama was unhappy when he saw the ads and demanded less drama.

"I don't think people will find that charge credible," he said, "and while I can make the case that it's true, I think it puts too much spin on the ball. Let's just lay out his position without feeling the need to scare people with some grandiose political scorecard terminology." The ads were changed. He did this time and again. If he thought an argument—positive or contrastive—felt like too much of a stretch, he pulled us back.

Before we jumped into advertising at our meeting, we talked about the strong rumors that a huge investment banking firm was about to go under. Bear Stearns' collapse had been unfathomable. According to our economic policy staff and outside advisers, losing another pillar of the financial industry could have a calamitous effect on the entire world financial system.

Obama wanted more ideas about what could be done, so we dispatched our economic team to have more discussions with our outside advisers and to develop a memo looking at options on how the government could play a constructive role in the unfolding financial crisis. Obama had been talking to some of our key advisers, like legendary investor Warren Buffett and former Treasury secretary Larry Summers, and he was clearly shaken by what he was hearing.

"You guys need to understand," he said gravely at our meeting, "that there's a possibility we could be dealing with global financial meltdown in the coming weeks. The election will seem almost irrelevant if that happens."

Flowing out of the economic discussion into message, I suggested we break convention in terms of our advertising and think about a longer-form address on the economy, perhaps a five-minute spot that we could run in the battlegrounds on TV and the Internet simultaneously.

"This could be an Oval Office–type address," I explained, "that would let us demonstrate both our proposed solutions to our economic troubles as well as steadiness and leadership qualities, in ways a thirty-second device just doesn't allow. And with all the negative ads flying around out there, it'll probably also be greeted with relief."

The airwaves in all our target states were cluttered not just with presidential-race ads, but with those from state and local candidates as well, almost all of them thirty seconds long and most of them negative. I thought that a longer ad like this had a chance of breaking through, and could become a "moment" when even those who did not view the spot would hear about it from their friends and neighbors. The takeaway would be that Obama had both a clear sense of what had gotten the country off track economically as well as concrete ideas to make the economy work again for all Americans, not just the special interests and privileged few.

It was also clear we were moving from economic slowdown to economic crisis, and that Obama was a master communicator who would be capable of displaying presidential leadership traits in a spot like this. Few in politics could pull off this kind of ad. Certainly, McCain couldn't, even if he had the money. He could be very effective in interviews and town halls, but direct-to-camera addresses were not his strength.

We discussed the idea for the spot at length. "Let's do it," Obama said finally. "People are scared, confused, and frustrated. An ad like this won't change that, but it should give them a strong sense that I have a plan, and hopefully some comfort that I'll be able to manage us out of this mess."

Larry Grisolano and Jim Margolis suggested two-minute ads, which would allow us to run them with a bit more frequency and across a spectrum of programming, coupled with an online component. Using this format could help ensure the ad would not be just a one-hit wonder—we'd have a chance to reach people over about a ten-day period.

I went back to the office to figure out how to pay for the spots. Ads cost money of course, and two-minute ads would cost a lot. Paying for them would add about $6 million per week to our budget, but we were able to cover most of this through more robust fund-raising than we had anticipated.

As I've said before, money counts, and we were counting on a lot. In June we had based our budgets and planning on raising $350 million for the campaign during the five months of the general election, with an additional $125 million raised through the DNC and state Democratic parties, giving us a global campaign budget of $475 million.

We projected the campaign cash flow as $50 million per month raised in June, July, and August, and $100 million a month in September and October, after the conventions and VP picks, when people would begin to get engaged at a white-hot level. In all campaigns, more money comes in toward the end of the race, and early planning needs to account for the steep rise. Underestimating can leave you sitting on a pile of money while needed investments are left wanting.

We had raised roughly $150 million in the summer months, right on schedule. Despite that, there was a raft of stories suggesting we were falling short of our finance goals and that perhaps we had made a mistake getting out of the federal system—our advantage over McCain might be smaller than anticipated. I have no idea where these stories came from. The few people who actually knew our budget and cash situation weren't talking, and in any case, they certainly didn't feel this way.

But as annoying as it was to read, I welcomed the stories. They would incentivize our donors and raisers to dig even deeper and make sure we had the resources to fund our muscular plan in all the states. We still needed to have great performance from our fund-raisers and large check writers. To this end, we had events scheduled all over the country with top-level surrogates, Biden, and a few marquee events with Obama.

But to reach the stratospheric number of $100 million in both of the last months—which would obliterate the previous monthly historical fund-raising record of $55 million we had set in February—we would need a massive performance from our existing grassroots donors, as well as to continually add new donors every day at an appropriate rate. We'd need to average at least $3 million and ten thousand new donors per day to make the math work.

As we reached the midpoint of September, it was clear that this was happening. We were way ahead of schedule (thank you, Sarah Palin). Soon we would blow past $100 million, and seeing this gave me the confidence to increase our communications spending. (The organization spending in the states had been locked in early at a high level, so most of any additional spending would go to advertising.)

Ultimately we raised a mind-blowing $150 million in September. We added over 2.3 million people to our list that month thanks to an aggressive advertising effort by our new media team, leaving us with over 11 million listed supporters by the end of the month. Our return on Internet advertising was unbelievable. Each dollar invested in list growth returned several times that—immediately. Over time, as these new recruits gave more money (and time), the return grew even greater. This result was highly unusual. Customarily, organizations are paying several dollars just to get someone to sign up on their list, only to see many people decline to take the next step of involvement, like contributing. Our numbers were another example of our enthusiasm gap and the extraordinarily important dividends that the gap was producing.

A total of over 3.1 million supporters had contributed by this point. Aside from the historic volume, the ratio of names on our list to actual donors is remarkable. About 30 percent of the people on our list had contributed, many multiple times. And almost all had volunteered.

These were not casual relationships, which was why we put such a premium on growing the list. With ratios of activism this high, both in time and money, getting people to join our list was akin to striking gold. So we mined everywhere we could—online and off—simply to build the list.

We had built an online fund-raising apparatus that grew consistently through the campaign, but the dam really broke in September, when we raised more than $100 million of our $150 million online. We sent out roughly ten fund-raising e-mails in September, increasing our ratio as we got closer to the election and time was running out; either we met our budgets or we would have to cut back, so the finance e-mails had an urgent tone.

On the days we directly asked for money, the contributions spiked. But even on days when we did not, the latent contribution level would often be over $1 million, sometimes $2 million. Much of this came from people— inspired by who knows what conversation, news report, or blog post—who simply came to our site unprompted and made a contribution, whether it be their first or tenth. Whenever I checked our fund-raising performance online, it was like watching a volcano erupt. There were times when we were raising $250,000, $300,000, even $500,000 an hour. It was remarkable, and critical. Every additional dime was being funneled into the battleground states.

By fall our campaign had really become an example in the art of the possible. The volume and passion of our volunteers meant we could do just about everything we wanted to on the ground. Register voters? Check. Try to talk to every sporadic-voting Democrat in a state? Check. Have multiple conversations, person to person, with target independents and Republicans? Check. It was a luxury few campaigns have. But our supporters and organizers constantly revised upward the capacity of our local organizations in terms of voter contact and vote goals.

We were also beginning to realize a similar dynamic on the advertising side, having gained the financial capacity to employ just about every tool at our disposal: we even ran ads on evangelical radio just to try to hold the Mc-Cain margin. The messaging was consistent throughout our ads, but the emphasis and focus of the issues discussed could be tailored closely to individual demographics. Our spots for those under thirty were very aspirational, a call to action, focusing on issues like Iraq and the environment, and calling on younger voters to get involved in shaping the future. A senior spot might focus on making sure we had economic, tax, and health care policies that would lift lower- and middle-income seniors.

It was quite an arsenal, and married to our ground forces, unprecedented in politics. I often repeated this point to younger staffers who were in their first or second campaign. "You are going to be completely spoiled," I told them. "Almost all campaigns never have enough money or people to do what they'd like. And most decision making around resources is of the cutting variety— you're falling short of your budget, so what gets axed? Not this campaign. It's like fantasy camp for political operatives, so relish it because you may never see it again."

———

Throughout much of the primary, I had continued to draft what we called "State of the Race" memos for the press, our staff, and key political and financial supporters. These offered a look at the race from our strategic perspective, for which as often as not we were being questioned and sometimes ridiculed. When writing the memos, I threw in a predictive component and offered a glimpse into positive numbers or developments we saw happening around the country. We posted them on our website but never distributed them directly to our grassroots supporters.

As I mentioned earlier, we didn't originally send these memos out to our whole list because (1) we did not want to be talking incessantly about the inside game, and (2) we thought our supporters on the whole were not interested in inside baseball.

This assumption couldn't have been more wrong, and not sending the memos to our grassroots supporters had been a big mistake. What we found when we researched things a bit more was that we were not doing enough internal communication to ensure that our supporters, and even staff, knew exactly what our strategy was and how their efforts fit into the puzzle. We had to fix that for the general election. If our electoral strategy was going to be questioned, I wanted our volunteers and contributors to hear directly from us why we were pursuing this path, so they would spend less time worrying about the pundit chatter and more time simply participating and executing.

This was a lesson we learned from the primary: even the staunchest supporters will get a bit freaked out if the chattering class is criticizing you. Our supporters wanted desperately to have the hood lifted a bit so they could understand what was really going on.

So lift it we did. With growing frequency through the fall, we sent out campaign updates to our entire list. More often these updates came in video form, usually from me but from other staff as well. The first couple of videos laying out our general-election strategy were received very well. We shot them on a laptop camera, in my office, with no lighting. Unpolished and unscripted, I liked to say.

Okay, perhaps they were a bit raw; the clips certainly did not look "presidential." Seeing the first update, one of our senior staff said, "Plouffe, you look like you're in a hostage video."

We tried the next one with better lighting and an actual high-definition camera. The results looked much more produced. Our supporters hated it. They thought it seemed inauthentic, staged, and less personal. So we went back to the hostage drama.

We began taping these updates on the fly and tried to send one out at least every seven or ten days. I'd often do them from the road, recording some in the middle of the night from wherever we were doing debate prep to give an even more intimate sense of what we were up to. We mixed in these videos with other types of e-mails. Some shared the content of Obama's issues and speeches; others asked people to contribute and volunteer, reminded them of deadlines like voter registration and early voting, and addressed issues that were state-specific. With so much coming across the transom, it could have been chaos. But the e-mail program, while perhaps not entirely symphonic, was well conducted.

We had hired an enormous e-mail team within new media that worked under Rospars's direction (I assume in future campaigns this department will be called digital strategy, not new media—it's not new anymore and it's not just media), and also made sure all the states had their own fully staffed new media and e-mail teams. There were dozens of e-mails a day from the campaign going out in the last sixty days—some high-impact, heavily scrutinized national e-mails, and some very regional ones to a county or two in a battleground state.

Coordinating this was a delicate dance, as we tried to get the right sequence of e-mails to the right people while balancing the demands of all the different campaign departments and states. Joe and his team navigated and arbitrated all that; I only weighed in on close calls or politically sensitive problems. Externally, it must have looked like a very smooth, corporate exercise. But like every other part of the campaign, in reality it functioned more like a M.A.S.H. unit day to day, trying to stay on course while negotiating the myriad obstacles, challenges, and opportunities that were dumped into our lap.

We sent out many updates that revolved around fund-raising, but the most effective video we did wasn't about raising money—it was about spending it. I wanted to pick one state to demonstrate why our supporters' dedication and assistance was so sorely needed, and why if they let up at all, we would lose. For this exercise I chose Florida, and we laid it all out in the video—our statewide budget ($38 million), where we were spending it by category, and how we thought we'd win the state. I covered everything, from turnout and registration to persuasion numbers and targets.

My overall message was simple: if we spend $34 million instead of $38 million we likely won't win. And if we fall short on our field metrics, we'll probably fail as well. Even after all the time and money you have given, I said, and as tough as it was to give, we need more. We built a campaign and a strategy predicated on you—on people. And if you let up now, the whole house of cards could come tumbling down.

This was not a mere tactic to get more money or volunteer time. It was what we believed. This video message was one of the most effective ones we sent; the response factors we could measure—contributions, spike in volunteer hours—unmistakably bore this out, but we also received a lot of anecdotal feedback from our staff in the states and in conversations our supporters were having with Chris Hughes's online organizing team. People felt like they were being leveled with, that we were explaining clearly how their time and money was being utilized. And they felt that we valued and needed them.

Some people questioned the wisdom of such a revealing video. Why would we lay everything out for all to see? From our perspective there wasn't much downside. McCain's campaign already knew fairly well what we were up to when it came to the basics—how much we were spending, where we were focusing our time and money organizationally. I'm sure they learned a few details from our presentation, but we thought this was small price to pay for the tradeoff of bolstering our supporters' trust in the organization.

The pressure we put on our supporters in the update also raised eyebrows. Many organizations that depend on volunteers tread gingerly when asking for help, emphasizing their gratitude and almost shyly or defensively asking for more: "We know you're busy, and it's a lot to ask, but if you could find any way to help again . . ."

We took the opposite tack. We saw our grassroots supporters as full partners and had designed a campaign with the belief that they could make the difference for us—financially, organizationally, and in helping us move message. So we pretty much laid it on the table for them: If you want change, you have to continue to fight and work for it. If you let up, we may not win. It's your decision—dig deeper or take a walk. The outcome of the election will turn on what you choose to do.

It worked. By the end of the campaign, I thought most of our volunteers really believed that if they did not show up on Saturday and knock on doors like they said they would, Barack Obama could lose. They felt that personally involved and responsible for his success. And they were right to.

———

Lehman Brothers did, indeed, collapse on Monday, September 15. Steady erosion in the markets and economic confidence was now threatening the foundations of the economy.

We were in unchartered waters as a country. And it was clear from our research even before Lehman went under that voters not only blamed Bush's policies for contributing to the worsening economic slide but also believed that the emerging crisis was not being managed intensively or with the right degree of urgency.

Americans went from feeling deep concern to being flat-out scared. And not just Main Street Americans—titans of finance and premier academics were also taking some deep breaths. No computer model had fully predicted this crisis, or could show an easy path out of it.

On the day of the Lehman collapse, voters thought our economy was going downhill, and fast. Early that day, Obama addressed the subject directly. He focused specifically on the lack of regulation and enforcement that contributed to the meltdown, but married this critique to our larger economic point: it was time to have a president, and a government, that was focused on improving the lives of the middle class, and not enabling the special interests to cash in while everyone else got stuck with dwindling 401(k)s and mounting job insecurity.

A bit later that morning, in Tallahassee, Florida, John McCain delivered some commentary on the crisis that flew directly in the face of what most of America was feeling. In many ways, along with Sarah Palin, the statement he made came to define his candidacy. While noting that Lehman was a very serious situation, McCain resurrected a line he had not used in months, and for which we had pounded him at the time. Despite the blow of Lehman's collapse, he said, "The fundamentals of our economy are strong."

Our press and research staffs were watching McCain's speech on the TVs in the bullpen, and when he dropped this bomb, they exploded. From my office I heard their collective cry—"Nooooo!"—and thought there must have been some tragic breaking news. "Oh no, he didn't!" someone yelled loudly.

I dropped the call I was on and walked down the hall to Dunn and Pfeiffer's office. Pfeiffer, generally less excitable than even me, was bouncing off the walls.

"What's going on?" I asked.

"That fool McCain," he said excitedly, "just said the fundamentals of the economy are strong!"

I looked up at the TVs. "No kidding? I thought they'd banned that phrase from his repertoire."

"I almost felt sorry for him," added Anita. "Almost. Because this is going to be one of the most brutal days of his political life."

Some commentators gave us great credit for how quickly we pivoted to McCain's comments and then punished him unmercifully for days across every platform. I thought we deserved little credit. It would have taken a Herculean effort to screw up the gift he had handed us.

Our response followed a standard formula. Insert a rebuttal to McCain's outrageous comment in Obama's next speech that day to create a back and forth, ensuring maximum coverage. Produce TV and radio ads for release by that afternoon and get them up in the states right away. Make sure all our volunteers and staff out in the states had talking points on this to drive home in their conversations with voters. Make sure all our surrogates campaigning for us, especially those doing TV interviews, relentlessly pushed the point. And make sure reporters understood that we thought this could be the defining moment of the campaign. There was no need to get clever on this one.

McCain tried to clean it up at his next event in Orlando, suggesting that what he meant was that the American worker was strong, not the whole economy, but this contorted explanation gained little to no traction. Part of

McCain's problem was that the gaffe served as another blow to his already shaky economic foundation with voters. From saying earlier in the campaign that he was not an expert on the economy, to ruminating that he would need a running mate with economic experience to balance out his lack of knowledge, to famously not being able to recall in a newspaper interview how many houses he owned (a moment that, had it been captured on video, might have rivaled this one in import), McCain had increasingly signaled to voters that he would be out of touch and out of his league when it came to dealing with the economic crisis.

Axelrod has a saying when evaluating how damaging a moment will be to a campaign: "The question is how many more bricks can the wagon carry?" In this case, McCain's economic wagon was already wobbly and teetering. His fundamentals gaffe was not a brick but a two-ton slab of cement. He would be crushed by it. The question was whether it would be merely crippling or a mortal blow.

Had this comment been a mere slip of the tongue, its shelf life and ultimate impact would have been fairly limited. But it rang true to people that McCain, out of touch and out of economic ideas, could actually believe that the fundamentals of the economy were strong. When Obama uncorked his infamous "bitter" comments back in March, they provoked concern but ultimately did not square with voters' perceptions of him. McCain's comment, however, confirmed what people were thinking about him. It accelerated the pace of a boulder that was already rolling downhill. For just this reason, confirmatory comments often have real legs in politics, as was certainly the case here.

It didn't help McCain that his comment came just as the worsening economic crisis threatened to shut out everything else in the news. The campaign was still being covered extensively but for the most part through the prism of the economy. For a moment it seemed the campaign was taking a backseat to the economy when it came to media coverage, and also in voters' minds. President Bush had used eerily similar language to describe his confidence in the economy, and it helped us to link McCain and Bush on one of the dominant electoral issues.

Then two huge campaign moments injected politics back onto the front pages and grabbed voters' attention. They also rivaled the "fundamentals" comment in terms of the damage they did to McCain's campaign.

Sarah Palin had conducted her first postselection interview with Charlie

Gibson of ABC News from Alaska the week after the GOP convention. The expectations for Palin going into that interview were absurdly low, especially as it related to foreign policy. We sensed that if she did not completely implode, the press would view it as a successful first effort; what voters thought, however, could be a different story.

Commentators thought she had a few rocky moments but generally believed she had acquitted herself well. When pressed about her foreign policy experience, she famously said in the interview, regarding Russia, "They're our next-door neighbors and you can actually see Russia from land here in Alaska—from an island in Alaska." This made for a lasting sound bite, especially after Tina Fey got hold of it on *Saturday Night Live*.

We were beginning to see in our research not merely a cooling off in terms of people's views of Palin, but downright concern about her qualifications. In focus group after focus group, voters essentially said, "She very well could be president. McCain is a cancer survivor and in his seventies, after all. She just doesn't seem to have the depth, understanding, or experience to take over. Hell, I'd love to have a beer with her. But I'd like to have a beer with a lot of people I know. And none of them should be president."

What interested me most in these focus groups was that voters didn't use their assessment of Palin to decide how they might vote. They almost always talked about her through the prism of John McCain. After expressing concerns about Palin, voters would go on to say, "I just don't understand how McCain could have picked her." They would talk about how political the pick was, even cynical, rushed, and desperate. They compared it very unfavorably to our pick and process.

Palin's next major interview was with Katie Couric of CBS News. This exchange will go down in political infamy. Couric took a much different tack than Gibson, instead allowing Palin to do more talking. Who knows if this created a dynamic where Palin was less on edge and therefore did not execute her prerehearsed answers?

Low points of the interview included Couric's asking Palin repeatedly for examples of McCain's push for greater oversight of Wall Street, only to be told by the smiling governor, on her third attempt, "I'll try to find you some and I'll bring 'em to ya."

My favorite responses, though, framed her foreign policy experience based on geographic proximity: "As Putin rears his head and comes into the air space of the United States of America, where do they go? It's Alaska. It's just right over the border. It is from Alaska that we send those out to make sure that an eye is being kept on this very powerful nation, Russia, because they are right there, they are right next to our state."

Though conservative commentators had labored to boost Palin's selection through most of September, these interviews caused many of them to start to turn on her. Kathleen Parker, a prominent conservative voice, captured in a column what many were privately thinking after the Couric debacle. "As we've seen and heard more from John McCain's running mate," she wrote, "it is increasingly clear that Palin is a problem. Quick study or not, she doesn't know enough about economics and foreign policy to make Americans comfortable with a President Palin should conditions warrant her promotion."

Parker went on to suggest that Palin withdraw, though this was further than many in the GOP were willing to go. But the buzz around the Couric interview was very strong, and millions of voters who did not see the broadcast watched it on YouTube and CBS's website. Our research suggested that many people who saw it were deeply troubled.

While many pundits—and, we sensed, the McCain campaign itself— viewed the race during this period through the prism of Sarah Palin, we never really did. And neither, it turned out, did voters. While gleeful at the troubles the interview caused the McCain campaign, we did not focus much on it externally. They had created an inferno. We could just sit back and watch it burn.

————

The first presidential debate would be held on September 26. The vice presidential debate would follow on October 2, leading in to the final two presidential debates on October 9 and October 16.

We thought these four encounters could very well determine the election, or at least have a significant impact on the outcome. While people watch fewer debates in campaigns for lesser offices than they did thirty years ago, they still tune in for presidential debates in huge numbers.

And what happens during these debates can play a major role in the campaign. In 2004, Kerry's strong performances in the first two debates closed the gap with Bush and proved the major reason the race grew so close at the end. Al Gore was judged as inauthentic and too aggressive in his debates with Bush, while Bush exceeded expectations, helping turn the tide in the 2000 election. In 1992, Governor Bill Clinton connected with voters' economic pain at a town hall debate while President George H. W. Bush impatiently checked his watch, seemingly tired of the interactions with voters; the contrast was devastating.

We thought our situation was most comparable to Ronald Reagan's in 1980. Like Obama, Reagan was an outsider criticized for his lack of Washington experience and sometimes accused of offering more sizzle than steak. The electorate was clearly ready for change, but they were not yet convinced Reagan was the necessary antidote. His convincing debate performance eased doubts about his capabilities, and a dead-heat presidential race opened up in his favor. It didn't hurt that Reagan also provided one of the campaign's only enduring lines—"There you go again"—while chastising Carter for some liberal cant.

Axelrod often cited the Reagan-Carter debate as a good guide for us. "Reagan's performance created a permission structure for voters," he explained. "After that, they felt it was okay to vote for Reagan. We need to do the same thing. Strong debates will allow people to feel it's acceptable to do what they're thinking about doing, but not quite there on—vote for the new guy with the strange name and little Washington experience."

Formal debate prep camp for the first presidential debate, to be held in Oxford, Mississippi, on Friday, September 26, opened on Tuesday outside of Palm Beach, Florida, at an old hotel called the Biltmore that was undergoing desperately needed renovations. During this period, Obama showed confidence but also some nerves. "If I can just have four and a half really good hours, we can win this thing," went his regular refrain. He wanted us all focused on achieving a strong performance. "Make sure we're being smart about prep and giving it enough time," he told me. "And I'll do my part—I'll take it more seriously than I did before."

Anita had witnessed some of our less than stellar debate prep sessions in the primary and knew we needed help from outside the campaign to manage this very cumbersome process. She recommended Tom Donilon and Ron Klain, who between them had prepped Kerry, Gore, and Clinton. Ax and I were initially skeptical—we didn't want the same old folks who had done this for other nominees; we felt we needed to have some fresh thinking. But once we met with Ron and Tom, we knew Anita was right—they were the folks for the job.

Prep was a daylong affair, with a break for Obama to campaign briefly in the local market. Ron and Tom drilled him during the day, working on different answers and spending extra time on areas where we needed improvement. At night we would do a full-length mock debate, starting at 9:00 p.m. EST, the same time the real debates would start. We even built an actual replica of the stage for each debate, practically right down to the carpeting. I initially resisted this idea because of the cost, but Ron and Tom convinced me it was worth replicating every detail of each night, so Obama could be familiar with how much room he would have to walk around, where exactly the moderator would be, and so on. It was wise counsel. The move added to Obama's comfort heading into the debates.

————

The financial crisis had altered the operation of our campaign. We now had at least one daily conversation, often more, about the economic crisis with some of our outside economic experts, like former Treasury secretaries Larry Summers and Bob Rubin. Jason Furman, our staff economic aide, and Austan Goolsbee now regularly dialed into our nightly phone roundup with Obama, and on many nights these economic discussions took up half the call. This meant that the calls started running long with some frequency, putting pressure on our schedule.

Obama was also talking to Treasury Secretary Henry Paulson, Federal Reserve Chairman Ben Bernanke, and congressional leaders, to stay abreast and offer his help and advice. Doing so let Obama stay plugged into all that was happening, but it was taxing in terms of time. Still, he seemed to thrive on it. He always preferred policy to politics, and I began to further appreciate his ability to stay very calm during a crisis, his efforts to stay one step ahead of the situation, and his hunger for information.

I mentioned this to Ax. "You know, we better win this thing," I told him. "I think our country really needs this guy to stay afloat."

"He's the smartest person I've ever met, and displays some of the best leadership qualities I've ever witnessed," Ax responded. "So don't blow it, Plouffe."

I wasn't so worried about me, but Washington, I thought, could easily blow it. At that moment, it wasn't clear that the so-called bailout plan to rescue the banks and thus the economy would pass Congress. Unsurprisingly, there was not much appetite among politicians to spend over $700 billion of taxpayer money on something that many voters neither understood thoroughly nor could see how it would benefit them.

Obama thought we needed to do more publicly to help pass the bailout. He was fearful of what would happen if Congress couldn't push through a capital infusion for the banks. His advisers were unanimous: the fate of capitalism and our economy hung in the balance.

"I don't care whether it helps in the election or not," he said on our nightly call after the first mock-debate session in Florida. "And I think McCain would feel the same way. He's clearly not wild about this bailout, and neither am I, but it's the only responsible thing to do." Obama wanted to call McCain about the possibility of putting out a joint statement that restated both men's general support for the concept. "It'll give cover to members of Congress," he said, "that the two nominees are holding hands and are willing to jump off the cliff with them."

Obama called McCain first thing the next morning. A couple hours later, as I was boarding a flight to Florida, Gibbs reported there was still no response from McCain. "He's up to something," Gibbs said. "I can feel it."

When I landed in Florida, there was still no word. On my way to the hotel, I got a call from Obama. "McCain finally called me back," he told me. "He says he may be willing to do a joint statement. But then he suggested maybe we needed to do more—he seemed to be hinting we should both suspend our campaigns, maybe even the debate. He wasn't very clear. Anyway, we agreed you would talk to Rick Davis and sort out where things stand. Where are you anyway?"

"A couple minutes from the hotel."

"We're right behind you." Obama had just been speaking at a rally in Dunedin. I heard him ask the service how long until they were back. "I'll be there in ten minutes."

"Alright. I'll call Davis and meet you when the motorcade pulls up," I said.

Talking to Rick Davis, it was immediately clear we would not be deciding anything jointly. "We're announcing in a few minutes that we're suspending our campaign to go back to Washington to help on the financial crisis and the bailout," he told me. "We're also going to announce that we won't be attending the first debate unless a deal is reached on the legislation. Senator McCain thinks that politics should take a backseat right now."

I almost laughed into the phone. Even in the backseat, this was politics at its most crass. "I see," I said. "I thought we were going to try and send out a message jointly to help the politics on the Hill."

Rick said, "We can do that. But we think much stronger action is required. We hope you guys join us."

"We'll have to talk it over," I replied.

"McCain is going out to talk to the press in a couple of minutes," Davis reported, and our conversation was over.

I tracked down Obama at the hotel, and as McCain made his announcement, I could tell Obama was peeved that McCain had gone to the press so quickly. "He left me the distinct impression that he was mulling this suspension deal over, not that he was running out to the cameras in a matter of minutes."

"That tells you all you need to know about this," I replied, "it's a high-stakes stunt. Not a whiff of principle involved. But we need to have an answer to this stinkbomb, and in a matter of minutes, too."

I asked Reggie to round up Gibbs, Ax, and Anita, and we all met in Obama's hotel room. All our BlackBerrys were buzzing with unsolicited, uniform advice: You have to follow McCain. If you don't he'll look big, and you'll look small. He'll look like a statesman and you'll look political.

I viewed our situation in the exact opposite way: this was a transparent stunt, very impetuous, and would be seen as such by the voters. Everyone in the room agreed and Obama quickly confirmed he had some instincts too.

"I think this is absolutely nuts," he said to us. "First, maybe McCain isn't on top of this like I am, but I know with certainty based on the umpteenth conversations I've been having with folks in Washington that if we turn this into a political circus, it will do much more harm than good. So if we truly want to help pass the bailout, the last thing we should be doing is taking the presidential campaign to D.C."

He also thought there was no more important time to debate than right at that moment. One of the two of them would be president in less than four months. People were scared, he said, and canceling presidential debates certainly wouldn't instill any confidence. Obama thought voters needed to take the measure of the candidates and argued that there was no better time for that than during a crisis.

"So," he concluded, "I want to go tell the press unequivocally that we are not suspending our campaign and that I intend to be in Oxford, Mississippi, on Friday night. You guys tell me what I am missing." We thought about it and decided he wasn't missing anything. From where we stood, the debate was on.

This was going to be like the gunfight at the O.K. Corral. We couldn't both win. One of the campaigns would pay a very heavy price for taking the wrong path. The stakes couldn't have been higher, but we were feeling loose. As much as we loved methodically combing through our data, making a decision on the fly always seemed to suit us.

Our press team hastily assembled the reporters traveling with us, and we wove our way through the corridors of the old hotel to where they were gathered. Obama announced our response to McCain's ploy, adding a terrific impromptu line in explaining why it was important to preserve the debate: "Presidents need to be able to do more than one thing at a time." That clip played over and over next to McCain suggesting postponement. We looked strong, confident, and steady. McCain looked erratic and a bit desperate.

We'd know soon enough if voters shared that view.

Back in Obama's room, we were celebrating his performance and the rush of taking the riskier path when Katie Johnson e-mailed me that Josh Bolten, the White House chief of staff, was urgently looking for me.

I ducked into the hallway and called him. "Listen, this wasn't our idea," he said, "but Senator McCain called the president and asked that we gather a meeting with the president and congressional leaders tomorrow in Washington, including him and Senator Obama, to try to nail down an agreement on the bailout package." I felt my grip tighten on the phone. "Whether this is a good idea or not, we'll see," he continued. "But we can't turn it down. I wanted to give you a heads-up and also discuss schedule. I know you guys are busy, and I want to make sure we hold it at a time you can attend."

While I appreciated the scheduling courtesy, my blood was boiling. I thought the White House was crossing a line, playing right along with McCain's political stunt and potentially providing legitimacy to his effort to be the white knight.

"You guys are playing politics with this," I told Bolten. "I just don't see how this meeting will be viewed as anything but a political handout from the White House. I feel like we're getting blindsided and played here."

Bolten seemed to be as even-keeled as Obama. "I understand how you could feel that," he said calmly. "But we're going to do everything we can to play it straight and who knows what will come out of the meeting. We just think we can't say no to holding it—and I'm not sure you'd want us to, but that's your evaluation to make. Anyway, my boss wants to reach out to yours. To talk about it principal to principal."

We arranged a time for Obama and Bush to talk. After hanging up, I thought about what Bolten said and realized perhaps I had not seen the whole picture clearly. If the White House refused to accept McCain's request for a meeting, McCain would surely make hay of that and his ploy would get even more oxygen. Now, with the meeting going forward, Obama would be in Washington, and if McCain tried to accuse him of choosing to campaign rather than stew in D.C., it would strike a discordant note—the one image voters would have would be McCain and Obama together at the White House, meeting about the bailout.

Obama reported that his conversation with Bush was interesting. "He doesn't seem all that thrilled about holding the meeting. Almost apologetic." Obama reported that the president said, "I know what it's like to be in the middle of a presidential campaign and have something like this dumped on you. And I know you're talking regularly to Paulson and Bernanke and they say you're being helpful. I'm not sure why McCain thinks this is a good idea. But I have to move forward. So I'll see you tomorrow."

We'd know soon enough if McCain was a genius and whether the White House was playing it straight with us. Meanwhile, we had real-world scheduling and logistical complications. We would hold our second mock-debate practice that night, Wednesday, and then Thursday morning Obama would fly to D.C. for the White House meeting. After that, though, we were going to have to completely wing it.

We decided to proceed as if the debate was going to happen, though all signs pointed against it. We couldn't risk being unprepared if for some reason McCain changed his mind or a deal on the bailout was struck. But we had no idea when we'd be prepping or where. Should we all fly to D.C. with Obama and prep there after the meeting? Should he fly back to Florida, since we had the stage and all our equipment there? If the debate were canceled, at least we'd be in a battleground state and could so some campaigning Friday. Or should we just get to Mississippi early and prep there? For a campaign that abhorred uncertainty, this was excruciating.

But there we were, forty-eight hours from a first presidential debate that looked like it wouldn't happen, facing a shocking shift of strategy from our opponent that would likely alter the race, and on our way to a high-stakes White House meeting that could have real consequences for the financial-rescue package.

Between the bizarrely impulsive VP selection process that yielded the Palin pick and now McCain's jumping around—suspending the campaign, unsuspending the campaign; not going to debate, now going to debate—a word entered the official lexicon of our campaign dictionary, a word we wanted every voter to think of whenever they thought of our opponent: *erratic*.

16

Plumbers and Radicals

On Thursday, September 25, Barack Obama left for Washington to meet with the president, McCain, and congressional leaders from both parties. On a conference call that day with the two Democratic leaders, Nancy Pelosi and Harry Reid, Obama suggested that he play point at the meeting. They readily accepted.

Thus, with a little more than twenty-hours left before the first, and now endangered, presidential debate, the two candidates met face-to-face, not at podiums but in the White House. When the meeting commenced, President Bush spoke first, and Obama followed, laying out the Democrats' principles regarding a final rescue package as well as what they saw as deficiencies in the existing Bush administration plan.

McCain, by contrast, was quiet, even sullen, according to what we heard from those in the room. His comportment seemed at odds with what was presumably his campaign's rationale in calling for the meeting: to showcase him as a leader capable of grabbing the reins in Washington and rescuing the country's finances. He was clearly peeved that Obama was taking a leadership role in the meeting, and, according to multiple participants, when he did speak, he came across as ill informed and offered only platitudes, with little grounding in the real economic situation.

John Boehner, the House Minority leader, who negotiated on behalf of the House GOP, had suggested that his people were close to accepting the outlines of the bailout legislation. However, at the White House discussion he reversed course and aggressively implied that the House GOP was far from agreeing to a deal. We assumed Boehner was in cahoots with the McCain campaign, though we could not be sure. It looked coordinated, even if just by happenstance.

The meeting quickly dissolved into acrimony and posturing. Clearly no deal was going to be struck that afternoon, and any fantasies McCain had of creating bipartisan peace were just that. The Republican congressional leaders (sans McCain) exited the meeting and went straight to the press camped outside, where they expressed strong reservations and offered slim prospects for a bailout deal anytime soon. The Democratic leaders (sans Obama) were less bleak but expressed frustration with the Republican posturing.

The press also began to report on McCain's role in the meeting, or lack thereof. "This is going to boomerang right back on them," I thought. The voters would score it that McCain's gambit yielded a typical Washington clusterfuck.

The meltdown at the White House seemed to decrease the likelihood that McCain would show up for the debate. He had said he would come down only if a deal was cemented, and we were now farther from resolution than we'd been when he'd issued his ultimatum.

After the meeting, Obama called Axelrod and me in Florida. There was a chance he'd have to attend another gathering in D.C. with congressional leadership later that night, which meant flying back down to Florida to resume prep was out. We had a plane on standby to bring some of the debate prep team up to him for a 9:00 p.m. session, but Obama suggested bagging the mock debate entirely, even though it was the last of our scheduled three.

"I think I should just review my materials tonight. We can do an abbreviated mock tomorrow, if the debate is on," he offered.

Ax and I were on speakerphone in Ax's hotel room; hearing this, we rolled our eyes at each other. Both of us knew that what Obama really wanted was a night to himself in a hotel room—reading his debate materials, no doubt, but with ESPN on the tube and no one poking at his answers and directing his every movement.

He tried to reassure us. "Guys, I know you're nervous about losing a night of prep. But I think we're in good shape, and some quiet reading wouldn't be the worst thing in the world."

Ax and I shrugged our shoulders. "Fine," Ax said, "but we really have to do some time tomorrow—I understand what you're saying but we still have to work through some of the exchanges we don't have nailed yet."

Barack laughed. "You two really are on edge," he commented. "We'll be fine. Figure out how prep will work tomorrow and let me know. Just make sure we aren't prepping right up to the debate—I want some time to decompress."

That was that. We were heading into a debate that could determine our fate and we were losing a third of our prep. Based on McCain's schedule and what we were hearing in the press, we assumed that McCain was not prepping very rigorously, but this was small consolation; we couldn't peg our effort on his. We had established a game plan and now it had been thrown out.

Ron and Tom were predictably apoplectic. "We're not where we need to be for this debate," Ron observed. "He's good to go on most stuff, but we still have to work through some things."

"I know, I know," I told them. "But we are where we are. Let's figure out how to salvage some time tomorrow and come up with a new game plan. We also have to decide whether to do it here in Florida or jury-rig something up in Oxford."

After a quick vote we decided on Oxford. I called Alyssa and told her we had a change of plans. We needed to get to Mississippi right away. The Oxford airport could not accept a plane as large as ours (many of the press were with us as well), so we had to land in Memphis, Tennessee, and have the advance team stationed in Oxford arrange volunteer drivers to transport our crew the hour and a half to Oxford.

We landed in Memphis well after midnight and clambered into the vans. We had something of a rolling conversation, if you can call it that, during the drive, as we all fell asleep for snatches of time. I would reply to something Ax said, but he would not answer. Joel Benenson, our leading national pollster, might instead. Then I would doze off. The ride was bumpy as hell. We got into Oxford around 3:00 a.m., stumbled into the hotel, and tried to get a couple of hours' sleep before the conference calls. The glamour of a presidential campaign . . .

———

We started telling the press that Obama was coming to debate no matter what; if McCain didn't show, we'd hold an event instead. We all thought there was a decent chance McCain would cave and show—it just wasn't in his DNA to duck a challenge, even if he would have to concoct a convoluted explanation for why he was changing course.

In between calls, I went for a quick run outside, largely to try to wake myself up. As I was running through the gorgeous Ole Miss campus, I came upon a sign reading CONFEDERATE DRIVE. I don't like to break pace when I'm running, but it stopped me dead in my tracks. I stared at the sign for a while. As I've mentioned, we were all so close to the race that it was hard to get any perspective when it came to the implications of Barack's run. Random things would occasionally provide a cue, and this sign was one of them. Looking up at the street name, it washed over me at that moment that Barack Obama, a major-party presidential nominee, would attend a debate that night—whether it happened or not—on the same campus where less than fifty years earlier, federal troops had had to protect James Meredith as he simply tried to attend classes.

My pace running back to the hotel was much quicker.

———

As Obama boarded his plane in D.C. to come to Mississippi, we still did not know if McCain was going to show. Then, at the last possible moment, they sent out a tortured statement saying he would come; he believed that because of his efforts, progress was being made to craft a better financial rescue package.

Total bullshit. They had blinked. Even worse for them, they had grossly miscalculated how all this would play out. We were thrilled, both because they looked weak and indecisive after royally screwing up a high-stakes game of chicken, and because we needed this debate—it was an important part of closing the deal with voters. Now, the McCain campaign was in a tough spot, with no good options. And they had boxed themselves into this unappetizing situation in pursuit of an ill-considered stunt.

We had a couple of good short prep sessions that afternoon in Oxford. During our walkthrough of the debate site, I stood in for McCain, and Barack and I bantered about the upcoming baseball playoffs as we tested the sound, he boasting of the White Sox's chances if they made it, I of the Phillies. He seemed ready for the spotlight and was feeling invigorated that we had held our ground while McCain had buckled. Psychologically it was a real boost for him and for all of us. "I felt comfortable up there," he said as we left the stage to drive back to our hotel. "I'm ready to make my case."

Obama won the debate convincingly. Polls afterward showed undecided voters who watched the debate giving him the win by a landslide. The pundit report cards weren't quite as emphatic but most thought we had won, if for no other reason than it was a foreign policy debate that McCain was expected to dominate. Anything beyond holding our own was seen by the political referees as a big win.

It helped us that despite the debate's ostensible foreign policy focus, a good chunk of the time was devoted to the domestic financial situation. Obama's economic answers focused like a laser on the middle class. This was a chief strategy of ours: to relentlessly make the case that as president, Obama would put the needs of the middle class first. We had prepped heavily on it, and Obama delivered beautifully on that score. McCain, though, had failed to display similar advocacy.

I mentioned this to Ax as the debate wrapped up. "Can you believe it? McCain didn't mention the middle class."

"I was just thinking that," he replied. "You're right, not once in the entire debate."

This we could capitalize on. Margolis's team immediately got cracking on an ad we would release the next morning that hammered home McCain's oversight. It was yet another miscue that made the young, rookie senator look like the steady leader in the race. We were in great spirits.

After the debate, Obama peeled off to head back to Memphis, but Ax and I called to congratulate him as we headed to the Oxford airport. For Obama, he was pretty charged up. "See, I told you guys you had nothing to worry about," he said.

I laughed. "Well, that doesn't mean we've set a precedent and will be cutting prep down to two days," I warned him. "Though I know a night of ESPN is probably the best reward you could get for winning the debate."

Obama chuckled. "That's right. But we only have two more debates. Let's leave nothing on the table. I can handle myself, but make sure you guys have Joe ready to go."

Biden's debate with Palin was coming up the next week.

Alyssa had arranged to have burgers and beers on the plane for the ride home. It was the best meal I'd had in an awfully long time.

––––––

We planned to have Biden prep in a battleground state as well, but he asked if he could prep in Delaware so he could be closer to his family—his son Beau, Delaware's attorney general and a member of the Guard, was deploying to Iraq shortly, and his mother-in-law was still ill. Of course we agreed.

Governor Jennifer Granholm of Michigan spent three days in Delaware with us, playing Palin, and she nailed the role perfectly. We assumed Palin would be a very effective debater with great one-liners, and that she would benefit from absurdly low expectations. We knew from reviewing her Alaska debates that she could hold her own, but given the blowback from the Couric interview and the high stakes of this particular matchup, just about everyone else was expecting Biden to wipe the floor with her. We had our work cut out for us managing these expectations.

On debate night, we landed in St. Louis to news that relegated the upcoming face-off to the backseat, at least for me. The press was reporting, without confirmation, that the McCain campaign was pulling out of Michigan.

I couldn't believe it. Recently we had opened up a slight lead in Michigan, in the mid- to high single digits. McCain had strong history in the state, and given that we had not campaigned there in the primary, it felt gratifying to be out in front, though our lead was hardly insurmountable. It remained a state in which we'd have to devote significant resources to walk away with a win.

But if McCain abandoned Michigan, it would have a powerful domino effect on the race. Ceding those seventeen electoral votes meant they really had to run the table, and made winning Pennsylvania—the last big Kerry state they were targeting—close to a necessity. Upon hearing the news, I hunted down Ax, who was talking to some international reporter—he had a hard time turning down any interview request—and pulled him aside. "This can't be true," I said.

"Michigan?" he guessed.

I nodded. "It makes zero sense strategically for them to do this. Is it some sort of head fake—get us to pull out ourselves and then jump back in with massive force?"

Ax laughed and put a hand on my shoulder. "Plouffe, can't you just accept some good news? I agree it's stupid but it sure looks like the real deal." He glanced around to make sure he wouldn't be overheard. "And anyway, I think a head fake might be beyond this gang."

Within the hour, the McCain camp confirmed it: they were suspending their campaign in Michigan, which for all intents and purposes meant they were waving the white flag. They said they needed to make hard decisions about resource allocation as Election Day drew closer and now thought Michigan was a less likely bet than Pennsylvania.

I was dumbfounded. We were playing electoral chess and these guys had handed over their queen. I understood making hard fish-or-cut-bait decisions on states that weren't realistically attainable; we had done so in Georgia and North Dakota. But those states were reaches for us, at the periphery of our strategy. Michigan had been ground zero in their efforts to win a big Kerry state so they could afford to lose a few Bush states and still reach 270 electoral votes.

This announcement was the most significant strategic moment of the general election to date. Our puzzle started to look almost complete, while theirs had just been given a swift kick and the pieces had scattered all over the map. I found this turn of events far more important to our chances than anything that would happen in the debate that night.

When I discussed it with Obama, he asked what I thought our new approach to Michigan should be. "I wouldn't change anything right away," I told him, "though let's not send you in again unless they reverse course. If, in the next few days, they are visibly pulling back, we should scale back our advertising and also maybe send some of our staff there to other states like Indiana."

He agreed but wanted to be cautious. "Just don't pull everything down too quickly. Let's make sure we're in the clear so we don't have to scramble back and redo everything we just disassembled."

McCain never reengaged in Michigan. His pulling out dominated the news in the Wolverine state for days and killed his numbers. We jumped to a nearly twenty-point lead in just a few days as a result of his decision.

Obama moved our discussion to the debate. "How's Joe going to do tonight?"

"He's in good shape for the most part," I replied, "but I'll be nervous until the debate is over—just like I am when you're up there."

"Thanks for that," Obama said sarcastically. "Should I call him and wish him luck or will that make him nervous?" I thought Biden would appreciate a pep talk and said so.

Our stomachs were in knots in the moments before the debate started, knowing that Biden would be graded on a tough curve. Even if he gave a stellar debate performance, the GOP ticket would still get credit for a great night if Palin made no unforced errors. But Biden was better than we could have hoped. He stayed relentlessly on message, proving a fiercely effective advocate for Obama on both economic and international matters, and a piercing critic on the merits of McCain's policies. He never took Palin's bait and never engaged with her directly—he kept the focus squarely on Obama and McCain and their differences in agenda and leadership. Most important, perhaps, he demonstrated beyond a shadow of a doubt that he was prepared to be president.

He also showed us he was a clutch player; onstage that night, he gave a terrific answer to the Iraq-funding question that he had struggled with all through the practice sessions without nailing. He now made the point that McCain, too, had voted against the bill because it contained a timeline for withdrawal, and keeping the focus on the two presidential candidates' big differences on Iraq. It was a near-perfect response.

Palin had no major unforced errors, and, as we had assumed would be the case, she was judged by many voters to have exceeded expectations. She came across as likable, but by all polling accounts, Biden won the debate hands down. Palin had done nothing to alleviate the deeper concerns voters had about her. They still couldn't see her as president, which reflected much more poorly on McCain than on her.

During the postdebate spin session, I was repeating an answer for the fifth time to another group of reporters when one of our advance staff grabbed me and said Biden wanted a word before he left. I navigated the back alleys and corridors to his motorcade, where he was waiting for me. He opened up his arms and shrugged, making a "Well, how did I do?" expression. I gave him a big smile and thumbs-up and then a big hug, telling him he couldn't have done any better. He had given the whole campaign a boost. "You know, I just got dialed in up there," he said. "All the practice helped, but you never can know. But honestly, when it started, I just had fun. I feel so good about Barack and what we're trying to do that it's an easy case to make."

I told him the hard part was over—now he could just head out to the trail for a month and pound our message home.

As he turned away from me, I witnessed a classic Biden moment. Frank Greer, a legendary Democratic media consultant, was helping us by volunteering as our stage manager at all four debates. Frank had a full head of thick gray hair, and as the folically challenged Biden grabbed him to thank him on the way out, he said, "Man, Frank, if I only had your hair I could have been the number one guy on this ticket!" And with that, our vice presidential nominee triumphantly entered his motorcade for the drive to the airport.

Ax and I once again headed together to the airfield for a quick flight to Chicago. I had told Alyssa that the burgers her team procured for the last flight brought us good karma; we needed them again. The burgers on this flight, however, were colder than the beer and had the consistency of hockey pucks. Still, as we climbed into the night with two debates down and two wins under our belt, they couldn't have tasted better.

The news from the states was even better than the outcomes of the first two debates.

One month from Election Day, the race had finally broken open a bit. This was especially important because in many key battleground states—North Carolina, Florida, Nevada, to name a few—early voting would begin in earnest in the next two-week window. Where the race stood at that point would be reflected in the early votes, and over 50 percent of the total vote in many of these states would come in early. We did not know it at the time, but 30 percent of the total national vote would be cast before the polls opened on Election Day, through mail ballots or in-person early voting.

All our indicators told us we were in strong shape, though by no means out of the woods. We led comfortably in every Kerry state, by at least mid-high single digits. We had comfortable leads in Nevada, New Mexico, and Iowa, and small but meaningful leads in Colorado, New Hampshire, and Virginia. The race was a dead-heat in Indiana, Ohio, North Carolina, and Florida, and we trailed narrowly in Montana and Missouri.

If we lost all toss-ups in this scenario, and won those in which we had either comfortable or smaller but meaningful leads, we would end up with 295 electoral votes. I looked at that as our base number. McCain needed to figure out a way to peel off at least 27 electoral votes. Even if the race turned against us toward the end, in those states where we had banked a huge number of votes early, the math got awfully hard for McCain.

For this reason, and also because we were so dependent on first-time and sporadic voters, we mustered an intense effort toward executing early vote. This effort consisted of radio ads reminding people of early vote and explaining how it worked; a fusillade of Internet ads to push the concept; repeated e-mail and text messaging to people on our list from these states; and a blizzard of door-knocks and phone calls to remind voters person-to-person about early vote. We also tried to make sure all our volunteers voted early so that they would be freed up to help on Election Day.

Some in political circles argue that the early vote doesn't matter—that the people who go to the effort to vote early are committed voters who will almost certainly show up on Election Day. We fervently believed that if a hurdle presented itself on Election Day—a family issue; a work emergency; transportation problems—nonhabitual voters are the most likely people to throw in the towel on making it to the polls. These are the folks we relentlessly encouraged to vote early and the yardstick to which we paid closest attention—

not how many early votes we were getting, but whose. Were enough first-time voters voting early? How about African American sporadic voters? In addition to allowing us to make sure we were voting large numbers of our most questionable turnout targets, it also gave us a window into overall changes in turnout from previous elections, which helped us determine whether we were really changing the electorate.

Jon Carson crunched numbers all day every day as reports from the states came in, and then summarized the trends for me, Jen O'Malley, our regional staff (who worked with a certain number of states out of HQ), and a handful of others in the campaign, so we could make adjustments, correct problems, or seize opportunities.

We needed everything to break perfectly to have a chance to win North Carolina, and it appeared that it just might happen. We saw that the African American turnout was ballooning, and turnout in white progressive areas was through the roof as well. Conversely, GOP base turnout looked depressed. We added even more trips from our principals into the state, a decision made easier by McCain's waiting until far too late to acknowledge the danger he was in, almost stubbornly refusing to spend time or money in North Carolina, despite overwhelming evidence that those fifteen normally reliable Republican electoral votes were in jeopardy. By my calculation there was no way McCain could win the election having lost North Carolina.

As we began moving deeper into early vote, one number caused alarm. Carson came into my office one afternoon. "I've been poring over the early-vote data," he said, "and we seem to have a problem. Or what could be a problem, I should say. We're meeting or exceeding our early-vote goals in most demographics across most states. But younger voters—under twenty-five—are off quite a bit."

"Let's move more money and bodies resources to it," I replied, "and maybe try some different messaging."

Carson agreed but also suggested doing some research among this group to try to find out why they were not voting early in great numbers. Did we have a motivation problem, an execution problem, or both?

I green-lighted the research, which yielded two very illuminating findings. First, many young voters were so excited by this election that they couldn't envision doing anything besides voting for Barack Obama in person at the polling location. When we raised with them the possibility of long lines, or the potential to free themselves up to volunteer, they simply wouldn't budge.

This was a big moment for them and they felt it would seem bigger if they voted at the polls. In any case, they were still dead-set on participating, which relieved us.

The second lesson was that there was still some confusion about who was eligible to vote early and how it worked. Armed with these findings, we made sure our communications to younger voters included even more remedial information about the nuts and bolts of early voting. Soon enough, their numbers began to climb. In many states we lowered our expectation for the under–twenty-five early vote (but not for overall turnout), and we eventually hit those numbers in most battlegrounds.

We prepped for the second debate—a town hall–style event to be held on Tuesday, October 7, in Tennessee—in our newest battleground, North Carolina. We were in Asheville, a beautiful town tucked into the foothills of the Smoky Mountains. This was by far Obama's favorite prep site—there was a great gym on site, and he enjoyed walking the golf course at dusk with his friend Marty Nesbitt. The comfort resulted in probably our best prep session. Obama was dialed in, his answers were crisp, and he was really looking forward to taking questions from regular Tennessee voters instead of the usual press inquisitors. "I guarantee you these questions will be the best of the three debates," he told us. "Very little political process, questions about issues grounded in their everyday lives, and questions not designed to make news themselves."

McCain was widely known as a master of the town hall format, having received rave reviews for his town hall performances in both the 2000 and 2008 primaries. We aggressively tried to hype this reputation and raise expectations for his performance, an effort that was helped by McCain's gambit to get us to agree to do a dozen joint town halls in the summer. We called him the best town hall performer in the history of American politics, echoing the 2004 debate run-up when the Bush campaign said John Kerry was the best debater since Cicero.

Hyperbole aside, we were genuinely concerned about this debate. McCain really was quite good in this format; it brought out his looseness with audiences and his irreverent sense of humor. We assumed he would correct his error of the previous debate and relentlessly portray himself as an advocate for the middle class; after all, the audience would be filled with middle-class Tennessee voters. With this in mind, we tried to find ways to maximize our performance, figuring that McCain would give his best showing yet.

It was at just this moment that a former radical from Obama's neighborhood in Chicago made his grand entry onto the general-election stage, complicating the campaign as well as our prep.

The issue of Bill Ayers had been raised during the primary, most notably during our inglorious debate before the Pennsylvania primary. Since then, conservative groups had begun running low-level TV ads in some battleground markets, slamming Obama for his association with Ayers. These attacks had gained little foothold; there was no context for voters to grasp onto.

William Ayers had once been a member of the Weather Underground, a 1960s-era radical group that became increasingly violent in its opposition to the Vietnam War. Ayers married Bernardine Dohrn, another member of the group. The Weather Underground's acts of domestic terrorism took some lives, including that of a New York City policeman. While Dohrn and Ayers were not directly involved in murderous incidents, they were ringleaders of the group, and Dohrn served some prison time for aggravated battery and bail jumping.

What does all this have to do with Barack Obama? Not much, really. But in politics, tangential associations can cause great damage. Obama's connections—Wright, Rezko, and other bogeymen for the right—were already a central thrust of our opponent's campaign.

By the time Obama met Ayers in the mid-1990s, he was not primarily known as a former radical. He was an education professor at the University of Chicago and deeply involved in school-reform issues. Ayers and Dohrn hosted a neighborhood coffee when Obama was running for state senate the first time—Ayers and Dohrn were both deeply ingrained in the Hyde Park political community—and Obama had also served with Ayers on the board of an education-reform nonprofit.

Ayers was not involved in Obama's presidential campaign and had never been a close adviser or political confidant. As Ayers himself put it, "I think my relationship with Obama was probably like that of thousands of others in Chicago and, like millions and millions of others, I wished I knew him better."

Five days before the second debate, the *New York Times* ran a story about Obama and Ayers's relationship that thrust the issue front and center into the campaign. The story was a green light for the rest of the media, and our opponents, to begin focusing white-hot attention on Ayers and the nature of his involvement with Obama, and, of course, to speculate on what it would mean in the campaign.

Another shitstorm to fight through. Axelrod in particular had been obsessing for months about Ayers and the challenge of dealing with this in a media world that would likely oversimplify the story; the specter of swiftboats had been dancing in the political community's head for months.

"It's about time they dragged this out," I said, trying to joke with him the night the story was posted online. "I was beginning to think your angst about it would be unfulfilled."

"Sadly, my angst is almost always on the mark," he replied. "We'll see. I think we can navigate through this but a lot will depend on how artfully the McCain campaign handles it."

"Making something of this requires a scalpel not a sledgehammer," I said. "Not really their MO so far. We also need to keep everyone calm internally. We've prepared for this, so we just have to muscle through it, hopefully quickly, and try not to get snowed under."

The traditional political play here was clear—McCain's camp would try to trump up the relationship with Ayers and question Obama's judgment for having anything to do with him, all in the interest of portraying Obama as too far outside the mainstream to be a safe pick. As Sarah Palin was fond of saying, "This is not a man who sees America as you and I do."

We had war-gamed the Ayers issue in focus groups and polling over the summer, long before this resurgence of interest, assuming it would eventually darken our doorstep. As we exposed voters to the likely Ayers-based attacks, it became clear we could not blow off the subject as simply more negative politics from McCain. The connection raised real questions in voters' minds: How close were Obama and Ayers? Was he going to be working in an Obama administration? When did Obama first learn of Ayers's past?

We found that as voters learned the facts, though, they were largely satisfied with the response, and the association did not alter their view of Obama. It helped that Ayers's acts of domestic terrorism were committed when Obama was eight years old, and that he was not an adviser to the campaign. The fact that Ayers had in the intervening years become a college professor and education expert also helped round out some of the sharp edges.

So we knew we would have to respond and defend ourselves—both in the press and through paid advertising—if and when the Ayers attack hit the airwaves. But we thought if we executed well, we could ultimately defuse it. That McCain waited so long to launch this line of attack helped us immeasurably. Voters tend to treat attacks late in campaigns with a high degree of skepticism. "If this is so important," they asked, "why is this the first time we are hearing about it seriously? What's really going on here?"

The McCain campaign also utterly flubbed their injection of the Ayers argument into the main artery of their communications. Sarah Palin—who had almost zero credibility and little standing with the broader electorate—was the tip of the spear, launching into the Ayers attack at a Colorado rally. Barack Obama is "palling around with terrorists," she told the crowd.

If anything, Palin did receive outsized press attention, and with something this controversial it was bound to explode into the media. For a week or two in mid-October, Ayers dominated the race, which must have made the McCain folks giddy. We were confident, though, that over time voters would eventually come to reject the notion that Barack Obama was spending his time with terrorists; it was just too much of a stretch. In addition to having the facts on our side, Palin's descriptive overreach made the behavior and motive of the McCain campaign part of voters' processing; in the long run, we thought, they had sacrificed more of their credibility to no foreseeable advantage.

While planning in advance for the Ayers assault, we had discussed different ways of blunting the impact of their argument, seeking an issue we could introduce that would raise questions about McCain's judgment and character. This was a traditionally political, tactical approach, but we did not want to backpedal without getting off a shot. We thought we should create some turbulence for McCain.

The obvious point was his involvement in the 1980s with Charles Keating and the savings and loan scandal. McCain had been one of five senators investigated for pressuring regulators on behalf of a major campaign contributor. They became notorious as the Keating Five, and McCain was reprimanded by his colleagues in the Senate. A tawdry episode, to be sure.

We thought Keating was much more relevant to the campaign than Ayers: some of the roots of the economic crisis lay in lax regulators and the influence that financial institutions carried in Washington. Looking at McCain's history with regulators seemed in bounds and relevant.

Obama told us he did not want to use Keating as a preemptive strike. Perhaps we could trot the issue out as a response, but he wanted to think hard about even doing that.

Most voters had hazy recollections or none at all of the twenty-five-year-old affair; if we decided to add Keating to the mix, we would have to find a way to tell the story in full, to both voters and the media. Our new media department suggested putting together a longer-form documentary that would objectively lay out the facts of Keating, McCain's involvement, and its relevance to the current economic situation.

I green-lighted a thirteen-minute video that featured lots of archival footage and a searing interview with one of the key regulators pressured by the Keating Five. When Rospars presented the finished product, the results were fantastic. We thought the piece was factually devastating and would be more readily accepted by voters than a thirty-second hit job.

I told Obama about the documentary and he liked the concept, both that it was factual and educational, and that we would release it only as a defensive measure. We had his approval to launch it if necessary.

Right before the second debate, the RNC prepared to launch TV attack ads focused on Ayers in all the battleground states. The press was enthralled with this issue, so we knew the move would get outsized attention. Not wanting to be the only candidate playing defense on a personal issue, I convened a call with a small group to discuss releasing the Keating documentary the next morning. Everyone agreed. Pfeiffer suggested tipping off some of the press that night to increase interest and lengthen the time the Keating pushback would be in the media bloodstream. I thought that was a good idea.

That night, after our first mock-debate practice at the hotel in Asheville, Obama headed upstairs and the prep team gathered in a meeting room. We were reviewing each answer from the mock debate so that in the morning we could review with Obama what worked, what didn't, and what needed some adjustment. He really disliked these review sessions. "You guys seem to enjoy telling me how many times I screwed up," he had frequently complained. Still, they were very helpful. He never agreed with all our assessments and suggestions, but when he did, grudgingly or not, the improvement would be noticeable and permanent.

As we were reviewing questions, Obama opened the door to the meeting room. This was very unusual; when he went up to his room he was almost always down for the night, reading or watching ESPN.

"Sorry, guys. I need the Davids for a minute." Ax and I looked at each other and went into the hallway. We both assumed there was a major problem of some sort.

"I was flipping through channels and saw that we are releasing the Keating documentary tomorrow morning," he said. "Why wasn't I consulted about it?"

I was stunned, thinking I had his agreement. I tried to explain, "We discussed it and I thought—"

Obama cut me off. "This is not a run-of-the-mill ad. This is a big bomb. And I should have made the final decision on whether to use it and when." He was clearly frustrated. "I must tell you, I think this is a mistake. Now, in the debate, when I suggest that McCain is engaging in the same old attack politics, he'll have an easy comeback: I'm doing the same thing. I'm really disappointed in you two for not handling this the right way."

Ax tried to explain how this would not affect our ability to defuse Ayers in the debate; the Keating issue was much more relevant. "It doesn't hem us in at all," Ax argued. "Ayers is more of the same phony politics of association—." But Obama cut him off, too. He felt blindsided and was not really focused on the substance.

I told him we wouldn't make this mistake again. And we didn't, though the Keating video ended up serving its political purpose. It competed with Ayers in the press coverage and pulled in a huge audience on YouTube. I saw it as a potential brushback pitch that could make the McCain folks think twice about how hard and irresponsibly to push Ayers and Obama's other associations. It also served as a subtle demonstration of our strength; we released the documentary only to the press and online, but they knew that if we wanted to, we had the financial ability to air it on TV.

Whatever the potential benefits, he felt that his campaign had gotten out of ahead of him, and the communications process between the two of us had broken down. The release of the Keating video did not quite rival the Clinton (D-Punjab) paper in terms of Obama's unhappiness with me and the campaign, but it was up there.

We spent a great deal of prep time hashing out responses for Ayers, but the bulk of the audience questions at the town hall debate addressed the issues affecting the voters and their families. Obama relentlessly linked his ideas to improving the prospects of the middle class. Inconceivably, McCain once again largely took a pass on burnishing his credentials with this group. Obama also engaged well with the questioners, an important factor in voters' evaluations of a town hall debate. McCain, though usually a master of this intimate format, seemed surprisingly uncomfortable and certainly not warm. We had expected him to joke with the crowd and really engage them, but instead he seemed tense, as if he was trying to remember the lines they had practiced instead of just letting it fly a bit. And surprisingly, he did not try to weave in Ayers.

Both our own research and the polls taken after the debate showed we won this contest even more decisively than the first. As we flew back to Chicago through the pounding Tennessee rain, munching on our superstition-mandated burgers and beers, I said to Ax, "One more. Get through one more goddamned debate and we could be in the clear."

"We're three for three if you count Biden," Ax replied as he downed his beer. "I don't think anyone's gone four for four, but I think we can. Our guy has really hit his stride."

"Yeah, he's in another gear now," I said. "It's almost like right before Iowa when it just clicked and everything seemed to slow down for him." We both considered this for a moment as we chewed silently. "We just need to make sure we don't have any letup," I continued. "The prep has to be rigorous. We'll be expected to win this next one, both because it's on domestic issues and we've already won the first two. Our expectations are soaring."

Ax smiled. "Will you settle down and just enjoy this one, at least until we land?"

I opened another beer and tried to do as he suggested. But with the big prize almost in our grasp, he had to worry about anything and everything that could knock it loose.

The third debate would be held in New York, but in keeping with our battleground tradition, we prepped in Ohio, at a state park lodge in Toledo. I flew into Detroit and drove down to meet up with the prep team the Sunday before the debate, having flown home to D.C. for a few hours earlier that day to visit my very pregnant wife and son. Landing in Michigan, it dawned on me as I deplaned that this was now our territory. An Obama flag was firmly planted in Michigan—the McCain folks really had abandoned ship.

The drive down took me from a state in which we had vanquished our opponent to one that was nothing short of a political war zone. Our lead in Ohio was narrow, and dominating the state's media for three days as Obama zigged and zagged from debate prep to public events gave us a huge boost. McCain was prepping at his ranch in Arizona and popping over to New Mexico for an event, a state that looked to us increasingly like a lost cause for him.

The team was gathering when I arrived in Toledo. Obama sat down a few minutes later for our initial discussion of the debate, but before we could dive in, he and Gibbs wanted to talk about an exchange he'd just had with a voter while knocking on doors in a neighborhood in northwest Ohio.

Not many presidential candidates go into neighborhoods and knock doors, but Obama had done it from time to time since the early days of the primary. It produced a nice image of him working hard for votes, engaging at a personal level. The pictures out of this Ohio visit were terrific—but there was one exchange with a voter that was beginning to percolate.

A resident of the neighborhood had come up to Obama as he was walking down the street and started to question him about his tax plan. The voter said he believed the Obama tax plan would hurt people like him who might one day want to buy or start a small business. Obama patiently explained that his tax plan would actually cut taxes for those in this position, and that the man would be far better off under an Obama tax plan than Bush's or what McCain was proposing.

But the man clearly had his mind made up and would not be assuaged by any of the explanations. In Barack's words, "He wouldn't take yes for an answer."

Gibbs added, "We couldn't have sold him a glass of water in the desert."

During the exchange on the street, Barack had used a phrase in defense of his tax philosophy that we knew McCain would pounce on: "redistribute the wealth." I blanched at the choice of words, but we were confident voters would understand that this referred to what Obama had been proposing all campaign: a restoration of balance in the tax code, cutting taxes for 95 percent of Americans, and allowing the Bush tax cuts for the wealthiest 2 percent of Americans to expire.

Axelrod didn't think the attack would resonate with voters because we had spent months pounding away in every battleground market that we were going to cut taxes for the middle class and small businesses. In one of the most significant but least appreciated developments of the campaign, in most states our research showed that voters believed Obama would be better than McCain on taxes for people like them. Republicans running for president almost always won this question by huge margins. We had turned the tables, and taxes were now an offensive issue for us, not something on which we had to contain damage.

Still, we knew what was likely to come from our opponents. "They don't have much going for them now," said Ax, "so they'll probably lean into this way too hard." I agreed. If McCain wanted to spend the closing debate and some of the last period of the campaign debating who was going to be more equitable on taxes, we should roll out the red carpet.

To sum it up, none of us were overly concerned about Obama's exchange on October 12 with the Ohio plumber Joe Wurzelbacher.

———

Ax was planning to stay behind in New York after the debate, ostensibly to travel with Obama for a couple of days. I suspected his decision had more to do with attending our last campaign fund-raising event the next night in New York, a concert with Billy Joel and Bruce Springsteen; Ax was a big fan of the Boss.

I was irrationally furious that he would not be joining me on the flight home for our postdebate burger-and-beer ritual. I had told him before the debate with deadly seriousness that he was screwing with our karma. There was a real chance, I said, that we could have a disastrous debate if he broke up our routine.

Concerned by my bizarre behavior, he offered to change his plans and fly back to Chicago, and then out to New York at 6:00 the next morning. I grudgingly reflected on the wear and tear my anxiety would cause him and said, "No, but if we lose the presidency, you'll know why."

The debate was at Hofstra University on Long Island, and our plane was flying into LaGuardia Airport. Barack, Ax, and I were standing and talking up in the front section of the plane as it descended into New York. One of the nice things about traveling on a private plane is that you don't have to sit down on approach—you can plop down in your seat right before you land. We were talking about sports and just then the skyline of New York City appeared out the window. Our conversation stopped and we all stared silently for several minutes. It's hard to fly by that skyline without being snapped back to that horrible September day in 2001.

The moment was also a piercing reminder that we were in a bubble and had been for a long time; seeing the city brought back memories of life during more normal times. For Ax, growing up on Manhattan's Lower East Side. For Barack, going to school at Columbia, where he first gained his seriousness of purpose. I had my own memories of special times with my wife and friends. None of us voiced our thoughts. Instead, we exchanged knowing looks and took our seats right before the tires of our plane touched down.

To our surprise and confusion, all McCain wanted to talk about on stage at Hofstra University was Joe Wurzelbacher. McCain raised "Joe the Plumber" in what seemed like every answer. All total, Joe's name was mentioned twenty-five times in this debate, almost as many times as health care and more times than creating jobs. Strategically, McCain needed to erode some of our surprising strength with voters on taxes. But with his broken-record reference to Joe, I thought McCain turned in a performance that sounded like a *Saturday Night Live* parody of himself.

We won the final debate by all measures, though not quite as convincingly as the first two. McCain was animated and attacked Obama with vigor throughout the debate. Expectations were lower because of our routs in the first two debates, and McCain did a better job of meeting and exceeding them.

I confess my attention was not focused 100 percent on the debate at every moment. My beloved Philadelphia Phillies had a chance to clinch the National League pennant against the Dodgers that night and had taken a big lead as the debate progressed. Ax and I insisted that one of the four TVs provided to us in the staff viewing room be tuned to the baseball playoffs. His Cubs and White Sox had bowed out early—he was incensed at the Cubs the night of the VP debate in St Louis—but my Phillies were defying their pitiful history and charging through the playoffs.

Not all our staff was wild about having baseball on and most ignored it, but my eyes were darting back and forth. At night's end we had gone four for four in presidential debates and the Phillies had put away the Dodgers, and were going on to the World Series. When I talked to Obama after the debate, he was more interested in talking about baseball.

"Honestly, Plouffe, if you had to choose, would it be winning the election or the World Series?"

"Honestly?" I asked. "It's a close call. I'd have to choose winning the election." I paused. "But we might need a recount."

17

Endgame

Barack was in a very light mood after the third debate. He had completed the last really hard thing the campaign trail demanded of him. We had run the gauntlet of the foreign trip, VP selection, convention, and debates, and not just survived but strengthened ourselves immeasurably. The campaign had executed well, but the real credit in the end goes to Barack Obama. "That was all you tonight," I told him on a call that night. "All of these big moments have been you. At the red-light moment, you're alone with the ball. You either make the shot or miss it, and you've made it every time. I could not be prouder of you."

I'm sure he appreciated the sentiment, but he snapped me back to reality. "Well, I've done my part," he said. "Now it's in your hands. I'll go out there every day and campaign hard and make the arguments we have to make. But from now on, what's happening on the ground is the most important thing." I could sense relief in his voice at having his toughest moments in the rearview mirror.

We stood twenty days out from the election, and the data coming in from the states increased our confidence. We were polling quite strongly across the battlegrounds, but in the states with early vote we were beginning to see actual trends in terms of who was voting; the result looked encouraging. Our base— African Americans, sporadic-voting Democrats, and younger voters—was turning out in larger numbers than McCain's base in most states. And independent voters who we thought were most likely to support us were turning out at greater levels than McCain's independent likely supporters. Given early-vote data like this, in states like Colorado, New Mexico, and Nevada, we thought we were heading into Election Day with double-digit leads with over half the votes already cast; McCain would have to win Election Day by a massive margin to carry these critical states.

You wouldn't have known this from spending any time with us. The conversations and demeanor in our HQ and state offices, and on the plane with Obama, revealed none of this confidence. Following his lead, we tended to be a very even-keeled outfit and had been through enough ups and downs in the primary to shy away from speculative remarks like, "Well, we should win this thing" or, "I don't see how McCain can pull this off." We just kept our heads down, tried not to make mistakes, and executed our responsibilities. Even though we knew we had the best staff and volunteer squad ever assembled in presidential politics, one that could potentially get us over the top in tied or close races, we did not let that cushion into our mind-set. We stayed focused on hitting our marks and metrics.

We also made sure our campaign counsel, led by Bob Bauer, had the most thorough, experienced, and dogged election protection team in place in all the states. A crack staff of hundreds of lawyers, almost all volunteers, would make sure the voters we were counting on—new registrants, younger voters, and minorities—were able to participate without facing the same degree of problems and malfeasance that had cropped up in recent presidential elections.

Every day, McCain, Palin, or both were hammering us on taxes, using Joe the Plumber as a device, even campaigning with him a couple of times—when he felt like showing up. At one event, McCain called Joe to the stage only to receive an awkward, silent response—and terrible coverage in the aftermath—when Joe was nowhere to be found. "Joe, I thought you were here today," said McCain to no one in particular. Pretty weak stuff.

And little of it was breaking through, anyway. Everything we heard and saw in the data confirmed that people weren't buying the notion of Obama as some socialist engaged in economic engineering—they still preferred him on taxes by a healthy margin in most states. And voters quickly grew sick and tired of Joe the Plumber; they were looking for authenticity.

———

The home stretch was in many ways the smoothest period of the entire campaign. Our organization was humming in the states, McCain's attacks were not resonating, and Obama's stumping crackled with energy. Absent some unforeseen earthquake, we had only to block and tackle well, and we would likely win the presidency.

Our e-mail list had reached 13 million people. We had essentially created our own television network, only better, because we communicated directly with no filter to what would amount to about 20 percent of the total number of votes we would need to win—a remarkably high percentage. And those supporters would share our positive message or response to an attack, whether through orchestrated campaign activity like door knocking or phone calling or just in conversations they had each day with friends, family, and colleagues.

On an issue like Ayers, what people on the ground said to one another was just as important, if not more, than what Obama said himself. When our supporter—let's call him John, a diner owner from Durango, Colorado—talked to his undecided neighbor Mary, we had to make sure John knew what to say. Through e-mailed talking points, postings on the website, and conversations with local field organizers, our volunteers were stressing the same arguments Obama, Biden, Ax, and Gibbs were delivering on any given day. Our philosophy was that John from Durango needed to be as current on the campaign as the candidate was. We wanted to build a message-delivery army in perfect harmony from top to bottom.

You couldn't put a price on it—regular people bringing Obama's message to their neighbors, serving as our ambassadors block by block throughout the battleground states. Especially in terms of character attacks, nothing was more potent when it came to reassuring target voters that they could trust Obama than hearing it from people who lived the same life and had the same values and experiences.

———

There were two bumps in our otherwise smooth landing—one planned and one that was sadly visited on us.

I was worried about the twenty-day lag time between the last debate and Election Day and thought we needed to create a major momentum-producing event that would excite our supporters, make one last high-profile pitch to lean-Obama supporters and undecided voters, and do something with a big enough footprint to dominate some of the endgame press coverage.

In early October, I floated with Ax and Grisolano the idea of doing a thirty-minute TV program to be aired the last week of the campaign. Of course the first issue they raised was cost. I told them not to worry about that, I'd figure it out. Our October fund-raising would not quite rival September's record-smashing haul, but we thought we'd easily surpass our initial $100 million target based on how we projected the month. We were firing on all cylinders—online money continued to explode, from both new and existing grassroots donors. And Julianna Smoot and Penny Pritzker's traditional finance operation continued to yield big dividends—they continued to cultivate new top-level fund-raisers, and even after two years of heavy mining, our raisers were still turning up new, large contributions. So the money for the program was there. The question was whether it made sense and how we would approach it.

We settled on focusing much of the program on stories of real Americans, struggling with the economy and health care. In this scenario, Obama would introduce the people, serving as an infrequent narrator, but he would not be the star of the show—the spotlight would stay on average Americans. Mark Putnam and Margolis pressed hard to have Obama come in live from an actual event site at the end of the program, to add some pizzazz to the production and spike interest. Putnam, one of the best producers in our party, had put together the remarkable video about Michelle for the convention. The candidate was skeptical.

"Going live seems awfully risky," he said. "What if there are technical issues? Or we mistime it at the rally? Wouldn't we better off, if we must go live, to do it from a studio somewhere where we have more control?"

"I think we can pull it off," I told him. "Look, we've been up on the high wire all campaign. So maybe this isn't a reasoned answer or clinical explanation, but it just doesn't feel right to pull up on the very last decision we have to make. Let's roll the dice."

Obama was quiet for a minute. "Okay," he said finally. "Let's do it." That was that. We were set for a nationally televised thirty-minute program, shown across the dial and of course streamed online, on Wednesday, October 29, just six short days before the election.

It was a ten-strike. The viewership was much higher than we anticipated. Over 20 percent of the country watching TV at the time was tuned in, a phenomenally high number. More important, in some key battleground markets like Palm Beach, Florida; Philadelphia, Pennsylvania; and Greensboro, North Carolina, the number was over 25 percent. And millions more watched the program or parts of it online, whether on our website or on various news and entertainment sites. Our research showed voters responding off the charts to the program's stories of real people. They were also almost universally surprised that the program wasn't just a long Obama speech or a Ross Perot–like production with pie charts. They told us it helped remind them what the election was really about: the economy, health care, and the human toll of our nation's veering off the tracks.

The program essentially dominated a forty-eight-hour period of news coverage during the last week of the race. It was an expensive way to block McCain, but well worth it. At the moment he could least afford to cede control of the campaign narrative, we showed up with a megaphone and he barely had a working mic.

Obama called me right after the live broadcast. "See, I told you guys there was nothing to it," he joked. He asked how it came across on TV, and I told him it could not have gone better. The show offered a nice contrast: the high-energy rally with the high-technology precision combined with the gritty true-life stories of the Americans.

Obama was psyched to have pulled it off. "I'm so pleased about how this went I won't even bend your ear about how it's eleven o' clock and I still have one more rally to do."

"This is the last Wednesday of the campaign," I told him. "And the last Wednesday-night rally you'll have to do until 2012, knock on wood."

The success of the thirty-minute program lifted our spirits. But personal tragedy also visited Barack at the end of the race, and it weighed on him a great deal.

His maternal grandmother, Madelyn Dunham, had been a rock for him throughout his life. She was the last person alive who had helped mold him into the man he was.

"Toot," as her grandchildren called her, was eighty-six and in failing health. Barack had spent a great deal of time with her during the August vacation in Hawaii. But she had been declining rapidly. He called me on a Saturday, seventeen days before the election, to say that his half-sister Maya, who was living in Hawaii and was with Toot constantly, reported that their grandmother did not have much time to live. "Do you think there's any way I could get back to Hawaii to see her?" Barack asked me. "She might make it past the election. But if she doesn't, I won't be able to forgive myself for not going back. I missed that chance with my mom and I don't want the same thing to happen with Toot."

Once again, it was really no decision at all; he had to go back. I talked to Alyssa and she suggested Obama fly to Hawaii the next Thursday, spend Friday with his grandmother, and then fly back overnight to resume campaigning on Saturday afternoon. He would be flat-out exhausted, but he said not to worry about it. And we would lose one day of the last twelve in the campaign, but Michelle would be out campaigning, and Biden of course, along with a host of surrogates. While there was no substitute in the battlegrounds for a Barack Obama visit, we knew we could flood the zone and make sure our case was being made in his absence.

He was subdued but relieved when I talked to him upon his return to the trail. "I'm so glad I was able to get back," he said. "She's meant so much to me. I'm not sure she'll make it to election day. I really hope she does—she is still following things so closely, even as weak as she is. But we're both at peace."

His grandmother passed away on Sunday, November 2. Barack was very serene, repeating how important it was that he had been able to say good-bye to her.

In an appearance in North Carolina Monday night, Barack, his emotions betraying how profoundly he felt her loss and with tears streaming down his cheeks, spoke of Toot and how much she meant to him, and what a strong and giving person she was. It had been a long journey and she would not be there to see its end.

Later that evening, ninety thousand people turned out at that rally in Manassas, Virginia, for the very last rally of his 2008 presidential campaign, a stone's throw from historic Bull Run, a key Civil War battleground. One hundred and forty five years after that battle, an African American was ending his presidential campaign in the heart of the old Confederacy, and likely to win the state, though it had been carried by Republicans for the past forty-four years.

I watched the coverage on television and felt proud of our discipline. We said Virginia would be perhaps the pivotal state in the election, and true to our word, our first and last events of the general-election campaign were held there. When we committed to something, we meant it.

Near the end of the rally Barack broke out, for the first time in the general election, the chant that had been such a constant in Iowa. "Fired up?" he'd shout. "Ready to go!" ninety thousand people shouted back in unison.

––––––

At the end, McCain's camp decided to throw everything they could into Pennsylvania, believing that if they could pull an upset and steal the Keystone State's twenty-one electoral votes, we would have to win a higher percentage of our targets. While that was true, we simply couldn't come up with a scenario—not one—where McCain could win Pennsylvania. Our lead was too strong and the state had become decidedly more Democratic in the last four years; we now enjoyed a registration edge of over 1 million. To win Pennsylvania, McCain would have to win about 55 percent of the independent vote and 20 percent of the Democratic vote. We did not think he could get anywhere close to that, and our data backed this up. Although McCain was essentially living in Pennsylvania at this point, we refused to take the bait and send Obama back there. Instead, as always, we stuck to our strategy and spent time in Florida, Ohio, Indiana, and North Carolina.

The night before the election, our last poll in Pennsylvania showed our lead slipping to just four points. These numbers didn't square with anything else we were seeing. I asked Jon Carson if he saw anything in the field data so far that day that suggested any erosion. "No, if anything we see strengthening," he told me. "The poll just seems way off."

Ax called me after seeing the Pennsylvania numbers. I relayed Carson's thoughts and said that I had been poring over different election scenarios and simply couldn't get McCain to 50 percent. His final ferocious effort might narrow the margin, but I was dead-certain we would win the state. Usually Ax was like a cat on a hot tin roof when we got bad polling numbers, but now he was calm. "Yeah, probably a screwy poll. I just don't see how this gets away from us tomorrow. It's weird to feel so confident."

I agreed and told him what a joy being on this journey with him had been. "Brother, the ride of our lifetimes," he responded. "Win or lose, I wouldn't have done it any differently or with different people. The hardest thing about tomorrow night will be that it's over. We've become a family and after tomorrow night, it'll never be the same again."

I hadn't really thought about that, but he was right. We all had gone through a political war together. Many of us had spoken nearly every day for two long years. We spent every waking hour together, talking all day long and sharing the highs, lows, and surprises. I would miss them all terribly.

One of the fundamental truths of the campaign's story, one that will always stick with those of us who went through it, is that we threw long. We refused to be defined by past electoral and American history, by what we were told we couldn't do. We tried to see things simply as they existed. We refused to accept the story that many thought would be written for us, and instead wrote our own chapter of history. The greatest treasure of the campaign was the chance to be my best self, and to share this with a band of brothers and sisters who were also their best selves, as we met and seized our moment.

As I hung up from that call with Ax, it dawned on me that it was all finally going to be over. Done. Finis. In about twenty-four hours. I was desperate to rejoin my family. Barring a Bush-Gore–style recount, this would happen at the crack of dawn Wednesday—unless our baby came on Election Day.

Even though it was midnight and I had to be up at 4:00 a.m. to do a round of the national morning shows, I left my short-term corporate apartment and walked down to Lake Michigan, past the apartment where my family and I had lived for most of the last two years. For at least an hour I stared at the water and the skyline. I tried to savor the memories of moments gone by and to get my arms around the idea that the verdict would be known in a matter of hours.

I chuckled aloud, recalling a board game I had often played as a kid with the improbable name Landslide. This may sound hard to believe, but it was actually a game based on the Electoral College. The goal of the game was to beat your opponents to 270 electoral votes, thus winning the presidency. Sometimes I would play against myself because, for some unfathomable reason, my friends and family weren't all that interested.

Now, thirty years later, I was trying to get to 270 for real. Win or lose, I knew how fortunate I was to be in this position, managing a presidential campaign on the precipice of achieving something that would have a profound and lasting effect. I felt lucky to be working with this candidate and this campaign team, and with all our passionate volunteers, at this moment in history.

As I looked at the Chicago skyline and its reflection shimmering on the lake, I felt at peace despite the mistakes we had made throughout the campaign. We hadn't left anything on the field and had run things the right way, trusting people, inspiring them, and thinking innovatively. It was hard to construct a scenario in which we would lose. But I had been down that road once before, on primary day in New Hampshire. If we lost on Election Day, it might take a lifetime to understand why, but it would not be because we screwed up the X's and O's of the campaign.

I took in a deep breath of the cool night air. I was ready for Election Day. And ready for it to be over.

What a difference the years had made. Though the campaign had started with little pressure or expectations of winning, I now felt weighed down by several factors that made the possibility of defeat unbearable.

I worried that if we lost, we could lose for a generation all the young and new volunteers and voters who got involved in our campaign. They poured their hearts into it; for many, it was the first time they'd ever taken this kind of leap, or even fathomed it. They believed in Obama, and in their capacity to affect the outcome of the election. Obama had ignited something very powerful in young people throughout the country. If that spark could be preserved, I was convinced we'd be a much stronger country for it.

As Obama often said: "I do not want to let them down."

"Them" meant people like the high-school-aged group of young men, a rainbow of ethnicities, that I saw on the street the day before the election, some wearing Obama gear, talking excitedly about states and polls and what they thought our chances were. I had stopped and pretended to tie my shoe while eavesdropping, wanting to soak in the moment, because I knew I might never witness another one like it. I felt a deep obligation to make sure these kids were celebrating the next night so they might be following and talking about elections for decades to come.

At least 95 percent of our six thousand employees were under the age of thirty, most under the age of twenty-five. It was hard for me to imagine the depths of their heartbreak if we came up short. Most of the staff were field organizers, the people who worked most closely with our volunteers out in the states. They would be personally devastated, and so would all their volunteers. I wanted to avoid that situation, if for no other reason than to fend off thousands of therapy sessions in the years to come. People felt that strongly about what we were doing and the necessity of winning.

I also felt growing pressure because of my changing assessment of Obama. In the beginning, Ax and I would often say we were pretty sure he had what it took to be a very good president, but we remained uncertain as to whether he could turn into a very good presidential candidate.

Well, he turned into one of the best presidential candidates ever to grace the stage. A brilliant communicator and motivator, he rarely made a mistake and in this most grueling of transparent processes actually ended up stronger than when he started. He wore well on the American people and grew in stature over the course of two long years. It was a remarkable feat for someone who burst suddenly onto the national stage and who even as recently as three months before Election Day had been an unknown quantity to many general-election voters.

And the grassroots movement we built, the well-oiled machine that funded so much of our campaign, moved our message person-to-person and organized volunteers and voters—this was all his making. Volunteers came to the campaign because they were interested in him. That interest became action, and then it became passion. Their commitment grew over time—perhaps it was tested in moments, but the faith our supporters had in him developed into a powerful force. In turn, his trust and faith in them was crystal clear, and this could not have been more motivating.

But I no longer thought Obama had the qualities to be merely a very good president—he might have the qualities to be an *excellent* president, even one for the ages. Grandiose, I know. But the problems the next president would inherit seemed to mount by the day, and I thought Barack's composure, intellect, desire to find common ground, and willingness to take on entrenched interests might meet the moment as well as any president had in recent memory, certainly going back to Reagan.

One night during the last week of the campaign, we did have a rare "What if I win" conversation. Sometimes we'd joke about it to lighten the mood in a rough moment: "Well, you think dealing with Ayers is bad, just wait until you have four seismic decisions on your desk in one afternoon." But this time was different.

"You know, David," he said, "when we started two years ago, I thought the stakes of this election and a change in direction could not be more important for the country. That need has only compounded. But the need for leadership and management and confidence building is more pronounced than we ever could've anticipated back then. And I think with the right help, I can provide that. And relish it."

"As crazy as this sounds," I told him, "I've thought for some time that you're better suited to the presidency than the campaign. Running critical meetings all day, gathering diverse, thoughtful opinions, making decisions, using the bully pulpit here and abroad to bring about change in nonlegislative ways, trying to open government back up to the people—in all those ways you're well suited to the job in normal times, but maybe even more so in extraordinary times.

"But let's snap back to the task at hand," I continued. "Or this conversation will go down in infamy."

———

It was hard not to think about the future, and even though we had an election to close out, Ax and I became more and more concerned about what would come next. We were utterly confident in Obama's capabilities, or his ability to put together a top-flight cabinet. But with the torrent of problems he would inherit, he would need a strong chief of staff. Without that, the promise of his candidacy would be sorely tested. Someone needed to be in charge, and right away, so his or her input would be reflected during the transition period if we won, when personnel decisions and priorities are established.

In my view, we needed that person in place the day after the election. The campaign would be over, and the structure we had spent two years building to surround Obama would cease to exist. We already had a transition process in place, managed by John Podesta, Bill Clinton's former chief of staff, in close consultation with Pete Rouse. They had been working for three months to present Obama with different options for administrative structure, cabinet short-lists, and a process to decide how to sequence legislative priorities. All this would be invaluable, and John and Pete had done heroic work. But we needed to make a decision on who would be tasked to head up the staff and run the ins and outs of government during and after the transition.

We needed a chief of staff who would be an uncommon leader, someone tough, with a huge bandwidth and the ability to transact business at the highest domestic and international levels. This need was made even more pressing by the worsening economic situation. We were facing an emergency. Obama would need a strong general.

Ax and I were convinced only one person could play this role—Rahm Emanuel, at the time the number three leader in the House and a legendarily intense Democratic operative. In baseball, a five-tool player refers to someone who excels at just about everything. Rahm was a five-tool political player: a strategist with deep policy expertise, considerable experience in both the legislative and executive branches, and a demeanor best described as relentless.

Obama thought about a range of people for this job, but before too long settled on Rahm as his first choice. When Obama first broached the idea with Rahm, he was turned down flat. Rahm knew to take the job would mean derailing a career that was heading toward a sparkling culmination with a role as Speaker of the House. And he had young kids and was very clear-eyed about what this would do to his family. When Obama suggested that the White House could be a family-friendly place, Rahm pushed back hard: "There's only one family White House service is good for—the first family."

I panicked at the thought Rahm might not go for it. The gap between him and the next best contender was a gaping chasm. But eventually he came around. I talked to him the weekend before the election, and while he was still officially mulling the chief of staff role, I could tell he had made the decision in his own mind. He was saying things like, "This is how I think we'll need to deal with Congress," and going over various personnel and cabinet ideas.

I felt a huge sense of relief. Even with all of Obama's skill, leadership qualities, and vision, he would need this spoke in the wheel, a partner in conceiving, executing, and staying on track in all his priority areas—and, of course, someone who could be trusted to manage the unexpected crises and events that visit every White House with great frequency.

I signed off my conversation with Rahm by saying, "Enjoy your afternoon, Mr. Chief of Staff."

"Fuck you," he replied. For Rahm, famously profane, it was like saying "See ya."

———

Election Day seemed like it lasted for a thousand days, but they were calm ones, at least. There were no major problems, only minor polling-place snafus, rain in Virginia, and some internal-reporting database breakdowns. But our huge and finely tuned organization was cranking on all cylinders. It looked like our turnout would be engorged in many places, and the GOP turnout modest.

The exit polls suggested an Obama landslide, but we had seen that movie before. We would wait until the actual votes came in before celebrating. The exits, if accurate, suggested that many of the narratives we fought through during the campaign would be turned on their heads. We looked to be winning Latino voters by almost forty points, a historic gap, and were doing better with white working-class voters than any Democrat since LBJ.

I spent the day in our Chicago HQ's boiler room, watching as the prediction machines starting firing up. As the media announced the early results, we were winning what we should win, McCain was winning what he should win, and all the battlegrounds were either too early or too close to call.

Indiana and North Carolina polls close early in the evening, and as we saw the raw votes coming in and compared them to our goals and projections, we knew we were headed for a very good night. The preliminary tallies suggested both states would be close finishes. In our wide-map electoral strategy, both of these states sat on the outer edges of necessity; states like Virginia, Colorado, and Nevada were much more likely and important. If we were going to be this close in these two longer-shot states, reason dictated that in friendlier turf, we should have more breathing room.

Someone at Fox News, of all places, sent our press staff an internal memo shortly after 8:00 p.m. EST. Based on the exit polls and the actual vote results Fox's number crunchers were looking at, they would be able to call the election for Obama at 11:00 p.m. EST. This was hard to get my head around. I felt like we were in a period of suspended animation, maniacally focused on crunching the data coming in even though it appeared the work would not be necessary. We had won.

All the networks called Pennsylvania when the polls closed at 8:00 p.m.—a devastating rebuke to McCain's last-gasp Pennsylvania strategy. He would now have to run the table to win.

Then, the big news: Ohio was called for Obama. I sent an e-mail to my wife at that moment that read simply, "We won."

With Ohio's result, the election was over. As long as there were no surprises out west in states that looked comfortably in our column, like California, Oregon, and Washington, we would be over 270 with a bunch of states still to be decided, many of them now looking like they would fall into our lap.

At 11:00 p.m. EST, on November 4, 2008, Barack Obama was declared the forty-fourth president of the United States.

Ax and I began our walk across the street to the Hyatt to join the president-elect. Our two-year odyssey was over. A new one was beginning, for Barack Obama, the country, and the world.

Epilogue

For me, the afterglow of winning a presidential campaign was fleeting. At about 1:00 a.m. in the same hotel where three hours earlier Obama and his family first learned he would be the forty-fourth president of the United States, Anita Dunn, David Axelrod, Robert Gibbs, and I sat down with a camera crew from *60 Minutes*. The interview was to focus on how we put together the campaign that yielded such an improbable victory, and it would run the next Sunday.

We were all exhausted. The campaign was finally over, but rather than cutting loose at last, we were going to be conducting an interview that would be seen by tens of millions of viewers around the world who would be watching to gain insight into Barack Obama, no longer our candidate, but America's new president-elect.

Given those stakes, it was perhaps ill advised for us to engage in some modest revelry. But after the two-year war we had just endured, putting off a valedictory brew any longer was simply not acceptable. Gibbs was losing his voice and fighting off a cold, and he and Anita smartly demurred. But Ax said he would join me for a nip. So we took our coffee cups, filled them with a little beer, and kept them in front of us during the interview. It could not have tasted better, and we seemed to handle Steve Kroft's probing questions just fine.

After the interview wrapped up, we left the hotel and lingered outside. Of course this would not be good-bye forever, but it was the end of the unique experience we had just shared. And as brutal and unrelenting as the campaign had been, it was a pleasure to have gone through it with these three colleagues and the rest of our team. We had truly become a family.

We already knew that Ax and Gibbs would be going into the administration. Anita and I would not be (though Anita did relent and agreed by the summer of 2009 to serve as White House communications director). This split would filter down through the rest of the staff. Some members would move forward with Obama on his journey, working night and day to fulfill the promise of his presidency. The rest of us would be helping in smaller and less time-consuming ways.

We exchanged embraces and my last hug was with Ax. We didn't say much and didn't have to. He simply said, "The pleasure of a lifetime, brother."

"Wouldn't have wanted to walk the road with anyone else," I responded.

And with that, the Obama for President campaign came to a close.

My flight out of O'Hare the next morning was scheduled for 6:00 a.m., so I just stayed up and watched the coverage of our victory. The history nerd in me had a lot to appreciate about the particulars of the results, notably the victory we appeared to be headed toward in good ol' Nebraska 2, which marked the first time the state's electoral votes had ever been divided. I left for the airport at 4:30 and arrived at the security screening area in a fatigue-induced daze, carrying two pieces of luggage and my computer bag. The security officer told me I had one bag too many and would have to go back and check it. If I did that, I could miss the flight. So I asked if I could lose a bag in the trash can. The guard looked at me quizzically and said, "Your call."

It was no decision at all. My wife was now three days overdue, the baby could come any moment, and I had promised my son I would be there on Wednesday to take him to school—for the first time in two years. I could not miss that plane. So I got on my knees, ripped open one bag, pulled my computer out and threw it in a suitcase, and started frantically rooting through the rest of my things. Finally I tossed one bag, much of its remaining contents, and a few clothes to boot in the nearby garbage. Now everything would fit in two bags.

Just then someone in line behind me said haltingly, "David Plouffe?"

I looked up to find a man I didn't know with a concerned expression on his face. "Yes?" I asked, perhaps a bit impatiently.

"Are you okay?" he replied. "We won, you know."

I laughed. I must have looked like a madman, sleep deprived and unshaved, tossing my possessions into a garbage can. It was a long way from the dignified pinnacle of a few hours before. And somehow it felt terrific. I stood up, picked up my two bags, and smiled. "Never been better."

I made the flight and two days later, in the early morning about fifty hours after the announcement of our victory, our daughter made her debut. May she always have such exquisite timing!

There was no question of my joining the administration. After the past two years and with a new baby to take care of, being a ghost father and husband was not an option. I had first discussed this with Obama in the spring, when I flirted with leaving as campaign manager after the epic march of the primaries. When I agreed to stay I told him flatly, "If we win, I have to be gone November 5. We have a baby coming and I have to dig in with my family."

And I did just that. While many of my colleagues from the campaign were working around the clock on the transition and inauguration and agreeing to administration jobs, I had ample time, albeit it usually at 4:00 a.m. with a baby sleeping on my chest, to reflect on some of the lessons of the campaign, and what they might mean moving forward.

———

We were essentially a start-up business. We had had nothing when we began—no lists, no equipment, no talent pool just waiting for the green light. Our candidate had had little experience on the national stage and almost no relationships or experience in the states that would decide our fate. It was an enormous challenge to launch this effort, under intense scrutiny, while we were still trying to get the phones turned on and the computers up and running. But that formative period created our identity, and many of the principles and decisions we employed at the outset were instrumental in allowing us to win. I presume these ideas would have some value to any enterprise.

We entered the campaign, and exited it, in the right mind-set, with a unique mixture of idealism and pragmatism. We believed that Obama offered great promise as both a candidate and a potential president, the kind of promise that most of us had assumed we would never witness, much less be a part of. This optimism was married to a keen appreciation of just how narrow our pathway to success would be. The odds from the start said we would not win. So idealism kept us going, but pragmatism kept us grounded. Both were necessary to our success.

We began with the belief that we needed a clear message as well as a single strategy. The message would encapsulate the emotion and substance we were offering voters, and the strategy would outline our theory for how we would succeed. Both of these were established at the outset and inviolable. There was no guarantee our strategy would work, but we needed to commit to one path, not many, and base every decision on it. And on both message and strategy, we did not pay much attention to what those on the outside were saying, whether we were perceived at that moment as up or down. We had our own radar and metrics and did not change course or rethink our fundamentals when the chorus of critics demanded it.

Everything in the campaign flowed through the prism of strategy, which made decision making relatively uneventful, a must for any organization. Taking the suspense out of why you say yes or no improves productivity, understanding, and morale, and makes it easier to reach sound decisions for the right reasons. This methodology also allowed us to make decisions quickly. In the beginning we had no choice, but as we got established, we carried that approach forward. There was simply no time to dither and second-guess. We knew that we wouldn't get all the calls right, and of course we didn't. But when we were wrong, we avoided wallowing or extended recriminations.

Technology played a key role in our success. Reaching an audience involves more than just figuring out who your audience is; it also means knowing how to find them. Part of the reason our campaign was so successful is that we were able to identify early that many of the people we wanted to reach were spending more of their time on the Internet. We realized that a smart, and large, Internet presence was the best way to provide people with the opportunity and the tools to get involved in the campaign—they were already immersed in the world of technology and would be more likely to encounter us there. We met people where they lived, instead of forcing them to deviate from their habits or lifestyle to seek us out. Our early commitment to a digitally based platform paid huge dividends.

From the outset, we tried to figure out how to communicate with target voters with a fresh set of eyes. Established tactics, like press interviews, TV ads, and mail pieces, would of course be important parts of our arsenal. But we put a huge premium on direct digital communication, as well as on the power of human beings' talking to human beings, online, on the phone, and at the door.

The principle underlying this was fairly simple: we live in a busy and fractured world in which people are bombarded with pleas for their attention. Given this, you have to try extra hard to reach them. You need to be everywhere. And for people you reach multiple times through different mediums, you need to make sure your message is consistent, so, for instance, they don't see a TV ad on tax cuts, hear a radio ad on health care, and click on an Internet ad about energy all on the same day. Messaging needs to be aligned at every level: between offline and on-, principal and volunteer, phone and e-mail.

We tried to be on our target voters' network TV, cable, satellite, and on-demand; on their radios; all over the Internet; in their mailboxes; on their landlines and their cell phones, if we could; at their doorsteps; and out in their communities. Balanced communications across all mediums is critical in any messaging effort today.

We measured our progress exclusively with our own yardstick. That takes discipline, but discipline without attention to the right metrics is meaningless. Whether it came to fund-raising, voter registration, our local press footprint, filling volunteer shifts, or ultimately reaching our vote goals, we had clear internal benchmarks that the campaign leadership used to measure our progress or lack thereof, and that all of our staff and volunteers could use to measure their own work. This is of chief importance—organizations tend to thrive when analysis of job performance is based on clear and incontrovertible standards. This way, any corrective action is based not on subjective measures but on clear, well-defined, objective ones.

Judging performance based on clear internal metrics leads to a healthy work environment, but it is just one part of a thoughtful and productive organizational culture. The culture established in the infancy of the Obama campaign carried us through for two years and had many other important facets. We placed a real premium on discretion and did not leak our internal discussions and business to the press or political community; we all felt that the mission was bigger than any of us individually; we tried to instill calmness, consistency, and clear rules of the road for employees; strong managers were hired and given great autonomy to reach strategic goals; and we were led by a candidate who each and every day quietly reinforced these principles, making any violation of them seem a betrayal of the cause.

We were a healthy organization, warts and all. There have been plenty of organizations that thrive, for a time at least, under leaders who yell and scream and fly off the handle and are propelled forward by a culture of intimidation and even fear. But I believe that, ultimately, organizations are collections of human beings. They will perform best and make their greatest achievements when there is clarity, calmness, conviction, and collegiality throughout the ranks.

Culture is about people. And the people of our campaign made this victory a reality. There is no more effective courier for a message than people who believe in it and have authentically embraced it. Our secret weapon, day in and day out, was our army of volunteers, real people who brought Obama's message and ideas to their neighbors, co-workers, and fellow citizens, guided by our extraordinary staff. The bonds of trust between individuals who shared values, goals, or even just living space were far stronger than anything we might hope to have forged through more traditional tactics. In many ways, the delivery of our message and the execution of our electoral strategy were successfully carried on the backs of these bonds.

And because these bonds are ultimately very fragile sinews, the trust contained within them cannot be abused. It took something special and true for people to put in the effort, day after day, at great personal and financial sacrifice. Yes, they believed in Obama's policy agenda and leadership abilities, and they thought the country needed to go in a fundamentally different direction. But all those factors led to votes, not historic levels of activism. The bond between the candidate and his supporters was intense and based on authenticity. Time strengthened it. Supporters knew in their hearts and in their guts that he treasured and respected their involvement and leadership in their local communities, and in the campaign. It was not *his* campaign—it was *their* campaign. That kind of loyalty and inspiration cannot be manufactured. Without it, we would have had a great webpage and social networking site, flashy but lacking humanity. Barack Obama and his supporters created something powerful and real, the likes of which we may not see for a very long time (with the exception of 2012, I hope).

I left the campaign extraordinarily confident about the future of the country, because of the talent and drive of the young men and women who made our victory possible. Certainly, we would not have won the primary or the general without a surging youth turnout in any number of states, Iowa most importantly. But their impact on the election goes beyond casting ballots. Most of our staff was under thirty, many of them under twenty-five, as were a sizable chunk of our most active volunteers. As I witnessed, sometimes in awe, their performance and desire to look beyond themselves and contribute to a better world (and they have a distinctly global outlook) it gave me extreme comfort to know that in the not so distant future they will be taking the reins and leading our companies, campaigns, and institutions. For my generation, the rocking chair beckons—these kids are that good. I can't wait to experience their leadership and vision in the years to come.

———

We started our campaign with the firm but risky belief that we could radically expand the electorate and that we could count on our grassroots supporters to execute our plan. This strategy proved wildly successful. Yes, we won states like Indiana, North Carolina, and Virginia because of that expansion. But you have to go a bit deeper into the numbers to understand just how effective that strategy was. If you consider only the people who voted in the Bush-Kerry election four years earlier, according to national exit polls, Obama beat McCain by a very small margin, 50–49 percent. In the 2004 election, Bush beat Kerry 51–47 percent among those same voters. A five-point swing is a big deal in itself, and it underlines Obama's appeal to traditional independent and even Republican voters.

But leaving it in the hands of only those voters would have produced another nail-biter election, which potentially could have been lost to a more strategic opponent. The reason we won comfortably, with the highest vote percentage for a Democrat since LBJ, was that among people voting for the first time in a presidential election—or for the first time in a long time—we won by a shocking 71–27 percent. Younger voters turned out in huge numbers. African American voters turned out at roughly the same rate as white voters for the first time in the country's history. The share of the electorate over sixty-five actually dropped between 2004 and 2008, not because fewer older voters turned out but because younger ones showed up in droves.

We—most importantly the candidate himself—refused to accept the electorate as it was. We thought we could make it younger and more diverse, and that's exactly what we did. That beautiful map of the 2008 vote, with Obama blue in some very unusual places, like Indiana and North Carolina, is a testament to our belief that we could reach the Holy Grail of politics. We tried to shoot high but remained grounded in a hard analysis of what would truly be possible.

President Obama is that way. He's not terribly interested in the same old arguments and debates or conventional reasons why things can't be done. He pushes and challenges, but he also doesn't want to tilt at windmills. Wiping the slate clean, looking at things differently—as we did in both the primary and the general—and deciding on a course based on sound analysis and research is an Obama hallmark, one that I believe will serve the country well.

Of course, when you do this, the cynics and purveyors of conventional wisdom howl in protest. In Washington, many focus more on what can't be done than on what can be. One of the president's great strengths, and therefore his organization's strength, is his discipline: once a course has been set, he is determined not to let a chorus of critics alter that game plan. I saw this commitment over and over again in the campaign when it came to message and strategy, and I can see it coming into play now as the White House tackles the hard work of stabilizing the economy, passing health insurance reform, and creating an energy revolution in America.

His efforts will be graded daily by the pundits, and polls will be thrown around as evidence of progress or setbacks, but he will keep the ship steady, focused on achieving an end result that will improve the lives of Americans. Without this discipline and long-range focus, change would be impossible to bring about in Washington, a city where every bump, real or imagined, is treated as a permanent setback. The president does not view his work and progress on these imperatives through the lens of daily political scorekeeping. He stays focused on whether his day-to-day work, most of which will never appear in the news, is leading toward the desired result.

As I write this, Washington is in a state of high agitation about health care. Some suggest that reform efforts are in deep trouble and question whether President Obama has bitten off too much, is too conciliatory, or is not conciliatory enough. It is a familiar dynamic from the campaign, akin to those moments when the press put us in the penalty box.

But this is where the president's long-term outlook and inner calm will serve the cause of health insurance reform and, therefore, the country, well. He is a chess player in a town full of checkers players. His eyes will remain focused only on the goal, and he will measure progress and make adjustments based on that, not on the current amount of hyperventilation going on in the political press.

It concerns me—and this is strictly a personal observation—that some quarters of the Democratic Party seem to worry that the effort it will take to pass health insurance reform, and then energy reform, could do damage to the party, because some recent polls have shown a not insignificant amount of unease among voters. In my view, this is looking three yards downfield instead of thirty. In the long run, the economy will be healed, and growing; landmark health insurance reform that has languished in Washington for seventy years will have been passed; and we will have done the hard work required to make us the worldwide leader in new energy and green jobs for generations to come. But to make that happen, we need to lay the groundwork now.

I hope Republicans will assist in these efforts. Only a few helped to push through the stimulus package, which I believe will come to be seen as an important cornerstone in our economic recovery. When the smoke clears, the Democrats will have a remarkable record of leadership that moved the country forward and will consequently have great political appeal. Contrast that with the Washington Republicans, who will likely have played little role, with the exception of a few principled individuals. And let's not forget that the economic policies they still embrace played a large role in creating this crisis.

When their fearmongering on health care proves to be just that—when reform passes and voters still have their choice of doctors, care remains unrationed, and Sarah Palin's death panels have killed only her political prospects—the Republicans in Washington will truly be exposed as the emperors with no clothes. They will have zero credibility. They are putting all their rotten eggs into one basket, using misinformation and outright lies to try to deny the president a victory.

This is the wrong approach for our country and a clear example of the Washington mentality that has prevented us from solving big challenges. But I believe it is also bad politics and at some point in the future will be seen as political malpractice. If the Republicans have little contribution to show when it comes to digging the country out of our greatest economic threat since the Great Depression or solving big issues like health care and energy, it could be a long, long road back to viability. They are already in bad shape with younger and Latino voters and will face only further damage when their overheated criticism on health care is proved to be demonstrably false.

I sincerely hope more in the Washington GOP decide to meet the moment by setting aside their misinformation campaigns and by working with the president and Democrats in Congress to find solutions that will benefit all Americans. But if they insist on treading their current path—a high-risk strategy of opposing everything and proposing nothing—they will pay an electoral price that, from my perspective, they will richly deserve.

———

Our belief in people did not end on November 4. As the president-elect said in his victory speech that night, "This victory alone is not the change we seek—it is only the chance for us to make that change. And that cannot happen if we go back to the way things were. It cannot happen without you. So let us summon a new spirit of patriotism; of service and responsibility where each of us resolves to pitch in and work harder and look after not only ourselves but each other."

When I talked to him on the phone the morning my daughter was born, he made clear his belief in the power of people not just to win an election but to change a country. "I know you're disappearing for a while to change diapers and play Mr. Dad," he said to me, "but just make sure you find time to help figure out how to keep our supporters involved. I don't think we can succeed without them." As I listened to him, I could hear Candidate Obama morph smoothly into President Obama. "We need to make sure they're pushing from the grass roots on Washington and helping to spread what we're trying to do in their local communities. And at the very least, we have to give them the opportunity to stay involved and in touch. They gave their heart and soul to us. This shouldn't feel like a transactional relationship, because that's not what it was. I want them along for the ride the next eight years, helping us deliver on all we talked about in the campaign."

His desire for a continued dialogue with the more than thirteen million people who signed up for the campaign led to the formation of a new group called Organizing for America (OFA). Run by Mitch Stewart and housed in the DNC, OFA ensures that the president can stay in touch with his millions of volunteers and supporters, communicating directly through the Internet and encouraging them to rally support and educate people in their local communities on what he is trying to accomplish on the economy, health care, energy, and other issues.

People talking to people, block by block, town by town, was an idea that Barack Obama believed in strongly as a candidate and still does as the president. The power of this interpersonal dialogue was never properly appreciated by our opponents or by the press and political community. But those quiet conversations, which took place in every corner of America, helped us win the election and will help the president succeed with his goals. In the end, they are far more important than the bickering politicians and pundits in the news media who get such outsize attention in our culture today. Of course this effort will not rival the campaign in size, intensity, or scope. But having millions of Americans absorbing ideas and message, understanding them, and sharing them—and having thousands on any given day organize conversations in their communities to show and build support for them—is an asset few presidents, if any, have enjoyed. This will be another piece of bringing about change to a city, Washington, that seems to abhor it.

President Obama's relative success or failure will be judged largely by the result of his legislative initiatives. And these are of course critical, especially when it comes to issues like health care, energy, and financial and regulatory reform. But he also believes strongly in the ability of real leadership to make a huge difference.

We saw voters looking at the human qualities of leadership throughout the campaign. His call for a new politics based on more civil and respectful dialogue, his risky and forthright speech on race during the Jeremiah Wright episode, and his challenge to parents "to turn the TV off and read to your kids" and to take more responsibility and involvement in their children's education—all these drove support for his candidacy.

The impact of his leadership qualities will likely not receive much attention in the daily box score of our political coverage, but I believe it could have a lasting impact. A generation from now, I suspect there will be a much smaller percentage of young people across the globe who choose the route of terrorism than might have, because President Obama will change the way many look at our country in the coming years. Studies may show a higher percentage of parents actively engaged in their children's education because of the president's leadership and the emphasis both he and the first lady are putting on parental involvement and responsibility in learning.

And even though there will be tough fights in Washington, the president will resist the low road. This attitude goes directly against the old dusty Washington playbook and may not be rewarded by the pundits. Outrage, anger, and attacks always get boffo coverage; reasonableness, measured responses, and seeing both sides of issues rarely do. But this is what the country is hungry for and what's called for if we hope to repair the tremendous damage done to our government and to our communities after so many years of a highly partisan approach to government. During the campaign, Candidate Obama treated the voters like adults, discussing issues and solutions in detail and, yes, with nuance, though he was often derided for doing so by many political observers. They said he was too professorial and did not engage in enough snappy, short lines of rhetoric. They are still criticizing him. But the president believes deeply that the American people want to have an honest and complex dialogue about the direction of the country.

And over time, I believe the American people, and maybe even a few politicians in Washington, will appreciate this change in tone; and perhaps years from now it will eventually become the norm instead of the exception.

Our election victory did not fully settle in for me until January 17, 2009, three days before the inauguration. I would still find myself hearing and seeing the words "President Obama," "incoming White House Press Secretary Robert

Gibbs," or "White House Senior Adviser David Axelrod," and I'd do a double take. It just didn't seem real.

And I was not alone. When I talked to the president-elect at some point in December, during the conversation where he encouraged me to write this book, he said, "Each day, it sinks in a little bit more. But there are still moments when it seems like an out-of-body experience. Then the reality that these will soon be my problems, that they're no longer theoretical, snaps me back. Not that we won. But that we have to govern. I actually haven't had a moment to really savor what we accomplished in the campaign. The election was over and the very next moment, we had a government to build, priorities to set with the problems getting worse by the hour."

The Saturday before the inaugural, my wife, son, and I joined the Obama and Biden families in a box on the steps of the Lincoln Memorial for an inaugural weekend concert that featured a dizzying array of talent, including Bruce Springsteen, U2, Stevie Wonder, and Beyoncé. It was a very nice gesture on their part to include us, though it has ruined all future concerts for my son; they will all pale in comparison. The president-elect was slated to speak briefly during the show and a few moments before he would stride to the microphone, I looked at him from behind. Everyone in our box was, and I assume the hundreds of thousands in the crowd were, fixed on the music performance onstage. But the president-elect was intently gazing in the direction of Abraham Lincoln's imposing statue rising up behind and above the stage. And ever the staff guy, I was observing him do so.

For me, this was the moment that his election finally became real. Watching our first African American president look quietly at Lincoln, the great emancipator, before taking the steps of the memorial built in his honor simply took my breath away.

Later that night, the Obamas had invited a small number of campaign staffers and key supporters to join them at Blair House, a government building where many foreign dignitaries stay when visiting Washington. It is directly across from the White House and the Obama family was staying there that weekend before they moved into their new home.

I asked the president-elect when I saw him, "Before you spoke today, were you looking up at Lincoln?"

He raised his eyelids, surprised perhaps that his private moment had been witnessed. "Very observant, Plouffe," he said. "It was emotional to be speaking on the Lincoln Memorial, given all the history involved. Reading the inscription reminded me of the weight of this office through history. It helped me gather myself. For all of our challenges, we've faced greater. Lincoln had to save the Union."

He paused. "So I also asked ol' Abe for wisdom and judgment and patience. We'll need it."

"Well, for me, it finally made all this real," I said. "Seeing you on those steps, drawing on Lincoln for inspiration, it was a remarkable moment in history."

He grabbed my shoulder and looked into my eyes. "It's real now for me, too. And, humbly, I think I'm ready. I can't wait to get to work and help change this country for the better."

I know he will.

Acknowledgments

When I sat down to write this book, my experience as a writer was limited to campaign memos and television advertisements. The scale and complexity of a book were daunting.

I have many people to thank for making sure I did not crash and burn.

First is President Barack Obama, who encouraged me to write this book, believing this story belongs not only to those of us who experienced it first-hand, but all whose lives it impacts, and, possibly, history. This campaign reflected the ability and willingness of a people to write their own history, and as such it deserved to be recorded accurately and thoroughly, and before the inevitable mythmaking warped its telling.

As the author of two best-sellers, the president can't know how seriously I took his joking admonition that "Your reputation, and the reputation of the organization, is pretty good coming off the campaign. Don't damage it by writing a bad book." While I can never approach his talents as a writer, I hope this book captures the spirit as well as the story of our campaign from a staff perspective. He was a remarkable candidate, is a remarkable person and leader, and my two years by his side are a most treasured period of my life.

Clare Ferraro of Viking, my publisher, went way out on the limb in agreeing to work with a first-time author, with no collaborator, on a tight schedule. Her confidence in my ability to write this book helped sustain and drive me.

Wendy Wolf, my editor, and her partner in crime, Kevin Doughten, helped shape this book in every meaningful way, and helped improve me as a writer throughout the process. I am immensely grateful for their patience, judgment, and skill.

Luckily for a novice author writing about a start-up campaign, Viking is staffed with seasoned professionals who took our breakneck schedule in stride. Everyone in managing editorial, design, and production worked far beyond the call of duty to see that we hit our marks, and the team from publicity and marketing tackled the launch by thinking outside of the box, as we did so often in the campaign. I'm grateful to all of these people for their time, effort, good judgment, and commitment to this project.

Bob Barnett, my agent, provided wise counsel and great advice throughout.

The audience I care most about is the Obama campaign staff and volunteers who were responsible for this story's occurring in the first place. I could have written a 200,000-word book and not had enough room to highlight the amazing work, accomplishments, and character of this campaign family. Your exploits are reflected in every page; I was humbled to work by your side and attempt to capture in this book all we accomplished together.

I want to single out David Axelrod and Katie Johnson for additional thanks. We simply would not have been the Obama campaign, or won, without David Axelrod. This is as much his story as mine, and I owe a special debt of gratitude to him for his collaboration, genius, and principles. He is a unique person in our politics, and I am fortunate to count him as a friend and collaborator.

Katie Johnson was by my side for two years, and without her, the campaign and I would have floundered. She could have done many jobs on the campaign as it progressed, because everyone who came in contact with her saw her talents and drive, but instead chose to stay as my assistant, helping me flourish and putting the campaign's needs first. She will make a difference wherever she goes.

Lynn Eisenberg and Jordan Burke played invaluable roles helping with the research for the book, often by necessity, at warp speed.

David Axelrod and Anita Dunn somehow found the time to read the manuscript and provide incisive guidance, additional perspective on important events, and, as always, terrific judgment. I am indebted to them now, twice.

There is no index following these acknowledgments as a recognition that our campaign was not a collection of individuals, no matter how talented, but a tight unit of staff and volunteers who were on every day, stronger as the sum of those parts. I hope this book honors that reality. But regardless, you'll need to read the book, not flip through and index, to find out.

The events and dialogue in this book reflect my recollections. I had plenty of source material to work from—e-mails, calendars, some notes, and the recollections of some of my former colleagues. But even though little time has passed, there is no doubt not every piece of dialogue is accurate to the word. But I am confident the spirit, content, and import of each exchange stands the test.

Our family was kept upright through the bouncy seas of this voyage by a network of friends and family. They kept us sane and focused; fed, housed, and listened to us; and wordlessly scrambled to retrieve the many balls we dropped while marveling aloud at how adept we were at juggling. We would not have survived without them.

My parents, brothers and sisters, and close friends gave enormous support and understanding during the campaign, as they have throughout my life. This book and any role I had in this amazing story are due to a lifetime of their love, guidance, and keeping me grounded.

I owe my wife, Olivia Morgan, gratitude on many levels, but two I can recognize in these pages. First, for encouraging me to embark on this improbable campaign journey, despite the sacrifices and burdens it required of her. She is my hero for that.

Olivia improved this book in large ways and small, and lived and breathed every word and chapter with me for many months. It is crisper, clearer as a result. She set as the guidepost a book that our children and their peers can read many years from now and understand that, for two years, Mom, Dad, and millions like them loved their country enough to change it.